ACCOUNTING THEORY
CONTEMPORARY ACCOUNTING ISSUES

DR. THOMAS G. EVANS
University of Central Florida

THOMSON
SOUTH-WESTERN

Australia · Canada · Mexico · Singapore · Spain · United Kingdom · United States

THOMSON

SOUTH-WESTERN

Accounting Theory: Contemporary Accounting Issues
Thomas G. Evans

Editor-in-Chief:
Jack W. Calhoun

Team Leader:
Melissa S. Acuña

Acquisitions Editor:
Sharon Oblinger

Developmental Editor:
Carol Bennett

Marketing Manager:
Julie Lindsay

Production Editor:
Heather A. Mann

Manufacturing Coordinator:
Doug Wilke

Compositor:
Navta Associates

Printer:
RR Donnelley & Sons
Crawfordsville, IN

Design Project Manager:
Michelle Kunkler

Cover and Internal Design:
Ann Small/a small design
studio, Cincinnati, OH

Cover Image:
©EyeWire, Inc.

Library of Congress Cataloging-
in-Publication Data
Evans, Thomas
    Accounting theory: contem-
porary accounting issues /
Thomas Evans.
        p.   cm.
    Includes bibliographical refer-
ences and index.
    ISBN 0-324-10784-6
    1. Accounting. 2. Accounting
—Standards. I. Title.

HF 5625 .E93 2003
657--dc21   2001055142

To my dear wife, Marilyn, with love.

Welcome to accounting theory. This course should be a new experience because an accounting theory course differs dramatically from other accounting courses previously taken. What makes theory unique is that emphasis is placed on an understanding of what is trying to be accomplished rather than on the techniques for accomplishing it. That is, theory emphasizes the *why* of accounting rather than the *how*.

This emphasis is necessary, and beneficial, because in the last decade business practices have become more complex causing accounting methods and pronouncements to become correspondingly more complex. Accounting practice mirrors the business environment in which it operates. As business environments have become more complicated, as a result of globalization, exotic securities, downsizing, stock options, write-offs, and other new developments, so have the accounting practices and procedures for these events. Accordingly, it is no wonder that most accounting courses today must focus on complicated practice procedures.

But underlying all those procedures are principles, concepts, and a theory framework that help tie the procedures together. This text concentrates on those concepts, principles, and the theory framework. It describes how concepts, principles, and theory have developed over the years, how they help explain current practice, how they can be used to evaluate current practice, and how they can guide accounting practitioners, financial statement preparers, and standard setters in the future.

It is not likely that students will remember all the practices and techniques that are taught in procedurally oriented courses. In fact, GAAP appears to be a vast number of overwhelmingly complicated procedures. One, however, should remember the basic principles that support those practices. These are fewer in number and tend to be easier to comprehend, which is one primary value of a theory course: knowing the *why* of accounting can be a guide for applying the basic principles to current practice problems.

Another fundamental value of a theory course is its benefit to the practice of accounting in the future. Because accounting mirrors the business world, accounting must cope with the increasing pace of the changes occurring in the world of business. As business continues to evolve and as new accounting problems arise and arise more quickly, traditional procedures may become increasingly less relevant or applicable. New problems will warrant new solutions. Again, knowing the *why* of accounting can help guide in the development of new practices to solve these future problems, and understanding the theory framework of accounting can help in formulating creative solutions to new problems that emerge.

Accordingly, this course switches gears and looks beyond familiar accounting procedures. Instead, it is concerned with the concepts and principles that explain them. By concentrating on concepts and principles, this book will provide an increased understanding of those concepts and principles and will aid in the preparation for solving new problems as they emerge in the future.

Overall, a study of accounting theory should benefit the reader in at least three ways:

- Stimulate and challenge the reader's reasoning ability regarding judgments necessary in the professional practice of accounting.
- Assist the reader in applying and using theory to solve controversial and complex practice problems. The reader will learn to use theory properly in resolving accounting problems and issues. Applying theory will help the reader perform well in complex analytical and conceptual situations and to solve real world problems.
- Help the reader to identify the controversial areas in accounting, and enable him or her to suggest solutions and evaluate alternatives by considering the broader economic and political context of accounting in framing solutions.

Accounting Theory: Contemporary Accounting Issues contains two distinct but integral parts. Part 1 focuses on two interwoven topics: historical theory formulation and standard setting. The first two topics of the course, theory development and accounting standard setting, are integrated in a chronological format to show how the two are related. The following topics are covered in Chapters 1 through 8:

1. *The nature of theory and its development.* What is accounting theory? What are the approaches to developing theory? What approaches should be used to formulate accounting theory? In addition, some of the benefits from having a strong accounting theory are discussed and analyzed, as well as some of the major difficulties that have been addressed in generating a theory. A major theme in the first part of the book is an analysis of some of the important past efforts in developing an accounting theory. Classic theory formulations before the Conceptual Framework project of the Financial Accounting Standard Board (FASB) are covered in detail to demonstrate how some of today's major theory concepts were derived. The Conceptual Framework project is examined closely because it is the reigning accounting theory and represents the most ambitious effort to formulate an accounting theory. The Conceptual Framework project has the greatest potential to influence accounting standards today and in the future.
2. *Accounting standard setting and its chronological development.* Each chapter contains a time line that shows standard setting and theory formulation milestones. How accountants have tried to set accounting standards, both in the past and in the present, is discussed. Past standard-setting bodies are examined to understand how they were structured and why they failed. The current body, the FASB, is examined in detail in order to understand more clearly how accounting standards are established today. The current political situation of the FASB is emphasized, and the effect of the movement toward international accounting standards is also described.

Part 2 of *Accounting Theory: Contemporary Accounting Issues* (Chapters 9 through 16) covers contemporary financial reporting issues as they relate to the FASB's Conceptual Framework. It examines the areas of contemporary financial reporting that are controversial, for example, income concepts and determination. This topic has dominated financial accounting for the past sixty years. Various income concepts are discussed, and different approaches to net income are considered, as well as the important issue of income determination on the Balance Sheet. The FASB's definition of comprehensive income is also discussed. In Part 2, the theme is the application of the definitions in the Conceptual

Framework to controversial accounting areas, such as accounting for cash flows, accounting for pensions, other postemployment benefits, and stock options. These controversial topics are examined in terms of how well the definitions of assets and liabilities in the Conceptual Framework are applied to specific accounting issues.

Thus this text is a blend of theory, practice, and research. The contemporary accounting literature uses theory as a reference point. Almost every issue of the major accounting journals contains the results of studies that help shape accounting. A bibliography is provided at the end of each chapter so that readers can dig deeper into issues that especially interest them.

DISTINGUISHING FEATURES

This book was designed with the following distinguishing features to facilitate your understanding of accounting theory:

- **Chronological Order**—Part 1 is presented in chronological order. The topics of accounting standard setting and theory formulation are interwoven chronologically to provide a sense of the dynamic flow of events as they occurred, which provides a better understand of the setting of important events. It also helps to explain why developments happened at a particular time and to show the relationship of events and developments that occurred at different times. The chronological development illustrates a clear picture of the important past events that led to the current state of affairs in accounting standard setting and theory formulation, namely the FASB and the FASB's Conceptual Framework project. Each chapter's time line emphasizes (in bold print) the relationship between standard setting and theory formulation for that chapter's time frame. Following this time line through the first part allows the reader to continually reinforce the past and present developments of accounting theory and standard setting. The time line also helps to illustrate what each chapter represents along the continuum.

- **Two Integrated Parts**—The two major parts of the book are linked and therefore dependent on each other. The first part promotes and facilitates the understanding of the second part. By understanding how accounting theory has been formulated and its relationship to accounting standard setting, one can better apply that theory to contemporary issues.

- **Historical Background**—Within the first part of the book, the reader is supplied the background for understanding current accounting theory, the FASB's Conceptual Framework. Knowledge of the major accounting theory formulations that preceded the Conceptual Framework project, such as the Accounting Principles Board's Accounting Research Study (ARS) #1 and ARS #3, helps the reader appreciate the effort that was necessary to produce the framework. Familiarity with preceding accounting theory formulations provides an understanding of how a number of specific accounting theory concepts originated, such as the asset-liability approach to net income determination. When one understands the "roots" of the concepts that appear in the current statement of theory, one grasps a deeper understanding of those concepts.

- **Understanding the FASB**—Within the first part of the book, the reader is given the background needed to understand the current institution that sets accounting standards, the FASB. By examining the accounting standard-setting bodies, such as the Accounting Principles Board, that preceded the FASB, one better understands the issues associated with setting accounting standards. Knowledge of past standard-setting efforts also helps you appreciate the difficulty in accomplishing that function. It also gives you a perspective on the FASB by knowing its "roots."

- **How the FASB Sets Standards**—Both the FASB and the FASB's Conceptual Framework project are covered in detail so you can understand how the FASB works in setting accounting standards and the theory it uses as part of that process. Because accounting standard setting is currently under the domain of the FASB, this is important information.

- **A Global Perspective**—Globalization is an important aspect of all business activities. The international dimension is interwoven within the major themes of accounting standard setting and accounting theory formulation. The global perspective is not presented as a separate issue and then forgotten; instead, it is covered where appropriate and relevant within a chronological development of accounting theory or standard-setting topic. Globalization is especially important to the topic of accounting standard setting within the context of global investment and financing.

- **Applying the Conceptual Framework to Contemporary Issues**—Part 2 demonstrates how the Conceptual Framework project (and especially the definitions of accounting elements) can be applied to selected contemporary accounting issues. This provides the reader with practical experience in using accounting theory. The topics are relevant for helping the reader to begin to apply theory because they are applicable to other issues beyond the scope of this book. A number of theory cases are presented and discussed to show how to apply theory in a specific situation. Thus one obtains experience in the application of theory and is prepared to deal with issues that arise as accounting evolves.

PEDAGOGICAL FEATURES

- **Chapter Objectives**—Each chapter begins with a statement of the objectives of the chapter. These represent the learning objectives you should accomplish by studying the material in the chapter.

- **Icons**—Helpful icons are presented in each chapter in Part 1 to identify key people, events, and organizations that helped shape the development of accounting.

- **Examples and Cases**—In Part 2, many examples and cases are presented to help reinforce the concepts.

- **Bibliography**—Bibliographic lists are provided in each chapter so that the reader can dig deeper into issues that are of special interest.

- **List of Abbreviations and Acronyms**—A handy reference list of abbreviations and acronyms is located inside the back cover of the book.

- **End-of-Chapter Material**—All chapters conclude with Review Questions that cover the major points of the chapter as well as Discussion Topics, which contain some application cases; some chapters have Research project suggestions. This material digs more deeply into the topics of the chapter.

- **Web site**—The web site of the book, http://evanstheory.swcollege.com, contains PowerPoint slides and links to other accounting sites for students and instructors. Future updates to the material, as needed, will be added to this site. The instructor will find the Solutions Manual, sample syllabus, and PowerPoint lectures posted to the Instructor's Resources link at this site.

- A printed Instructor's Manual with end of chapter solutions (ISBN 0-324-10785-4) is available to instructors upon request.

ACKNOWLEDGEMENTS AND THANKS

This book benefited greatly from the contributions of many individuals and organizations. The following are recognized for contributing materials or providing permission to include materials:

- Professor Jerry Kreuze, Western Michigan University, for the application problems in Chapters 9 through 15
- The following cases: "The Lottery Ticket Case (Part 1)," "The Lottery Ticket Case (Part 2)," "The Lottery Ticket Case (Part 3)," "The See-through Office Building Case," "The Longevity Bonuses Case," "The Bonus Case," "The Income Tax Carryforward Case," and "The Asset Disposal Case" are taken from T. Johnson and K. Petrone's *The FASB Cases on Recognition and Measurement*, Second Edition, copyright 1995, the Financial Accounting Standards Board, 401 Merritt 7, P.O. Box 5116, Norwalk, Connecticut. Portions are reprinted with permission; complete copies of the documents are available from the FASB
- The APB's response to ARS #1 and ARS #3 (Copyright 1962 from the *Journal of Accountancy* by the American Institute of Certified Pubic Accountants, Inc. Opinions of the authors are their own and do not necessarily reflect policies of the AICPA, reprinted with permission); the definition of accounting from ARS #1 (© 1961); the basic postulates of accounting from ARS #1 (© 1961); the basic principles of accounting from ARS #3 (© 1962); and the twelve objectives of the Trueblood study (© 1973)
- Pages 409–422 from T. Evans, M. Taylor, and R. Rolfe, *International Accounting and Reporting*, Third Edition, © 1999. Reprinted with permission of South-Western College Publishing, a division of Thomson Learning (fax 800-730-2215)
- The charge to the committee to prepare *A Statement of Basic Accounting Theory* (ASO-BAT); the four goals of ASOBAT; the definition of accounting; the four objectives of accounting, and the comments of Russell Morrison; reprinted with permission of the American Accounting Association
- The front cover and pages 4–20 of the 1931 General Electric annual report. Reprinted with permission by General Electric Corporation
- Portions of FASB Concepts Statements, copyright Financial Accounting Standards Board, 401 Merritt 7, Norwalk, Connecticut 06856-5116, U.S.A, are used with permission; all rights reserved; complete copies of the FASB documents are available from the FASB

I am deeply indebted to my editor, Carol Bennett, for all her great suggestions and advice. The work of the two accounting reviewers, Professor John Hassell of Indiana University and Professor Jerry Kreuze of Western Michigan University, was very helpful. Both reviewers provided me with excellent advice on the content of this book. John Hassell also did a lot of editorial work on the manuscript, and I think the publisher owes him a big box of red pens. My thanks to the production and marketing people at South-Western Publishing whose professionalism greatly assisted the process. Finally, as is traditional, I accept responsibility for any errors in the book (since I probably made them anyway).

PART 2

THE STUDY OF CONTEMPORARY ACCOUNTING ISSUES
WITHIN THE CONCEPTUAL FRAMEWORK

PART 1

STANDARD SETTING AND
THEORY FORMULATION

INTRODUCTION

The first part of this book (Chapters 1 through 8) examines standard setting and accounting theory formulation. This first chapter begins a chronological presentation of both topics. These two topics are discussed together because they are dependent, related, and interwoven. As shown in Part I, standard setting without a theory is virtually impossible and theory formulation without a standard-setting organization as one of its primary users is largely irrelevant or of minor, esoteric value.

A second important reason for presenting both topics chronologically is that it helps provide the background to understand the beginning of the "new view" of accounting. This new view emerged from standard setting and theory formulation with the formation of the Financial Accounting Standards Board (FASB) in 1973 and the initial efforts at creating the FASB's Conceptual Framework theory project. From this standpoint, accounting is an important part of the macroeconomic fabric of the American and world economies because of its important role in capital allocation through capital markets.

In the new view, accounting is defined at a macro level, on a total or centralized basis. Accounting is viewed as a link between all firms and the capital markets, both domestic and international. Accounting plays a significant role in those markets and thus in the welfare of society. This new view elevates accounting to a higher level and gives it much more importance than it had in the past.

Under this new role, accounting provides financial information about economic entities to investors and creditors, who have an investment in business firms but are not actively managing those entities.

Their investments are an important part of their wealth and, in aggregate, important to the economy; therefore, accounting is important to the fabric of the economy and to society. This view will be discussed in depth in Chapter 4.

A third reason for presenting these topics chronologically is to facilitate understanding of current accounting theory, the FASB's Conceptual Framework. Most of this framework was formulated between 1973 and 1985 and is consistent with the new view of accounting. In fact, some consider it a blueprint for this new view. The Conceptual Framework contains a number of new ideas for accounting—the importance of users, an emphasis on cash flows, the importance of relevance over objectivity, and so on. But one may wonder: Were these ideas new to the Conceptual Framework or had they been advanced before? Or, simply, "Where did the FASB get those ideas?" An understanding of the chronological development of theory formulation shows that these were not new ideas but rather ideas that had been presented as parts of prior accounting theory formulations. So they are not as radical as some thought then (and still think now). Thus an understanding of the chronological development of theory helps explain current theory; it gives one the proper perspective from which to view it.

The following timeline provides an overview of Part 1 and how the individual chapters and their subparts are related. To help keep the proper perspective on the overall flow, this time line will be shown at the beginning of each chapter, with the current chapter's coverage highlighted in bold.

STANDARD SETTING	1900	THEORY FORMULATION
STANDARD SETTING I		THEORY 1
PRE-CAP	1900-1938	NATURE OF THEORY
SEC	1934	
STANDARD SETTING II		
CAP I	1938	
STANDARD SETTING III		
CAP II	1938-1958	
STANDARD SETTING IV		THEORY II
APB	1959-1962	
	1961-1962	ARS #1 AND #3
STANDARD SETTING V		THEORY III
APB	1963-1966	
	1966	ASOBAT
STANDARD SETTING VI		
DEMISE OF APB	1970	
STANDARD SETTING VII		
TRUEBLOOD	1973	
WHEAT	1972	
TRIPARTITE STRUCTURE	1973-2001	
		THEORY IV
	1977	SATTA
		POSITIVE ACCOUNTING 1980s
STANDARD SETTING VIII		THEORY V
	1973-2001	CONCEPTUAL FRAMEWORK PROJECT
STANDARD SETTING VIII		
FASB: PRESENT AND FUTURE STANDARD SETTING: DOMESTIC AND INTERNATIONAL	2001	
	2002	

CHAPTER 1

FOUNDATION: STANDARD SETTING AND THEORY

LEARNING OBJECTIVES

After studying this chapter, you should be able to

> Appreciate the linkage between standard setting and theory formulation in accounting.

> Understand the role and importance of key change factors in accounting.

> Understand the factors that led to the creation of the Committee on Accounting Procedure.

> Describe the three purposes of accounting theory and the two main approaches to the formulation of a theory.

> Explain the two needs of an accounting standard-setting body.

STANDARD SETTING	1900	THEORY FORMULATION
CHAPTER 1		
STANDARD SETTING I		**THEORY 1**
PRE-CAP	**1900-1938**	NATURE OF THEORY
SEC	**1934**	
STANDARD SETTING II		
CAP I	**1938**	
STANDARD SETTING III		
CAP II	**1938-1958**	
CHAPTER 2		
STANDARD SETTING IV		THEORY II
APB	1959-1962	
	1961-1962	ARS #1 AND #3
CHAPTER 3		
STANDARD SETTING V		THEORY III
APB	1963-1966	
	1966	ASOBAT
STANDARD SETTING VI		
DEMISE OF APB	1970	
CHAPTER 4, 5		
STANDARD SETTING VII		
TRUEBLOOD	1973	
WHEAT	1972	
TRIPARTITE STRUCTURE	1973-2001	
CHAPTER 6		
		THEORY IV
	1977	SATTA
		POSITIVE ACCOUNTING 1980s
CHAPTER 7		THEORY V
	1973-2001	CONCEPTUAL FRAMEWORK PROJECT
CHAPTER 8		
STANDARD SETTING VIII		
FASB: PRESENT AND FUTURE STANDARD SETTING: DOMESTIC AND INTERNATIONAL	2001	
	2002	

CHRONOLOGICAL DEVELOPMENT

This chapter begins by examining the past, the chronological development of standard setting and theory formulation. The objective is to learn from the past, not just to study it for historical interest. The focus is on the present and future, but it is important to know what happened when and to understand why these things happened in order to see how the present situation developed. Knowing how past developments contributed to the current situation not only helps to explain current standard setting and theory formulation but also provides some clues for the future.

KEY CHANGE FACTORS

PEOPLE

EVENTS

ORGANIZATIONS

In the examination of chronological development, it is important *to identify key change factors.* These are key people, events, and organizations that caused significant change to occur in business and/or the practice of accounting. The chronological development of accounting shows that key people, events, and organizations have caused major shifts in the progression of accounting practice and theory. Some of the changes are seen as positive, others as negative. Some of the key events are economic, such as the Great Depression, and others are political, such as passage of the law that created the corporate form of business organization or the income tax law of 1913. Key change organizations can be internal to accounting, such as the creation of the Committee on Accounting Procedure (CAP), or external to accounting, such as the Securities and Exchange Commission (SEC).

Through the years some key individuals have also been the "right person at the right place at the right time" and therefore had a dramatic impact on accounting. For example, as shown subsequently, if Carmen G. Blough, the SEC chief accountant in 1938, had been unable to attend some important meetings at the SEC in 1938 in Washington, D.C., because of a flat tire on the commute to the office or illness, the Securities and Exchange Commission might have assumed full authority for issuing accounting standards instead of delegating that authority to the accounting profession, as Blough persuasively argued. One can only imagine what a difference that would have made in the following years of accounting practice, auditing, business practice, investments, and professional careers in accounting. Blough is an example of the right person at the right place at the right time.

Identifying key people, events, and organizations will help you to understand what factors cause change and help you to identify those factors in the present and the future.

Chronological development begins with standard setting, which preceded theory formulation and set the context for it. The following discussion is centered on the primary organizations that were involved: the CAP and the SEC.

STANDARD SETTING I
PRE-CAP

BEFORE ACCOUNTING STANDARDS

The first official standard-setting body in the accounting profession was the Committee on Accounting Procedure (CAP), established in 1936 by the American Institute of Accountants

(AIA). However, to understand why the CAP was established, it is necessary to begin earlier, looking at the world of accounting in the early 1900s. Important developments in accounting practice were happening, and they help explain the context, "the setting," of the times in which the CAP was formed.

ORGANIZATION

ACCOUNTING IN THE EARLY 1900S

Informative financial accounting reports were published by firms before being required by the SEC or accounting standard-setting bodies. Around the turn of the century through the early 1900s, accounting practice was unregulated. Business firms (preparers) considered their accounting practices confidential, internal policies for reporting to their owners and loan-capital suppliers. This was understandable because there was little public investment or public ownership in firms. Instead, firms relied on loan-capital, which was supplied by outside creditors and bankers. Thus the accounting records and reports were not prepared for public owners; instead, they were prepared for the managers of the firms and for the firms' creditors and bankers. Bankers and other creditors were primarily interested in cash flows and the ability of the firms to repay their debts (liquidity and solvency). These elements were emphasized in the underlying accounting records and reports. Because each firm followed its own accounting practices, no comparability between two firms existed and neither did consistency for the same firm over time. However, because there were few investors, this situation wasn't a major concern at that time. But, as illustrated in a subsequent section, things changed rapidly.

THE GENERAL ELECTRIC 1931 ANNUAL REPORT

Surprisingly, some industrial firms' accounting practices flourished in this unregulated environment. That is, even in the absence of regulation, some companies were inspired to adopt accounting practices that were advanced and progressive in terms of disclosures. For example, the General Electric (GE) annual report for 1931 shown in the appendix at the end of this chapter was noted for its detail and financial disclosure. Exhibit 1.2 shows the condensed balance sheet for GE.

The GE Annual Report for 1931 contained a comparative Statement of Income and Expenses for 1930 and 1931 and a condensed Balance Sheet for the same years, although the balance sheet was not condensed by today's standards. It was two pages and provided a great deal of detail on the assets, liabilities, and capital (owners' equity). For example, six lines of Current Assets were presented. As shown in the appendix, a report on manufacturing plants was also presented. It provided much detail on plant expenditures, such as the total that GE had spent on manufacturing plants during its formation in 1892 and the additional amount in 1931, as well as depreciation for 1931 and the cost of plants sold or dismantled. Notes were also provided to cover details concerning such topics as investments in other firms, foreign business, inventories, capital stock, and pension plans. The audit opinion was issued by Peat, Marwick, Mitchell & Co. of New York.

Not all of the accounting procedures in the 1931 GE report are generally accepted today. For example, it reported investment in marketable securities at the lower of par or market value. It also followed a reporting format that is not used today by industrial corporations: Assets in the Balance Sheet were listed in reverse order of liquidity, with long-term tangible assets first, followed by current assets, and cash listed last. The audit opinion

EXHIBIT 1.2
General Electric Annual Report Condensed Balance Sheet

1931   *General Electric Annual Report*

CONDENSED BALANCE SHEET
December 31, 1931 and 1930

ASSETS

	1931	1930
Fixed investments:		
Manufacturing plants at cost, including land, buildings, and machinery	$199,129,732.92	$198,303,962.66
Less: General plant reserve and depreciation	153,068,713.66	152,436,033.08
	$ 46,061,019.26	$ 45,867,929.58
Other property	228,445.67	252,609.47
Furniture and appliances (other than in factories)	1.00	1.00
Patents	1.00	1.00
Total fixed investments	**$ 46,289,466.93**	**$ 46,120,541.05**
Associated companies and miscellaneous securities	179,308,010.36	204,810,328.13
Current assets:		
Inventories	57,335,498.53	60,063,418.56
Installation work in progress	10,063,820.42	16,229,589.20
Notes and accounts receivable	39,192,433.60	41,676,727.47
Marketable securities (at the lower of par or market) . . . $ 7,122,820.00		
Cash 115,056,113.22	122,178,933.22	141,717,851.25
Less; Advance payments on contracts	$228,770,685.77	$259,687,586.48
	9,684,175.13	17,123,037.38
Total current assets	$219,086,510.64	$242,564,549.10
Deferred charges	241,948.86	476,403.83
	$444,925,936.79	$493,971,822.11

LIABILITIES AND CAPITAL

	1931	1930
3½% Debenture bonds due 1942	$ 2,047,000.00	$ 2,047,000.00
Current liabilities:		
Accounts payable and accrued liabilities.		
Dividends payable	16,301,469.11	28,422,154.65
Total current liabilities	12,181,318.95	12,181,296.35
	$ 28,482,788.06	$ 40,603,451.00
Reserves for self-insurance, workmen's compensation, etc.	4,063,496.81	7,974,385.38
Charles A. Coffin Foundation	400,000.00	400,000.00
General reserve	14,517,597.21*	39,763,664.68
Special stock:		
Authorized 5,500,000 shares, par value $10; issued 4,292,963½ shares . .	42,929,635.00	42,929,635.00
Common stock and earned surplus:		
Common stock (authorized 29,600,000 shares no par value; issued 28,845,927 36/100 shares)		
Earned surplus on January 1st	180,287,046.00	180,287,046.00
Deficit (1931) and surplus (1930) for the year (page 5)	179,966,640.05	171,200,881.34
Total common stock and earned surplus	7,768,266.34	8,765,758.71
	$352,485,419.71	$360,253,686.05
	$444,925,936.79	$493,971,822.11

*After applying $25,246,067.47 in reduction of book value of "Associated companies and miscellaneous securities."

(shown in the appendix) contained language that would not appear in today's audit opinion, such as "we certify," "the valuations of the investments . . . are conservative," and "we
have confirmed the cash and securities by count and inspection." A modern reader of this
annual report would be impressed with the amount of detail that GE provided to its stockholders during an era when no such disclosures were required.

FINANCIAL REPORTING IN GENERAL

However, the absence of any rules and regulations did not inspire most firms to adopt progressive accounting practices with the same level of disclosures as GE. Instead, firms continued to adopt those standards that primarily met their needs and the needs of their
loan-capital suppliers, not necessarily the needs of the external stockholders. The emphasis was on the adequacy of cash to meet the debts as they came due.

FIRST PUBLIC INVESTMENT BOOM AND BUST

The relative unimportance of stockholders as a user group of financial accounting reports
changed dramatically after World War I. The key change factor was the decision
of the U.S. government to fund the war by issuing Liberty Bonds. This process   EVENTS
gave the general public its first real opportunity to "invest" and earn a return,
interest. Because the war effort involved people from all walks of life, this chance to invest
in a financial instrument was significant. It must also be noted that World War I was a big
boost to the U.S. economy. Prior to entrance into the conflict, the United States became
the chief supplier of materials to the Allies, which helped make Americans more wealthy
than they had ever been and paved the way for the post–World War I period.

    During that period, the U.S. government made the decision to retire the Liberty Bonds
it issued to finance the war. (Yes, the government actually paid off the war debt it incurred
to finance the U.S. involvement in WWI!) This repayment was coupled with a time of
general prosperity in America: low inflation, increasing productivity, and a new-product
market that was causing quite a stir—automobiles. After World War I, the auto industry
became the main growth industry in the United States, and many investors became quite
excited about the investment opportunities in auto firms. Auto firms were equally excited
because they needed massive amounts of capital to fund their operations. These factors
caused a big change in pubic investing and accounting—one that continues today. The
repayment of the war bonds resulted in an investment boom in stocks. It seems that the
"common person" discovered investing in stocks and the rewards and risks involved.
Investing in stocks became popular and profitable in the 1920s as the rewards of investing
were emphasized over the risks.

    The tremendous popularity of the stock market led to the first modern
investment boom. Unfortunately, the investment boom led to a bust: the crash of   EVENTS
the stock market in 1929. One of the reasons for the steep climb of the stock
market before the crash was financial trickery, and unfortunately, accounting was partially
involved. That is, people were *sold stock* rather than *investing* in it, and accounting was
one of the tools used to sell stock. Certainly, with no standard-setting body to set uniform
standards, accounting practices and procedures could not react to the change in business
investment. Accounting standard setting geared toward the new investment-oriented
market lagged behind the growth and development of investment in stock, and thus,

accounting was readily available for use in duping eager investors. The absence of a standard-setting body allowed firms to use accounting principles that presented the view management wanted. And naturally, accounting received some of the blame for the crash of the market. But this transformation of U.S. capital markets represented a new role for accounting in the allocation of capital through the stock market. That transformation is the beginning of the new view of accounting that emphasizes the important role of accounting in capital allocation in the national economy.

In fact, during this time, some financial writers spent much of their time criticizing contemporary accounting. For example, two financial writers, Harvard economics professor William Z. Ripley and J. M. B. Hoxsey of the New York Stock Exchange, became famous as critics of corporate accounting practices in the 1930s.

After the crash of the stock market, with accounting taking part of the blame, the accounting profession (the AIA) began to look for ways to improve its practice and its public image. Note that the key change factor at work here was the growth in public investing in the stock of American corporations.

THE NEW YORK STOCK EXCHANGE OVERTURE

In this environment, one opportunity for the accounting profession to set standards came along by way of the New York Stock Exchange (NYSE). After the crash of the stock market, the NYSE had a vested interest in restoring investor confidence in stocks and investing. So as part of its program, it contacted the AIA, asking it to develop a list of accounting principles that could be required of firms listed on the Exchange.

In response, the AIA formed a committee, called the Special Committee on Cooperation with Stock Exchanges, which eventually generated a list of five principles that were recommended to the NYSE in 1932.

1. Unrealized profit should not be credited to net income ("the income account"). Profit is realized when a sale is completed.
2. Additional paid-in capital (capital surplus) should not be charged with items that are more appropriately charged to net income.
3. Retained earnings (earned surplus) of a subsidiary should not be added to consolidated retained earnings.
4. In rare circumstances (not defined), treasury stock may be considered an asset of the firm, but dividends on such shares should not be considered as revenue.
5. Officers', affiliates', and employees' notes receivable should be separately disclosed.

Note that these principles dealt mainly with what elements should be included in determining current net income.

These five principles were approved by the NYSE and communicated to listed firms but never implemented as requirements. Later, this was accomplished by the SEC.

A sixth principle was also generated by the AIA. It dealt with the situation when stock was issued at par for property and later donated back to the corporation. The principle does not allow the par value of the stock issued to be considered as the cost of the property acquired. All six principles were adopted by the membership of the AIA, and the five listed earlier were adopted by the CAP, which was formed later. However, there are two significant things to consider. First, this was the first real attempt to codify accounting principles by the profession. Second, to describe this list, the phrase "accepted accounting principles" was coined (this was later changed to generally accepted accounting principles, or GAAP).

THE SECURITIES AND EXCHANGE COMMISSION

Another result of the stock market crash of 1929 was the creation of the Securities and Exchange Commission (SEC) by Congress in 1934. It was created primarily to regulate the sale of securities in capital markets to protect investors. The 1933 Truth in Securities Act regulated only the initial offering and sale of securities through the mail. The Federal Trade Commission administered it. The Securities Exchange Act of 1934 regulated the trading of securities on secondary markets. The SEC was created by this act to administer both the 1933 and 1934 acts. It was given authority over the form and content of financial information filed by firms. This authority was consistent with its mandate to oversee the sale of securities and to protect investors.

ORGANIZATIONS

As part of fulfilling its mandate, the SEC was given legal authority over accounting practices of regulated firms. It became questionable as to whether the SEC should become active in setting accounting standards. Remember that the early SEC staffers would have had legal backgrounds and been more oriented toward the regulation of firms and the sale of securities, not the firm's accounting practices. A heated controversy developed within the SEC as to whether the SEC should create a set of accounting standards to be followed by firms when filing with the SEC. The chief accountant, Carmen G. Blough, was successful in overcoming strong opposition and in convincing the SEC to delegate this important function to the accounting profession (i.e., the AIA).

PEOPLE

STANDARD SETTING II
THE CAP I

FORMATION AND ORGANIZATION

It seems an unwritten rule of any organization that when something needs to be done or some crisis is addressed, the natural response is to form a committee. Although the AIA created the Special Committee on Development of Accounting Principles in 1933, it was inactive. This committee was replaced with the CAP in 1936. Unfortunately, the CAP was also relatively inactive in its early years.

SEC PRESSURE

The accounting profession did not seem to respond quickly to the opportunity to accept the delegation of authority from the SEC and begin setting accounting standards. Because no standard-setting body had existed before, perhaps the profession did not know how to begin. Or maybe the delegation of authority was not clear to the profession. For whatever reason, it was soon clear to the SEC that the accounting profession was reluctant to exercise standard-setting authority, and by 1937, it was apparent that unless the SEC acted, the profession would not formulate accounting standards. So in 1938, the SEC pressured the accounting profession by issuing Accounting Series Release (ASR) #4, which required that accounting practices filed with it have "substantial authoritative support." Substantial authoritative support could be provided by the accounting profession or by the SEC. Thus the SEC put the accounting profession on notice that unless it made some progress in standard setting, the SEC would take over and withdraw the delegation of authority it made previously. Note that in 1937 the SEC became an active change factor to spur the accounting profession into active standard setting.

EVENTS   Another development that prompted the SEC to issue ASR #4 was the McKesson and Robbins scandal, which occurred in 1938. This firm was convicted of massive fraud, involving $19 million of fictitious inventory and accounts receivable. This case revealed to the SEC the potential abuses in financial reporting and the need for regulations and rules to govern the process.

THE COMMITTEE ON ACCOUNTING PROCEDURE

The CAP became active in 1938 in response to the SEC's issuance of ASR #4. Initially, this committee was made up of eight members. Apparently, the AIA expeditiously decided to staff this new committee with the heads of the seven currently existing committees with the president of the AIA as ex-officio. Later it was expanded to twenty-one members. The expansion was designed to staff the committee with representatives from organizations whose support was required for the pronouncements to be accepted. The membership included one member from each of the eight national public accounting firms as well as other CPAs and AIA officers.

The members all served part-time on the CAP because they were fully employed and thus not independent of their firms. The CAP operated with a small staff and only a part-time research department. All members were AIA members and thus reflected a bias toward the AIA. Therefore, users, such as investors or creditors; preparers, such as chief financial officers of corporations; and academics or professors who were not AIA members could not serve on the CAP.

CAP THEORY EFFORT

Initially, the CAP wanted to develop a theory of accounting (a comprehensive set of accounting principles) to help in the solution of accounting problems. However, the CAP estimated that this effort would take about five years, so it was abandoned in favor of issuing standards to address specific issues. In light of the earlier problems with the SEC, the CAP felt that the SEC would not wait five years for this committee to issue accounting standards. Thus, the CAP correctly sensed the need for theory but gave up and tried to address specific accounting controversies, *without a theory.* Therefore, standard setting became a political process among the members of the CAP. In effect, the CAP adopted a short-run rather than a long-run approach to standard setting. This choice is crucial for understanding standard setting throughout the rest of the 1900s.

PRONOUNCEMENTS

In terms of authority, the CAP did not have the direct support of the SEC. That is, the SEC never specifically identified the CAP as the major source of accounting standards; its support was indirect and informal. However, the CAP's pronouncements were considered as having "substantial authoritative support."

The CAP issued fifty-one pronouncements, called Accounting Research Bulletins (ARBs). These pronouncements were interestingly named. They were not based on any actual research; instead, they represented largely the opinions of CAP members. They were not "bulletins" in any sense of the word, such as a late-breaking event. But they were considered as having substantial authoritative support by the SEC and nonetheless could be considered standards. However, they were not binding on CPAs at this time. It is interesting that these ARBs are part of present-day GAAP and are binding on CPAs under the FASB's GAAP hierarchy. Time has validated them.

Many of these ARBs broke new ground and represented the first codification of accounting principles in particular areas. As a first step, the ARBs were very important; they represented a benchmark of accounting practices and principles. Many of the principles contained in these bulletins were the only authoritative word on accounting for a particular area for over two decades.

STANDARD SETTING III
THE CAP II

CAP TENURE

Over its twenty-one year term, the CAP did accomplish a great deal as the first "official" accounting standard-setting body. Most importantly, it kept standard setting in the private sector and made some progress to improve practices. However, concerns about the CAP emerged: it was too slow in decision making, did not represent all public accounting firms and preparers, did not include users in the standard-setting process, was not open to stakeholder input, and did not base its decisions on research or theory. Thus many of the CAP's decisions were unpopular. And the CAP ran into conflicts with the SEC over such issues as the CAP's favoring the current operating view of the income statement, whereas the SEC favored the all-inclusive view.

Toward the end of the CAP's tenure, the body of GAAP had grown such that firms were able to select from among a number of equally accepted accounting principles. This created major comparability problems for investors and others who wanted to use accounting information in their decision models to compare two or more firms. For example, firms had considerable flexibility in selecting accounting methods for inventories, depreciation and depletion, income tax allocation, pensions, research and development costs, goodwill, and so forth. The different accounting methods resulted in material differences in reported net income between similar firms.

The growth in GAAP is not surprising. One of the purposes of theory is to evaluate practice. That is, with theory, a standard-setting body can periodically evaluate the effectiveness of various accounting practices to keep GAAP updated and relevant. Without a theory, that cannot be done. So under the tenure of the CAP, new accounting practices and methods were proposed from a number of sources. To be available to preparers, the accounting methods only needed substantial authoritative support, which could be found in CAP bulletins, SEC rulings, or the authoritative literature. With no one to evaluate the resulting GAAP, it is natural that GAAP grew over time.

Thus without theory and with only indirect authority from the SEC, the CAP lacked the two necessary factors to be successful as a standard setting body.

SECOND INVESTMENT BOOM

To make matters worse for the CAP, during the end of its tenure in the 1950s, America experienced its second public investment boom. This boom in the post–World War II period was even greater than the post–World War I boom. It was based on the need to expand the national economy through capital investments by industry. This boom caused almost a doubling in the number of American stockholders in the space of a decade. By the early 1950s, there were about seven million stockholders; by the early 1960s, this number increased to almost twenty million. Thus a large part of the public were involved in investing in stock. This put accounting back into the spotlight because financial accounting information became the most important source of information about corporations. Accounting became a topic in the financial press, and the general consensus was that the situation was not good. As mentioned previously, the CAP's efforts had not narrowed the range of acceptable accounting practices, and this flexibility was not seen as a positive element in the investment boom. Thus accounting again came under much criticism, and a crisis of confidence in accounting emerged once more by the late 1950s.

THE END OF THE CAP

TROUBLE

Under the CAP, GAAP had grown. Although this might sound like a positive development, it was not. The wide diversity of accounting methods provided preparers with flexibility in reporting results. This flexibility, in conjunction with a renewed interested in investing by the public, caused a crisis for the accounting profession. During the post–World War II period, from 1940 to 1960, the number of investors grew dramatically from four million to twenty million. This put the spotlight on accounting as these investors had major problems with the lack of comparability among firms. Clearly something had to be done to narrow the diversity of accounting methods. In Chapter 2, the chronological development of standard setting is continued.

THEORY I
NATURE AND PURPOSE OF THEORY

The fact that the CAP initially saw its most basic need as the development of a theory, a comprehensive set of accounting principles to use in solving accounting problems, leads us to the topic of the nature and role of accounting theory. To explain this further, the next section describes the nature of theory, its definition, its role, and approaches to theory formulation.

At the onset, it's important to recognize that the study of theory is different from the study of other accounting topics. Three major differences exist in the study of theory compared to the study of accounting practices.

1. In theory, the fundamental underlying nature of a discipline, its basic concepts, ideas, and laws, rather than current practices, are considered.
2. When studying theory the substance, the underlying essence, is examined not necessarily its current form (the "essence" is timeless).
3. The essential concepts and principles and the reasons *why* are the focus in studying theory, not the current applications.

As an example of these differences, assume a firm purchased a plant asset five years ago at a cost of $10,000. The firm recognized depreciation on this piece of productive equipment totaling $8,000 to date and now sells the asset for $3,500 cash. The following accounting entry records this event:

Cash	$3,500	
Accumulated Depreciation	8,000	
Plant Asset		$10,000
Gain on Sale of Asset		1,500

This represents the correct view of this transaction from an accounting treatment perspective.

But for theory, we look at things differently, with our emphasis on different aspects of the transaction. *In theory, we examine practice in terms of how well it achieves the objectives of accounting.* For example, if the objective of accounting is to provide financial information to investors to use in evaluating the management of the firm, this treatment of the sale of the asset may be misleading. That is, did the firm really have a gain from this transaction? In this situation, the amount of the gain is driven by two factors: the selling price the firm received and the amount of the depreciation it recognized on this asset. Because the amount of depreciation recognized is at best an estimate, one could question the determination of the amount of the gain. One could also question whether the signal that this entry sends to the users of financial statements is correct.

If this was the only transaction of its kind that the firm experienced during the current reporting period, the gain would be presented in the financial reports and the investor would be pleased that the managers of the firm sold an asset at a gain. However, is this appraisal correct? First, does it signal higher future dividends? Should the share price increase? Second, the central question in selling an asset is: What was it replaced with? The firm is not in the business of selling assets; it's in the business of selling products or providing services. So the important aspect of this transaction focuses on the replacement decision. Thus the reality of the transaction is that unless management replaced this asset with one that is more efficient or cost-effective, this transaction may not have been positive for the firm. Indeed, management may have been better off continuing to use the asset that was sold. But the accounting for this event is silent on those issues and thus may mislead the users of this firm's financial statements. Theory asks those kinds of questions and looks at those issues. Therefore, this illustrates how different the study of theory is from the main body of accounting content, which is primarily composed of current procedures.

THEORY

To understand theory in accounting, we need to define generally what theory is and then consider what an accounting theory is. A basic definition of theory is:

Theory is a coherent set of hypothetical, conceptual, and pragmatic principles forming a general frame of reference for a field of study.

This definition reveals much about the nature of theory. It shows that a theory consists of a set of principles and that this set is a coherent set; all the principles are related and combined. The principles in this set consist of the following three types:

- hypothetical—unsupported by facts, assumed, or unproven
- conceptual—a general notion or idea
- pragmatic—useful or utilitarian

Note the purpose of this collection of principles: to form a general frame of reference for a field of study. This provides a framework for understanding the field of study, like a road map of the knowledge landscape.

Theory should give us the "big picture" for a particular discipline or field of study. The world is complex, with many variables and complicated interrelationships among those variables. Theory aids in understanding the world, identifying the relationships between phenomena and variables that exist, and helping to find stability that leads to predictions about the world. Theories do this by simplifying the complexities in the world so they can be grasped and understood. This understanding enables identification of causal relationships and predictions for future use.

ACCOUNTING THEORY

Applying this general definition of theory to accounting leads to the following definition of accounting theory: "a coherent, coordinated, consistent body of doctrine expressing the standards by which corporation accounting may be judged."[1] Theory in accounting can benefit accounting in a number of ways. The next section focuses on the three most important ones.

THREE PURPOSES OF ACCOUNTING THEORY

Given the nature of theory, accounting theory performs three purposes (or roles) for the discipline of accounting:

1. *To explain current practice* so that it is better understood by both accountants (practitioners) and nonaccountants (users)
2. *To evaluate practice*, providing a frame of reference to judge current practice and eliminating unnecessary diversity of accounting practices
3. *To facilitate the development of future practice*, extending accounting to new frontiers, to be fertile to create new procedures that solve new problems.

Many benefits to accounting and standard setting accrue from having a theory of accounting. Theory can assist standard setters in evaluating current practice to keep the body of GAAP up-to-date and composed of relevant practices. Theory can help develop new practices and procedures as new phenomena are encountered. This aspect of theory is extremely important in light of the rapidly changing national and international business environment with which accounting must cope. Without theory, there is no general agreement on what accounting is. Theory can help to define the objectives of accounting, developing relevant accounting concepts to aid in the understanding of accounting, the promotion of consistency in accounting, and the basis for the evaluation of practice. Thus, with these benefits in mind, one can readily understand why the CAP initially wanted to develop a theory. However, its abandonment of the theory project helped set the stage for its own failure.

THEORY VERIFICATION

Additional insights about the nature of theory can be obtained by looking at ways that theory can be verified. One way is to see if theory correctly predicts the phenomena with which it is concerned. In other words, does the theory help to predict future events? A second way looks at the internal logic and consistency within the theory. Has the theory been properly formulated and the approach correctly followed? A third method compares the theory with empirical data. Does it agree with the facts? Is it a guide to reality? All three show some important qualities of theory: It should work, be correctly specified, and be consistent with the actual world.

APPROACHES TO THEORY FORMULATION

Given that most disciplines (including accounting) would benefit greatly from a theory, there are obviously a number of ways that a theory may be developed to generate a body of propositions. These range from an unexpected intuitive "(lightning) flash" to a thinker sitting under a tree to scientifically studying observed regularities in a laboratory. But in accounting theory formulation, two traditional methods found strong support: *the inductive approach and the deductive approach.* Both methods have been used in other disciplines to develop theories and thus are well-tested models.

THE INDUCTIVE APPROACH

The inductive method attempts to bring order to a disorderly, chaotic world. It attempts to see the overall structure in seemingly unorganized phenomena. It involves reasoning from the specific to the general and has been very useful in the physical sciences. The basic procedure is to make detailed observations in the field of some phenomena or a sample of the phenomena and attempt to draw generalized conclusions from the observations. The goal is to describe what's going on and to explain existing world relationships.

To utilize the inductive approach to formulate a theory, a threefold procedure is followed:

1. *Limit the field of inquiry.* Some limits are placed around the investigation, which defines what is being attempted to accomplish. Think of this as a fence.
2. *Observe the data.* Attention is focused on the phenomena under study, which is examined. The items within the fence are examined, looking for regularities.
3. *Generalize conclusions.* Broad statements about commonalties in the items within the fence are searched for. These statements are principles.

The result of step three is a series of principles that comprise the theory. In this approach, data are gathered to support the premise, and principles are based on the actual observations made.

As noted previously, this approach has been used to develop many familiar theories, especially those in the physical sciences. For example, the theory of gravity was formulated following the inductive method.

The inductive method has the following advantages: (1) It is realistic because it is based on actual phenomena; (2) It is based on the scientific method; and (3) it is not highly structured, so it can be applied in a variety of circumstances.

The disadvantages are: (1) The results are necessarily biased by the particular sample of observations used in the process; (2) the results are easily biased by the observer who has done the examination; and (3) the conclusions are hard to change once adopted because the whole experiment would have to be replicated.

THE NORMATIVE DEDUCTIVE APPROACH

The deductive approach tends to be normative, emphasizing what should be. It represents a desire to improve the current situation in a particular discipline.

This approach has been popular in the social sciences, nonphysical sciences, and philosophy. It involves reasoning from the general to the specific, that is, from a premise to a conclusion. It involves a highly structured form of reasoning. It begins with objectives, then postulates are stated, and from them principles are developed that when applied, will achieve the objectives. Under this approach, if no logical mistakes are made and the premises are true, then the conclusion will also be true.

One advantage of the normative-deductive approach is that it is fertile; if faithfully followed, it should produce a theory. Another advantage is that it represents a complete, coordinated, and consistent approach to theory formulation; that is, it is orderly and logical.

The normative-deductive approach has two major disadvantages. It is a fragile approach; unless each part is done correctly, the results are flawed and the conclusion is invalid. Also, it can produce unrealistic results because no actual observations are necessarily used in the process. Of these two major approaches, the normative-deductive approach found more support in accounting probably because it had been popular in the social sciences and is an orderly and logical approach.

TWO NEEDS OF A STANDARD SETTER

An accounting standard-setting body needs *a theory of accounting* to be successful. Theory is like a compass to guide the standard-setting process. Without a theory, the three purposes of accounting theory probably cannot happen and standard setting would be very limited. Without theory, accounting standards would rest solely on opinion or political power, which could lead to standards that are inconsistent with other standards or lack support because of the compromise that led to their issuance.

A second needed element of a standard-setting body is *authority*. Obviously, if a standard-setting body is expected to regulate the practices of business firms, it needs authority to ensure that its pronouncements are followed. Because the SEC has legal authority to prescribe accounting practices, it must clearly delegate this authority to the accounting standard-setting body. Unless there is a change in U.S. security laws, however, the SEC cannot give this statutory authority to the standard-setting body. At the maximum, therefore, because authority must be delegated, any accounting standard-setting body must operate in the shadow of the SEC and only with the SEC's explicit approval.

Although both theory and authority are necessary factors for the success of an accounting standard-setting body, they may not be sufficient to guarantee the long-term success of that body. Additional factors are needed to accomplish that, which are discussed in Chapters 2 and 3.

SUMMARY

This chapter provides the foundation for further study of accounting standard setting and accounting theory formulation; it shows the importance of external key change factors in this process. Key factors, such as the public investment in stock, served as stimuli for accountants to begin to codify accounting standards. Important linkages in the change factors were noted: the stock market crash caused the creation of the SEC, which led to the delegation of accounting standard setting to the AIA's CAP, which led to the issuing of accounting standards. The chronological development also shows that accountants were always dependent on external change factors for internal changes. Accountants rarely took the initiative to resolve problems. This pattern of behavior seems to have been set during these years.

Two primary factors, *theory* and *authority,* are important for the success of a standard-setting body. Theory is important to accounting as well. The three roles of theory are to explain practice, evaluate practice, and facilitate the development of new practice. The deductive has the greatest potential for theory formulation in accounting and ultimately has the strongest impact on theory formulation.

A crisis of confidence in the CAP developed in the late 1950s. Without a theory but with authority delegated from the SEC to set accounting standards, the CAP was not successful in managing the growth of GAAP. As the public invested more in stock, investors needed to rely more on accounting information. Unfortunately, the CAP could not stop the unstructured growth of GAAP, which led to major comparability problems. These problems reflected back on the CAP. Something radical had to be done to solve the problem.

REVIEW QUESTIONS

1. Give two reasons for examining standard setting and accounting theory formulation together.
2. What are some characteristics of the "new view" of accounting?
3. Select three key change factors (people, events, or organizations), and label them as having a positive or negative impact on the development of accounting.
4. List and explain some reasons why we should be concerned with the chronological development of accounting.
5. In what way did the context or the times influence the early years of the CAP?
6. What role did World War I play in the development of public investing in the United States?
7. What motivated the New York Stock Exchange to seek the development of accounting principles?

8. What was significant about the list of five accounting principles that the AIA Special Committee on Cooperation with Stock Exchanges provided to the New York Stock Exchange?

9. What was so important about the creation of the SEC in 1934?

10. Why do you think the CAP was relatively inactive in its early years?

11. How did the McKesson and Robbins scandal affect the SEC?

12. Identify one advantage and one disadvantage of the size of the CAP after it expanded to twenty-one members.

13. Why did the CAP decide not to attempt to formulate an accounting theory? How did this decision affect the CAP over its tenure?

14. What were the major accomplishments of the CAP over its tenure?

15. How has time changed the authority of the ARBs issued by the CAP?

16. When you decided to take a course in accounting theory, how would you have defined theory? How does that compare to the definitions of theory in this chapter?

17. How can theory help any discipline?

18. Two approaches to the development of accounting theory were described in this chapter. Briefly describe each and list three advantages and disadvantages. Why do you think accountants adopted the deductive approach to develop their theory of accounting?

19. What are the two needs of a standard setter? How did they apply to the CAP?

20. What role does accounting theory perform in the discipline of accounting? What other benefits are derived from developing an accounting theory?

DISCUSSION TOPICS

1. **Application Problem.** Read through the 1931 GE annual report (Exhibit 1.2 and appendix), and respond to the following questions:

   a. Describe the level of disclosures in this annual report. In general, how would that level compare to the level of disclosures in current annual reports? (Characterize the comparison as more, less, or about the same, and support your answer.)

   b. Review the accounting principles used in the financial statements. Identify those that are not currently generally accepted accounting principles.

   c. Describe any interesting disclosures that you would not have expected to find. Would you find similar disclosures in current annual reports?

2. Discuss the following quotation from the beginning of another accounting theory book, now out of print:

   "There is no generally accepted theory of accounting."

   If we accept this disclaimer as valid, what are the implications for accounting? List and briefly describe three important implications for accounting today.

3. Do you agree or disagree with the following statements:

   "Why should we be concerned with the chronological development of accounting standard setting or theory formulation? After all, what's past is past. We can't

go back to the future and rearrange anything. We should just be concerned with the present."

Support your position.

4. In the period of standard setting and theory formulation covered in this chapter (1900–1960), we've noted some key change factors (people, events, and organizations) that had a significant impact on accounting. Select one factor from each category (people, events, and organizations) and describe the impact it/they had on accounting.

5. Although it lasted for over twenty years, the CAP ultimately failed as a standard-setting body. List and briefly explain the three most significant major criticisms of the CAP that contributed to its failure.

6. What role did the growth in public investment in capital markets have on the development of accounting in the period covered in this chapter (1900–1960)? In what ways is this consistent with the "new view" of accounting described in the introduction to Part I?

7. What similarities (if any) do you see between the period after World War I when the new automobile industry was flourishing and the mid-1990s–2000 when the new dot.com industry was flourishing?

8. Many people believe that new breakthroughs in thinking occur with an intuitive flash or similar dramatic event rather than through a formal process, such as inductive or deductive reasoning. What are the advantages and disadvantages of both approaches? Which do you prefer?

NOTES

1 Paton and Littleton, vi.

REFERENCES

Dennis, Anita. "No One Stands Still in Public Accounting." *Journal of Accountancy* (June 2000): 67–74.

Edwards, James Don. *History of Public Accounting in the United States.* Tuscaloosa: University of Alabama Press, 1978.

Hoxey, J. M. B. "Accounting for Investors." *Journal of Accountancy* (May 1937): 252–61.

Kerlinger, F. N. *Foundations of Behavioral Research.* New York: Holt, Rinehart, and Winston, 1964.

Kohler, Eric. "Theories and Practice." *The Accounting Review* (September 1939): 316–321.

Paton, William, and A. C. Littleton. *An Introduction to Corporate Accounting Standards.* Ann Arbor, MI: American Accounting Association, 1940.

Ripley, William Z. *Main Street and Wall Street.* Boston: Little, Brown, 1927.

Sterling, Robert A. "On Theory Construction and Verification," *Accounting Review* (July 1970): 444–57.

Storey, Reed K. *The Search for Accounting Principles—Today's Problems in Perspective.* New York: American Institute of Certified Public Accountants.

Zeff, Stephen A. "1926 to 1972 Chronology of Significant Developments in the Establishment of Accounting Principles in the United States." In *Corporate Financial Reporting*, edited by A. Rappaport and L. Revsin, 219–33. Chicago: Commerce Clearing House, 1972.

Zeff, Stephen A. "Some Junctures in the Evolution of the Process of Establishing Accounting Principles in the U.S.A.: 1917–1972." *The Accounting Review* (July, 1984): 447–68.

Zeff, Stephen A. "A Perspective on the U.S. Public/Private-Sector Approach to the Regulation of Financial Reporting." *Accounting Horizons* (March 1995): 52–70.

FORTIETH
ANNUAL REPORT
GENERAL GE ELECTRIC
COMPANY

1931

DECEMBER 31, 1931

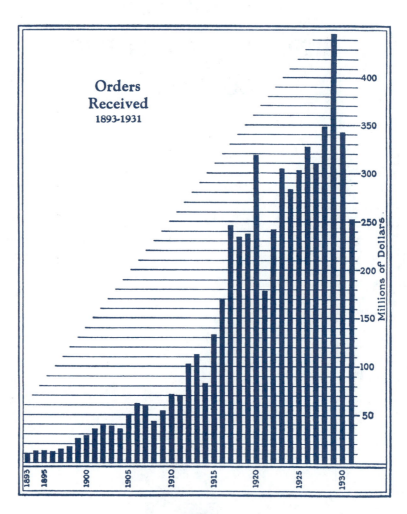

Orders Received
1893-1931

Millions of Dollars.

GENERAL ELECTRIC COMPANY

RECORD OF EARNINGS AND DIVIDENDS

The table below shows the profit available for dividends on common stock per share of average common stock outstanding in each of the last twenty-nine years:

Year	Amount	Year	Amount
1903	$17.76	1918	$14.93
1904	14.59	1919	20.93
1905	15.17	1920	16.62
1906	15.52	1921	12.92
1907	10.17	1922	14.86
1908	7.37	1923	18.40
1909 (11 months)	9.96	1924	21.13
1910	16.66	1925	20.49
1911	14.55	1926	6.14*
1912	16.20	1927	6.41
1913	12.88	1928	7.15
1914	11.03	1929	8.97
1915	11.56	1930	1.90*
1916	18.31	1931	1.33
1917	26.50		

For more than thirty-two years cash dividends have been paid continuously on the common stock, and from April 1900 to and including April 1926 the rate was uniformly $8 per share per annum with an extra Red Cross dividend of $1 per share in 1917. In May 1926 four shares of no par value common stock were exchanged for each $100 par value share. Cash dividends at the rate of $3 per share per annum were paid on the new stock from July 1926 to April 1927 inclusive. In July 1927 an extra cash dividend of $1 per share was paid and at the same time the regular cash dividend rate was increased to $4 per share per annum, which was paid regularly through 1929. Extra cash dividends of $1 per share were also paid in July 1928 and in January and July 1929. In December 1929 a regular cash dividend of $1.50 per share was declared, payable in January 1930. In January 1930 three additional shares of no par value common stock were issued to the holder of each share of no par value common stock then outstanding, and in April 1930 a regular quarterly cash dividend of $.40 per share was paid, which rate has been continued quarterly without change.

In addition, the following distributions of stock per share of General Electric common stock have been made during the last twenty-nine years:

1912—30% in common stock
1917—2% in common stock
1918 to 1921 inclusive—4% annually in common stock
1922 to 1925 inclusive—5% annually in special stock†
1924—1 share of Electric Bond & Share Securities Corporation stock
1926—$1 in special stock†

---

*Number of shares of common stock increased four for one in 1926 and again in 1930.

†Special stock, par value $10 per share, paying 6% annual dividends.

Schenectady, N.Y., March 26, 1932

To the Stockholders of the
General Electric Company:

Orders received during the year 1931 were $252,021,496, compared with $341,820,312 in the year 1930, a decrease of 26 per cent.

Unfilled orders at the end of the year were $49,308,000, compared with $56,062,000 at the end of 1930, a decrease of 12 per cent.

COMPARATIVE STATEMENT OF INCOME AND EXPENSES

	1931	1930
Net sales billed	$263,275,255.37	$376,167,428.42
Less: Costs, expenses, and all charges except interest	234,884,372.57	335,717,167.11
Net income from sales	$ 28,390,882.80	$ 40,450,261.31
Income from other sources:		
Associated companies and miscellaneous securities	$ 8,657,110.67	$ 13,453,654.25
Interest and discount	3,819,280.21	3,258,498.99
U.S. Government and other marketable securities	21,533.46	1,757,715.15
Royalties and sundry revenue	501,422.20	1,605,334.28
	$ 12,999,346.54	$ 20,075,202.67
Total income	$ 41,390,229.34	$ 60,525,463.98
Less: Interest payments	$ 433,344.73	$ 313,078.69
Addition to general reserve		2,721,470.03
	$ 433,233.73	$ 3,034,548.72
Profit available for dividends	$40,956,995.61	$ 57,490,915.26
Less: 6% cash dividends on special stock	2,575,005.15	2,574,952.95
Profit available for dividends on common stock	$ 38,381,990.46	$ 54,915,962.31
Less: Cash dividends on common stock	46,150,256.80	46,150,203.60
Deficit (1931) and surplus (1930) for the year	$ 7,768,266.34	$ 8,765,758.71

5

CONDENSED BALANCE SHEET
December 31, 1931 and 1930

ASSETS

	1931	1930
Fixed investments:		
Manufacturing plants at cost, including land, buildings, and machinery	$199,129,732.92	$198,303,962.66
Less: General plant reserve and depreciation	153,068,713.66	152,436,033.08
	$ 46,061,019.26	$ 45,867,929.58
Other property	228,445.67	252,609.47
Furniture and appliances (other than in factories)	1.00	1.00
Patents	1.00	1.00
Total fixed investments	$ 46,289,466.93	$ 46,120,541.05
Associated companies and miscellaneous securities	179,308,010.36	204,810,328.13
Current assets:		
Inventories	57,335,498.53	60,063,418.56
Installation work in progress	10,063,820.42	16,229,589.20
Notes and accounts receivable	39,192,433.60	41,676,727.47
Marketable securities (at the lower of par or market) . . . . $ 7,122,820.00		
Cash 115,056,113.22	122,178,933.22	141,717,851.25
	$228,770,685.77	$259,687,586.48
Less: Advance payments on contracts .	9,684,175.13	17,123,037.38
Total current assets	$219,086,510.64	$242,564,549.10
Deferred charges	241,948.86	476,403.83
	$444,925,936.79	$493,971,822.11

6

CONDENSED BALANCE SHEET
December 31, 1931 and 1930

LIABILITIES AND CAPITAL

	1931	1930
3½% Debenture bonds due 1942	$ 2,047,000.00	$ 2,047,000.00
Current liabilities:		
Accounts payable and accrued liabilities.	16,301,469.11	28,422,154.65
Dividends payable	12,181,318.95	12,181,296.35
Total current liabilities	$ 28,482,788.06	$ 40,603,451.00
Reserves for self-insurance, work-men's compensation, etc.	4,063,496.81	7,974,385.38
Charles A. Coffin Foundation	400,000.00	400,000.00
General reserve	14,517,597.21*	39,763,664.68
Special stock:		
Authorized 5,500,000 shares, par value $10; issued 4,292,963½ shares	42,929,635.00	42,929,635.00
Common stock and earned surplus:		
Common stock (authorized 29,600,000 shares no par value; issued 28,845,927 36/100 shares)	180,287,046.00	180,287,046.00
Earned surplus on January 1st	179,966,640.05	171,200,881.34
Deficit (1931) and surplus (1930) for the year (page 5)	7,768,266.34	8,765,758.71
Total common stock and earned surplus	$352,485,419.71	$360,253,686.05
	$444,925,936.79	$493,971,822.11

*After applying $25,246,067.47 in reduction of book value of "Associated companies and miscellaneous securities."

7

Committees of the Board of Directors reviewed the valuation of manufacturing plants, investments in associated companies and miscellaneous securities, inventories, and notes and accounts receivable, and the figures used in this report are the result of such reviews.

MANUFACTURING PLANTS

From the formation of the General Electric Company in 1892, there had been expended on manufacturing plants to December 31, 1930		$327,225,297.35
Added during 1931		9,600,173.80
		$336,825,471.15
Dismantled, sold or otherwise disposed of to December 31, 1930	$128,921,334.69	
Dismantled, sold or otherwise disposed of during 1931	8,774,403.54	137,695,738.23
Cost of present plants		$199,129,732.92
General plant reserve and depreciation, December 31, 1930	$152,436,033.08	
Added by charges to income during 1931	8,859,062.05	
Proceeds from sale of dismantled equipment, etc., during 1931	548,022.07	
	$161,843,117.20	
Less: Cost of plants dismantled, sold or otherwise disposed of during 1931	8,774,403.54	153,068,713.66
Net book value, December 31, 1931		$ 46,061,019.26

Expenditures for manufacturing plant in 1931 amounted to $9,600,173.80, compared with $13,566,076.00 in 1930. The more important projects were the construction of a building for the manufacture of transformer tanks at Pittsfield works, a new refrigerator warehouse at Erie works, and the beginning of construction at Schenectady works of the first outdoor fuel-burning generating station in the United States. This station will consist of a mercury boiler and turbine unit, which will generate 20,000 kilowatts (26,800 horsepower) of electric energy besides making sufficient steam to produce 33,000 kilowatts (44,220 horsepower) in a steam turbine. It will be operated under lease by the New York Power and Light Corporation. Electric energy and

8

steam will be supplied to Schenectady works, while excess electric energy will be fed into the Power Company's system. This combination of public utility and industrial usage, with its attendant improvement in efficiency, distinctly advances the power art.

Annual reports of the past, notably those for 1926 and 1928, have outlined a policy of plant depreciation and valuation. Depreciation goes on whether plant is used to capacity or partially idle. Very little of the plant, except the land on which it is located, remains until used up or worn out; more is replaced by buildings and equipment which are superior or better adapted to the job to be done. A manufacturing organization's progress may be measured to some extent by the rapidity of its change in plant, bringing about better methods, improved quality of products, and lower costs. With lower costs come reduced selling prices, followed by increased business, and a greater use of plant. When plant value is low on the books, management is more responsive to the introduction of new methods and better tools.

ASSOCIATED COMPANIES AND MISCELLANEOUS SECURITIES

Investments in associated companies and miscellaneous securities were increased during 1931 by $17,782,549.22, and amounted to $222,592,877.35 before revaluation on December 31, 1931. This amount has been reduced by reappraisal, according to methods stated below, to $179,308,010.36. These investments include advances to associated companies as well as securities, inasmuch as most of the advances are required permanently in the business. The decrease resulting from revaluation was charged in part to the General reserve (page 12) and to other reserves set aside from earnings of previous years.

The larger investments during the year were in Electrical Securities Corporation, United Electric Securities Company, and International General Electric Company, Inc.

Interest and dividends received from associated companies in the United States, and from Canadian General Electric Company, Ltd., and International General Electric Company, Inc., are included in the "Statement of income and expenses" as

9

part of "Income from associated companies and miscellaneous securities." Total income from associated companies and miscellaneous securities amounted to $8,657,110.67, which is 4.5 per cent of the average net value of these investments at the beginning and end of the year. This compares with 6.9 per cent return in 1930.

Your Company's share of income earned by associated companies during 1931 (disregarding revaluations of their securities) exceeded your Company's share of the dividends distributed by approximately $5,000,000, which is equivalent to 17 cents per share of the common stock of your Company outstanding on December 31, 1931.

Investments in associated companies are of a more or less permanent character, and may well be considered as investments in plant and working capital of companies closely associated with your Company in the development of its business on a broader base and in a more effective manner than could be done by your Company itself. Accordingly, investments in associated companies in which your Company has a majority interest are appraised on a basis similar to that used in the valuation of your Company's assets. Investments in other companies are appraised after consideration of cost, net worth, return on investment, market price, if any, and foreign exchange, but in no case is an investment or security appraised at a higher valuation than the market price on a recognized exchange on December 31, 1931, with due allowance for foreign exchange rates.

In determining the value of your Company's investment in International General Electric Company, Inc., these same methods of appraisal were applied to securities of foreign companies held by International General Electric Company, Inc. and its subsidiaries.

Foreign Business

Canadian General Electric Company, Ltd. reported net profit for the year 1931 of $2,308,155, compared with $3,765,798 for 1930. Dividends of 7 per cent were paid on $8,557,750 of preference stock, and 8 per cent on $9,442,250 of common stock outstanding.

10

International General Electric Company, Inc. conducts the export and foreign business of your Company outside of Canada, and, for 1931, reported a profit available for interest on capital advances and dividends of $2,963,222, compared with $3,897,818 for 1930. Interest and dividends paid in 1931 amounted to $2,846,667, compared with $3,878,619 in 1930.

Electrical Securities Corporation

The capital of Electrical Securities Corporation was reduced $18,750,000 in December 1931, by the surrender by your Company of 750,000 of the 1,000,000 shares of common stock without par value outstanding. As your Company owned all of the common shares, the surrender did not affect its equity position. This action was taken as a result of depreciation in the market price of securities owned by Electrical Securities Corporation, and the amount of the capital reduction was set aside as a reserve against losses on securities.

Earnings of Electrical Securities Corporation for 1931 were $2,675,199, compared with $2,339,048 for 1930, and regular dividends were paid out of earnings at the annual rate of 5 per cent on the preferred stock, and 50 cents per share on the common stock during each of the first three quarters and $2 per share (on the reduced number of shares) in the last quarter.

CURRENT ASSETS

Inventories

Inventories in factories and warehouses and on consignment have been valued, in accordance with the custom of your Company, at the lower of cost or market. After deducting reserves, they were carried at $57,335,498.53, compared with $60,063,418.56 at the end of 1930.

The following table shows the relation of inventories to shipments billed in each of the last twelve years:

11

Year	Inventories at end of year	Net billing	Per cent of inventories to billing
1920	$118,109,173.99	$275,758,487.57	42.8
1921	64,848,188.87	221,007,991.64	29.3
1922	75,334,561.79	200,194,294.09	37.6
1923	83,746,031.05	271,309,695.37	30.9
1924	68,485,161.08	299,251,869.15	22.9
1925	67,798,190.20	290,290,165.97	23.4
1926	65,295,154.88	326,974,103.84	20.0
1927	67,213,705.87	312,603,771.53	21.5
1928	63,776,149.05	337,189,422.43	18.9
1929	80,835,545.38	415,338,094.39	19.5
1930	60,063,418.56	376,167,428.42	16.0
1931	57,335,498.53	263,275,255.37	21.8

CURRENT AND CONTINGENT LIABILITIES

Total current liabilities amounted to $28,482,788.06, compared with $40,603,451.00 at the end of 1930. Your Company had no notes payable or any obligation bearing its endorsement outstanding, and none of the companies in which your Company owns a majority interest had any funded debt or any loans owing to banks or to the public. Your Company's only contingent liability was that of guarantor for $1,846,724 in connection with the employees home ownership plan (reviewed on page 15), which was adequately secured.

WORKING CAPITAL

Working capital (total current assets less total current liabilities) amounted to $190,603,722.58, compared with $201,961,098.10 at the end of 1930, a decrease of $11,357,375.52.

GENERAL RESERVE

The general reserve, which amounted to $39,763,664.68 on December 31, 1930, has been drawn upon in 1931 in connection with the revaluation of associated companies and miscellaneous securities, and on December 31, 1931, amounted to $14,517,597.21.

12

CAPITAL STOCK AND DIVIDENDS

There were no changes during the year in the special or common stock outstanding. Regular dividends of 15 cents per share on the special stock and 40 cents per share on the common stock were paid quarterly.

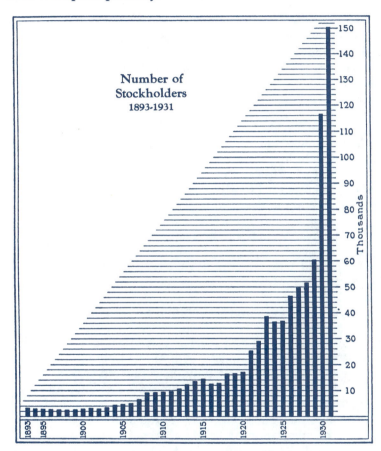

Number of
Stockholders
1893-1931

STOCKHOLDERS

On December 18, 1931, there were 150,073 holders of common and special stock, half of this number (exclusive of

13

corporations, institutions, etc.) being women. This compares with 116,750 on December 19, 1930, and 60,374 on December 16, 1929, an increase in 1931 over 1929 of 149 per cent.

ORGANIZATION CHANGES

Theodore W. Frech, who was given leave of absence on January 1, 1930, resumed his position as Vice President in charge of the Incandescent Lamp Department in April 1931.

Dana R. Bullen, Assistant Vice President, retired on pension July 1, 1931.

EMPLOYEES AND PAYROLLS

The average number of employees of your Company during 1931, not including those of associated companies, was 65,516, compared with 78,380 during 1930. Total earnings of these employees amounted to $106,656,000 for 1931 and $140,905,000 for 1930. Average annual earnings per employee were $1628 and $1798 respectively, a decrease of 9.5 per cent. The cost of living, according to the index of the National Industrial Conference Board, decreased 9.9 per cent from 1930.

Compared with the year 1923, average annual earnings of employees for 1931 were 1.2 per cent more and the cost of living was 13.3 per cent less.

Supplementary compensation of 5 per cent of annual earnings has been paid for sixteen years to employees having five or more years of service and receiving salaries or wages of less than $4000 per year. Payments for 1931 amounted to $3,007,263, and were made to 39,264 employees, compared with payments of $3,408,657 to 38,452 employees for 1930. The long continued depression made it necessary to give notice on December 28, 1931, in accordance with the terms of the plan, that this supplementary compensation (which is a fixed charge, and does not fluctuate with the earnings of the Company) would be discontinued after payments for the year 1932.

The several plans of extra compensation (or profit sharing), referred to in previous reports, yielded $1,940,257 payable to

14

1,731 employees for 1931, compared with payments of $3,971,153 to 2335 employees for 1930.

VARIOUS EMPLOYEE PLANS

Plans dealing with group life and disability insurance, home ownership, savings, pensions, unemployment, and employment guarantee were described at length in the 1930 Annual Report.

Group Life and Disability Insurance

At the close of 1931, approximately 62,200 employees were insured for $73,000,000 under the policy paid for by the Company, and for $98,400,000 under the Additional Insurance Plan paid for by employees, a total of $171,400,000.

Death and disability benefits paid during 1931 amounted to $1,156,294, of which $397,890 was free insurance, and $758,404 was additional insurance. Since the inauguration of the first plan in 1920, $7,936,663 has been paid as death benefits to the families of 3677 deceased employees, or as disability payments to 450 employees.

Home Ownership

During 1931, 144 homes, having a value of $1,010,000, were financed under the Home Ownership Plan. In the last eight years, 2706 homes, representing a value of about $20,000,000, have been acquired or built by employees. Payments of upwards of $7,850,000 have been made on these homes, the balance being in the form of first and second mortgages held by regular financial institutions.

Savings

The G.E. Employees Securities Corporation has continued through the depression to be a very satisfactory medium for employees' savings. The bonds, which are sold to employees for cash or on an installment plan, bear 6 per cent interest, to which the General Electric Company adds 2 per cent as long as the original purchaser remains in the employ of the Company and retains the bonds. On December 31, 1931, approximately 33,900

15

employees owned or were paying for bonds having a total value of $43,471,870. This compares with approximately 36,500 employees and $40,430,080 of bonds on December 31, 1930.

Pensions and Retirement Payments

Company pension and retirement payments aggregating $1,517,667 were made during 1931 to 2141 retired employees, the larger share of which was paid by the Pension Trust. On December 31, 1931, there were 1953 on the pension and retirement rolls, whose average age was 68.0 years, average active service to date of retirement 29.6 years, and average annual payment $885. Pension and retirement payments amounting to $5,513,400 have been made since the inauguration of the plans in 1912.

The General Electric Pension Trust on December 31, 1931 held assets of $20,125,255, compared with $16,505,168 on December 31, 1930.

Contributions by employees to the Additional Pension Plan during the three and one-half years since its establishment amounted, with interest, to $4,098,382. This amount is deposited in a trust fund to the credit of 50,037 employees.

The Additional Pension Plan added $43,275 to pensions paid during 1931.

The Trustees of these two Trusts hold title to their respective assets, which are therefore not reflected in your Company's balance sheet.

Employees Unemployment Pension Plan and Employment Guarantee

The 1930 Annual Report stated that the Employees Unemployment Pension Plan was adopted in the second half of 1930, and that the normal contributions paid into the fund amounted to $381,251, one-half contributed by the participants and one-half by the Company. This amount was placed with the G.E. Employees Securities Corporation by the Trustees, and on December 31, 1931, amounted, with interest, to $396,431.

During the thirteen months from December 1, 1930, when the Unemployment Emergency Plan began to operate, to December 31, 1931, collections from piece-work and hourly-

16

rated employees eligible for benefits under the Plan amounted to $540,000, collections from other employees amounted to $570,000, and the Company's contributions amounted to $1,110,000, which, with interest and adjustment of loans and refunds, make a total of $2,255,756. Disbursements under the Unemployment Emergency Plan until November 1, 1931, and under the Employment Guarantee during November and December, amounted to $1,357,481, leaving an unexpended balance in the fund on December 31, 1931, of $898,275.

The Employment Guarantee in the Incandescent Lamp Department for the year 1931, which was described in the 1930 Annual Report, has been renewed with some modifications for the year 1932. Instead of a guarantee of thirty hours per week, the 1932 Plan guarantees fifteen hundred hours of work during the year, less time lost through illness or through fire, flood, strike, or other extreme emergency.

The cost to the Company of the Employment Guarantee in the Incandescent Lamp Department for 1931 was approximately $25,000. The employees put aside in the savings fund $40,930.

SUGGESTION SYSTEM
"There Is Always a Better Way"

The Suggestion System is designed to stimulate the initiative of employees and to encourage suggestions for better ways of doing things. It has been in operation for many years in most factories and many offices of your Company, and during the past year was broadened by the establishment of a routine to further facilitate the consideration and adoption of suggestions made by supervisory, technical, clerical, and other salaried employees.

Response from employees continues to be most gratifying. Factory employees submitted 19,595 suggestions in 1931, or 428 per thousand of eligible employees, of which 32.6 per cent were adopted and for which awards amounting to $55,739 were made. Suggestions submitted in 1930 totaled 29,919, or 536 per thousand of eligible employees, of which 32.1 per cent were adopted and for which awards amounting to $94,091 were made. During the last nine years, since the plan became system-

17

atized, awards of $517,907 have been made to factory employees in cash or G.E. Employees Securities Corporation bonds.

ACCIDENT PREVENTION

It is gratifying to report that, as a result of intensive effort to equip machinery with safeguards and to educate employees in methods of safety, lost-time accidents have been reduced to less than one-third of what they were in 1920. It is a matter of further gratification that during 1931 the number of fatal accidents to employees while at work was lower than in any year since 1915.

Cost of hospitalization and workmen's compensation has risen steadily, despite the constant reduction in number of lost-time accidents, and, in 1931, amounted to approximately $800,000. The increasing cost has arisen from the creation of better hospitalization facilities and medical attention for injured employees, and from the steadily mounting expenses imposed by State laws in connection with workmen's compensation payments.

CHARLES A. COFFIN FOUNDATION

When the Board of Directors created the Charles A. Coffin Foundation in 1922, it was announced that the Foundation was formed "as an expression of appreciation of Mr. Coffin's great work, not only for the General Electric Company, but also for the entire electrical industry and with the desire to make this appreciation enduring and constructive, as Mr. Coffin's life and work have been."

The following awards were made during the year under the provisions of the Foundation:

In June 1931, the Committee of the National Electric Light Association awarded the Charles A. Coffin Medal to the Virginia Electric and Power Company, and in September 1931, the Committee of the American Electric Railway Association made a similar award to The Milwaukee Electric Railway and Light Company, for having made, during the previous year, distinguished contributions to the development of electric light and power and of electric transportation respectively for the convenience of the public and the benefit of the industry.

18

In addition to the medal, $1000 was given to the employees' benefit association of each of the companies granted the award.

The Committee representing the American Institute of Electrical Engineers, the Society for the Promotion of Engineering Education, and the National Academy of Sciences awarded Charles A. Coffin Fellowships to nine graduates of American colleges who desired to carry on postgraduate research work and who needed and were found worthy of assistance. Since the creation of the Foundation, seventy-two fellowships have been granted to fifty-nine individuals (thirteen having received fellowships two years in succession), who have received approximately $44,500. These students graduated from forty-eight different institutions (some having degrees from more than one) and continued their studies at twenty-four, the two groups of institutions being located in twenty-nine states and three foreign countries.

The Advisory Committee of your Company awarded thirty-eight Charles A. Coffin Foundation Certificates of Merit, carrying with them honorariums in cash, to employees for meritorious work and distinguished service. Among them were seven workmen in the shops, six tool designers and expert mechanics, five foremen, twelve engineers, and eight members of the commercial and administrative organizations.

The certificate of the accountants, testifying to the correctness of the published financial statements, will be found on page 20.

By order of the Board of Directors,

OWEN D. YOUNG, *Chairman*

GERARD SWOPE, *President*

19

PEAT, MARWICK, MITCHELL & CO.
Accountants and Auditors

40 Exchange Place, New York, March 4, 1932

TO THE BOARD OF DIRECTORS OF THE
   GENERAL ELECTRIC COMPANY,
     120 BROADWAY, NEW YORK,

Dear Sirs:

We have examined the accounts of the General Electric Company for the year ended December 31, 1931, and certify that the Condensed statement of income and expenses and Balance sheet appearing on pages 5-7 of this report are in accordance with the books and, in our opinion, set forth the results of the operations of the Company for the year and the condition of its affairs as at December 31, 1931.

We have confirmed the cash and securities by count and inspection or by certificates which we have obtained from the depositories. The valuations at which the investments in Associated companies and miscellaneous securities are carried have been approved by a Committee of the Board of Directors and, in our opinion, are conservative. Our examination has not included the accounts of companies controlled through stock ownership (other than International General Electric Company, Inc. and G.E. Employees Securities Corporation), but financial statements of these Companies have been submitted to us.

We have scrutinized the notes and accounts receivable and are satisfied that full provision has been made for possible losses through bad and doubtful debts.

Certified inventories of merchandise, work in progress, and materials and supplies have been submitted to us and we have satisfied ourselves that these inventories have been taken in a careful manner, that ample allowance has been made for old or inactive stocks, and that they are conservatively stated on the basis of cost or market, whichever is lower. Provision has also been made for possible allowances or additional expenditures on completed contracts.

Expenditures capitalized in the property and plant accounts during the year were properly so chargeable as representing additions or improvements. Adequate provision has been made in the operating accounts for repairs, renewals and depreciation, and for contingencies.

Yours truly,

PEAT, MARWICK, MITCHELL & CO.

20

CHAPTER 2

THE ACCOUNTING
PRINCIPLES BOARD I

LEARNING OBJECTIVES

After studying this chapter, you should be able to

> Trace the events leading to the formulation of the Accounting Principles Board.

> Understand A. Jennings's dual approach to theory formulation and standard setting.

> Identify the elements of the normative-deductive approach to theory formulation.

> Describe the content of ARS #1 and ARS #3, and explain why they were rejected by the accounting profession.

STANDARD SETTING	1900	THEORY FORMULATION
CHAPTER 1		
STANDARD SETTING I		THEORY 1
PRE-CAP	1900-1938	NATURE OF THEORY
SEC	1934	
STANDARD SETTING II		
CAP I	1938	
STANDARD SETTING III		
CAP II	1938-1958	
CHAPTER 2		
STANDARD SETTING IV		THEORY II
APB	**1959-1962**	
	1961-1962	ARS #1 AND #3
CHAPTER 3		
STANDARD SETTING V		THEORY III
APB	1963-1966	
	1966	ASOBAT
STANDARD SETTING VI		
DEMISE OF APB	1970	
CHAPTER 4, 5		
STANDARD SETTING VII		
TRUEBLOOD	1973	
WHEAT	1972	
TRIPARTITE STRUCTURE	1973-2001	
CHAPTER 6		
		THEORY IV
	1977	SATTA
		POSITIVE ACCOUNTING 1980s
CHAPTER 7		THEORY V
	1973-2001	CONCEPTUAL FRAMEWORK PROJECT
CHAPTER 8		
STANDARD SETTING VIII		
FASB: PRESENT AND FUTURE STANDARD SETTING: DOMESTIC AND INTERNATIONAL	2001	
	2002	

In this chapter, the examination of the standard-setting and theory formulation efforts of the accounting profession continues, focusing on the dissolution of the Committee on Accounting Procedure (CAP), the establishment of the Accounting Principles Board (APB), and the first major attempt to formulate a theory of accounting. This chapter covers some major developments in the chronology of standard setting and theory formulation.

To help keep the events in perspective, refer to Exhibit 2.1 and note that this chapter's coverage is indicated by the bold type.

THE ACCOUNTING PRINCIPLES BOARD

TROUBLE

In the late 1950s, the accounting profession was in trouble. Under the CAP, GAAP had grown, but this resulted in the problem that firms had remarkable flexibility in their selection of accounting practices. This flexibility, in conjunction with a renewed interested in investing by the public, caused a crisis for accounting. During the post–World War II period, from 1940 to 1960, the number of investors grew from four million to twenty million. This dramatic growth in investing put the spotlight on accounting as these investors had major problems with the lack of comparability between firms. Something clearly had to be done to narrow the diversity of accounting methods.

Zeff[1] identified five forces at work that led to the termination of the CAP.

1. Serious divisions existed in the CAP over the solutions to a number of major accounting problems. A prime cause of the division was the lack of an accounting theory. Without agreement on the basics of accounting and its underlying principles, CAP members could not agree on the best solution to accounting problems.
2. Members of the Controllers Institute of America (now the Financial Executives International [FEI]) were disgruntled that they had no opportunity to comment on proposed bulletins before issuance. That is, the preparers of financial statements were not given the opportunity to provide their input during the process.
3. Many accountants saw the American Accounting Association (AAA) as being more progressive in its view of accounting standards than the CAP.

PEOPLE

4. One of the most powerful of the managing partners of the eight national public accounting firms was Leonard Spacek of Arthur Andersen. He was a frequent and outspoken critic of the CAP.
5. The CAP had a number of conflicts with the SEC during its tenure and the relationship between the two was strained.

These are serious problems that faced the CAP. It is understandable that eventually the accounting profession felt something had to be done to regain the respect of the parties affected by accounting standard setting.

ALVIN JENNINGS

The period toward the end of the CAP's existence was the first watershed period for accounting, a time when significant change began. This change had long-lasting effects on accounting standard setting and theory formulation. It was instituted by Alvin Jennings, the president of the American Institute of Certified Public Accountants (AICPA). In light of the difficulties noted previously, at the 1957 annual meeting, he responded to the crisis by calling for a new, radical approach for standard setting.

This new approach had dual elements: A theory of accounting should be developed, and then accounting standards should be based on that theory. Jennings was not satisfied with the CAP's approach to standard setting without a guiding theory. Instead, he felt that a new effort to formulate a theory of accounting should be undertaken, and when completed, it would be the main guide for the standard-setting body. This dual approach would narrow the areas of difference and inconsistency in accounting practice and provide the information that investors needed. Jennings believed that this approach would solve the current crisis in accounting.

THE APB AND THE ACCOUNTING RESEARCH DIVISION

In response to his call, the AICPA set up a Special Committee on Research Program in 1957. This committee considered the lack of research on accounting and the lack of understanding and agreement on the basic postulates and principles of accounting. In 1958, it called for the dissolution of the CAP and its part-time research department and its replacement with two new bodies: a new standard-setting body, the Accounting Principles Board, and a related research organization, the Accounting Research Division (ARD). Note that the profession did not feel that simply tinkering or tweaking the structure and operations of the CAP was the answer. Instead, the profession wanted to start over with a new standard-setting body, coupled with a new research division to formulate a theory of accounting. Based on the experience of the CAP, this appeared to be a sound approach.

Jennings's recommendation was accepted by the AICPA in 1959, and both the APB and ARD were created with the following three objectives:

1. to advance the written expression of GAAP;
2. to narrow the areas of diversity; and
3. to lead in the solution of unsettled and controversial areas.

It was expected that the ARD, which was semiautonomous and had its own director, would sponsor research and issue Accounting Research Studies (ARSs) on controversial topics and issues.

The ARSs were designed to provide professional accountants and other interested parties with discussion and documentation of accounting problems. They were supposed to be informative but not conclusive. In other words, they were a vehicle for exposure of matters for consideration prior to the issuance of an Opinion by the APB.

The APB would issue standards (called Opinions) based on these ARSs. (Why the APB's pronouncements were called Opinions is not known. The use of this term may have weakened the impact of these pronouncements.)

Both the director of the ARD and the chairman of the APB conferred on the topics to be studied by the ARD. It was hoped that the ARD would find "accounting truth" and that the APB would adopt it. Thus both organizations would work together to issue standards based on theory and research rather than on the personal opinions of APB members.

APB STRUCTURE: ORGANIZATION AND SIZE

A board is usually an organization that has authority to pass motions, and because accounting practice was based on accounting principles, the APB's name was appropriate. The APB was structured to have eighteen to twenty-one members, all CPAs, which was very large for a standard-setting body. Imagine a committee trying to come to a decision on some topic; in general, a smaller-size committee will decide things more quickly. The larger the committee, the longer it takes to come to a decision, and often, more compromise is involved. The APB was designed as a large committee to ensure that all groups had representation. The AICPA insisted that the big eight CPA firms be represented by their managing partners on the APB. Other representatives were drawn from large and small CPA firms, academia, and industry, but all the representatives were required to be CPAs.

The members all served part-time. Each had a full-time "day job" to which that person was necessarily more committed than to the APB. Although members took their position on the board seriously, their primary allegiance was to their full-time professional position. As professionals, they tried to be independent and objective when deciding accounting issues, but the reality was that these issues directly affected their full-time professional position, and thus, objectivity was virtually impossible to attain. Another factor at work here was the knowledge of the big eight CPA firms and the industrial firms (the preparers) that the pronouncements of the APB would directly affect their firms. Some firms became "APB watchers" and tried to work out a position for their firm on APB issues. No doubt these positions were developed with the input of the firm's members who sat on the APB. And these positions would also have been communicated to any of the firm's members who sat on the APB.

The APB operated with a two-thirds vote required to pass any Opinion. The board lasted fourteen years (until 1973) and issued thirty-one Opinions. No due process or open deliberation process to obtain feedback or views on proposed standards was established for the APB until much later in its tenure.

AUTHORITY

An essential aspect of standard setting is to have the power or authority to expect compliance with the results of the standard-setting process. Unfortunately, the APB was not specifically empowered by the SEC. Of course, indirectly through substantial authoritative support, APB Opinions were accepted by the SEC in filings. But the SEC never went beyond that to officially or directly endorse the APB. As will be shown in Chapter 3, the SEC challenged the APB very early in its history, and because the SEC had legal authority to specify accounting standards, the SEC prevailed.

NORMATIVE-DEDUCTIVE APPROACH IN ARS #1 AND ARS #3 THEORY II

The ARD started off with a "great theory search." The Special Committee on Research Program laid the basis for the new research program of the ARD. From the beginning it was understood that major research projects would be undertaken to discover the basic postulates of accounting followed by a statement of a "fairly broad set of coordinated accounting principles" based on the postulates. These were intended to provide the foundation for the entire body of future pronouncements by the APB.

The first head of the ARD, named the Director of Accounting Research, was Professor Maurice Moonitz of the University of California at Berkeley. He decided to use the normative-deductive approach to formulate a theory composed of postulates and principles. (See the discussion on the deductive approach in Chapter 1.) In fact, he concluded in ARS #1 that the ARD was driven to "heavy reliance" on the normative-deductive approach so as to solve problems by looking at what "ought" to be the solution not just what "is" the solution. This position was consistent with the popularity of the normative-deductive approach. Although no prior major effort using this approach had been undertaken, the normative-deductive approach had intuitive appeal to the accounting profession as the best approach to use.

NORMATIVE-DEDUCTIVE APPROACH

To many scholars, especially those involved in the "great theory search" debate in accounting in the 1960s, the normative-deductive was the only approach that should be used to develop or formulate a theory of accounting. It had general acceptance with accountants. Because the majority of attempts at accounting theory development used this approach, it has had the greatest influence on accounting and justifies a closer examination here in conjunction with ARS #1.

ELEMENTS OF THE NORMATIVE-DEDUCTIVE APPROACH

The typical normative-deductive model has four structural elements, which are listed in the proper sequence in which they are developed: objectives, postulates, principles, and rules. A detailed discussion of each follows.

Objectives   The starting point for developing a theory using the normative-deductive approach is to state the objectives. *The objectives answer the question: What are we trying to accomplish with the theory?* This important first step guides the development of the theory in the subsequent steps and has enormous influence on all that follows.

The objective is critically important. For example, compare tax accounting and financial reporting. Both aim at different objectives: financial reporting attempts to provide financial information to decision makers outside the firm for investment and credit decisions, whereas tax accounting determines how much a taxpayer owes the government according to the tax code (laws). Given these very different objectives, we can understand why financial accounting and tax accounting are very different in structure. The objectives are what we wish to accomplish through the application of the theory. We can conclude that the theory is correctly applied when the objectives are accomplished.

In terms of accounting, the objectives should define three areas: (1) the audience, those to whom accounting data is directed (the *who* issue); (2) the function, for what purposes the data are to be used (the *why* issue); and (3) the content, what data or information are communicated (the *what* issue). A good statement of objectives will clearly specify all three.

Postulates   The next step is to develop a set of postulates, or basic propositions about the economic, political, and sociological environment in which accounting operates.

Postulates are broadly descriptive of the environment of a particular discipline. Usually they are few in number and must be accepted as valid because they are usually so basic as to be unproven.

Postulates should have three characteristics. They should: (1) be relevant—they must apply to the particular field of study under question; (2) be accepted as valid—they generally cannot be proven; and (3) be fertile—they must be productive as the source of the principles. Postulates can be generally descriptive of the environment of accounting, procedural (focus on the procedures of accounting), or normative, indicating what should be done.

Principles   *Principles are the general rules or laws adopted as a guide to action.* They represent a settled ground or basis of conduct or practice. They are controlling propositions that are the best possible guides in the choice of alternatives. They can be descriptive or normative. What's vitally important about the principles is that their application will achieve the stated objectives.

Rules   Rules are the final step in the formulation of the theory and are specific, detailed guides to action. *Rules represent the detailed application of the principles to specific situations.*

Next these four elements and their application to accounting by Moonitz and Sprouse in ARS #1 and ARS #3 are examined.[2]

ARS #1 AND ARS #3

Moonitz organized a two-part project. First would be the objectives and postulates project, followed by the principles project, based on the first project. He decided to do the objectives and postulates parts of the project himself and asked Dr. Robert Sprouse of Stanford to work with him on the principles phase of the study.

A six-person project advisory committee was organized for each study. These advisory committees were designed to review the plans for the study, act as a source of feedback both to the authors and the ARD during the project, and then to advise the Director of Accounting Research on the suitability of the project for publication. The Director had the authority to publish the study. Advisory committee members had the right to have their comments, positive or negative, included in the study.

The theory projects were begun in an atmosphere of great enthusiasm and optimism. The accounting profession had confidence in the dual approach and believed that it would resolve the crisis. The profession had great hopes that by following the dual approach of Alvin Jennings, accounting standard setters would have a theory of accounting and a set of principles based on that theory that could be used to solve accounting problems.

ARS #1: THE BASIC POSTULATES OF ACCOUNTING

ARS #1 was published in 1961. It contained the objectives of accounting and a presentation of the basic postulates of accounting.

OBJECTIVES

In ARS #1, a classic definition of accounting was presented that listed five objectives for the function of accounting. Although these were not specifically labeled as the objectives of accounting, they worked as such:

The function of accounting is to (1) measure the resources held by specific entities; (2) reflect the claims against and the interests in those entities; (3) measure the changes in those resources, claims, and interests; (4) assign the changes to specifiable periods of time; and (5) express the foregoing in terms of money as a common denominator.[3]

These five functions of accounting are also presented early in ARS #3 as a statement of the functions of accounting.

If we analyze this statement of the objectives using the three criteria previously discussed in Chapter 1 for the objectives statement in the normative-deductive model, we conclude:

1. *The who issue:* Moonitz's definition is silent on who will be the user of this information.
2. *The why issue (for what purpose is the information to be used):* The definition is silent on the purposes for which this information can be used.
3. *The what issue (what information is communicated):* This is precisely stated in the definition.

Thus based on the three criteria, the conclusion is that the objectives statement appears deficient. It provides no information about the users of accounting information and the uses of accounting information. Instead, the single emphasis is on what information is to be communicated, probably because at that time, accounting was seen as a body of technical principles. Although this definition can be considered the best one up until 1961 and certainly superior to those that came before it, it does lack two of the three elements sought in an objectives statement.

THE POSTULATES

Fourteen postulates were presented in ARS #1.[4] They were organized into three categories: those stemming from the economic and political environment, those stemming from the field of accounting itself, and the imperatives. Five postulates were given in the first category, four in the second, and five in the third. Following are the postulates and explanatory comments.

Group A, Economic and Political Environment Postulates   This group of five postulates is based on the economic and political environment in which accounting exists. The postulates represent generalized descriptions of those aspects of the environment that are relevant for accounting.

A-1. Quantification. Quantitative data are helpful in making rational economic decisions, i.e., in making choices among alternatives so that actions are correctly related to consequences.

This postulate deals with the basis for decision making and how individuals process data in their decision-making models. This postulate is quite relevant to accounting because financial statements are useful and play an important role in decision making. This proposition paves the way for other postulates that deal with the most appropriate form and content of financial statements.

A-2. Exchange. Most of the goods and services that are produced are distributed through exchange and are not directly consumed by the producers.

The second postulate describes the basis for distribution in our economy, the transaction. This is the basic building block of accounting.

A-3. Entities (including identification of the entity). Economic activity is carried on through specific units or entities. Any report on the activity must identify clearly the particular unit or entity involved.

The third postulate deals with how our economy is organized. It describes the basic economic unit, which later becomes the focus for accounting.

A-4. Time period (including specification of the time period). Economic activity is carried on during specifiable periods of time. Any report on that activity must identify clearly the period of time involved.

This postulate describes the temporal nature of economic activity.

A-5. Unit of measure (including identification of the monetary unit). Money is the common denominator in terms of which goods and services, including labor, natural resources, and capital are measured. Any report must clearly indicate which money (e.g., dollars, francs, pounds) is being used.

This proposition deals with two related issues. The first describes the medium of exchange in our economy, money. The second issue relates to identification of the money used, in light of the number of currencies used in the world.

Group B, Accounting Postulates The second group of postulates focuses on the field of accounting. The four propositions are designed to act as a foundation and assist in constructing accounting principles.

B-1. Financial statements. (Related to A-1.) The results of the accounting process are expressed in a set of fundamentally related financial statements which articulate with each other and rest on the same underlying data.

Financial statements provide information on the resources of an entity and the changes in those resources over time. They are related to each other and are dependent on each other in a systematic way; therefore, they are *not* independent.

B-2. Market prices. (Related to A-2.) Accounting data are based on prices generated by past, present, or future exchanges which have actually taken place or are expected to.

The second postulate of this group is related to postulate A-2, that goods and services are distributed through exchanges (transactions). It focuses on a measure of the transaction: the prices involved. These prices can be past, present, or future prices. The exchange price is further described as having a high degree of validity when used to initially record a transaction because that price was a measure of the sacrifice given up in exchange for something else.

B-3. Entities. (Related to A-3.) The results of the accounting process are expressed in terms of specific units or entities.

This logically follows from the Group A postulate: if economic activity is conducted by specific economic entities, then accounting reports should likewise be expressed in terms of those same entities.

B-4. Tentativeness. (Related to A-4.) The results of operations for relatively short periods of time are tentative whenever allocations between past, present, and future periods are required.

The last postulate in this section refers to the time issue. Because economic activity is conducted during specifiable time periods, the accounting reports likewise should take the time period in account when processing transactions. Uncertainty about both the future and the allocation process adds a tentative quality to the resulting measures.

Group C, Imperative Postulates   The third group of five postulates differs fundamentally from the first two groups. They are not primarily descriptive statements but instead represent a set of normative statements, which emphasize what should be rather than what is.

C-1. Continuity (including the correlative concept of limited life). In the absence of evidence to the contrary, the entity should be viewed as remaining in operation indefinitely. In the presence of evidence that the entity has a limited life, it should not be viewed as remaining in operation indefinitely.

The first postulate in this group is made necessary because of the change in the way business was conducted. Early in the history of commerce, business activities were conducted in separate ventures. Over time, this changed to a pattern of continuous activity. In light of that change, accounting reports should focus on the continuity of the firm.

C-2. Objectivity. Changes in assets and liabilities and the related effects (if any) on revenues, expenses, retained earnings, and the like, should not be given formal recognition in the accounts earlier than the point of time at which they can be measured in objective terms.

The second postulate deals with the need for objectivity in accounting measurements. Accounting measurements should rest on evidence that is reliable and subject to verification. As a source of information for decision making, it is incumbent on accountants to serve that role objectively.

C-3. Consistency. The procedures used in accounting for a given entity should be appropriate for the measurement of its position and its activities and should be followed consistently from period to period.

This postulate concerns the ability of users of accounting information to compare the same firm across time.

C-4. Stable unit. Accounting reports should be based on a stable measuring unit.

The fourth postulate is related to the third; to be consistent, accounting needs to use the same measurement unit from period to period. Because money is not necessarily a stable measuring unit, accountants should ensure that they use a stable measuring unit. Most accountants understand this proposition to advocate price-level adjustments when changes in the price level and inflation cause material changes in the purchasing power of money.

> *C-5. Disclosure. Accounting reports should disclose that which is necessary to make them not misleading.*

The last postulate deals with disclosures. In rather broad terms, it advocates the reporting of all information whose absence would make the reports misleading.

ANALYSIS OF POSTULATES

Postulates were defined previously as basic propositions about the economic, political, and sociological environment of accounting. They may be either descriptive (what is) or normative (what should be). Postulates should have the following three characteristics: They should be (1) relevant to accounting; (2) accepted as valid at face value; and (3) productive as a source of principles.

A review of the postulates as a group shows that, in general, they do describe the basic ideas of accounting. Group A appears to describe the economic environment of accounting, and Group B describes the process of accounting. Group C postulates are normative but also focus on the process of accounting. Note that some postulates are logically derived from others: B-1 refers to A-1; B-2 refers to A-2, and so on. We find a number of basic accounting concepts described in the postulates, for example, the entity concept (A-3 and B-3), periodicity (A-4 and B-4), going concern (C-1), consistency (C-3), and objectivity (C-2). However, we note the absence of any postulates directly related to two other major accounting concepts: the matching approach used to compute net income and historical cost.

Because the companion study, the principles study, was not published when ARS #1 was issued, it was impossible to evaluate whether these postulates would be fertile and produce sound principles.

REACTION TO ARS #1

ARS #1 did not evoke much of a reaction. Reaction was delayed until the principles project was published in 1962 as ARS #3 and they could be considered together. Frankly, the companion project was of much greater interest, especially to practicing accountants, because it would more directly relate to GAAP.

PEOPLE 🔑 One member of the advisory committee, Leonard Spacek, the head of Arthur Andersen and Company, published his dissent with ARS #1 in the document as "Comments of Leonard Spacek." His main concern with the study was that the postulates were "self-evident observations that cannot serve as the basic foundation on which sound accounting principles can be established."[5] He did not believe that it accomplished the objective for which it was written. He thought it followed the historic and customary approach to theory formulation and that that approach was not adequate. What was needed was a new approach, in his opinion. He was a strong advocate of one basic postulate: fairness. By that he meant fairness to all segments of the business community. He concluded strongly, "In my opinion, this monograph does not adequately describe the real purposes and objectives of accounting, and the concepts set forth as being postulates cannot provide a basic foundation from which to build a sound framework of accounting theory."[6]

The staff of the AICPA tabulated the letters written to the AICPA after the publication of ARS #1. Fifty-two such letters were received. In general, supportive letters came from academics (five letters), whereas negative letters came from practitioners (four letters). The largest number of letters did not comment on the study as a whole but dealt with specific aspects of the study (forty-three letters).[7]

A later section examines the reaction to both ARS #1 and #3, as well as evaluates the postulates fully.

ARS #3: A TENTATIVE SET OF BROAD ACCOUNTING PRINCIPLES FOR BUSINESS ENTERPRISES

This companion study to ARS #1 by Robert T. Sprouse and Moonitz was published in 1962. It was based on ARS #1 and completed the theory project. Sprouse wrote the first draft of the study, which was then entirely reworked, in light of ARS #1, to integrate the two studies. In ARS #3, the role of principles is viewed as meeting the needs of all interested groups. In a dynamic world, detailed rules would change as circumstances change, but the broad principles would not change.

The study also provided definitions of assets, liabilities, cost, financial statements, depreciation accounting, owners' equity, invested capital, and net profit.

According to Sprouse and Moonitz, they attempted to do three things in ARS #3: (1) ensure that the principles were compatible with the postulates in ARS #1; (2) explain the principles and their implications—but *not* produce a set of rules for accountants to follow; and (3) formulate recommendations that could be applied to practice in the present and future.

ARS #3 PRINCIPLES[8]

The substance, or core, of ARS #3 was the list of broad principles of accounting; eight groups of principles were presented. Exhibit 2.2 contains a summary of the principles.

ANALYSIS

These principles seem reasonable and largely consistent with current practice, although analyzing these principles today is very different from their first analysis in the early 1960s. In fact, they could have been written recently by the FASB. But one must realize that they were written in 1962 and remember that they were presented to accountants whose contemporary environment was 1962, not the twenty-first century. These accountants were familiar with 1962 GAAP and interpreted these principles from that context.

Objectively, the list of principles in ARS #3 is comprehensive. It covers almost all basic accounting topics of interest: net income, asset measurement, inventories, plant and equipment, investments, intangible assets, liabilities, and owners' equity. The principles are presented as general guides to action. They appear related to each other and internally consistent. Sprouse and Moonitz explained:

> . . . *the emphasis in the postulates study on the measurement of wealth in the hands of economic entities becomes more specific in this study as an examination*

EXHIBIT 2.2
Summary of Principles from ARS #3[8]

A. Profit is attributable to the whole process of business activity.

B. Changes in resources should be classified among the amounts attributable to:
   1. changes in the dollar (price level changes);
   2. changes in replacement costs;
   3. sale or other transfer; and or
   4. other causes.

C. All assets of the enterprise should be recorded in the accounts and reported in the financial statements.

D. The problem of measuring (pricing, valuing) an asset is the problem of measuring the future services, and involves at least three steps:
   1. a determination if future services do in fact exist;
   2. an estimate of the quantity of services; and
   3. the choice of a method or basis or formula for pricing the quantity of services arrived at under 2 above. In general, the choice is to be made from the following:
      a. a past exchange price, e.g. acquisition cost;
      b. a current exchange price. e.g. replacement cost;
      c. a future exchange price. e.g. anticipated selling price.
   4. All assets in the form of money or claims to money should be shown at their discounted present value or equivalent.
   5. Inventories which are readily salable at known prices with readily predictable costs of disposal should be recorded at net realizable value and the related revenue taken up at that time. Other inventory items should be recorded at their current replacement cost and the related gain or loss shown separately.
   6. All items of plant and equipment in service, or held in standby status, should be recorded at cost of acquisition or construction. with appropriate modification for the effect of the changing dollar either in the primary statements or in supplementary statements.
   7. The investment (cost or other basis) in plant should be amortized over the estimated economic life.
   8. All intangibles should be recorded at cost and those with limited life should be written off.

E. All liabilities of the enterprise should be recorded in the accounts and reported in the statements.

F. Those liabilities which call for settlement in goods or services (other than cash) should be measured by their selling prices.

G. In a corporation, stockholder's equity should be classified into invested capital and retained earnings.

H. The statement of the results of operations should reveal the components of profit in sufficient detail.

of the assets and liabilities, and related revenues and expenses, gains and losses, of business enterprises.[9]

The major controversy in ARS #3 eventually centered on the recommended recognition of all objectively determined changes in assets, including the recognition of price-level changes, changes in replacement values, and changes from other causes.

Previously, it was noted that in the normative-deductive model, principles are designed to achieve the objectives. If we examine the five functions of accounting and examine these ARS #3 principles, the principles appear to fulfill the objectives.

REACTION TO ARS #1 AND ARS #3
GENERAL

Once ARS #3 was published in 1962, the set was complete and both studies could be evaluated as a whole; reactions were quickly received. One of the first was the official reaction, which appeared in a News Report section of the *Journal of Accountancy* in May 1962:[10]

> *In the opinion of the Director of Accounting Research [Dr. M. Moonitz] these two studies comply with the instructions to the Accounting Research Division to make a study of the basic postulates and broad principles of accounting. Prior to its publication, Study No. 3 has been read and commented upon by a limited number of people in the field of accounting. Their reactions range from endorsement of the ideas set forth in the study of Broad Principles to misgivings that compliance with the recommendations set forth by the authors would lead to misleading financial statements.*
>
> *The Board is therefore treating these two studies . . . as conscientious attempts by the accounting research staff to resolve major accounting issues which, however, contain inferences and recommendations in part of a speculative and tentative nature. It hopes the studies will stimulate constructive comment and discussion in the areas of the basic postulates and the broad principles of accounting. . . .*
>
> *The Board believes, however, that while these studies are a valuable contribution to accounting thinking, they are too radically different from present generally accepted accounting principles for acceptance at this time.*
>
> *After a period of exposure and consideration, some of the specific recommendations in these studies may prove acceptable to the Board while others may not. The Board therefore will await the results of this exposure and consideration before taking further action on these studies.*

(This reaction was later published as APB Statement No. 1.)

The overall AICPA evaluation, the bottom line, was that the principles were too much of a departure from present practice to act as a foundation for the APB, and thus, the AICPA rejected them.

As the preceding quote indicate, there was some serious disagreement among people who read the studies. The range of reactions was quite wide, from enthusiastic support to outright rejection. It is interesting that the first part of the quote seems to put responsibility for publication of the studies on Moonitz, who also happened to be an author and co-author of the studies, respectively. One cannot help wonder that if someone else had been the Director of Accounting Research, would these studies have been published?

ADVISORY COMMITTEE CONCERNS

As expected, a firestorm of criticism broke out after the publication of ARS #3. An overall negative reaction came from the two advisory committees for the studies. Of the twelve members of the two advisory committees, nine members included their comments in ARS #3;[11] only one fully supported it. Following are their summarized comments, explaining what some of the issues were that led to the negative reaction to the studies and the overall rejection of this theory formulation.

- Paul Grady wrote the longest and most detailed comment. He had prepared detailed comments on an earlier draft of ARS #3 and added to them for inclusion in the document. He disagreed with the methodology of the study, the normative-deductive approach, and preferred the inductive or pragmatic approach. He thought the study should simply be a brief summary of the generally accepted accounting principles currently in practice (an inventory of GAAP), with theoretical explanations and reasons as appropriate.
- Andrew Barr believed that the work of Moonitz and Sprouse was normative and a significant departure from current practice. But he cautioned against a hasty acceptance of the postulates and principles without a long period of testing and further explanation.
- John Zebley saw little positive in the studies: they neither could be used to narrow diversity nor could they be used without further explanation and study.
- Carmen Blough gave a lengthy criticism of the principles in ARS #3. He characterized them as untried and not tested or practical. In light of this, he was very concerned with the principles that advocated recognizing changes in asset values and the use of market, or current, values.
- Herbert Miller was concerned about the lack of a transition plan for implementing the postulates and principles. He also was concerned that the principles made the accounting process more subjective.
- William Wertz took exception to the lack of a distinction between currently accepted practice and mere proposals. He did not favor the publication of the study, but said if they did, they should clearly identify their proposals early in the study.
- Leonard Spacek believed that the two monographs presented the authors' opinions rather than accounting principles in a sound framework of theory. He did not believe that the accounting principles presented were adequately supported or defended.
- Oscar Gellein thought that the publication of ARS #3 would "serve no useful purpose." He was deeply concerned that the changes proposed in ARS #3 had not been tested nor shown to be an improvement over current practice. He wanted proof that the new proposals were more useful than the old.
- Arthur Cannon's reaction was the only positive one. He characterized their efforts as "an excellent job." He supported the efforts of Moonitz and Sprouse, particularly their proposals regarding the use of current market values on the balance sheet. He also countered the comments of two other advisory committee members, Grady and Spacek, and defended Moonitz and Sprouse. He faulted Grady for being a defender of the status quo and Spacek for stating his personal opinion.

McDonald[12] provided a synopsis of the comments of the advisory committee members, which presented their positions organized by the background of the members:

Representative from	Number	Favorable	Unfavorable	Neutral	No Comment
Public Accounting	7		4	2	1
Academia	2	1			1
Government	1			1	
Industry	2	1			1
Total	12	2	4	3	3

According to McDonald's analysis, only four of the advisory committee members were unfavorable toward the studies, but their number was double the number of committee members in favor. By representation, more than half of the public accounting members were unfavorable, and none were counted as favorable. The only two favorable committee members were from academia (a professor) and from industry. It is interesting to note the ambivalence in the positions of one-half of the members. In light of the controversial issues raised in ARS #1 and ARS #3, it is difficult to understand how anyone could have been neutral or had no comment.

But the reactions by the advisory committee members to the studies help us understand the reason for the ultimate rejection by the APB.

SUMMARY OF SPECIFIC CONCERNS

A number of specific concerns were raised when both studies are considered as a whole. They are presented below, organized by study.

For the postulates

1. The postulates in Group C (the imperatives) represented value judgments. Postulates should be descriptive, not normative. This invalidated these postulates.
2. Some of the Group B postulates appeared to be reasoned from those in Group A. Postulates should formulated independently and not be derived from other postulates; this was not appropriate.
3. The postulates were organized into three groups then ranked and numbered. The ranking of postulates in the three groups was questionable.
4. Postulate C-4 (Stable unit: Accounting reports should be based on a stable measuring unit) was seen as the key postulate because the essence of a measuring system is the unit used. But the way it was stated unfortunately led to a dual interpretation problem. As written without further delineation, it could support either historical cost or current cost, two distinctly different measuring systems. (It's interesting that this postulate turned out to be "explosive.")

For the principles

1. The general emphasis in the principles was on value, either current or market, rather than on historical cost. This emphasis represented a material departure for accounting and caused many to believe that Moonitz and Sprouse were against historical cost.
2. The emphasis on measuring changes in values when they were objectively measurable inferred a broader view of realization than was currently used. The traditional view of realization, which required an arm's-length transaction, was discarded.

3. There was an overemphasis on theory and logic that wasn't practical. Many were concerned that these new principles had not been tested in the real world. They would have preferred a more pragmatic approach, which would have involved testing before adoption.
4. The measurement principles were not seen as additive. The principles would produce a balance sheet that was a mix of many different values for the assets (some at historical cost, others at replacement cost, and still others at market values). One couldn't add the different values to get a meaningful sum.
5. The study was silent about the users of accounting. Throughout the principles study, users were not mentioned. No consideration of users' needs was presented.

For both studies

1. The studies failed to show how the principles were derived from the postulates. There was no direct linkage presented in the studies, nor could one see how the principles were associated with the postulates. Some would have preferred a more explicit presentation, that is, one that would allow specific principles to be tied to specific postulates from which they were based.
2. There appeared to be no principles from the Group A postulates. Some tried to relate specific principles to specific postulates but found no principles that appeared to be linked to that group.
3. The studies failed to show how a transition from current practice to their principles would be accomplished. They lacked specific guidance on how to transition from current practice to a practice dominated with the new principles. Given the radical nature of change recommended by the studies, some felt that a transition plan or timetable should have been provided.
4. The studies failed to show support for the new principles, and there was no justification or extensive support for the new principles. Instead, they were simply presented as the logical deductions from the postulates and objectives. To many, logical deduction was not enough. They wanted explanations, reasons, and justifications for the new principles.

Overall, this once-heralded attempt to use the current technology, the normative-deductive method, to formulate a theory of accounting for the use of the new standard-setting body, the APB, was a dismal failure. The rejection of ARS #1 and ARS #3 by the accounting profession was clear, overwhelming, and unambiguous. Therefore, the APB started its standard-setting tenure without a theory, and its first major initiative was rejected. In hindsight, the accounting profession's reaction doomed the APB and led to the APB's eventual failure.

When reviewing historical material, one must consider time when considering the measure of success for a theory formulation. Since their initial appearance, ARS #1 and ARS #3 have had a dramatic impact on the practice of accounting. In one sense, Moonitz and Sprouse were ahead of their time. Although rejected by the APB as the foundation for future Opinions, these studies have had a dramatic impact on future theory developments and practice.

SUMMARY

This chapter examines the continuing efforts of the accounting profession to formulate a theory of accounting and establish a standard-setting body that would be successful. Unfortunately, as the events reveal, they were not very successful in either endeavor. After a very serious and widely heralded attempt to develop theory, the accounting profession rejected the theory. Using the approach that was expected of them, the normative-deductive approach, Moonitz and Sprouse produced a two-part theory consisting of postulates and principles. Unfortunately, their formulation was not acceptable and was branded as "radical," caused by the forward-looking principles of ARS #3. Although these principles were, in general, properly deduced from the postulates, they were not the principles that the accounting profession was prepared to accept in 1962.

The failure of the profession to embrace ARS #1 and ARS #3 had significant implications. First, those that followed Moonitz and Sprouse in attempting to formulate a theory of accounting would never again feel that the normative-deductive approach was the best approach for developing theory. In fact, the normative-deductive approach was somewhat stigmatized by the failure of Moonitz and Sprouse to formulate an acceptable theory.

Second, the accounting profession revealed a series of "sacred cows" in its reaction to Moonitz and Sprouse. The concepts of historical cost, matching, and realization were firmly held views among accountants that were not easily changed. The reaction to Moonitz and Sprouse clearly showed that those concepts were held sacred by the accounting profession. No theory formulation that attacked those sacred cows could hope to be popular in the near future without a compelling argument.

Third, it seriously derailed the dual approach that Jennings recommended and the accounting profession had accepted. Everyone who applauded this approach and believed in it had a serious problem with cognitive dissonance in the aftermath of the failure of Moonitz and Sprouse's theory. With the rejection of ARS #1 and ARS #3, the APB embarked on its standard-setting voyage alone, without the theory it needed to guide it. Chapter 3 focuses on the fate of the APB under those circumstances, and as you might expect, it was not positive.

However, the pioneering nature of Moonitz and Sprouse's theory formulation must be noted. Although written more than forty years ago, the postulates and principles sound remarkable contemporary to today's readers. In fact, one may easily conclude that today's GAAP is more consistent with ARS #1 and ARS #3 than the GAAP at the time they were published. Although not adequately recognized in the early 1960s, Moonitz and Sprouse made a positive contribution to theory formulation and standard setting.

REVIEW QUESTIONS

1. What forces were at work to terminate the CAP by the late 1950s?
2. How was Alvin Jennings an example of a key change person to accounting in the early 1960s?
3. What were the two elements of Jennings "dual approach"? How were these two elements related?

4. What was the organizational relationship between the Accounting Principles Board and the Accounting Research Division?

5. Why did Moonitz and Sprouse decide to use the normative-deductive approach to formulate a theory of accounting? In general, did they appear faithful in applying the method?

6. Reread the list of ARS #3 accounting principles (see Exhibit 2.2). Which do you think were the most controversial in 1962? Are these still as controversial today?

7. What concerns were raised about ARS #1 and ARS #3? Attribute the concerns to the three stakeholder groups: public accountants, users, and financial statement preparers.

8. Although the overall reaction to ARS #1 and ARS #3 was negative, what were some positive results?

9. What are the two needs of a standard-setting body? How did they apply to the APB in 1963?

10. Complete the following table for the APB and CAP, and comment on the differences that are revealed:

SIMILARITIES AND DIFFERENCES: APB AND CAP		
Aspect	**CAP**	**APB**
Organizational location		
Members: full-time vs. part-time		
Number of members		
Qualifications for members		
Theoretical support		
Authority		

DISCUSSION TOPICS

1. How did the problems of the CAP in the late 1950s relate to the increased emphasis on investing by the public?

2. Hopefully, we learn from our mistakes. Compare and contrast the original structure of the APB with that of the CAP. In what ways was the APB structured to overcome or solve problems that were seen with the structure or operation of the CAP? Were these improvements effective? That is, did they improve standard setting for the APB as expected?

3. What's considered as radical in one era can become accepted in a later era. Given the overall "flavor" of ARS #1 and ARS #3, in what ways were they forward looking and a signal of the way that accounting would develop in the future?

4. How did the principles of ARS #3 change historical cost and the realization principle? Were these changes more in line with GAAP today than with GAAP in the 1960s?

NOTES

1 Zeff, (1984), pp. 459–62.
2 In case you were wondering why the second part of the theory was not issued as ARS #2 it was because ARS #2 was issued in 1961, "Cash Flows and the Funds Statement," by P. Mason. It is unknown why the ARD did not reserve "ARS #2" for the second part of the theory.
3 Moonitz, 23.

4 Sprouse and Moonitz, 6.
5 Moonitz, 56.
6 Ibid, 57.
7 AICPA (1963).
8 Sprouse and Moonitz, 55–59.
9 Ibid, 53.
10 Accounting Principles Board.
11 Sprouse and Moonitz, 76–83.
12 McDonald, 72.

REFERENCES

Accounting Principles Board. "Statement by the Accounting Principles Board." Statement No. 1 (Accounting Principles Board) 1962.

American Institute of CPAs. "Comments on the basic postulates." *Journal of Accountancy* January 1963: 44–55.

American Institute of CPAs. "Accounting Principles Board Comments on 'Broad Principles,'" *Journal of Accountancy* (May 1962): 9–10.

McDonald, Daniel L. *Comparative Accounting Theory.* Reading, MA: Addison-Wesley, 1972.

Metcalf, Richard W. "The Basic Postulates in Perspective." *Accounting Review* (January 1964): 16–21.

Moonitz, Maurice. *The Basic Postulates of Accounting.* New York: AICPA, 1961.

Sprouse, Robert and Maurice Moonitz. *A Tentative Set of Broad Accounting Principles for Business Enterprises.* New York: AICPA, 1962.

Vatter, William J. "Postulates and Principles." *Accounting Review* (July 1963): 179–97.

Zeff, Stephen A. "Some Junctures in the Evolution of the Process of Establishing Accounting Principles in the U.S.A.: 1917–1972." *Accounting Review* (July 1984): 459–62.

———. "A Perspective on the U.S. Public/Private-Sector Approach to the Regulation of Financial Reporting." *Accounting Horizons* (March 1995): 52–70.

3

CHAPTER

THE ACCOUNTING PRINCIPLES BOARD—II - ASOBAT

LEARNING OBJECTIVES

After studying this chapter, you should be able to

> Analyze what factors caused the APB to struggle as a standard-setting body.

> Describe the content of a Statement of Basic Accounting Theory.

> Evaluate the content of ASOBAT.

> Compare and contrast ARS #1 and 3 and ASOBAT.

> Understand what caused the APB to fail.

STANDARD SETTING	1900	THEORY FORMULATION
CHAPTER 1		
STANDARD SETTING I		THEORY 1
PRE-CAP	1900-1938	NATURE OF THEORY
SEC	1934	
STANDARD SETTING II		
CAP I	1938	
STANDARD SETTING III		
CAP II	1938-1958	
CHAPTER 2		
STANDARD SETTING IV		THEORY II
APB	1959-1962	
	1961-1962	ARS #1 AND #3
CHAPTER 3		
STANDARD SETTING V		**THEORY III**
APB	**1963-1966**	
	1966	**ASOBAT**
STANDARD SETTING VI		
DEMISE OF APB	**1970**	
CHAPTER 4, 5		
STANDARD SETTING VII		
TRUEBLOOD	1973	
WHEAT	1972	
TRIPARTITE STRUCTURE	1973-2001	
CHAPTER 6		
		THEORY IV
	1977	SATTA
		POSITIVE ACCOUNTING 1980s
CHAPTER 7		THEORY V
	1973-2001	CONCEPTUAL FRAMEWORK PROJECT
CHAPTER 8		
STANDARD SETTING VIII		
FASB: PRESENT AND FUTURE STANDARD SETTING: DOMESTIC AND INTERNATIONAL	2001	
	2002	

In Chapter 3, the examination of the chronological development of standard-setting and theory formulation efforts in accounting in the United State continues, focusing on the tenure of the Accounting Principles Board (APB) and another major effort at theory formulation. That effort came from the American Accounting Association (AAA) and was published as *A Statement of Basic Accounting Theory* (ASOBAT) in 1966.

To help keep the events in this chapter in perspective, refer to Exhibit 3.1 and note that this chapter's coverage is highlighted in bold type. The discussion begins with the APB's efforts during the 1960s, and then moves to ASOBAT.

STANDARD SETTING V
APB (2)

INITIAL PROBLEMS

If ever an organization started off with promise, optimism, and with high hopes for a successful tenure, the APB did. The AICPA thought Jennings's dual approach was appropriate for solving the problems that developed with the Committee on Accounting Procedure (CAP). Unfortunately, the rejection of ARS #1 and ARS #3 by the accounting profession was an early failure that was to haunt the APB for its entire existence. It placed a limitation on the APB. Certainly, if the APB's stated view was accepted, a theory was needed on which to base pronouncements. It believed this to be the best approach to issuing accounting standards—base them on theory. Without a theory, by default, the pronouncements would be founded on personal opinions of the APB members. Perhaps the APB was being especially foresightful in naming their pronouncements Opinions, because that is what mostly occurred. It should be noted that after ARS #1 and ARS #3, the Accounting Research Division (ARD) continued to fund studies on specific accounting topics and some subsequent APB Opinions were based on this research. But the studies on specific topics did not constitute a comprehensive accounting theory. And that was the situation they wanted to avoid by having a theory.

FIRST MAJOR PRONOUNCEMENT

Another problem developed in the APB's formative years that would have lasting significance. The problem erupted over the proper accounting for an innovative, fiscal macroeconomic tool, the investment tax credit, that the new Kennedy administration had adopted in 1962 to jump-start the recovery of the American economy, to move the country quickly out of a recession.

President Kennedy's economic advisors thought the investment tax credit was an appropriate tool for this. Under the tax credit, American firms that invested in fixed or productive assets could take a tax credit (not a deduction) on their federal income tax bills for the year in which the investment was made. The advisors hoped that this would spur spending in the capital asset segment of the economy. They believed that this growth, through the multiplier effect, would drive even greater growth in other parts of the economy and result in a recovery from the recession. This appeared to be a sound macroeconomic decision.

The APB's involvement centered on the issue of how to account for the new tax credit.

Obviously, if firms were to obtain a tax credit from their investment in plant, property, and equipment, guidance was needed on how to record this credit in their records and report it in their financial statements. Because the investment tax credit was a new development, GAAP was silent on how to account for it. No prior pronouncements covered investment tax credits. The APB had a free hand to set an accounting standard. This was a golden opportunity for the new standard-setting body. It was also an opportunity to set an accounting standard that impacted the national economy. Therefore, this opportunity had many implications.

Two alternative basic approaches were developed and considered by the APB to account for this tax credit: the flow-through and deferral methods.

1. *The flow-through method viewed the tax credit as a decrease in the income tax expense of the firm in the year the firm made the investment and obtained the credit.* The resulting asset would be recorded at its full cost, and that cost would be depreciated over its life. This approach produced an economic impact in the short run. It was called the flow-through method because the credit flowed through the income statement in the year in which it was taken, that is, the financial benefit was recognized in the current year.

2. *The deferral method viewed the tax credit as a reduction in the cost of the asset and reflected this over the life of the asset through reduced depreciation charges.* This accounting spread the tax credit over the life of the asset. This approach produced an economic impact over the long term. It was called the "deferral method" because it deferred the benefit from the credit over the life of the asset. Because plant, property, and equipment were at issue here, the economic life would be long term, that is, the financial benefit was spread out over the life of the asset.

It is likely that the Kennedy administration was concerned with the short run and thus not particularly interested in a long-term benefit to the economy. Instead, it wanted to jump-start the economy and wanted the immediate benefit of the tax credit in the first year to achieve that goal. So they considered the first approach, the flow-through method, as more consistent with the purpose of the legislation. If business firms viewed the tax credit as a benefit accruing to them over the long life of an asset, the long-term effect might have decreased the attractiveness of the credit to them.

Using the technical knowledge that senior accounting professionals acquire over their careers, the APB decided to adopt the deferral method and issued Opinion #2 in November 1962. The Opinion allowed only the deferral approach and did not allow the use of the flow-through method. No research study was conducted to precede the pronouncement. The board reasoned that the credit really was a reduction in the cost of the asset and thus properly should be spread over the life of the asset. The APB did not accept the idea that the tax credit represented a one-time reduction in the tax expense of the firm as the Kennedy administration intended.

The decision was controversial. The Opinion was adopted by a 14 to 7 vote, the minimum two-thirds that was necessary. Four of the "Big 8" CPA firms' representatives voted against it. The board seemed to be unaware of the economic consequences of its action when it issued APB Opinion #2.

The reaction to Opinion #2 was dramatic and immediate. Three of the Big 8 CPA firms disagreed with the Opinion and told their clients not to follow it. Many business firms (i.e., the preparers) opposed the Opinion. Perhaps companies preferred the flow-through method because they viewed it as a way of lowering their tax bills and increasing their bottom lines, net income after taxes. A more serious challenge to this pronouncement came from the SEC. In January 1963, it issued Accounting Series Release (ASR) #96, which allowed firms to follow either approach, in essence, validating the flow-through approach. ASR #96 directly contradicted APB Opinion #2 and challenged the authority of the APB. However, because the SEC had legal authority to issue accounting standards, the APB wisely backed down in this standoff. The APB issued Opinion #4 in 1963, which reversed their position in Opinion #2 and allowed firms to use either the flow-through or deferral methods.

Clearly, the APB started its standard-setting tenure in the worst possible way. It stumbled in its golden opportunity to set an accounting standard that helped the economy move from recession to prosperity. This missed opportunity also plagued the APB in another way. It showed that the APB was inconsistent and subject to a higher authority. Both of these outcomes were negative for the stature and authority of the APB in the long term. With all the hope and optimism associated with the dual approach of Jennings, nothing seemed to work out according to expectations.

Therefore, the APB faced two disasters early in its term: the rejection of its accounting theory set forth in ARS #1 and ARS #3 and the problem with accounting for the investment tax credit, with subsequent overruling by the SEC. Thus the APB began its tenure without theory to guide them and without direct support of the SEC. The APB lacked the two main factors that a standard-setting body needs to be effective: theory and authority.

AICPA SUPPORT FOR APB

In 1964, the APB received some welcome support from the AICPA. The AICPA's council (its governing body) declared the authority of APB Opinions and stated that departures from APB Opinions would involve a violation of Rule 203 of the AICPA Code of Professional Conduct. The AICPA's position was that a public accounting firm would no longer issue a clean audit opinion if the accounting was inconsistent with APB Opinions. Although the AICPA rule was not a very direct or dramatic show of support for the APB, it was helpful. However, in the conspicuous absence of any delegation of authority from the SEC, this support was relatively weak.

THEORY III
ASOBAT

AAA'S ROLE

After the failure of the theory project of the Accounting Research Division (ARD) of the APB (ARS #1 and #3), accounting theoreticians did not give up. Instead, the mantle was passed to another accounting organization, the American Accounting Association. The AAA differs markedly from the AICPA. It is composed largely of accounting academics and professors rather than public accountants and those in private practice. Although any accountant can be a member of the AAA, the membership is usually composed of accounting professors from major public and private universities, colleges, and community colleges in the United States.

Certainly, if any group of accountants would appear to have a comparative advantage in the formulation of a theory of accounting, the academics would. Why? First, they are not hindered by practical constraints in their careers or daily work as public accountants and preparers. Second, they tend to be more theory oriented than practicing accountants. Academics tend to view problems from a theoretical rather than a practical standpoint. Third, because most of them possessed Ph.D.'s, they probably studied the work of Moonitz and Sprouse as part of their doctoral programs and thus were more familiar with past theory formulations than practicing CPAs would have been. Thus it was natural for them to take up the banner of accounting theory formulation from the AICPA, freeing it to focus its attention on the more pressing issue of narrowing the diversity in GAAP. In fact, the AAA had previously published a number of statements on accounting principles, standards, and theory; it was experienced in this arena.

GENESIS

So based on their past experience, the AAA Executive Committee decided to embark on a new and different type of theory effort. The AAA saw this as a natural extension of its past work on accounting theory. In 1964, it authorized the appointment of a committee to do the following:

> develop an integrated statement of basic accounting theory which will serve as a guide to educators, practitioners and others. . . .
>
> Among the subjects the committee may want to consider are the role, nature, and limitations of accounting, both now and in the future; the appropriate conceptual framework for a coordinated statement of accounting theory; and the possibility of implementing its conclusions.[1]

This committee consisted of nine members—eight well-known academics at major universities (including some who also had served on the advisory committees for Moonitz and Sprouse) and one practitioner. All served part-time without compensation while they continued their normal teaching and research efforts (some may have had their teaching loads reduced by their academic deans to provide them with time to serve on this important national-level committee) or public accounting activities. The committee took two years to produce the statement, meeting eight times (for a total of twenty days) during the process. They organized into subcommittees to complete the work. The operating principles of the committee allowed the publication of its statement if at least two-thirds of the committee members agreed. In fact, all nine members agreed, and the AAA published its statement in 1966, entitled *A Statement of Basic Accounting Theory* (ASOBAT).

EVENT

CONTENT

The monograph is divided into five broad categories, each with a separate chapter. The first chapter is an introduction, which includes various definitions and explains the need for accounting information. The second chapter deals with the standards for accounting information and guidelines for communicating this information. In the next two chapters, ASOBAT applies the standards to accounting for external and internal users. The final chapter suggests some of the possibilities for the future of accounting.

OBJECTIVES

Early in the process, the committee stated four goals for the project.

1. To identify the field of accounting so that useful generalizations about it can be made and a theory developed
2. To establish standards by which accounting information may be judged
3. To point out possible improvements in accounting practice
4. To present a useful framework for accounting researchers seeking to extend the uses of accounting and the scope of accounting subject matter as needs of society expand.[2]

The committee decided to emphasize the second goal.

ACCOUNTING DEFINED

ASOBAT contained an interesting definition of accounting, which telegraphed much about their approach and subsequent standards: "the process of identifying, measuring and communicating economic information to permit informed judgments and decisions by the users of the information."[3]

The writers of ASOBAT viewed accounting as an information system. This view differed significantly in a number of ways from the way that most practicing accountants viewed accounting in the mid-1960s. One major difference in ASOBAT was the inclusion of communication as one of the processes of accounting. Most accountants in 1966 would have readily agreed that the accounting process involved identifying and measuring but would have stopped there. Although the accounting process does culminate in the reporting of financial statements, in general, practicing accountants thought that preparing the financial statements concluded their part of the communication process. In a sense, just composing and sending the message meant communication. ASOBAT would add to that responsibility. ASOBAT, based in part on communication theory, would broaden the process of accounting to include the communication phase.

A second example of ASOBAT's difference from contemporary views concerns the phrase, *economic information*. Notice that according to ASOBAT, accounting deals with economic information. Most practicing accountants would have preferred to see their subject matter specified as financial information, since financial information would include a narrower set of information than economic information. It would appear that ASOBAT broadened the type of information that accountants dealt with. In fact, ASOBAT defined economic information as "concerned with any situation in which a choice must be made involving scarce resources." ASOBAT also noted that its definition was broader than any expressed before; it did not limit the kinds of information that might qualify as accounting information. It also attempted to show that accounting information based on nontransaction data would meet the standards for inclusion in accounting statements. This position was a major departure from conventional accounting thinking.

A third example is its formal inclusion of "users." Notice that this definition specifically identifies users, (but no details were included,) as the end product of accounting. The primary purpose for which users need accounting information is for decision making. That decision making was further delineated as information judgments and decisions.

So from the beginning, ASOBAT took a different approach to accounting than Moonitz and Sprouse and contemporary conventional accounting thought.

USERS' NEEDS

Note that in addition to formally mentioning users in their definition of accounting, the writers of ASOBAT specified four informational needs of users. These needs were not based on any survey of users but represented general categories for this information. ASOBAT indicated that the objective of accounting is to provide information for the purposes of:[4]

1. making decisions concerning the use of limited resources, including the identification of crucial decision areas and determination of objectives and goals
2. effectively directing and controlling an organization's human and material resources
3. maintaining and reporting on the custodianship of resources
4. facilitating social functions and controls

These four items were seen by ASOBAT users' needs. Accounting was interpreted as an information system that would provide economic information to meet these needs. ASOBAT did not specify the exact informational needs of users. It did state that some of the informational needs of users were known and others could be inferred from these. In fact, ASOBAT declared that it wasn't necessary to know all the exact needs of a diverse group of users to be able to report some accounting information that is relevant to them. However, the emphasis was on external users.

An important distinctiveness in ASOBAT concerns the fourth purpose, facilitating social functions and controls. The ASOBAT committee viewed accounting as playing an important role in various social functions, such as taxation and governmental regulation. The committee believed that accounting should aim at facilitating the operations of organized society for the welfare of all. This view elevated and broadened the role of accounting to one of major importance in the national economy and society. This view was quite a change from the previous view of accounting, which was much narrower. The previous view, a microview, saw accounting as linking the firm and its owners. ASOBAT introduced a macroview in which accounting is linked to the national economy and society's welfare. This view of accounting from the mid-1960s became the dominant view with the creation of the FASB in 1973 and the FASB's theory formulation, the Conceptual Framework.

A forward-looking statement, an indicator of things to come, concludes the first chapter of ASOBAT: "important changes in accounting practice should be made."[5]

STANDARDS FOR ACCOUNTING INFORMATION

ASOBAT differed from the Moonitz and Sprouse approach by refusing to identify important accounting principles and fundamental concepts from which they are derived. Instead, ASOBAT defined four standards for evaluating accounting information and five guidelines for communicating the information.

In light of the view of accounting as an information system, the core of ASOBAT was its four standards for accounting information, which it used to develop accounting information that would be useful to users. The usefulness, or utility, of information was related to its ability to reduce uncertainty about the state of the world for the user.

It recommended the following four standards for accounting information:

1. Relevance
2. Verifiability
3. Freedom from bias
4. Quantifiability

Taken as a whole, these four standards provided criteria to be used in evaluating potential accounting information. If the standards were not met, the information was not acceptable and should not be communicated. The standards could also be used to evaluate accounting methods indirectly by evaluating the information they produce. Accounting methods that did not produce information that meets these standards would be unacceptable.

The foremost standard was relevance. It was the primary standard and a necessary characteristic for all accounting information. It could not stand alone, however. Relevance was directly related to decision usefulness and defined as the appropriateness of the information with regard to the decision or action it is designed to facilitate.

Although the idea of relevance was not new, listing relevance as the primary standard was another major departure from conventional thought in the mid-1960s. Accounting had long emphasized objectivity and verifiability rather than relevance. Compared to objectivity, relevance was seen as more subjective. Relevance is in the "eyes of the beholder" and thus emphasizes the users, whereas objectivity stresses evidence. Relevance puts more emphasis on the users and their needs; objectivity places more emphasis on the accountants' processes and evidence.

The second standard was verifiability. This standard assured users that the information was dependable. It was defined as the ability of information to be tested or evaluated with evidence and be upheld, based on the ability of two or more individuals working independently to come to the same results.

ASOBAT recognized that relevance and verifiability might conflict. For example, some highly relevant information may not be verifiable (such as a management forecast), and some highly verifiable information may not be relevant (such as the historical cost of a sunk cost).

The third standard, freedom from bias, referred to the ability of information to be impartial and neutral, that is, not being biased toward anyone or any side. Accounting operates in an environment with competing users. To be fully useful, accounting must be careful to not slant its information toward one set of users to the disadvantage of another set of users. Interestingly, ASOBAT did not use the term *objectivity*. Avoiding that term may have been a conscious attempt to block those who used the term merely as a way to thwart any nonhistorical cost valuation scheme from consideration. Many practicing accountants would object to using market-to-market accounting as not being objective.

Quantifiability, the fourth standard, was defined as the association of a number with a transaction or activity. This is how accounting operates like a measurement system. A measurement system operates as follows: It examines an object and finds many attributes of that object; then it selects one attribute and associates a measure with that attribute, and that measure represents the object. In accounting the most frequently measured attribute is economic usefulness, and the most frequently used measure is dollars. The result is always a single value as compared to a range of values.

It's important to understand exactly how accounting operates as a measurement system. For example, when shopping for a new car, an individual will appreciate many attributes of the automobile: exterior color and shape, interior color and layout, make, size and power of the engine, number of luxury options, new-car smell, and price or "deal." But when an accountant records the purchase of a new car by a firm, the only attribute the accountant records is the purchase price. The dollar amount and asset account represent the car in the accounting records. One issue in measurement systems is the appropriateness of the attribute to represent the object.

COMMUNICATION GUIDELINES

In addition to specifying the four standards of accounting information, ASOBAT described the communication process in accounting and provided five communication guidelines.

1. Appropriateness to expected use
2. Disclosure of significant relationships
3. Inclusion of environmental information
4. Uniformity of practices within and among entities
5. Consistency of practices through time

These guidelines were provided to help accountants do a better job of communicating. The guidelines implied that, in ASOBAT's opinion, accountants needed to do a better job in this area.

The first guideline suggested that reports should be prepared with the intended users' needs in mind. This was a major theme in the ASOBAT. Following this guideline would produce reports that were both timely and relevant. This guideline also signified that different reports would contain different information, depending on the users.

The second guideline related to levels of summarization and aggregation. Accountants had been criticized for excessive summarization and aggregation in financial reports. ASOBAT recommended that they provide reports that permit the observation of significant financial and operational activities of the firm. Often this was not possible because data was hidden in large totals or important segments of the data were buried in those totals.

The third guideline advocated the inclusion of environmental information in accounting reports. This involved describing the conditions under which the data were collected and the report prepared. ASOBAT recommended that the background information and setting associated with information be presented to permit informed judgments.

The fourth guideline involved uniformity of practice within and among entities. It referred to consistent classification and terminology, which facilitates comparisons. Otherwise, differences in terminology, classification, or measurement units may make accounting reports misleading.

The final guideline referred to consistency of practice through time. To facilitate the determination of trends and analysis of a series of data, accounting measurement and reporting practices should be consistently applied from year to year.

MULTIPLE MEASURES

The most controversial of the proposed changes in accounting practice advocated by ASOBAT dealt with historical cost. ASOBAT declared that much of the dissatisfaction with accounting at that time could be traced to the deficiencies and limitations of historical cost. Although historical cost–based information was high in verifiability (because it was based on transactions), it was only adequately relevant. Current cost information, however, was higher in relevance, especially because it reflected not only the transactions of the firm but also the impact of the environment on those transactions. ASOBAT admitted that current cost information was somewhat lower in verifiability. In a radical departure from traditional accounting practice, ASOBAT recommended that both historical and current costs be reported. That is, firms should prepare multivalued reports that present historical cost and current cost information side by side in columns. This dual reporting would allow users to compare the figures under both systems. Their recommendation included both current cost information using replacement costs and general price-level cost adjustments. To illustrate what they advocated, an appendix presented sample reports, a balance sheet, and an income statement.

As could be expected, accounting practitioners had many problems with the recommendation that multiple measures be reported. Recall that at the time accounting practice was grounded in verifiability and objectivity. Accounting practitioners were concerned that their audit procedures would have to be greatly expanded to deal with the new information and the new audit programs being developed.

ESSENCE OF ASOBAT

ASOBAT was a departure from previous theory efforts and conventional thinking in the following ways:

- For the first time, users were specifically mentioned in a theory formulation and ASOBAT gave them preference.
- ASOBAT emphasized accounting as an information system, placing a corresponding emphasis on the communication side of accounting. Much emphasis was accorded this topic, indicating the relative neglect that accountants had for this aspect of accounting.
- Consistent with the communication approach, ASOBAT emphasized relevance as the most important aspect of accounting information. Declaring the primacy of relevance was a departure from conventional thinking, which made objectivity or verifiability the primary standard.
- A broader view of accounting dominated ASOBAT. Nontransactional data could be included.
- The multi-measure recommendation of ASOBAT earned it the reputation as being against historical cost and in favor of current cost.

As an interesting note, the longest chapter in ASOBAT deals with managerial accounting. This was a first—theory formulation that included internal management accounting. Some questioned the wide scope of ASOBAT and suggested that a chapter entitled, "Accounting Information for Internal Management," didn't belong in a statement about theory formulation.

CONCERNS ABOUT ASOBAT

As expected, no theory formulation is ever presented without criticism. Certainly, ASOBAT was no exception; its publication generated a number of diverse interpretations. Three major criticisms are examined.

MORRISON'S COMMENTARY CONCERNS

One committee member, Russell Morrison, the only practitioner, agreed to the publication of ASOBAT but submitted his comments with the request that they be published in ASOBAT as a commentary at the end of the document. In his opinion, ASOBAT was a "thoughtful and . . . useful study." However, he concluded the following:

PEOPLE

> *But it offers little in the way of basic accounting theory as a foundation for a body of sound accounting principles governing the treatment of accounting information. Thus, in this respect I believe that an essential part of the statement of basic accounting theory which the committee was charged to prepare remains to be developed.*[6]

Morrison noted three specific items with which he disagreed: (1) the reporting of current cost, which he believed to lack verifiability; (2) the inclusion in ASOBAT of a chapter on managerial accounting; and (3) the inclusion of the last chapter (Chapter V, "Extensions of Accounting") on areas of accounting that warrant further research.

SORTER'S EVENT SCHOOL CONCERNS

A second major criticism of ASOBAT came from committee member Professor George Sorter.[7] Although he noted that for many the most controversial aspect of ASOBAT was its recommendation that both historical and current cost be reported in a dual-reporting format, he believed that another aspect of ASOBAT was even more startling. That aspect was the emphasis on a *value approach,* or *user need approach,* in which it is assumed that users' needs are known and well specified enough to allow accountants to produce information to meet those needs. He came from an opposite direction, the *events approach* (or school), and his article describes the Events school versus User Needs school.

PEOPLE

Sorter stated that ASOBAT was written following the User Need school. It assumed that accountants know enough about users' needs to prescribe information for them that will act as optimal input values for decision-making models.

Sorter believed the User Need school erred because of two factors.

1. Accounting information can be applied to a variety of uses. There is a wide range of possible uses for accounting information, and this makes it very difficult to assume to know all users' needs.
2. For any particular use, there are different users. These users all have different decision models, and this makes it impossible to assume to know all models.

In light of these factors, Sorter believed it impossible to describe, detect, and specify optimal information for users. As an alternative, the Events school, he proposed that accountants provide "events" and let them choose appropriate information based on them.

The Events school suggests that accounting's purpose is to provide information about relevant economic events that might be useful various decision models. A major area of contrast between the User Need and the Events schools concerns the level of aggregation and summarization in accounting. In the User Need school, the accountant is the aggregator and evaluator; the accountant decides which data to aggregate, the level of aggregation, and the format for reporting that data. Notice that the accountants, in these activities, are acting as though they know what is best for the users. In the Event school, the accountant would provide data in disaggregated form so that users could generate their own input values for use in their own decision models.

An example from normal daily life will clarify the difference. Look, for example, at weather forecasting. Some weather forecasters assume they know our needs and will state their forecast as, "It will rain tomorrow, so be sure to take an umbrella with you." Other forecasters will state "The probability of rain tomorrow is 60 percent." Notice that the second forecaster does not specify what the listener's action should be; it simply provides data. If a listener's minimum probability threshold for avoiding rain is 50 percent, he or she will take an umbrella; if it is 70 percent, he or she will not. Therefore, the User Need school is like the first forecast; the Events school is like the second.

Sorter did not approve of ASOBAT because of its inherent assumption that accountants know the users' needs and could produce optimal input values in the form of accounting information for these needs. He wanted his article to contrast the two approaches and to stimulate discussion of using the events approach for making accounting more responsive to users' needs. Although this article was published in 1969, it is an interesting precursor to an idea that became popular in the beginning of the twenty-first century in financial reporting using a technology known as relational databases. As discussed more fully in Chapter 16, "Financial Reporting: Disclosure," many firms are considering providing financial data in the form of online relational databases for investors to access in addition to published financial statements. The online disclosures would be available much earlier than the published statements. With a database, users could download data and perform a wide variety of computations and analyses. This process sounds similar to what Sorter was proposing in the late 1960s.

STERLING'S REVIEW CONCERNS

PEOPLE   One of the leading academic theoreticians of the 1960s, Robert Sterling, wrote a review about ASOBAT.[8] He began by noting that the committee was given a very big job in their charge, and subsequently, he wasn't surprised that they failed. He really did not find much new in ASOBAT; in fact, according to Sterling, much of what appeared in the theory formulation had been presented elsewhere in accounting theory literature.

He did see three new items in ASOBAT and commented on them.

One concerned the methodology used to formulate ASOBAT. Remember that methodology, or approach to theory, was an important factor in the early 1960s. But the approach used in ASOBAT was not explicitly stated nor apparent. In some places, ASOBAT sounded inductive and in other places, deductive. But which method was used was not clearly stated, defended, or supported. So, Sterling questioned, if the approach is not explained, how can we know it is valid?

The second new factor in ASOBAT was its view: It viewed accounting as a measurement information system, which was laudable. However, given that, relevance is obvious. Sterling pointed out that although viewing accounting as a measurement information system is praiseworthy, ASOBAT's conclusion that relevance is primary is not equally commendable because it is an obvious conclusion. A measurement system can never measure all the attributes of an object; one must be selected, and therefore, relevance is natural. ASOBAT should take no credit for selecting relevance as the primary characteristic of accounting information.

Additionally, if relevance is the primary standard for judging accounting information, why did ASOBAT recommend that multiple measures (both historical cost and current cost) be reported? Doesn't this conflict with relevance? Are both relevant? If not, why report both? This appeared to violate the standard of relevance.

Related to this was Sterling's concern that ASOBAT did not take the issue of capacity constraints into consideration. In communication, an important factor is consideration of the limits of your capacity to communicate. But ASOBAT suggested at least doubling the data being transmitted to users (both historical cost and current cost), which might cause "information overload." That concern should have been addressed by ASOBAT.

The third comment by Sterling was that the support for current cost was weak and indirect. It was not enough to say that the primary reason for supporting current cost measures was because historical cost was "bad." If historical cost is inadequate, it doesn't necessarily lead to the conclusion that current cost is better. Sterling questioned the lack of support or justification for current cost in ASOBAT. Support for current cost appeared to stem only from dissatisfaction with historical cost. Sterling wanted to see a direct justification for current cost. In fact, if historical cost is inadequate, why report it at all? Why not disregard historical cost and replace it with something better?

Overall, Sterling found ASOBAT to be inconsistent. In some places, it is pure theory, and in other places, it takes positions on contemporary issues. Elsewhere, it looks to the future. He did not see enough support for the positions, development of the main arguments, precision in the recommendations, or logical rigor for the arguments.

However, in a positive sense, he viewed ASOBAT as a good collection of agreed-upon ideas by theorists.

During the period of time when ASOBAT was the focus of accounting, things continued to go badly for the APB. The next section covers those developments.

STANDARD SETTING VI
DEMISE OF THE APB

By the late 1960s, the APB began to run into more problems with their Opinions again. Over its term, the APB issued 31 Opinions, many of which were preceded by an ARS. Many of its Opinions tackled important issues in accounting: pensions, earnings per share, income tax allocation, business combinations, and goodwill. In 1971, the APB installed procedures for gathering input on issues, and public hearings were introduced.

But as time went on, it became increasingly clear that the APB was not effective. The following concerns about the APB began to surface:

- Either because of the absence of theory or the early reversing of its position on the investment tax credit, the APB was not seen as a strong standard setter. Certainly, the threat of an SEC reversal always hung over the APB.
- The board members were part-time.
- No users were on the board. Although accounting is a service activity, designed to provide information to users, users were never included in the APB.

- A technical, mechanical approach to accounting appeared to dominate the board. This was clearly seen in its approach to accounting for the investment tax credit.
- The APB was too large in terms of the number of members. Although eighteen to twenty-one members provided wide representation (but did not include users), it was too large and cumbersome.
- It was weakened by major controversies, especially early in its tenure.
- It failed to narrow diversity, and without a theory, it adopted a fire-fighting approach.
- It failed to resist outside pressure. Once public accounting firms and the preparers knew they could get the SEC to overrule the APB, the pressure was on the APB. This did not create a positive atmosphere in which to attempt to set accounting standards.

Thus by the 1970s, it became apparent that the APB needed to be replaced with a new structure. Accountants were painfully aware of the failure of their second effort at establishing a standard-setting body. And yet, this was their best, most comprehensive effort to date.

INTERNATIONAL STANDARD SETTING

At this point in the chronological development of accounting theory and standard setting, it is appropriate to consider how other nations were setting accounting standards. An examination of the accounting standard-setting structure in two other nations, The Netherlands and Japan, provides an international perspective on the deliberations occurring in the United States. The comparisons reveals that vastly different approaches were being followed in other nations.

To provide an overview of this topic, four broad categories of approaches to setting accounting standards are listed next.[9]

1. A *purely political approach,* which relies on legislation to establish the accounting standards
2. A *private, professional approach* in which the accounting standards are set by the accounting profession
3. A *public-private approach* in which the accounting standards are set by a private-sector agency that acts as a public agency
4. A *mixed approach,* which combines private, public, governmental, labor, and other groups in setting the accounting standards

These categories are used to discuss the accounting standard setting process in the Netherlands and Japan in the early 1970s.

The Netherlands   The Netherlands is an example of the private, professional approach. The main professional accounting organization is the Netherlands Institute of Registered Accountants (Institute), which was founded in 1895. In 1970, the Act on Annual Accounts of Enterprises was issued by the government in The Netherlands. This act required the auditing of large Dutch companies by registered accountants (members of the Institute). In the early 1970s, Dutch GAAP was informal and had not been codified in formal pronouncements by the Institute. Instead, accounting practitioners followed the technical papers and reports on various accounting topics published by the Institute. A large body of accounting literature written by Dutch academic accountants supplemented these papers and reports.

Japan   In Japan, a public approach to setting accounting standards was followed. In national accounting matters, the Japanese Ministry of Finance was the dominant standard-setting body, not the Japanese Institute of CPAs. In fact, in the early 1970s, the Japanese Institute of CPAs was a small organization with little influence over setting standards. Within the Ministry of Finance, the Business Accounting Deliberation Council was the single most authoritative source of Japanese GAAP. This council was composed of thirty members, all of whom are experts in accounting appointed by the Ministry of Finance. Accounting standards were then enacted into the Japanese Commercial Code.

SUMMARY

The focus of this chapter is on the Accounting Principles Board's tenure and another major effort at theory formulation—this time from the American Accounting Association, *A Statement of Basic Accounting Theory,* in 1966. Neither the APB nor ASOBAT was well received by the accounting profession and preparers of financial statements.

Although it started with optimism and hope, without a theory, the APB soon fell victim to political problems. By the 1990s the APB was in trouble as an accounting standard setting body for various reasons.

The AAA had a natural advantage in formulating a theory of accounting. But unfortunately, the resulting theory set forth in ASOBAT was not accepted. Thus neither standard setting nor theory formulation was going particularly well for accounting in the early 1970s.

REVIEW QUESTIONS

1. What issue caused a major problem for the APB early in its tenure? What aspect of that issue was the most troublesome?
2. How strong was the AICPA support for the APB in 1964? What alternative ways could the AICPA have more strongly supported the APB?
3. How does the membership of the AAA differ from that of the AICPA?
4. Why are academics more oriented toward theory than practitioners or public accountants?
5. What process was followed to develop ASOBAT? What are some of the pros and cons of that process?
6. In what ways was the definition of accounting in ASOBAT a departure from contemporary accounting thinking in the mid-1960s?
7. How were users of accounting information covered in ASOBAT?
8. How was ASOBAT's emphasis on relevance different from accounting thinking at the time?
9. Summarize Morrison's, Sorter's, and Sterling's concerns about ASOBAT.
10. Compare and contrast ASOBAT with Moonitz and Sprouse's accounting theory project in the following table.

	ASOBAT	Moonitz and Sprouse's Project
Authors		
Sponsoring agency		
Major approach		
Major conclusions		
Reaction		
General acceptability		

11. What evidence appeared in the late 1960s to early 1970s that signaled the demise of the APB?
12. List the four broad categories of approaches for setting accounting standards.

DISCUSSION TOPICS

1. If you had been a member of the APB in January 1963, how would you have felt when the SEC overruled Opinion #2 with ASR #96?
2. Examine the four goals stated for ASOBAT. How do these compare to the three purposes of accounting theory?
3. What was the essence of ASOBAT? Which element was most controversial in your opinion?
4. Of the three major criticisms of ASOBAT, with which one do you most agree?
5. Examine the instructions given to the ASOBAT committee in 1964 (see p. 69). Did they accomplish them or not?
6. Do you think the fact that the only member of the ASOBAT committee that disagreed with the results of the committee was a practitioner has any significance? Can you suggest some reasons for this?
7. What was significant about ASOBAT's mention of the importance of accounting information for social functions and controls as one of the informational needs of users?
8. If you had to choose between relevance and objectivity as the central objective of accounting, which would you select? Defend your choice.
9. How would you evaluate the structure and operations of the APB? What was positive about them? What was negative? Is your overall evaluation positive or negative?
10. Of the four broad approaches to setting accounting standards, which do you think is most efficient? Support your answer.
11. **Application Problem.** Using the web site containing the addresses of standard-setting bodies around the world, http://accounting.rutgers.edu/anet/accounting_services/assns/acctg_associations_toc.html, select two and obtain information from their sites about how they set accounting standards. Categorize them according to the four broad approaches cited in the chapter.

NOTES

1 American Accounting Association (1966), p. v. (The committee consisted of Norton Bedford, R. Lee Brummet, Neil Churchill, Paul Fertig, Russell Morrison, Roland Salmonson, George Sorter, and Lawrence Vance; it was chaired by Charles Zlatkovich.)

2 Ibid., p. 1.

3 Ibid.

4 Ibid., p. 4.

5 Ibid., p. 6.

6 Ibid., p. 97.

7 Sorter.

8 Sterling.

9 Daley and Mueller, pp. 40–41.

REFERENCES

American Accounting Association. *A Statement of Basic Accounting Theory,* (Evanston, IL: American Accounting Association), 1966.

Daley, L. A. and G. G. Mueller. "Accounting in the Arena of World Politics." *Journal of Accountancy* (February 1982): 40–41.

Deinzer, Harvey T. *Foundations of Accounting Theory* (Gainesville: University of Florida Press), 1971.

Fertig, Paul E. "A Statement of Basic Accounting Theory." *New York CPA* (September 1967): 663–671.

Hicks, Ernest L. "Comments on 'A Statement of Basic Accounting Theory.'" *Journal of Accountancy* (September 1966): 56–60.

Sorter, George. "An Events Approach to Basic Accounting Theory." *Accounting Review* (January 1969): 12–19.

Sterling, Robert. "ASOBAT: A Review Article." *Journal of Accounting Research* (Spring 1967): 95–112.

Zeff, Stephen. "A Perspective on the U.S. Public/Private-sector Approach to the Regulation of Financial Reporting." *Accounting Horizons* (March 1995): 52–70.

Zlatkovich, Charles T. "A New Accounting Theory Statement." *Journal of Accountancy* (August 1966): 31–36.

CHAPTER 4

THE NEW TRIPARTITE STRUCTURE

LEARNING OBJECTIVES

After studying this chapter, you should be able to

> Compare and contrast the mission of the Trueblood Committee and the Wheat Committee.

> Explain the new view of accounting and contrast it with the old view.

> Describe the international developments that affected the new view of accounting.

> Distinguish between the three elements of the new tripartite structure of standard setting.

> Define the mission, membership, and authority of the FASB.

STANDARD SETTING	1900	THEORY FORMULATION
CHAPTER 1		
STANDARD SETTING I		THEORY 1
PRE-CAP	1900-1938	NATURE OF THEORY
SEC	1934	
STANDARD SETTING II		
CAP I	1938	
STANDARD SETTING III		
CAP II	1938-1958	
CHAPTER 2		
STANDARD SETTING IV		THEORY II
APB	1959-1962	
	1961-1962	ARS #1 AND #3
CHAPTER 3		
STANDARD SETTING V		THEORY III
APB	1963-1966	
	1966	ASOBAT
STANDARD SETTING VI		
DEMISE OF APB	1970	
CHAPTER 4, 5		
STANDARD SETTING VII		
TRUEBLOOD	**1973**	
WHEAT	**1972**	
TRIPARTITE STRUCTURE	**1973-2001**	
CHAPTER 6		
		THEORY IV
	1977	SATTA
		POSITIVE ACCOUNTING 1980s
CHAPTER 7		THEORY V
	1973-2001	CONCEPTUAL FRAMEWORK PROJECT
CHAPTER 8		
STANDARD SETTING VIII		
FASB: PRESENT AND FUTURE STANDARD SETTING: DOMESTIC AND INTERNATIONAL	2001	
	2002	

In this chapter, the examination of the development of accounting standard setting and theory formulation continues, focusing on the dissolution of the Accounting Principles Board (APB) and the events occurring before and after its dissolution. The second watershed period for accounting standard setting and theory formulation is covered. Organizational developments—the Trueblood Committee and the Wheat Committee—and international developments are all examined.

The chapter then focuses on the major change in accounting: the new view of accounting. This leads into a discussion of the sweeping change in standard setting that was implemented in 1973. The chapter ends with a discussion of the new tripartite structure (Financial Accounting Standards Board [FASB], Financial Accounting Foundation [FAF], and Financial Accounting Standards Advisory Council [FaSAC]).

In order to keep the events in this chapter in perspective, preserving the chronological development begun in Chapter 1, refer to Exhibit 4.1. Note this chapter's coverage is highlighted in bold.

STANDARD SETTING VII
DISSOLUTION OF THE APB

APB'S TROUBLES, 1970

By 1970, the APB faced two major obstacles. These problems were serious and threatened the existence of the APB. The first problem was criticism of corporate financial reporting. The second problem was the lack of a framework for developing accounting principles.

PEOPLE   The criticism of corporate financial reporting came from users (investors and creditors) and regulators. For example, Professor Abraham J. Briloff became a popular and outspoken critic of accounting and disclosure practices. He believed that U. S. GAAP was too diverse and that too many alternative accounting principles existed that afforded preparers the opportunity to influence their reported results. The criticisms resulted in a growing lack of confidence in the standard-setting ability of the APB, which meant serious problems, both for the APB and for the accounting profession.

The second problem was related to the first. As noted in Chapter 3, the APB issued opinions. It issued a total of thirty-one Opinions. Although some of them were preceded by a research study conducted through the Accounting Research Division (ARD), none were issued following a general frame of reference (an accounting theory). They were based on the personal views of the members of the APB (whose membership did not include users), and since the membership changed from year to year, the Opinions differed from one another and were sometimes inconsistent. This inconsistency contributed to a lack of confidence in the APB and its standard-setting activity.

As an example of the internal dissension and disagreement in the APB and the resulting difficulty in issuing Opinions, Zeff analyzed twelve substantive single-issue Opinions of the APB from 1959 through 1970.[1] He analyzed Opinions on topics such as depreciation methods, the investment tax credit, leases, pension plans, net income, income taxes, convertible debt, earnings per share, business combinations, and intangible assets. Of the Opinions on these twelve important accounting issues, nine were issued with major disagreement.

AICPA'S REACTION

The APB's situation was desperate enough to warrant a meeting in January 1971 in Washington, D.C., of thirty-five prominent CPAs, representing twenty-one major public accounting firms. This meeting was called by the president of the AICPA, Marshall Armstrong, to decide what to do about the two major problems facing the APB. The result was a recommendation that two study groups be established: one to look at the objectives of accounting and the other to review how accounting standard setting should be structured.

As a result of these and other concerns about the APB, the AICPA had to act. The President, Marshall Armstrong called for a comprehensive review of standard setting. This set the stage for what followed. This was the second watershed period for accounting standard setting and theory formulation. The actions taken in 1971 had long-lasting effects on accounting, many of which are still being felt today.

TWIN COMMITTEES

The AICPA established the two committees, The Study Group on the Objectives of Financial Statements, and The Study Group on the Establishment of Accounting Principles. Each committees was named after its chairperson: the Trueblood Committee and the Wheat Committee, respectively. Thus the fate of accounting was in the hands of these twin committees.

The state of standard setting and theory formulation was so grave that even the American Accounting Association (AAA) was about to take action. The 1971 AAA executive committee called for the establishment of a blue-ribbon committee to make a comprehensive study of how accounting principles should be established. However, the committee was never established in light of the response of the AICPA's formation of the Trueblood Committee.

THE TRUEBLOOD COMMITTEE

OBJECTIVES

The Trueblood Committee was established in October 1971 and was chaired by Robert Trueblood, a practitioner with Touche, Ross, and Company. There were nine members: three academics, three public accountants (including Trueblood), two preparers (industrial firms), and one investment analyst. The committee issued its report in 1973.

Due to concerns about corporate financial reporting, the Trueblood Committee was charged by the board of directors of the AICPA to find the answers to four questions.

1. Who needs financial statements?
2. What information do they need?
3. How much of the needed information can be provided by accountants?
4. What framework is needed to provide the needed information?

Notice the "themes" in the questions: uses and users of accounting information and the theory needed to meet those users' needs. These topics were addressed by the AAA in ASOBAT in 1966, but the AICPA was determined to find its own answers to these questions.

METHODOLOGY

The committee made a serious effort to find the answer to these questions. It assembled a staff of academics, public accounting professionals, and others, including consultants and observers. It conducted surveys and solicited the views of more than five thousand corporations and other organizations. The committee held more than fifty interviews and thirty-five meetings, including a three-day public hearing in May 1972. Note that for the first time, the committee did not limit its inquiry to the views of committee members or the accounting literature. Instead, it ventured beyond the committee to obtain feedback from those who used accounting reports and those who prepared them.

This was not an easy topic to address. Just as everyone has opinions on the basic issues of life, accountants held a wide variety of views about what the objectives of accounting should be. The feedback obtained on issues such as the objectives of financial statements would be subjective and hard to tally and summarize. The committee itself had substantial internal debate about the issues and admitted that its final conclusions were only an initial step in establishing objectives.

THE TRUEBLOOD REPORT

The Trueblood report was issued in the fall of 1973. It was not regarded as a final report by the committee; the committee saw it as a first step and noted that significant effort should continue to be made on the topic.

In addition to other information, the report listed the following twelve objectives for financial reporting:[2]

1. The basic objective of financial statements is to provide information useful for making economic decisions.
2. An objective of financial statements is to serve primarily those users who have limited authority, ability, or resources to obtain information and who rely on financial statements as their principal source of information about an enterprise's economic activities.
3. An objective of financial statements is to provide information useful to investors and creditors for predicting, comparing, and evaluating potential cash flows to them in terms of amount, timing, and related uncertainty.
4. An objective of financial statements is to provide users with information for predicting, comparing, and evaluating enterprise earning power.
5. An objective of financial statements is to supply information useful in judging management's ability to utilize enterprise resources effectively in achieving the primary enterprise goal.
6. An objective of financial statements is to provide factual and interpretive information about transactions and other events which is useful for predicting, comparing, and evaluating enterprise earning power. Basic underlying assumptions with respect to matters subject to interpretation, evaluation, prediction, or estimation should be disclosed.
7. An objective is to provide a statement of financial position, useful for predicting, comparing, and evaluating enterprise earning power. . . . Current values should also be reported when they differ significantly from historical costs. Assets and liabilities should be grouped or segregated by the relative uncertainty of the amount and timing of prospective realization or liquidation.

8. An objective is to provide a statement of periodic earnings useful for predicting, comparing, and evaluating enterprise earning power. . . . Changes in the values reflected in successive statements of financial position should be reported, but separately since they differ in terms of their certainty of realization.

9. Another objective is to provide a statement of financial activities useful for predicting, comparing, and evaluating enterprise earning power. This statement should report mainly on factual aspects of enterprise transactions having or expected to have significant cash consequences. This statement should report data that require minimal judgment and interpretation by the preparer.

10. An objective of financial statements is to provide information useful for the predicting process. Financial forecasts should be provided when they will enhance the reliability of users' predictions.

11. An objective of financial statements for governmental and not-for-profit organizations is to provide information useful for evaluating the effectiveness of the management of resources in achieving the organization's goals. Performance measures should be quantified in terms of identified goals.

12. An objective of financial statements is to report on those activities of the enterprise that affect society which can be determined and described or measured and which are important to the role of the enterprise in its social environment.

Based on their research, the members of the Trueblood Committee concluded that *the primary purpose of accounting is to provide information that is useful in decision making*. This purpose was designed to serve users—those without the ability, resources, or authority to obtain that information directly. Instead, users rely on accounting as a primary source of information.

The Trueblood report concluded that the major need of those users was information that would help them predict, compare, and evaluate potential cash flows. The information should further help them assess those cash flows in terms of amount, timing, and uncertainty. The users primarily concerned with cash flow information were investors and creditors. The committee further recommended that a statement that specifically focused on the cash flows of the firm be created.

Another topic of interest was information on the earning power of the business entity. Users needed information to help them predict, compare, and evaluate the earning power of the business and how management's decisions affected that earning power.

The issue of current costs was addressed. The report concluded in Chapter 6, "Financial Statements—Historical Cost and Value Considerations," that the objectives could not be served by the use of a single valuation basis such as historical cost. Rather, it concluded that different valuation bases should be used for different assets. Forecasted information was also called for in the report along with disclosure of the societal aspects of a firm's operations.

EVALUATION

The report of the Trueblood Committee was forward-looking. The primacy of users, the usefulness of accounting, and the emphasis on cash flow information were all steps forward for accounting. A broader view of accounting was also included, as shown in objective 12, which put accounting in the context of society and its welfare. Notice, however, that relevance, as a concept, was conspicuous in its absence in the stated objectives. Instead, it was covered in Chapter 10, "Qualitative Characteristics of Reporting," as a characteristic of information to satisfy users' needs.

Unfortunately, the Trueblood report also did not provide any guidance on the implementation of its objectives. This was viewed as beyond its scope.

A comparison of the twelve objectives to the four questions originally charged to the committee, reveals the answers to three of the four questions.

1. Who needs financial statements? Objectives 2 and 3: users (investors and creditors).
2. What information do they need? Objective 1: information for decision making; objective 3: information about cash flows; objective 4: information about earning power; objective 5: information to judge management; and objectives 6 through 12.
3. How much of this information can be supplied by accounting? This answer is similar to the answer for question 2.

The Trueblood Committee report does not answer the fourth question: What framework is required to provide the needed information?

In addition, four other considerations should be taken into account when evaluating the report. First, it should be noted that the Trueblood Committee did its work in a difficult atmosphere because the Wheat Committee was also working on a related topic, how to set accounting standards. These two committees were interdependent. What objectives you establish for accounting will be largely impacted by how you set accounting standards. In addition, the primary benefactor of a statement of the objectives of accounting is the standard-setting body. And that issue was uncertain as the Trueblood Committee started its work.

Second, it is significant that the AICPA decided to solve its problems by first establishing a committee to study the objectives of accounting. The existence of this committee implied that accountants were either uncertain about the objectives of accounting or disagreed on those objectives. That was a sad commentary on the accounting profession of the early 1970s. It would be more understandable if a committee had been set up in the 1870s to determine the objective of accounting. Most other professions (e.g., medicine and law) had agreement on their objectives much earlier than accounting. And that fact was conspicuous as the Trueblood Committee began its work.

Third, by starting with the objectives, the AICPA ended up following the same pattern as set forth by the normative-deductive approach to theory formulation. Under that approach, the first priority is a statement of the objectives of the discipline. Therefore, one would think that the committee was going to follow the normative-deductive approach again; however, it was purely coincidental that the AICPA started with objectives. At the time, no one would have seriously considered trying the normative-deductive approach again after the failure of Moonitz and Sprouse's theory formulation. The normative-deductive approach had been stigmatized.

The fourth consideration is timing. Timing worked against the Trueblood report in two ways: (1) The report was issued after the Wheat Committee's report, which greatly overshadowed it because the Wheat report dealt with the more prominent issue, how to set accounting standards. (2) When the Trueblood Committee finished its report, it was submitted it to the ACIPA, its sponsor. But by October 1973, the AICPA was no longer in the standard-setting business. As of July 1, 1973, a new FASB standard-setting structure was in place. So the Trueblood committee submitted the final report to the AICPA, asking it to forward the report to the FASB.

REACTION

The Trueblood report was issued in a rather uncertain time for accountants. As the Trueblood Committee worked on finishing the project, attention was increasingly focused on the Wheat Committee as it completed its work on a new procedure to establish accounting standards. Many saw this as the more pressing issue.

Reaction to Trueblood was somewhat mild. Some thought that the objectives stated were rather obvious. Others wondered why the report did not prioritize the objectives. As an example of these concerns, consider Ross Skinner. He criticized the report as being bland and noncontroversial. For example, he characterized it as "the good gray prose . . . fuzzy abstraction . . . careful balancing of one hand and the other."[3]

One cannot help but see similarities between the reaction to Trueblood and the reaction to ARS #1. Remember that the objectives in ARS #1 were not as controversial as the principles in ARS #3. Of course, the Wheat Committee issued its report before Trueblood. The Wheat Committee's sweeping changes to standard setting were accepted by the AICPA and implemented before the Trueblood report was published, thereby overshadowing Trueblood.

THE WHEAT COMMITTEE

The Wheat Committee, The Study Group on Establishment of Accounting Principles, was created in March 1971 and charged with studying how accounting principles should be established and was committed to a comprehensive review of how to set accounting standards. Its chair was Frances M. Wheat, a former commissioner of the SEC and a past critic of the APB and accounting standards. The committee consisted of seven members.

The Wheat Committee finished its report in March 1972, recommending major changes in the establishment of accounting standards. It did not simply make changes in or adjust the structure or operations of the APB. It recommended wholesale changes. These wholesale changes involved moving accounting standard setting from under the organizational authority of the AICPA and making it an independent process. In addition, it expanded the structure for standard setting to a three-part (tripartite) structure, which was larger than the dual structure previously used (APB and ARD). The three parts would be the Financial Accounting Foundation (FAF), the Financial Accounting Standards Board (FASB), and the Financial Accounting Standards Advisory Council (FaSAC). The AICPA accepted the recommendation in June 1972 and implemented it on July 1, 1973.

These three groups are discussed in the last section of this chapter. The next section discusses the changes in the environment of accounting that led to these changes, as background for understanding why the sweeping changes were seen as necessary and were adopted.

NEW VIEW OF ACCOUNTING

To appreciate the changes that were adopted in July 1973, you must understand the new view of accounting. This understanding will provide the needed background to understand standard setting under the new conditions that began to exist in the early 1970's signaling the need for major changes in accounting standard setting. Although the new view of accounting has been mentioned in previous sections, this section focuses on it in more detail and contrasts it with the old view.

OLD VIEW FOCUS

Under the old view of accounting, the focus was on a microlevel, an individualized, or decentralized, structure. Accounting was seen primarily as a link from the firm to its investors and creditors. Accounting was not seen as important beyond that level. Although important to investors and creditors, it was not viewed as having a higher level of scope. That is, accounting was not seen as playing an important role in the national economy, the world economy, or the welfare of society. Accountants were considered to be "bean counters."

NEW VIEW FOCUS

All that changed under the new view. Now accounting was defined at a macrolevel, on a total, or centralized, basis. Accounting was seen as the linkage between all firms and the capital markets, both domestic and international. Accounting was viewed as playing a significant role in those markets, and thus, in the welfare of society, thereby elevating the importance of accounting.

ACCOUNTING'S NEW ROLE AND IMPORTANCE

Under the new view, accounting is seen as providing financial information about economic entities to investors and creditors.[4] Investors have a significant investment in business firms but are not actively engaged in managing those firms. Their investments are an important part of their wealth and, in aggregate, an important part of the economy. Creditors provide loan-capital to firms and expect to be repaid. Therefore, accounting is important to the very fabric of the economy and of society. The links between accounting and investors and capital markets are briefly described in the following paragraphs. In each of the numbered paragraphs, a summary is provided.

1. For the goals of any society to be achieved, its economy must be efficient because the welfare of society is linked to its economy. That is, no society will ever prosper unless its economy operates efficiently. Therefore: **To achieve society's goals, we need a strong economy.**
2. To have a strong economy, there must be adequate capital resources. These capital resources can be equity or debt capital. Therefore: **To achieve an economy's goals, it must have adequate capital resources.**
3. For an economy to have adequate capital resources, there must be a supply of and demand for capital resources. Some mechanism must exist to allocate those capital

resources to firms, that is, from suppliers to consumers. In Western economies, capital resources are allocated through capital markets. Capital markets are arrangements or locations at which the suppliers of and consumers for capital resources determine the market prices that equate supply and demand. Therefore: **Capital resources are allocated through capital markets.**

4. The allocation process involves many decisions by suppliers and consumers. That is how capital markets operate to equate supply and demand. Both capital suppliers and consumers make decisions that allocate capital. Capital markets use expected returns and risk as inputs into allocation decisions. Therefore: **The allocation process involves a large number of decisions by capital suppliers and capital consumers.**

5. For allocation process decisions to be made, some information must be available to be used by suppliers and consumers. The decisions made to allocate capital should not be made without the benefit of information. As important as capital allocation is to the economy and to society, the decisions should be grounded in information rather than be made intuitively. Because capital markets use expected returns and risk as decision-making factors, information can be helpful to reduce uncertainty about future events and circumstances. And because capital is a financial asset and the allocation decision involves finance, some of the information used to allocate capital should be financial information. Therefore: **The decisions by capital suppliers and consumers are based on financial and other information.**

6. If suppliers of and consumers for capital need financial information to make decisions, accounting has an important role. That is, because accounting deals with financial information, it can serve as a source of that information for capital allocation decisions. Accounting's important role in the economy results from its ability to provide this financial information about suppliers through financial statements. Therefore: **Accounting is an important source of financial information, playing an important role in economy and society.**

THE NEW TRIPARTITE STRUCTURE OF STANDARD SETTING

It is in the 1970s' context of the new view of accounting that the AICPA began to implement the recommendations of the Wheat Committee to make radical, sweeping changes in the procedures for setting accounting standards. The changes were sweeping because they dissolved the old dual structure of the APB and ARD and replaced it with an entirely new tripartite structure. The changes were radical because the new structure was independent of the AICPA. All past standard-setting agencies were organizationally under the authority of the AICPA. Now standard setting was set free of the AICPA and had "to stand on its own two feet."

The three parts of the new structure—the FAF, the FASB, and the FaSAC—are discussed next, in terms of their structure.[5] The operations of the tripartite structure are explained in Chapter 5. Exhibit 4.2 shows the relationship of the three components of the new structure along with their respective functions.

EXHIBIT 4.2
Components of the Tripartite Structure

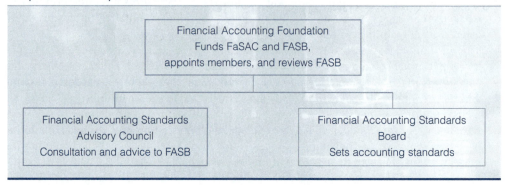

THE FINANCIAL ACCOUNTING FOUNDATION

The FAF is the parent organization of the tripartite structure. It is incorporated as an Internal Revenue Code Section 501(c)(3) foundation, which operates exclusively for charitable, educational, scientific, and literary purposes. This organization has basically three broad functions.

1. *Raise money.* The FAF receives contributions and approves the budget for the FASB and FaSAC. The tripartite structure is independent in terms of budget. It is expected to raise its own funds and be financially viable. It depends on funds received from contributions and the sale of literature and literature services (subscriptions). Its major expense is personnel costs.

2. *Appoint FASB and FaSAC members.* The FAF decides who will serve on the other two parts of the structure. In light of the importance of the FASB and its small number of members, seven, this is an important function.

3. *Review administrative performance of FASB.* The FAF is responsible for general oversight of the FASB. However, this oversight extends only to the administrative operations of the FASB and focuses on whether the FASB has followed its procedures correctly. The review does not include the FASB's decisions on accounting standards.

It is important that the FAF be able to raise resources for the tripartite structure because independence comes at a cost. The initial budget of the tripartite structure was expected to be $3 million. Without the AICPA or another organization financially supporting the new structure, resources are needed. Additionally, contributions made to the FASB do not flow directly to the FASB; they go to the FAF first and then are distributed. This process helps keep the FASB independent because it doesn't allow an element of its constituency to make a large contribution and expect the FASB to consider this donation when setting accounting standards.

The FAF is independent of the other two parts and governed by a board of sixteen foundation trustees. This board has a chair and cochair. Eleven trustees are nominated by the eight sponsoring organizations of the FAF: AAA, AICPA, Association for Investment Management and Research (AIMR), Financial Executives International (FEI), Government

Finance Officers Association, Institute of Management Accountants (IMA), National Association of State Auditors, Comptrollers, and Treasurers, and the Securities Industry Association (SIA). Note the wide representation in the list of sponsoring organizations: public accounting (AICPA), academia (AAA), preparers (FEI and IMA), users (AIMR and SIA), and the government. Five trustees-at-large can be nominated by organizations other than the sponsoring organizations. The trustees-at-large represent the general public. Thus in the FAF we see the wide variety of constituents reflecting the new view of accounting. Accounting links the firms to their investors and creditors and is an important part of the national economy and society. These sectors are all represented on the FAF board of trustees.

THE FINANCIAL ACCOUNTING STANDARDS ADVISORY COUNCIL

The second element of the new structure is FaSAC, also referred to as the council. It is composed of more than thirty members who consult with the FASB about technical issues on the Board's agenda, project priorities, matters likely to require the attention of the Board, and selection and organization of FASB task forces. The chair of the FASB can ask the council for any advice that he or she thinks the FASB needs.

The council's members broadly represent preparers, auditors, and users of financial information and serve part-time. Generally, members are technically competent with regard to financial reporting matters and are experienced accountants. The chief accountant of the SEC is also a member (ex officio). The council elects its chair.

The council is an important element of the tripartite structure. It serves as a link to the current developments in practice and is a source of vital information for the FASB. The council monitors current developments and can provide the FASB with contemporary information about what's happening on a number of fronts. Because the reporting environment is dynamic, FaSAC represents a set of eyes and ears to keep track of important developments.

THE FINANCIAL ACCOUNTING STANDARDS BOARD

The third element is the FASB, or the Board. It is the standard-setting body and the most prominent aspect of the tripartite structure. In fact, the FASB is the only part of the tripartite structure many people have ever heard about.

Mission   The mission of the FASB is to establish and improve standards of financial accounting and reporting for the guidance of the public, including issuers, auditors, and the users of financial information.

This mission reflects the new view of accounting. The Board recognizes that accounting information is essential to the allocation of resources in the economy and that financial information is also used by the public in making many kinds of financial decisions.

The Board seeks to accomplish this mission in the following five ways:

1. Improving the usefulness of financial reporting
2. Keeping standards current and changing them when changes in the business world and economic environment occur
3. Considering new standards promptly when areas of deficiency in financial accounting are noted or opportunities for improvement are seen

4. Promoting the international comparability of accounting standards
5. Improving the common understanding of the nature and purposes of information contained in financial statements

Membership   The Board is composed of seven members who are selected by the FAF. These members serve full-time on the Board and are required to dissolve their relationships with their current employers when they join. Understand that this does not simply mean that they just take a leave of absence or sabbatical with the prospect of reemployment later. Instead, it means that they must resign their current position without a long-term agreement with their employer to rehire them after their term on the Board expires.

Board members serve five-year terms. They may serve a maximum of two terms. Members have diverse backgrounds but with accounting connections. They must possess a knowledge of accounting, finance, and business and be concerned with public interest in manners of financial accounting and reporting. For example, Board members in 2001 have the following backgrounds: public accounting (three), academia (one), industry (preparers; two), and security analysis (user; one). However, no strict formula for determining the Board from constituencies is followed. Board members have extensive experience in financial accounting and a number have served on FaSAC or FASB task forces. Salaries reflect this experience: Board members in 2001 receive $345,000 annually; the chair collects $425,000 (in 1973 salaries started at $75,000 and $100,000). The Board elects its chair; the first was Marshall Armstrong, former president of the AICPA. In 2001, the first female served on the FASB.

A staff of approximately forty professionals with backgrounds in public accounting, industry, academia, and government assists the Board. The Board also receives support from a full-time director of research and technical activities.

Authority   As noted in Chapter 1, a standard-setting body needs two factors to be successful: authority and a theory. One of the most conspicuously absent factors about the CAP and the APB was their lack of authority. Neither agency received any direct support from the only legal source of authority in financial reporting, the SEC. In fact, in some instances, the SEC demonstrated its authority over the CAP and APB by overruling their pronouncements. Thus a critical element in this new structure was the authority given to the FASB; it was important in both source and extent.

Both the SEC and the AICPA formally recognized the authority of the FASB. The SEC, in Accounting Series Release (ASR) #150 in 1973, officially recognized the FASB as authoritative. (Note that this ASR was reissued as Financial Reporting Release [FRR #1], in 1982 when the SEC revised its system of pronouncements.) The SEC stated that FASB standards are officially sanctioned as the basis for statutory reports filed with the SEC. The commission intended to look to the private sector for leadership in establishing and improving accounting standards.

In addition, the AICPA added their support through Rule 203 of the AICPA Code of Professional Conduct, which was amended in May 1973.

ANALYSIS OF STRUCTURE

The FASB began its operations with a solid foundation in terms of authority and organizational structure. Its structure reflected the environment of financial reporting and the new view of accounting.

The FASB was independent in appearance and fact. There was a division of functions that contributed to the independence of the elements. The financial needs of the FASB were the responsibility of the FAF, and the FAF selected the members of the FASB and FaSAC.

INTERNATIONAL DEVELOPMENTS

There were similar major changes in the world economy occurred at that time that had implications for the new view of accounting.

WORLD CURRENCY MARKETS

In the early 1970s, the Bretton Woods Agreement[6] of 1945, which established an international monetary system based on fixed exchange rates linked to the U.S. dollar, unraveled because of a number of problems that developed over the twenty-six year tenure of the system. It was replaced in 1973 with a floating rate system in which currencies no longer had fixed exchange rates. In this floating system (or nonsystem, as some call it), exchange rates are determined by supply and demand. This event ushered in a new era for businesses in the world economy. The relatively stable exchange and interest rates under the Bretton Woods Agreement were gone, replaced with volatility. Firms faced a brave new world.

One of the effects of the changing world currency markets was the development of the European Joint Float in 1972. The nations of Europe involved in the Common Market, in light of the large amount of business they conduct between themselves, joined their currencies together as a group to "float" against the other currencies of the world. The nations agreed to keep their individual currencies within certain relationships with each other as a way to stabilize their currencies and enhance their intergroup trade. This was successful and became the forerunner of the European Monetary System (in 1978), which in turn became the European Monetary Union (in 1986), which led to the introduction of a single currency, the euro (€), in 2000.

DEMOLITION OF WORLD ECONOMIC BARRIERS

Another major international development that began in the early 1970s was the demolition of barriers to world trade and investment through the advances of telecommunications and information technology. Slowly at first but then at increasing rates, factors such as merchandise, information, labor, services, technology, and capital began to flow more freely throughout the world economy. Other factors were also at work here: a vast expansion of economic freedom and property rights (coupled with a reduction in the scope of government) and soaring increases in trade and investment, and a quickening of innovation and technological advances. The effects of the changes are still being felt.

GROWTH IN WORLD CAPITAL NEEDS

Another change, the size and pace of international investment flows began during the seventies and has since skyrocketed. This new development was caused by a number of factors. As communism crumbled and economies became more open, two to three billion people were added to the free-market economy during the period of 1970–2000. Developing nations sought capital for growth and development; many nations began to privatize state-owned enterprises and therefore needed capital. Businesses in developed countries saw the growth potential of these newly emerging markets and needed capital to serve them. Advances in telecommunications and computer technology made international investing fast and easy. This growth resulted in three developments: (1) more investors and capital suppliers sought investment opportunities, (2) more securities were sold internationally, and (3) more capital began to flow internationally. These developments caused a fundamental change in the world order.

CHANGE IN THE WORLD ORDER

THE OLD WORLD ORDER

One major outcome of all these changes to the world economy and the economies of many of the nations of the world was a fundamental shift in the order of the world.[7] The previous world order—after World War II to the end of the cold war—was basically a bipolar one. It was organized around two dominant superpowers based on military might: the United States and the Soviet Union. In this world order, the potential confrontation was war between hostile powers. Alliances between nations were based on military treaties, such as NATO. Very few nations were allowed to be neutral; most nations were forced into aligning themselves with one side or the other. Most of the economic cooperation on both sides was secondary to their military alliances and motivated by rivalry

THE NEW WORLD ORDER

The new world order represents a major redistribution of power. The new economic superpowers are the United States, Japan, and the European Union. These three powers represent about 75 percent of the world's total economic output. Of these three nations, only the United States continues to also be a military superpower. Because economic power is the new basis for this new order, potential confrontations are trade wars. Alliances are based on trade pacts, such as the European Union or North American Foreign Trade Agreement (NAFTA). Under the new world order, many nations are left out of economic alliances; invitations to join trade pacts are selective. Although all the nations of the new world order compete with each other, they all realize that they must, to increasing degrees, cooperate with one another if they are to prosper. (This new world order may result in economic giants and military pygmies.)

SUMMARY

This chapter examined the second watershed period for accounting standard setting and theory formulation: the dissolution of the APB and the surrounding events. Organizational developments—the Trueblood Committee and Wheat Committee—and international developments contributed to a major change in accounting.

The chapter also focuses on a major change in accounting, the new view of accounting, which led to the sweeping change in standard setting in 1973. The resulting new tripartite structure (FASB, FAF, and FaSAC) represents a major improvement over the structure of the CAP and APB and held much promise for the setting of accounting standards consistent with the new view of accounting. The SEC gave authority to the FASB to promulgate accounting standards, and the AICPA Code of Professional Conduct requires public accounting firms to adhere to FASB standards when issuing audit opinions.

REVIEW QUESTIONS

1. By 1970, what two major problems faced the APB? How were these two problems related? How did the AICPA attempt to solve these problems?
2. Do you think the Trueblood Committee was addressing the right questions? How well did it answer the four questions it was asked to address?
3. What process did the Trueblood Committee follow to come to its conclusions?
4. Examine the twelve Trueblood objectives discussed in the chapter. What major themes are evident?
5. Compare and contrast the Trueblood and Wheat committees in terms of their purpose, their success in achieving their goal, and their importance to accounting.
6. What special problems did the Trueblood Committee face in light of the parallel work of the Wheat Committee?
7. Describe the special timing problems associated with the issuance of the Trueblood Committee's report in 1973.
8. What factors led to the emergence of the new view of accounting?
9. Describe the role of accounting before 1973 and after 1973.
10. What international developments were concurrent to the development of the new view of accounting?
11. In what two ways was the implementation of the tripartite structure a major change from the past in terms of standard setting?
12. What are the three components of the tripartite structure and how do their roles differ?

DISCUSSION TOPICS

1. What key change factors are described in this chapter? For each, characterize it as a key person, event, or organization, and describe the significant impact it had on accounting standard setting or theory formulation.
2. In what way was the time period covered in this chapter another watershed period for accounting standard setting and theory formulation?
3. Do you believe that the AICPA reacted properly in early 1970 to the crisis of confidence that surrounded the APB? Support your answer.
4. Evaluate the twelve objectives of the Trueblood Committee in terms of the three qualities of objectives given in Chapter 2.
5. Why wasn't the Trueblood Committee report as severely criticized as other past theory formulations, such as ASOBAT?

6. Which of the four international developments appears to be the more significant in your opinion? Defend your choice.
7. Hopefully, lessons are learned from previous mistakes. What were the three most significant problems with the structure or operation of the APB, and how did the initial or original structure of the FASB represent an improvement or remedy to those problems? In the longer term, were the FASB improvements beneficial?
8. There is a progression in the parts of the subsequent standard-setting bodies: the Committee on Accounting Procedure (a single body) was replaced by the Accounting Principles Board and Accounting Research Division (a dual approach). This in turn was replaced with a tripartite structure, the Financial Accounting Foundation, the Financial Accounting Standards Board, and the Financial Accounting Standards Advisory Council. Projecting into the future, do you think the replacement of the tripartite structure will be a four-part organization?

NOTES

1 Zeff, "Some Junctures in the Evolution," p. 461.
2 American Institute of CPAs, pp. 61–66.
3 Skinner.
4 This section is based on Miller, Redding, and Bahnson, pp. 11–13.
5 Descriptions of the structure of the FAF, FASB, and FaSAC are based on *Facts about FASB*, 2000, Financial Accounting Standards Board (Norwalk: CT, 2000). Current information about the FAF, FaSAC, and FASB and their activities is available at the following web site: http://www.fasb.org.
6 In 1944, the representatives of the major nations held a meeting in Bretton Woods, New Hampshire to establish a postwar international monetary system that would facilitate the restoration of an industrial world after World War II.
7 The discussion on the change in world order is based on Evans, Taylor and Rolfe, pp. 409–10.

REFERENCES

American Institute of CPAs. *Objectives of Financial Statements*. New York: AICPA, 1973.
Anton, Hector. "Objectives of Financial Reporting: Review and Analysis." *Journal of Accountancy* (January 1976): 40–51.
Berton, Lee. "Arthur Young Professors Roundtable: The FASB—the First Decade and After." *Journal of Accountancy* (July 1983): 28–36.
Evans, Thomas G., Martin Taylor, and Robert Rolfe. *International Accounting and Reporting*, Third Edition. Houston, TX: Dame Publications, 1999.
Financial Accounting Foundation. *Tenth Annual Report*, Stamford, CT: FAF 1982.
Financial Accounting Standards Board. *Facts about FASB*. Norwalk, CT: Financial Accounting Standards Board, 2000.
Kirk, Donald J. "The FASB's Second Decade," *Journal of Accountancy* (November 1983): 86–96.

Miller, Paul, R. Redding, and P. Bahnson. *The FASB, the People, the Process, and the Politics,* Fourth Edition. Boston, MA: Irwin, McGraw Hill, 1998.

Pacter, Paul A. "The FASB after Ten Years: History and Emerging Trends," *FASB Viewpoints*, April 7, 1983.

Skinner, Ross. "The Trueblood Report: Brave New Beginnings or Dead End?" *Chartered Accountants Magazine* (December 1973): 100–113.

Sorter, George and Martin S. Gans. "Opportunities and Implications of the Report on the Objectives of Financial Statements." *(Journal of Accounting Research Supplement)* pp. 1–12.

Thompson, Robert C. "How Do You View the FASB?" *Financial Executive* (May 1984): 38–42.

Zeff, Stephen. "Some Junctures in the Evolution of the Process of Establishing Accounting Principles in the U.S.A.: 1917–1972." *The Accounting Review* (July 1984): 447–468.

Zeff, Stephen. "A Perspective on the U.S. Public/Private-Sector Approach to the Regulation of Financial Reporting." *Accounting Horizons* (March 1995): 52–70.

CHAPTER 5
FASB: OPERATIONS

LEARNING OBJECTIVES

After studying this chapter, you should be able to

> Describe the due process operations of the FASB.

> Distinguish between the different types of output of the FASB.

> Explain the three forms of politics that affect the FASB.

> Understand the three national political experiences of the FASB.

STANDARD SETTING	1900	THEORY FORMULATION
CHAPTER 1		
STANDARD SETTING I		THEORY 1
PRE-CAP	1900-1938	NATURE OF THEORY
SEC	1934	
STANDARD SETTING II		
CAP I	1938	
STANDARD SETTING III		
CAP II	1938-1958	
CHAPTER 2		
STANDARD SETTING IV		THEORY II
APB	1959-1962	
	1961-1962	ARS #1 AND #3
CHAPTER 3		
STANDARD SETTING V		THEORY III
APB	1963-1966	
	1966	ASOBAT
STANDARD SETTING VI		
DEMISE OF APB	1970	
CHAPTER 4, 5		
STANDARD SETTING VII		
TRUEBLOOD	**1973**	
WHEAT	**1972**	
TRIPARTITE STRUCTURE	**1973-2001**	
CHAPTER 6		
		THEORY IV
	1977	SATTA
		POSITIVE ACCOUNTING 1980s
CHAPTER 7		THEORY V
	1973-2001	CONCEPTUAL FRAMEWORK PROJECT
CHAPTER 8		
STANDARD SETTING VIII		
FASB: PRESENT AND FUTURE STANDARD SETTING: DOMESTIC AND INTERNATIONAL	2001	
	2002	

OPERATIONS OF THE FASB STANDARD SETTING VII

In this chapter, the examination of standard setting continues, looking closely at the current standard-setting body, the FASB, and focusing on the due process operations of the FASB and related issues. The chapter includes an evaluation of the FASB and the political problems it experienced.[1] Emphasis on the chronological development of theory formulations and standard setting also continues. Exhibit 5.1 provides the chronological perspective for this chapter.

FASB DUE PROCESS

BACKGROUND

In Chapter 4, the FASB's initial structure was discussed. This chapter focuses on its operation and how the FASB goes about the business of setting accounting standards. Remember that there was a concern about standard setting under both the CAP and the APB. Both were criticized for not doing things to the satisfaction of the interested parties, the stakeholders. One criticism of the CAP came from financial executives, who were responsible for statement preparation but had no opportunity for input in the promulgation of accounting bulletins by the CAP. Another criticism was that the APB did not establish open hearings at which interested parties could comment on proposed Opinions until very late in the process. In both cases, outside parties wanted to be heard and considered in the standard-setting process. This makes sense, especially when the new role of accounting in the economy and the impact of resulting accounting standards are considered. Surely, the FASB would learn from those past shortcomings, and it did.

Rules of procedure require the FASB to follow an extensive due process mechanism for major issues, or problems, on which the FASB (the Board) will issue a Statement of Financial Accounting Standard (SFAS). The Board also issues other pronouncements, such as implementation guides for existing standards. The due process mechanism for those pronouncements is less rigorous.

The due process for a potential SFAS is designed to give all interested parties (1) notification of what issues the FASB is currently studying, how the issues are being resolved, and at what stage the issues are in the overall process (a public record) and (2) an opportunity to provide input or be involved in the FASB's standard-setting process. The first goal is one of informing the public and interested parties about the activities of the Board. The second goal is to give those groups the opportunity to be a part of the process by providing input and feedback. Thus one could characterize due process as having two characteristics: open, because nothing is carried on in secret and almost all activities are in the "sunshine" (meaning nothing is done in private and all deliberations are subject to public observation), and evenhanded, because all interested groups are treated the same and no one has any advantage.

EVENT

In fact, the procedure is modeled after the Federal Administrative Procedures Act (FAPA) issued in 1946, which is a procedural guide for federal agencies. The FAPA requires a federal agency to provide opportunity for interested parties to present their views before the agency issues a regulation. However, the FASB's procedures are more elaborate than those required by the FAPA for federal agencies.[2]

THE SIX STEPS

The due process mechanism is highly structured and can be categorized into six steps. These are shown in Exhibit 5.2 and discussed in this section.

EXHIBIT 5.2
Six Steps in FASB Due Process

Step 1	Preliminary Evaluation of Issue
Step 2	Agenda Admission
Step 3	Early Deliberations
Step 4	Tentative Conclusion
Step 5	Further Deliberations
Step 6	Resolution

STEP 1: PRELIMINARY EVALUATION OF AN ISSUE

There is no scarcity of requests for the FASB to act on a particular issue. In fact, the Board typically gets many such requests from all sectors of the economy and financial world during the year. But the FASB cannot take on all issues; with limited resources and time, it must be selective. The FASB welcomes the referral of problems for solution but must maintain strict control over its technical agenda. So, how does it decide? What criteria does it use to make a decision?

To help it choose which issues to address, an advisory task force of outside experts may be appointed, and studies of existing literature may be conducted. Outside experts and studies of existing literature provide assistance to the Board in evaluating the issue. How the FASB decides to admit an issue to the agenda is step 2.

STEP 2: AGENDA ADMISSION

To be admitted to the technical agenda by the Board, an issue must be considered against the following four factors:

1. *Pervasive and persistent.* First of all, is the issue pervasive and is it permanent? For the FASB to justify devoting its resources to the attempted solution of a problem, it must be pervasive throughout the economy or important sectors of the economy. Secondly, the problem must be relatively permanent, only these are considered.
2. *Available solutions.* Alternative solutions must exist for the issue, and these solutions should represent an improvement over past financial reporting.
3. *Solvable problems.* The alternatives must be workable and feasible.
4. *Generally accepted solution.* The solution will be generally accepted and well received by preparers, public accountants, users, and regulators.

These four factors are considered for each problem that is accepted for placement on the FASB's agenda. Of course, the importance associated with each factor for each problem can differ. But by using the same four factors for each issue, the Board can make its admission decisions consistent.

STEP 3: EARLY DELIBERATIONS

Once an issue has been admitted to the agenda, accountability begins. That is, once admitted, the FASB must now take action and keep track of the progress of the issue through the remaining steps of the due process.

Task Force   During this step, a task force of about fifteen people is appointed. This task force will include preparers, auditors, users, and others (including experts from other disciplines). Each member of the task force must have direct knowledge of the issue, or topic, and the Board attempts to have many different views of the topic represented on the task force.

The task force is the basic organizational unit in the due process mechanism, and it heads the project throughout the process, meeting with and advising the Board and its staff. The task force holds open meetings and hearings on the topic and serves as the primary focal point for the agenda item.

Discussion Memorandum   A tool used by the task force to organize the factors associated with the problem and educate users and preparers, as well as acting as a basis for obtaining both written and oral feedback, is the discussion memorandum (DM). These are often prepared by the task force after extensive literature surveys or research. DMs generally define the problem and its related issues, explain the scope of the project, organize the project so as to relate the parts of the project back to the whole, discuss the relevant accounting literature and research results, define the financial and reporting issues, and present alternative solutions to the problem, including advantages and disadvantages of each alternative. As one can imagine, a DM on a topic is an excellent source of "everything you ever wanted to know but were afraid to ask" on a given topic. DMs are widely distributed to all interested parties and generally post a deadline for comment or feedback to the task force. Sometimes the DM concludes with a prepared form to help individuals organize and structure their comments according to the issues.

Open Public Hearings   As part of the due process, the Board will schedule a public hearing, which will be open to interested parties. Generally, these meetings are announced sixty days before being held and any interested party can attend, space permitting. The meetings are structured, not open-ended, casual discussions.

These hearings represent an opportunity for the Board and its staff to interact with respondents, ask and answer questions, and obtain information on differing views about the topic. In general, questions are based on written materials submitted prior to the meeting.

An individual who wishes to make a presentation at the hearing should make a request to be heard at the meeting, and the FASB's staff will make every effort to accommodate such a request. However, most of the time for the public hearing is reserved for Board member and staff interactions with the respondents. Those who cannot make the hearing in person can submit comments. All comments, oral and written, from all parties are preserved in the public record of the hearing.

Written Input   In addition to an open public hearing, respondents are able to respond to the issues in the DM in written form. These written comments are transmitted to the FASB and analyzed. The FASB's staff attempts to analyze the views of the respondents beyond just tallying how many favored certain alternatives and how many did not. The Board is actively seeking as much input as possible to ensure that all views are given the opportunity to be heard. It is only then that the Board begins to deliberate on the issue.

The FASB's deliberations can take the form of any number of Board meetings, which are scheduled and open to the public. But public observers do not participate in the Board's discussions. Much of the material considered in meetings is written. As mentioned earlier, the FASB's staff spends significant time and effort summarizing positions on the issues or researching alternative viewpoints. All this information is conveyed in writing to the Board and placed in public record.

STEP 4: TENTATIVE CONCLUSION

When the Board feels it has heard the major arguments and is ready to reach a conclusion, it signals the staff to prepare an exposure draft (ED). This important document, distributed to all interested parties, presents the proposed SFAS on the issue, the effective date and method of transition, background information, and an explanation of the basis of the Board's conclusion.

The exposure period is generally sixty days or longer. During that period, respondents are encouraged to comment on the proposed SFAS. At this stage, respondents have a definite proposal to which they can respond. Written comments are especially important. If necessary, the Board may schedule more open public hearings on the ED. These additional public hearings will be conducted as described before but will have a much sharper focus, that is, the proposed SFAS. If necessary and feasible the FASB can arrange a field test to be conducted with existing business firms during these sixty days. Field tests are helpful to observe the real impact of a proposed SFAS. Field tests are like simulations, but they use real-world data. During the exposure period, the FASB's staff is busy analyzing the written comments received. The staff's summaries are presented to the Board members, and more Board meetings may be held.

STEP 5: FURTHER DELIBERATIONS

If the written feedback so dictates, another ED could be issued as a revised exposure draft (RED). That will happen only when the comments lead the Board to believe that substantial modifications should be made to the ED. When an RED is issued, there will be a new period of time to receive written input. A public hearing may also be scheduled if modifications to the original ED are extensive. As before, all input is analyzed by the staff and presented to the Board.

STEP 6: RESOLUTION

After completing the first five steps, two possible outcomes exist. First, the Board may decide to terminate the project. This will happen when the feedback so indicates or the Board or staff feels that there are no acceptable or feasible solutions to the problem. In this case, the FASB will then terminate the project.

The second outcome is the logical conclusion of the whole process: the issuance of a new SFAS on the topic. This is the final resolution of the issue. The new SFAS takes its place with other standards in GAAP.[3]

Once one of these two outcomes occurs, the issue has been finally resolved. But once in a while, that isn't the end of the story. On a few occasions, the Board has reopened past issues covered in existing SFASs. This process is called *subsequent review,* and it can be triggered by a number of reasons.

1. *The Board has received extensive and consistent negative feedback during the implementation of a particular SFAS.* Remember that not all new SFASs are field-tested before they are issued. Only occasionally are "beta versions" of the SFAS given to firms during the exposure period to see if it works and to iron out the bugs. Therefore, it not unexpected when some implementation problems arise after a new SFAS becomes effective. Normally, if the implementation problems are not too extensive, an implementation guide can be issued (discussion follows). However, if the standard has many or complicated implementation problems, the Board may reconsider the SFAS.

2. *The SFAS may produce negative economic consequences.* That is, the implementation of the SFAS may cause more harm than good or unintended results. Firms implementing the standard may find that it doesn't accomplish its objective and, instead, produces results that are contrary to what was intended. This situation would move the Board to reconsider the standard to avoid negative economic consequences.

ACCOUNTING OR POLITICAL PROCESS

After considering all of the rules of procedure (due process mechanism) of the Board, does this seem like an accounting process? Actually, it lends itself more to a political or legal process. It is modeled after the public policy area; so naturally, it has similarities to those processes. But the process hasn't really been applied or adopted for any of the particulars of accounting. For example, notice that input on an ED is democratic—all written input is treated the same. Some input is from experts in accounting or from people who are more informed about accounting procedures than others. Should their input count more? Presently, a letter from a high school student on an ED is treated equally to correspondence from managing partner of a Big 5 CPA firm. Although some high school students may be capable of brilliant insights into accounting issues, in general, one would expect the managing partner of a CPA firm to have a more informed opinion. And yet, both letters are considered equally.

PARTICIPATION

The FASB's rules of procedure are characterized as open and orderly. The openness of the process gives interested parties (preparers, public accountants, users, analysts, etc.) many opportunities to provide input. Remember that the two previous standard-setting bodies, the CAP and APB, did not provide this opportunity. But under the FASB's rules of procedure, preparers and others have unprecedented opportunities to influence the standard-setting process.

Many firms recognize this opportunity and take advantage of it. The opportunity to serve on FASB task forces and to provide written input on an ED, has become a serious issue with preparers and CPA firms. In fact, many of the *Fortune* 100 firms have established a special unit within their chief financial officer (CFO) departments to provide formal input to the FASB. This unit is usually headed by a CPA who has worked for the firm in the controller's department and is staffed with accountants or financial analysts from within the firm. The unit's first objective is to monitor the FASB and be aware of issues that are under consideration by the Board. Many such units have extensive subscriptions with the FASB and thus receive almost every written document that the FASB produces, in order to keep fully informed. The unit's second objective is to consider each new ED in terms of how the ED would affect their firm, that is, the implications for their firm. These units also act as a central point for gathering input from the executives on each ED. Finally, a third objective is to draft responses from the firm to EDs and then prepare written comments for submission to the FASB. The unit may also write the comments to be presented by senior financial executives from the CFO department at an open hearing conducted by the FASB.

For the due process procedures to work effectively, input from preparers and public accountants is necessary. To help motivate them, Dennis Beresford, former chair of the Board, and William Ihlanfeldt wrote an article for *Strategic Finance* titled "You Can Influence Accounting Standards."[4] In it, they describe how executives could get involved. First, they need to understand how the FASB operates. Second, a number of accounting organizations are involved with the FASB and their views on FASB activities are available. Firms should subscribe to the FASB's newsletter, Action Alert, which covers the status of every technical issue before the Board. Beresford and Ihlanfeldt also provide guidelines on how to prepare an effective comment letter on an ED. The authors note that any firm can send a letter on any issue to the FASB at any time, but most written input occurs during the formal comment periods. They recommend that firms concentrate on aspects of the ED that most affect their firm in their letters. Firms should provide careful reasoning in support for their position and, if possible, should cite the Conceptual Framework in their support. One aspect that preparers are uniquely qualified to comment on is the expected effects of the proposed SFAS on their firm. The Board is quite interested in this aspect of a proposed SFAS, and only preparers are able to provide it. Firms can also provide concrete examples of how the SFAS would affect them and can address implementation problems they expect to encounter if the proposed SFAS is issued.

As you might expect, the FASB receives all kinds of letters in response to its request for input. Effectiveness of the letters varies considerably. As an example of what *not* to do, consider the letter in Exhibit 5.3. Notice how this letter does not conform to any of the guidelines presented in the previous paragraph. It is emotional, negative, and has no support for its arguments. If anything, this letter is counterproductive. It would be read by the staff of the Board and cataloged as part of the written input on that particular issue (accounting for pensions, SFAS 87). But other than perhaps providing a chuckle for the staff, it would not be effective.

Exhibit 5.4 shows an example of an effective letter. Notice that the tone of the letter is factual and nonemotional even though the writer disagrees with the proposed SFAS on stock-based compensation. The letter conforms to Beresford and Ihlanfeldt's suggestions. It is reasonable and provides two bases for its conclusion: conceptual and practical. It also shows how the proposed new SFAS is expected to affect their firm. Additionally, the letter

---

EXHIBIT 5.3
Example of Ineffective Comment Letter

December 15, 1982

Director of Research and Technical Activities
File Reference No. 1032
Financial Accounting Standards Board
High Ridge Parkway
Stamford, CT 06905

Gentlemen:

I rarely write to the FASB on its pronouncements because experience has taught me that it's usually a useless exercise. However, the Board's preliminary views on accounting for pensions cry out for a response from every financial executive.

In all my years in the financial arena, I have never seen such an absolutely ridiculous proposal. This is the ultimate triumph of academics over common sense. Pension liability estimates are just that—estimates. There is a great potential margin for error, especially in smaller plans. So to dignify these "actuarial" estimates by recording them as assets and liabilities would be virtually unthinkable except for the fact that the FASB has done equally stupid things in the past (SFAS 8 says it all)!

Should the present thinking on this subject become the law of the land, we will refuse to recognize it and encourage all of our peers to do likewise.

For goodness sake, use common sense just this once.

Sincerely,

xxxxx

---

applies the FASB's Conceptual Framework in its comments, showing that the writer has done some "homework." Although this single letter would not necessarily convince the FASB to withdraw its proposed SFAS, it would have a greater impact on the due process procedure than the letter shown Exhibit 5.3.

A study of the effect of participation on the due process procedure was conducted by the Financial Executives Research Foundation and published in 1989.[5] It is one of the relatively few comprehensive studies on the effects of comment letters. In the study, conducted by two professors, thirty SFASs issued by the FASB between 1973 and 1988 were randomly selected and the written comment letters from preparers, public accountants, regulators, academics, investors, and financial analysts were analyzed with four research questions in mind.

1. What was the degree of participation of the various stakeholder groups? Which groups tended to write comment letters more often than others?
2. What was the level of agreement between the different groups on the accounting issues? Across different groups, was there a great extent of agreement or not?

EXHIBIT 5.4
Example of Effective Comment Letter

December 23, 1993

Leader International Corporation
San Jose, CA

Dear Sirs:

On behalf of the Leader International Corporation, I am commenting on the proposed SFAS, "Accounting for Stock-based Compensation." Our firm is opposed to the implementation of this proposal on two grounds: conceptual and practical.

Conceptual: We do not agree that compensation expense should be recognized as a result of a grant for fixed stock options. We believe your rationale that leads to this conclusion is flawed. There is no economic loss to a firm from the grant of stock options. The effect on the stockholders is recognized through the dilution of earnings per share. But the firm granting the stock options incurs no present or future cost and no liability, and no future cash outflows are required. Thus, we don't believe the proposed SFAS is consistent with the FASB's Conceptual Framework.

Practical: As a practical matter, the results of this proposal, both accounting and disclosures, are not reliable and will not be understood by the majority of financial statement users. In terms of our firm, we project that the effect of the proposal would lower 1994 net income by approximately $1 million dollars, or 7%. Our firm is a hi-tech firm that uses fixed stock options to attract experienced management. Such a financial impact is material for our firm and may endanger its future.

We strongly encourage the Board to withdraw this proposal.

Sincerely,

xxxx
Controller and CFO

(Based on Miller, Redding, and Bahnson, 1995, p. 83.)

3. What was the level of agreement within each group on the accounting issues? Among the members of a particular group, was there a great extent of agreement on the issues or not?
4. What influence did the comment letters appear to have on the FASB in the issuance of the particular SFASs?

The study found the following:

1. Preparers comprised the largest group and also wrote the largest number of comment letters.
2. All groups tended to send comment letters that opposed the proposed SFAS rather than letters that supported the standard.

3. Between groups, there was little consistent agreement or disagreement on the proposed SFASs. One group's views on a proposed SFAS did not necessarily agree with another group's views.
4. Within groups, there was little consistent internal agreement on the proposed SFASs. The two groups to exhibit the least amount of internal agreement were investors and financial analysts.
5. Public accountants have the greatest association between their comment letters and the form of the final SFAS issued on the topic; regulators were second; preparers were third, and academics were last.

The study concluded with the following suggestions for improving the effectiveness of written comment letters to the FASB:

1. Comment letters should emphasize theoretical concerns related to the proposed SFAS rather than more pragmatic, self interest-based concerns.
2. Preparers should consider communicating their views on the issues to their public accountants as a way of influencing public accountants' views.
3. Preparers should mobilize themselves to achieve more internal agreement on proposed SFASs. This mobilization could be implemented through various industry associations and other organizations.
4. Greater influence can be attained by earlier involvement in the proposed standard-setting process, such as serving on the task force that is established early in the due process procedure.

FASB OUTPUT

The FASB publishes several types of pronouncements. For example, as discussed earlier the FASB issues Statements of Financial Accounting Standards, which establish GAAP. The FASB also issues Interpretations, which clarify, explain, and elaborate GAAP. These are issued after a less extensive due process procedure. The Board's Conceptual Framework consists of Statements of Financial Accounting Concepts (SFACs).

Technical Bulletins are issued by the Research and Technical Activities staff of the FASB, but they are not voted on by the FASB. They are issued with a very limited due process that involves some exposure in a public hearing and discussion by the Board. They usually have a sharp focus and deal with a particular situation. They may provide guidance on issues not directly covered in SFASs or deal with narrow technical issues in the application of existing SFASs.

EVALUATING THE FASB

No accounting standard-setting body has operated without criticism. One reason for this is the wide variety of views or opinions on accounting issues. Almost every accountant has an opinion on how standards should be set, views on issues that need to be addressed, opinions on issues that have already been addressed and views on myriad other issues. Since its creation in 1973, the FASB has been criticized numerous times. Rather than discuss them individually, selected responses to some criticisms by Dennis Beresford and R. Van Riper will be included here. These are general criticisms, not criticisms addressed to particular topics on which the Board had issued standards or were considering new standards.

At the request of the Financial Accounting Foundation (FAF), Beresford and Van Riper listed what they saw as the eight major criticisms of the Board as of early 1992 and responded to each of them.[6] Their responses provide a helpful way to understand the general concerns that have arisen about the operation of the FASB. The eight criticisms, an explanation of each, and the response of the Board to counter it follow.

1. *The Board ignores input.* This criticism is that the Board ignores the input it receives and doesn't listen to the views communicated to it by various stakeholder groups. According to the FASB, it receives a "mountain" of mail on most major projects, between three hundred to one thousand letters. Board members and the FASB's staff read all letters; the Board does pay attention to the input. But the Board is not required to follow what that input dictates. That is, the Board does listen to the input but doesn't necessarily follow it when issuing new pronouncements.

The situation here is similar to the two different views of elected government representatives in political science. One view is that the elected representatives are there to vote the will of the people who elected them. In this view, representatives must poll their constituencies and vote the will of the majority. An opposing view is that representatives are elected to use their best judgment when voting on issues. The representatives will listen to the views of their constituencies on the issues but then make up their own minds and vote using their own best judgment. The Board's behavior falls within the latter view. However, this concern—that the FASB ignores input—is serious. If it were true, the FASB would seriously damage the due process mechanism because it would be futile for interested parties to take the time and effort to provide input if that input were ignored.

2. *The Board doesn't apply the cost-benefit rule.* This criticism states that the Board does not apply the cost-benefit rule when issuing standards and, thus, issues standards whose costs exceeds the benefits. Under the cost-benefit rule, each proposed standard would be evaluated in terms of its costs and benefits and only those standards whose benefits exceeded their costs would be issued. Although this sounds like an excellent idea, it is very hard to implement. No formulas exist for determining the costs and benefits of accounting standards. In general, it is easier to determine the cost of a new standard by asking the preparers to calculate the cost of its implementation. But the result is an inexact figure, given the existence of common costs. It is virtually impossible to determine the benefit of an accounting standard because those benefits accrue unevenly to different user groups. So calculating the benefit would not be feasible. Cost-benefit analysis is currently unworkable.

3. *The standards are too long and complex.* This criticism reflects the view of many preparers and public accountants. It is true that some SFASs are long and complicated. However, this complexity is not always within the control of the FASB. As the pace of change in the business environment quickens and new, complicated business practices emerge to deal with these changes, the resulting accounting standards will also have to be longer and more complex. Something as complex as accounting for a derivative cannot be condensed into a simple two-page accounting standard. Beresford and Van Riper also explained that accommodating the views of the preparers has often led to these long and complicated standards. For example, as the Board worked on the change in accounting for income taxes (SFAS No. 96), preparers wanted the adoption implementation to be spread over a three-year adoption window. The Board agreed to this request and put it in the final standard. But in doing so, the three-year adoption window added complexity to that standard.

4. *The Board should field-test every standard first.* This criticism arises because new SFASs are usually not field-tested before issuance. Therefore, many implementation problems are unknown when the new standard is issued, and these problems can crop up quickly. That's why some have stated that all FASB standards should be field-tested before issuance. This is a quality control issue; field tests should help discover implementation problems. Then problems can be rectified before the final standard is issued. However, field testing is not easy. Few firms are interested in participating because it is expensive in terms of executive and accounting costs. It also is seen as risky because the field test reveals the firm's internal accounting system to outsiders, raising competitive concerns. Of course, there is also no agreement on how long field tests should be or what constitutes a successful field test. Field testing would delay the issuance of new standards as well.

5. *The Board should adopt a sunset law.* A *sunset law* deems that certain rules will expire unless they are reviewed and renewed by a certain deadline, or expiration date. In terms of accounting standards, this would imply that all SFASs would be issued for a certain time period, their effective period. At the conclusion of that time, unless the Board specifically renews the standard, it would expire and no longer be effective. This is seen as a way of making sure that the group of accounting standards would continue to contain only relevant standards. Those whose effectiveness has lapsed would expire. However, Beresford and Van Riper countered that this would imply that all new SFASs were tentative until renewed by the Board. Additionally, the Board has conducted some postenactment review of standards and made modifications in those needing change.

6. *The Board's staff is too important.* This criticism states that the staff exercises too much influence over the Board. Certainly, any organization with busy members has a powerful staff. Initially, some employees of the FASB had been with the Board since its inception and appeared to have considerable power. Staff members read all comment letters, prepare analyses of the letters, and make recommendations to the Board, so they have a lot of visibility and play an important role in the standard-setting process. However, the Board has taken steps to make regular changes in the staff. To increase turnover, the FASB has introduced a number of revolving staff positions, bringing in temporary staff from academia, preparer firms, and public accounting. This process has helped to dispel the notion of a powerful, permanent staff associated with the Board.

7. *Academics dominate the Board.* There are some who believe that the Board is unduly influenced by academics. Beresford and Van Riper counter this with the facts that very few members of the staff of the Board are professors and only one member of the Board is an academic. In fact, they believe that academics are not involved enough in the standard-setting process only. A limited number of research studies for the Board have been conducted by academics, and a few professors have their students write comment letters to the Board in response to EDs.

8. *The Board has excess capacity.* This criticism states that the Board is not productive enough and should take on additional projects. In fact, the authors of the article noted that the Board regularly turns away potential projects because of a lack of resources. The Board frequently needs additional resources to respond to the needs of the reporting environment.

OTHER MAJOR CONCERNS

In addition to these eight criticisms, three other concerns about the FASB warrant discussion.

The first concern is that the FASB takes too long to resolve an accounting issue. Although many examples can be cited, consider the issue of insubstance debt defeasance. This became an accounting issue when in July 1982, Exxon Corporation found it could cover existing long-term debt with an investment in U.S. government securities and show a $130 million gain (after taxes) from the transaction. Interest rates had changed so much over the life of Exxon's long-term debt that current investments would pay interest equal to the interest payment requirements on the debt and cover the principal payment when due. The cost of the investment was less than the book value of the long-term debt, and Exxon reported a gain on the transaction. Once Exxon did this, others followed, and a number of firms used this technique to cover their long-term debt and report a gain. But was this the proper accounting for that transaction? GAAP was silent. So the FASB took on the project in August 1982, and after going through their due process procedure, issued SFAS No. 76 in November 1983. No discussion memorandum was issued nor were any public hearings conducted for SFAS No.76. By November 1983, most firms had already completed their insubstance debt defeasance transactions, the standard was too late to affect practice.

The counterargument to this concern is that the due process mechanism takes time. It provides a number of steps that must be completed before a new standard can be issued. Although this slows down the FASB, it is a necessity.

The second concern is that voting procedures of the FASB have been questioned. When the FASB started with seven members, the rules of procedure required a 5 to 2 favorable vote to issue a new SFAS. A five-vote majority was considered to be consistent with the idea of GAAP, because the "generally" part of the GAAP was believed to be more than just a simple majority. The 5 to 2 procedure was followed until 1978.

In 1977, the rules were changed, effective January 1, 1978, to allow a 4 to 3 affirmative vote to issue a new standard. In 1981, a number of individuals and some of the Big 8 public accounting firms wrote to the FAF and seriously questioned the wisdom of allowing accounting standards that are called "generally accepted" to be issued by a 4 to 3 vote. Concern was also stated that if a standard were issued by a 4 to 3 vote, then if one member of the Board changes, the standard could be reversed. But the FASB continued this simple majority rule until 1990, when it switched back to the 5 to 2 vote, which had now become known as the *supermajority*. During the period of 4 to 3 voting, a number of issues were adopted with the simple majority vote. Many of these issues were controversial (for example, SFAS No. 76 mentioned in the previous paragraph), and the fact that the new SFAS was issued by a one-vote margin only added to the controversy. A concern with the move back to the 5 to 2 was the effect of this change on the output of the Board. The concern is that the new voting procedure will further slow down the Board's activity.

The third area of criticism of the FASB concerns the theory formulation efforts of the Board and the resulting theory, the Conceptual Framework. These criticisms will be covered in Chapter 7.

FASB POLITICS

THREE FORMS OF POLITICS

One concern that has been more evident with the FASB than previous standard-setting bodies is the effect of politics in setting accounting standards. The term politics here refers to getting things done through or with other people. It involves cooperation and obtaining results when they cannot be mandated by law. Politics in three forms (national, stakeholders, and local) operates within the FASB.

The first form of politics is local, within the Board itself. The Board comprises seven members who consider and vote on new standards, oftentimes when the right decision is not always clear. The decision process on a new standard involves the Board members in back-and-forth discussion, individual lobbying, persuasive arguments, and other personal activities. Some limitations prevent politics from becoming the dominant force on the Board. For example, no more than two Board members at a time can meet privately. But politics also makes the Board work. There is no way to keep track of the level of politics within the Board, and one cannot naïvely assume that none exists.

A second form of politics concerns the stakeholders, or the constituents, of the Board. These groups—preparers, public accountants, users, the public, analysts, and regulators—have self-interests, which they pursue by lobbying the Board toward their position. Many of the ways that they accomplish this are officially sanctioned through the due process mechanism. Two of the characteristics of the due process procedure are openness and evenhandedness. Both provide safe channels for the political pressures that naturally arise from the stakeholders.

FAF, as a separate organization from the FASB, is designed to stop one form of stakeholder politics: the idea that the major contributors to an organization dominate that organization. Because the FASB has no source of revenues and as a private-sector body does not get any government funds, those who contribute to the FASB may become a concern. But in the case of the FASB, that form of politics or pressure has been greatly limited by the FAF. No major contributor dollars go directly to the FASB. Instead, they are contributed to the FAF which then funds the FASB. So the FAF acts as a shield for the FASB in this regard.

A third and powerful form of politics, national, is still working at the FASB. It has two sources, the Securities and Exchange Commission (SEC) and Congress. The 1934 U.S. law that gives legal authority for setting accounting standards to the SEC has never been revised. As in the case of the CAP and APB, the FASB operates in the shadow of the SEC. As noted earlier, however, for the first time, the SEC has delegated direct authority to the FASB. However, that authority is delegated; the actual authority still resides in the SEC. As a governmental agency in the public sector, the SEC has more interaction with politics than the FASB, which is in the private sector. On a few occasions, the SEC has used political pressure on the FASB to obtain the results it believes to be in the best interest of the country. So the politics that started with the APB has not changed.

The second source of politics at the national level, Congress, established the SEC by law and is still involved in accounting standard setting. One aspect of the political process surrounding the issuance of accounting standards is the lobbying of Congress by interested parties, usually statement preparers. In general, when lobbied on accounting standards, Congress puts pressure on the SEC; therefore, Congress becomes involved indirectly. In a few, but relatively important, cases, Congress has become directly involved in the accounting standard-setting process. Two examples of this, accounting for oil and accounting for stock options, are discussed later in this chapter.

EFFECTS OF POLITICS

A problem with the effect of politics on a standard-setting body is that it tends to produce some unwanted results. Two such results are discussed next.

For example, politics tends to produce standards that are inconsistent over time. Politics is a function of those in power, and as that changes, the accounting standards change. A change in power or the power of groups will be magnified on the standard-setting process and cause inconsistency. This is illustrated by comparing SFAS No. 2, which generally requires expensing almost all research and development costs, and SFAS No. 86, which generally allows firms to capitalize software development costs.

The administrations in Washington also influence accounting standards. During the Carter years, with inflation raging in the United States, the FASB issued SFAS No. 33, which required firms to account for inflation. Under the Reagan administration, the Board issued SFAS Nos. 82 and 89, which rescinded SFAS No. 33. There are many other examples to support this point.

An additional problem with politics is that it causes changes to occur slowly because those in power do not support change. They prefer the status quo; there must be compelling reasons for change. If changes threaten the existing powers, they won't be made. Compromise is often necessary to make even the smallest change. In a dynamic and fast-paced business world, slowness is not appropriate to a standard-setting body that desires to keep pace. Three examples of national political situations for the FASB are described next.

NATIONAL POLITICAL EXPERIENCES I

Congress   The first major national political experience of the FASB occurred in the mid-1970s and involved congressional subcommittees. The staff of two Congressmen, Senator Lee Metcalf and Representative John E. Moss, discovered while researching on Fortune 100 firms that they were all audited by only eight public accounting firms. That appeared to be a concentration of power, and concentrations of power are viewed suspiciously by Congress. Things got more interesting when it was discovered that the eight firms had no regulator directly over them; they were self-regulated. So the staff recommended that this be investigated, and Metcalf and Moss opened subcommittee hearings regarding the possible concentration of power. As part of the hearings, the Big 8 managing partners came to Washington to testify before the committee about their so-called monopoly power and their self-governance procedures. The FASB also became involved because the partners testified that they simply audited records kept according to the standards issued by the FASB. Although the FASB was not the target of the investigation, being involved gave it some initial experience with Congress and congressional investigations. It turned out to be a dress rehearsal for things to come.

In 1985, Congress was once again interested in accounting, especially the FASB. The

 EVENT

issue here was much more tangible: the failure of banks and savings and loan (S & L) asso-

PEOPLE

ciations. The investigation was conducted by Representative John Dingell ("Big John" from the southeastern sector of Michigan) who was the senior member of the Commerce Committee. He wondered about two accounting issues: (1) Why did many of the banks and S&Ls that failed have clean audit opinions in the years prior to their failure? and (2) Why didn't the financial statements of these failed institutions signal their financial troubles? In the first case, Dingell wondered if the failures were business failures or audit failures. In the second case, he wondered if accounting standards were contributing to the problem rather than helping solve the problem. Given Dingell's seniority, these became important questions.

Public accounting firms once again went to Washington to explain to the committee about the scope and implications of audits. To answer the question of whether the accounting standards issued by the FASB contributed to the failure of these institutions by masking their financial problems, the chair of the FASB, Don Kirk, testified. Although nothing tangible with regard to audit standards or the operation of the FASB was affected by the outcome of the investigation, it was another political experience for the FASB.

STAKEHOLDER POLITICAL EXPERIENCES

Statement Preparers' Onslaught   In addition to the national level, political problems arose at the stakeholder level. The primary group involved was the preparers, the American business firms that are subject to the pronouncements of the FASB for both their accounting procedures and reported results. Although you could argue that businesses hold a special place in the standard-setting process, they are considered just another stakeholder group as far as the FASB is concerned. But businesses didn't see it that way. In response to what they felt were unfair pronouncements, they decided to act in the late 1980s. Frustration over recently enacted statements resulted in what could be characterized as the "statement preparers' onslaught."

ORGANIZATION

The leading group in this political process was the Business Roundtable, composed of the two hundred largest U.S. industrial firms in conjunction with the Financial Executives International (FEI; an international group of CFOs of industrial and financial institutions). In 1987, the Business Roundtable established a subcommittee to consider the structure and operation of the FASB. The Business Roundtable had three concerns about the FASB: (1) the FASB was not accountable to any organization, (2) the agenda of the FASB was outdated, and (3) the FASB's project review procedure was inappropriate.

This subcommittee realized that to really influence the FASB, one had to operate through two other organizations, the FAF and the SEC. Both organizations had authority over the Board and could be more easily influenced; therefore, operating through them was more effective than a direct assault on the FASB. So the Roundtable established contact with both organizations and, in 1988, proposed an oversight committee for the FASB, outside the tripartite structure. This proposal prompted the SEC to bring together all groups in an effort to resolve their differences. The FAF created a committee to review the procedures of the Board, which led to the change in the voting procedures (from a 4 to 3 to a 5 to 2) as discussed earlier

One outcome of this process to change the voting was that some members of the SEC ended up agreeing with the Roundtable group. As a result, in October 1990, one SEC commissioner publicly expressed concern that SFASs make U.S. firms less competitive internationally. No one came to the rescue of the FASB except Representative Dingell. He became aware of what was happening and recommended that the SEC support the FASB in light of these attacks. One cannot help but wonder why the only support for the FASB in this controversy came from outside the public accounting profession and not from the AICPA or from public accounting firms.

The preparers' onslaught continued in 1996; this time it was led by the FEI.[7] The FEI believed the FASB to be too big, too slow in its deliberations, and antibusiness in their approach, and it proposed eleven changes to remedy those problems. Four of the most significant proposals are (1) shrink the membership of the FASB from seven to five, keeping two of the five preparers; (2) require a positive vote from four of the five before any new SFAS could be issued; (3) make membership in the FASB part-time; and (4) reduce the size of the FASB staff. These were sweeping and radical changes, many of which harkened back to the structure of the CAP and APB; these proposals represented features that turned out to be serious limitations for the earlier standard-setting groups. But the four proposals received little support outside of the FEI.

However, there was a significant by-product of the FEI proposals. As part of the controversy, the chairman of the SEC, A. Levitt, became involved and was concerned about the composition of the FAF trustees, mainly the small number of trustees representing the public interest. Consistent with the new view of accounting— the importance of accounting to the capital markets and the public—he thought that the public interest should dominate the board of trustees. So he decided to fix that situation and began to negotiate with the chair of the FAF. In these negotiations, Levitt prevailed. In July 1996, the FAF and SEC issued a joint announcement that the FAF trustees would be restructured to reduce the number of seats held by preparers and increase the number held by users and the public interest. By December 1996 the representation of users and public interest on the board of trustees increased to 56 percent. Levitt achieved his goal. Notice that the FEI's efforts resulted in a net loss of power to the preparer community but an increase in the power to the users and the public interest. This is consistent with the new view of accounting in that it emphasized the role of accounting as a part of the national capital markets and national economy.

NATIONAL POLITICAL EXPERIENCE II

It seems like each accounting standard-setting body studied so far has had a defining political problem develop early in its tenure that changed the complexion of standard setting from that point on. The FASB's event dealt with accounting for oil and gas. It is interesting because it brought together politics at the national level and stakeholder level. It was an interesting case of interplay between standard setting, economic phenomena, and politics, bringing to mind "Dallas" the popular TV series of the early 1980s.

In retrospect, the controversy appears ridiculous in light of the economic phenomena that sparked it: dry holes. Dry holes are oil exploration efforts that are not successful. No oil is discovered, and the oil exploration firms end up with a dry hole rather than a producing oil well. It would appear very clear as to how the dry hole should be accounted for.

Although to most people, dry holes are worthless and thus an expense, the structure of the oil industry in the United States had an effect on the answer.

The U.S. oil industry is made up of two entirely different types of firms: a large group of small firms that primarily do oil exploration (the "Wildcatters") and a small number of very large firms (the "Big Sisters") that do little exploration but are integrated in terms of refining, distribution, and retailing. Because most of the exploration is done by the small firms that are dependent on bank loans to keep them in business, dry holes were considered assets. That is, small oil firms argued that to find a productive well, one had to drill many dry holes. So, the cost of the productive well encompassed the cost of the dry holes that were drilled prior to it. An analogy was made to agriculture in which a number of seeds must be planted to produce a good plant; the cost of the good plant would encompass all the seeds that were sown, not just the one that germinated. This method was called the full cost method by these oil firms, and it was widely used by wildcatters as a way of protecting their Income Statement by deferring dry hole costs on their Balance Sheet until a productive well was discovered.

The Big Sisters didn't drill too many wells, so they followed another accounting method, the successful efforts method. This method treated dry holes as an expense and kept them separate from productive wells. Because oil exploration wasn't a significant part of the operations of the Big Sisters, this worked fine for them.

Thus two different accounting methods were used by oil firms for the same phenomena.

The APB decided to examine this area and commissioned a research study through the Accounting Research Division in 1964. It was published in 1969 as ARS #11, and it recommended that the successful efforts method be used by all firms. The APB planned to adopt this recommendation but found that it was in conflict with the Federal Power Commission which required the full cost method be used by extractive industries. So the APB deferred the issue and moved on to other issues. The issue would not stay dormant. In 1972, the SEC looked at the issue and recommended the full cost firms should also report what their net income would be under the successful efforts method. However, this proposal drew an onslaught of complaints from the oil industry. So the SEC recommended that the new accounting standard-setting body, the FASB, take up the gauntlet. But this was not on the original agenda of the FASB, and it politely refused.

EVENT   In 1973, worldwide economic events changed the mind of the FASB. The OPEC oil embargo on the United States caused a national crisis for the American economy, and for American drivers. (Although many have forgotten, some remember the days of gas rationing when one could only buy gasoline on certain days depending on whether or not your street address was an even or odd number; getting up at 4:00 AM to line up at a gas station to be among the first one hundred cars to be able to fill up with gasoline; and paying much more than the 30 cents per gallon for gasoline that had existed before the embargo.) The national crisis put oil and gas in the spotlight, especially because during this period gasoline shortages and higher energy prices, the large petroleum firms (Big Sisters) reported record profits ("obscene profits" as they were characterized). The public reaction to this was understandably negative, and by 1975, the SEC let the FASB know that either it had to take on the issue of accounting for oil exploration or the SEC would take over the setting of accounting standards. Wisely, the FASB accepted and added the item to its agenda.

After extensive fast-tracked due process that involved a discussion memo and public hearings, the FASB concluded that successful efforts was the only acceptable method and issued SFAS No. 19 in December 1977, which the SEC endorsed. The problem was solved . . . so they thought. But it unleashed a firestorm of reaction that ultimately caused the FASB to recant.

The oil industry mounted a furious attack on SFAS No. 19 through their Washington lobbying organization, the American Petroleum Institute. This attack ultimately involved the Federal Department of Energy, Department of Justice, and Federal Trade Commission. Their charge was a strong one: SFAS No. 19 was in restraint of trade. By requiring only the use of the successful efforts method, the FASB was in effect killing off the wildcatters, who would be unable to raise capital and would go out of business. This would leave the oil industry composed of the Big Sisters, who still had a major public relations problem with the American public. In the times of the mid-1970s, that result was unthinkable. Mounting pressure caused the SEC to reverse itself, and in 1978, it issued ASR #253, which allowed firms to use the full cost method; therefore, the FASB had no choice but to recant also. In 1979, it issued SFAS No. 25, suspending No. 19. This was the national political "baptism of fire" for the FASB.

NATIONAL POLITICAL EXPERIENCE III

Although the APB had only one bad experience with national politics in its handling of the investment tax credit, the FASB found itself repeating the oil and gas political controversy a number of times during its tenure with other accounting issues. We cannot leave our discussion of national political experiences of the FASB without a contemporary example of what perhaps was the most intensive experience: accounting for employee stock options.

ECONOMIC PHENOMENA: STOCK OPTIONS

Employee stock options have been around for a long time. They represent a way that firms can retain and motivate key employees by giving them an opportunity to invest in the stock of the firm at a discounted price. In the 1960s and 1970s, a firm would give an employee the right to purchase the stock of the firm for a particular price, which is normally below the current market price, for a period of time. When the stock option was granted to the employee, the firm measured the compensation expense element of the transaction by the difference between the market price of the stock at that time and the lower option price. This type of option plan is called a *performance stock option*. The accounting procedures for nonqualified plans were established in 1972 by APB Opinion #25.

A new type of stock option emerged in the new economy of the 1980s and 1990s, called an incentive stock option plan. Instead of providing an exercise price that was lower than the current market price for the stock, firms began to provide option plans with exercise prices that equaled or exceeded the current market price. And generally, the incentive stock option could not be exercised until a given period of time had lapsed. So for employees with this type of stock option, the only way they could financially benefit from the option was to work to improve the market price of the stock during the exercise period. This plan became very significant in the emerging high-tech industry in the United States, especially for the firms in northern California's Silicon Valley. Many of these firms were startups and could not afford to hire experienced executives. So the incentive stock option plan became the standard way for these firms to hire experienced executives at lower salaries. For many U.S. executives at both high-tech and more traditional firms, incentive stock options became 30 percent of their annual compensation packages (in some smaller high-tech firms, it was nearly 60 percent). Unfortunately, these plans did not fit into the accounting of APB Opinion #25, so the compensation expense was not recorded and became a form of "stealth compensation." But once the press became aware of this stealth compensation, it quickly became a public issue, especially to stockholders and analysts.

To resolve this problem, in 1984 the AICPA and seven of the Big 8 public accounting firms urged the FASB to put incentive stock options plans on its agenda. The Board agreed, and this project started through the due process procedure.

STOCK OPTION EXPOSURE DRAFT

In June 1993, the FASB issued the ED of SFAS No. 123, "Accounting for Stock-Based Compensation," in which it proposed that firms measure the compensation expense of incentive stock option plans at the grant date. Firms should use the Black-Scholes model, a finance model to measure the market price of unlisted options. The Black-Scholes model attempts to measure the value of the option to the recipient, which is a measure of the expense associated with the options.

As part of the due process, the FASB received more than seventeen hundred comment letters on this ED; field-tested it under the supervision of KPMG Peat Marwick (one of the Big 6 firms); and held six days of public hearings in both Connecticut and California. By and large, the feedback on the ED was negative. The two major concerns were that the proposed standard would either drive high-tech firms, especially those in Silicon Valley, out of business by destroying their profitability or severely limiting their access to experienced executives and that the Black-Scholes model was inappropriate to measure the compensation expense and was too complicated to implement. The opposition included the Big 6 public accounting firms, the FEI, and the AICPA. In fact, the Big 6 and the AICPA now urged the FASB to drop the idea. However, the Board was convinced that its ED was the best way to solve the problem of stealth compensation.

The debate over the stock option ED quickly became bitter. The Board's initial decision to continue with the ED frustrated many high-tech firms. Those firms saw many negative economic consequences to their industry at a time when it was the world's leading industry; it had become a driver of the new economy and a crown in the economy of the United States. So these firms worked through their trade organization, the American Electronics Association, which approached national leaders in Washington with the story that the FASB was trying to kill off the high-tech industry. The following is a list of the Washington politicians who were involved in the controversy: senators, representatives, the chairman of the Federal Reserve, the chairman of the SEC, the secretary of commerce, the president and vice president of the United States, the secretary of the U.S. Treasury, the senate securities subcommittee, and the United States Senate. In reaction to the perceived dangers associated with this ED, bills were introduced in both the Senate and House of Representatives, which would limit the standard-setting authority of the FASB.

The chair of the FASB during this period of time was Beresford. Fortunately, he has a sense of humor. But as an example of the intensity of the controversy over the ED, at a point in time he joked (he thought) with a reporter that he had received death threats over this issue. This report became a rumor that was widely reported.[8]

After all this reaction, the Board had no choice but to back down on the plan to issue the ED as a new SFAS. So in January 1995, the Board voted 5 to 2 to seek only footnote disclosure of the expense associated with incentive stock option plans and issued SFAS No. 123 to accomplish that. This illustrates that even when the FASB loses a major battle over an accounting standard, it still accomplishes something. For the first time ever, SFAS No. 123 required exposure of the expense associated with stock options in a standardized manner.

These three examples of the FASB's national political experiences demonstrate how accounting standard setting has changed under the new view of accounting. Although the new view of accounting as a significant factor in the capital markets in the economy is uplifting to accounting, it brings with it a heightened visibility. If accounting is important to the national economy of the United States, then we can expect national political attention to be directed to accounting. That is true for the FASB for now and for the future.

SUMMARY

This chapter examines the standard-setting process adopted by the FASB and some of the operational and political problems it has encountered. Although the due process mechanism was designed to be open and evenhanded, its application did not forestall the emergence of politics and political pressure on the FASB. Although some political functioning on any standard-setting body is expected, there is concern that politics has become a dominant factor for the FASB.

The due process mechanism appears to work well for the vast majority of issues that come before the Board. Only a few issues have gone beyond the due process and spilled into national politics. Although these become the more prominent ones, they should be put in the perspective of the normal operations of the Board, which does not involve such actions.

REVIEW QUESTIONS

1. In what ways did the due process procedure of the FASB address concerns about the operation of the CAP and the APB?
2. What are the due process procedures of the FASB modeled after?
3. How does the FASB decide to admit an issue, or problem, to its agenda? Do you agree with its criteria?
4. What is the role of the task force in the due process procedure?
5. What is a discussion memorandum, and what role does it play in the due process procedure?

6. Describe how FASB public hearings are conducted.

7. What two options does the FASB have at step 6, of the due process procedure, Resolution?

8. Is the due process mechanism similar to accounting or politics? Why or why not?

9. Describe how interested parties can participate in the FASB due process procedure. What advice would you give a firm that was planning to provide written input to the FASB?

10. Describe the various types of output produced by the FASB. Which create GAAP and which do not?

11. Of the eleven concerns and criticisms of the FASB listed in the chapter, which three are the most significant in your opinion?

12. What are the three forms of politics that affect the FASB?

13. Which of the three national political experiences of the FASB described in the chapter is the most significant in your opinion?

14. What was the outcome of the statement preparers' onslaught?

15. Evaluate the significance of politics in the operation of the FASB. Do you agree with it, or in your opinion, should politics be more or less significant?

DISCUSSION QUESTIONS

1. Critically evaluate the due process procedure of the FASB. What are the advantages and disadvantages of the present form? What improvements are needed? Should it have been as extensive as it is or could it be shortened? Should it be modeled after the FAPA or should it have been modeled after some other agency or procedure?

2. Consider the four factors used by the FASB to admit an issue to their agenda. Are the factors effective in limiting the topics accepted by the Board? Should the Board simply accept all topics that are suggested to it as a public service?

3. Should the FASB make its open hearings *more* open? Should individuals who wish to address the board be required to obtain permission, or should they just be able to comment as they see fit?

4. **Application Problem.** Consider the two views of representation in political science presented in the chapter. Which of the views do you support? Do you think the FASB was correct in adopting the position of the second view?

5. **Application Problem.** Discuss some of the reasons why accounting standards are long and complex. What are the advantages and disadvantages of shorter accounting standards?

6. Visit the FASB web site: http://www.fasb.org. Describe the current board members, including their background, experience, and education; the topics currently under consideration by the FASB; and other topics that are listed.

RESEARCH PROJECTS

1. **Research project:** Obtain some of the comment letters to the FASB on a current topic, and evaluate the letters using the criteria described by Beresford and Ihlanfeldt.

2. **Research project:** Select a topic under consideration by the FASB, obtain a copy of the exposure draft, and draft a comment letter consistent with the criteria cited by Beresford and Ihlanfeldt.

NOTES

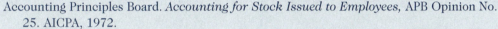

1 Remember that current information on the FASB is available at its web site: http://www.fasb.org.
2 We should mention here that many mistake the "F" in FASB for federal, but that's not correct.
3 Note that the new standard is not an "FASB." The FASB doesn't issue anything called an FASB. Its standards are SFASs.
4 Beresford and Ihlanfeldt.
5 Mezias and Chung.
6 Dennis Beresford and R. Van Riper.
7 For a blow-by-blow description of the events in this controversy, see Miller, Redding, and Bahnson, pp. 184–194.
8 Stephen Barr, p. 35.

REFERENCES

Accounting Principles Board. *Accounting for Stock Issued to Employees,* APB Opinion No. 25. AICPA, 1972.

Barr, Stephen. "The FASB Under Siege," *CFO Magazine* (September 1994): 34–46.

Beresford, Dennis. "What's Right With the FASB?" *Journal of Accountancy* (January 1990): 81–85.

———. "What Did We Learn from the Stock Compensation Project?" *Accounting Horizons* (June 1996): 125–30.

Beresford, Dennis, and William J. Ihlanfeldt. "You **Can** Influence Accounting Standards," *Strategic Finance* (March 1999): 53–56.

Beresford, Dennis and R. Van Riper. "The Not-So-Mysterious Ways of the FASB," *Journal of Accountancy* (February 1992): 79–83.

Brown, Victor. "Accounting Standards: Their Economic and Social Consequences," *Accounting Horizons* (September 1990): 89–97.

Corporate Reporting. "The Role of the FASB from Three Vantage Points," *Financial Executive* (September/October 1990): 52–58.

Field, Robert E. *Financial Reporting in the Extractive Industries,* Accounting Research Study No. 11. AICPA, 1969.

Financial Accounting Foundation. *Report of the FAF Structure Committee on FASB Voting Procedures* (October 1989).

Financial Accounting Standards Board. *Financial Accounting and Reporting by Oil and Gas Producing Companies,* Statement of Financial Accounting Standards No. 19, 1977.

———. *Suspension of Certain Accounting Requirement for Oil and Gas Producing Companies,* Statement of Financial Accounting Standards No. 25, 1979.

———. *Accounting for Stock-based Compensation,* Proposed Statement of Financial Accounting Standards, 1993.

———. *Accounting for Stock-based Compensation,* Statement of Financial Accounting Standards No. 123, 1995.

Kirk, Donald. "FASB Standards: Too Many or Too Few?" *Journal of Accountancy* (February 1983): 75–80.

———. "FASB Voting Requirements," *Accounting Horizons* (December 1990): 108–113.

Loomis, Carol. "Will 'FASBee' Pinch Your Bottom Line?" *Fortune* (December 19, 1988): 93–108.

Mezias, Stephen and Seungwha Chung. *Due Process and Participation in the FASB,* Financial Executive Research Foundation, Madison, NJ, 1989.

Miller, Paul, Rodney Redding, and Paul Bahnson. *The FASB, The People, the Process, and the Politics,* Fourth Edition. Boston, MA: McGraw-Hill, 1998.

Pacter, Paul, Elizabeth Fender, and Paul Jones. "Taking Stock of Statement 123," *Financial Executive* (November/December 1995): 41–44.

Point/Counterpoint. "Should the FASB Be Neutral or Responsive?" *Journal of Accountancy* (March 1990): 35–40.

Sunder, Shyam. "Properties of Accounting Numbers under Full Costing and Successful Efforts Costing in the Petroleum Industry," *Accounting Review* (January 1976): 1–8.

Wyatt, Art. "Accounting Standards: Conceptual or Political," *Accounting Horizons* (September 1990): 83–88.

———. "Accounting Standard Setting at a Crossroad," *Accounting Horizons* (September 1991): 110–114.

Zeff, Stephen. "A Perspective on the U.S. Public/Private-Sector Approach to the Regulation of Financial Reporting," *Accounting Horizons* (March 1995): 52–70.

6

CHAPTER

STATEMENT ON ACCOUNTING THEORY AND THEORY ACCEPTANCE AND POSITIVE ACCOUNTING THEORY

LEARNING OBJECTIVES

After studying this chapter, you should be able to

> Explain what distinguished the Statement on Accounting Theory and Theory (SATTA) from past theory formulation efforts.

> Describe the SATTA conclusions and SATTA's significance to theory formulation.

> Understand Kuhn's view of the process that disciplines of knowledge go through to advance.

> Define the positive approach to accounting and the positive theory of accounting.

THEORY IV

Chapter 5 discussed the topic of standard setting and the FASB's process. In this chapter, the focus changes to the topic of theory formulation. The American Accounting Association (AAA) reentered the theory formulation arena and produced *A Statement on Accounting Theory and Theory Acceptance* (SATTA). This represented a marked difference from the previous AAA theory formulation (see Chapter 3), *A Statement of Basic Accounting Theory* (ASOBAT).

As part of the examination of SATTA, the related topic of how change occurs in accounting, by evolution or revolution, is considered. This is an important topic, considering the rapidly changing environment of accounting. Accounting has always been a reactive discipline; one that does not typically take the initiative to change but changes in response to changes in the environment of accounting. In its discussion of theory acceptance, SATTA included the approach of Thomas Kuhn, which will be examined in detail. The chapter concludes with an examination of positive accounting, a major research emphasis that developed in the 1980s that had important implications for theory formulation and standard setting.

As in previous chapters, to help keep the topics of this chapter in perspective, refer to the time line in Exhibit 6.1. The current chapter's coverage is in bold type.

AAA—BACK TO THEORY, 1973

As the FASB was becoming established, the AAA reconsidered accounting theory once again. The timing was excellent because since ASOBAT was issued in 1966 there had been many changes in accounting, and it was time for a revision. Additionally, because a new standard-setting body was being established, any new work on a general theory of accounting formulation would be welcome at that time.

COMMITTEE ON CONCEPTS AND STANDARDS FOR EXTERNAL FINANCIAL REPORTS

The AAA committee charged with this work was the Committee on Concepts and Standards for External Financial Reports, a nine-person group. The original charge to the committee in 1973 was to update ASOBAT and apply it to the current time, that is, to write a statement that would provide an updated version of ASOBAT.

However, by the time the committee prepared its report, major changes had occurred. The project had gone through two committees (each with two-year terms): the original committee (1973–1974) and a second committee (1974–1975). Each committee included nine accounting academics who devoted part-time efforts toward the assignment. To provide continuity, six members from the first group were also part of the second. But the committees decided that such big changes had happened to accounting during the previous years that its initial charge needed to be modified. Instead of updating ASOBAT, the committee adapted its charge to better meet the current situation.

SATTA

SATTA

REPORT ISSUED, 1977

The final report was not a statement of accounting theory and theory acceptance but rather a statement on or about theory and theory acceptance. Although it may appear to be a subtle distinction, this was actually a big difference. If the report had been titled a statement of accounting theory, then we would have expected another ASOBAT, a distillation of current thinking on accounting theory. But the committee followed a different route, dictated by recent changes in accounting, which led them directly to conclusions that contradict the first title. SATTA was an attempt to reflect those accounting changes.

PURPOSES OF SATTA

Update ASOBAT   The initial commission by the executive committee of the AAA was to update ASOBAT, that is, to modify it for the many changes that had taken place in accounting since 1966.

The Current Status of Theory   But instead of fulfilling its original charge, the committee decided to produce a statement about accounting theory and theory acceptance. SATTA was a survey of the current literature on financial accounting and a statement of where the profession stood relative to accounting theory. It was a benchmark exercise, an examination of where accounting theory stood. The committee concluded that a single, universally accepted basic accounting theory did not exist at that time. This is surprising given that the AAA had been more interested in accounting theory than either the AICPA or the SEC for a long time and that the newly established standard-setting body, the FASB, was about to embark on a theory formulation effort of its own.

CONCLUSIONS

SATTA resulted from a survey of the accounting literature. It provided a deeper understanding of the nature of alternative accounting theories, how they differed from one another, and what issues could be used to select from among them.

No Single Theory   SATTA noted a persistent, widely held belief among accountants that they could find a single theory of accounting that would be universally recognized. But after the committee's survey and consideration of the literature, it concluded that such a theory did not exist. Instead, accountants had a collection of theories, each of which was capable of coping with narrow areas of accounting. The committee understood that this conclusion would be controversial and noted the long debate in accounting over theory and the inescapable conclusion that these debates did not resolve the issues. Therefore, the committee believed that SATTA would contribute to a greater understanding of theory, reducing the unrealistic expectations regarding "authoritative theory pronouncements."

User Differences   SATTA noted that almost all accounting theory formulations focus on accounting as a source of economic information about entities that is provided to external users. But SATTA further explained that little agreement exists on *who* the users are and for *what* accounting information is used. SATTA recognized that there is a wide variety of different users, and in conjunction with numerous users, there are many different applications for accounting information. SATTA's view was that until there was agreement on users and uses, accounting theory could not be applied to resolve problems in accounting practice.

No Dominant Approach   The report touched on the different approaches to accounting theory. It noted that three approaches to theory had been popular in accounting: (1) classical "true income" (normative-deductive) and inductive models; (2) decision usefulness, which is subdivided into decision and decision makers models; and (3) information economics (an application of economics to accounting problems). Moonitz and Sprouse's theory was included in the first group, and ASOBAT was included in the second group. But SATTA concluded that although these three approaches differed, no one was able to reconcile the differences, and none of these three approaches had risen to a position of singular prominence in contemporary accounting thought.

No Consensus on Theory   The authors of SATTA reviewed six major reasons as to why no theoretical approach has achieved consensus acceptance in accounting. Their coverage of these reasons was not designed to criticize the various approaches to theory; instead, it was designed to explain why none of these approaches had achieved consensus acceptance, that is, why none of the theory approaches had produced a sufficient and compelling basis for acceptance.

1. *The problem with relating theory to practice.* Many practical day-to-day problems faced by practicing accountants cannot be solved. Most theories have practical limitations, and accounting is a pragmatic discipline. For example, all theories have omissions that limit their guidance in practice. Many theories are based on unrealistic assumptions. For example, many economic theories start with the general statement, "Holding all other things constant . . ." But in reality, nothing is held constant, all is in a constant state of change. Realism and theories are thus often incompatible.
2. *The difficulty with allocation.* Accounting practice relies heavily on allocation, which is inherently arbitrary. No theories incorporate allocations; therefore, they are limited in their application to practice.
3. *The problem with normative standards.* Many theories and theory approaches emphasize the normative, what *should* be. Numerous questions arise immediately with this approach. How are normative standards related to the real-world decision makers and their decisions? What do normative standards mean? How are they applied in practice, and who decides what should be applied?
4. *The problem of interpreting security market price-behavior research.* Much of the security market research in accounting has been empirical research based on the efficient market hypothesis. This research has attempted to explain how investors, acting in the aggregate, use accounting information. But many of these studies have limiting assumptions and experimental problems. There are disagreements on the basic fundamentals such as research design and results. As long as these basic fundamentals are not understood or agreed on, this research cannot support theory.
5. *The difficulty of applying cost-benefit analysis in accounting theories.* Accounting theory formulations do not contain cost-benefit analysis applied to the recommendations, without which recommendations cannot be defended as optimal.

6. *The limitations of data expansion.* A theoretical approach has emerged that concludes that more information is always preferred to less information. However, this conclusion is questioned by many, and thus, the approach has not achieved widespread acceptance.

No Closure on Theory   SATTA concluded that theory closure could not be dictated. The statements, standards, and pronouncements of authoritative bodies could not be expected to lead to a resolution of conflict in accounting. Part of the reason for this was the recognition of the new view of accounting. SATTA stated that external financial accounting had a wider scope than was generally perceived. Unless major issues associated with this wide view were resolved, such as the desirability of the regulation of accounting practice by a standard-setting body, the committee viewed the ability of accounting theories to help with policy decisions as limited or only partially helpful.

THEORY ACCEPTANCE IN SATTA

One of the major contributions of SATTA was its discussion of why it has been so difficult to obtain consensus on accounting theory. SATTA noted that in the past, accounting professional and academic groups have sponsored accounting theory formulations with the expectation that these would lead to a single theory that would provide the needed guidance in setting accounting standards. Even the process of formulating these theories and the resulting arguments should lead to some sort of agreement. But none of this has happened. Why?

SATTA believed the answer was found in an alternative view of how change occurs in disciplines of knowledge, such as accounting. Many naturally see that change as happening evolutionarily. That is, progress is made in little steps, some forward, some backward. But the progress is always forward, with each new step adding incrementally to the body of knowledge. However, another view, professed earlier by Thomas S. Kuhn, saw the process of change in the sciences as being revolutionary, not evolutionary.[1] And SATTA espoused that this view was a better explanation for accounting. In fact, the committee believed that Kuhn's view provided a better explanation as to why there has been such slow progress in achieving accounting theory consensus and that accounting had a lot in common with the sciences Kuhn wrote about.

In light of the importance of Kuhn's view, the next section discusses his significant work and its implications for accounting.

REVOLUTION IN ACCOUNTING À LA KUHN

When one reads the views of any expert in accounting, one naturally questions, "How well accepted are these views?" That inquiry raises the questions: How do new views become accepted in accounting? How do we make progress in a discipline like accounting? How do new ideas get added to the knowledge database that is accounting?

Kuhn wrote *The Structure of Scientific Revolutions* (often called a "philosophy of science") to provide answers to the following questions:[2]

1. How does scientific development take place?
2. What role do paradigms play in the research and theory formulations of a particular discipline?

3. What happens after a group of experts accept a paradigm?
4. How do scientific revolutions occur?

Acceptance Pattern: Evolution or Revolution?   Many people believe that progress works in a cumulative fashion. As new ideas are presented, they are added to the old information, and over time, the knowledge database expands. Some old ideas die out and are forgotten, replaced with new ideas that are added to the knowledge base. Kuhn, a physicist, found that just the opposite has happened in the sciences. After studying the development of the natural sciences, he discovered that the pattern represented a revolution not an evolution.

To explain his conclusion further, he coined the term, *paradigm*. According to Kuhn, a paradigm is a shared view of phenomena, universally recognized as the solution to problems. A paradigm is shared by the experts and practitioners of a particular knowledge base who form a community of scholars. To enter and become a member of that knowledge discipline, one is taught to accept the paradigm. In that way, the paradigm becomes established and continues. It is taken for granted and guides the research and thinking of the group of experts. Through this process, the paradigm becomes dominant.

A detailed view of the sequence of the events in Kuhn's pattern is shown in Exhibit 6.2.

EXHIBIT 6.2
Steps in Kuhn's Pattern

1. Preparadigm stage at which there is no set of core beliefs in the knowledge domain. Members of the discipline are questioning and addressing various issues without clear agreement.
2. Emergence of the dominant paradigm consensus (shared by all members of the discipline). It is adopted and becomes the foundation for future growth of the discipline and the guide for all research.
3. The normal science stage when the paradigm evolves and is used to advance the boundaries of the discipline.
4. The crisis stage when anomalies emerge that cannot be explained by the paradigm and members of the discipline begin questioning the paradigm.
5. A competing paradigm emerges to contest the dominant one.
6. The revolution stage when the new paradigm overthrows the old and becomes the new dominant paradigm.
7. The resumption of the normal science stage at which time the new dominant paradigm is used to expand the boundaries of the discipline.

The sequence of change in a knowledge domain can be simplified in the following steps:

1. At any point in time, an area of knowledge or a discipline is dominated by an established pattern of ideas that are generally accepted, a paradigm.
2. Over time, the members of the knowledge community expand the dominant paradigm through research and the accumulation of knowledge.
3. Anomalies (inconsistencies and unpredictabilities) develop and are observed that cannot be explained by the dominant paradigm.

4. A crisis stage is reached in which a search for a new dominant paradigm is started. This process concludes with a revolution: A new dominant paradigm overthrows and replaces the old one.

Although the dominant paradigm rules in a particular discipline, competing ideas emerge. These often contradict the dominant paradigm and are often squashed or dismissed because they don't agree with the main line of thinking.

However, anomalies develop eventually that cannot be explained fully by the dominant paradigm. These anomalies cause insecurity in the discipline, followed by a crisis. This crisis leads to a revolution as a new dominant paradigm—that explains the anomalies—is adopted, overthrowing the old paradigm. This is the revolution, a noncumulative development event in which an old paradigm is replaced by a new one.

Example: Flat or Round Earth?   As an example of this sequence of events from the world of science, consider the view that Earth was flat. That view, based on physical observation and evidence, was widely held by scientists. Some evidence supported this view. A number of ships sailed to the horizon and then disappeared, "falling off the edge." No ship ever returned; therefore, the conclusion: Earth was flat. It had an edge, and if you went beyond it, you fell off.

Now there were some "heretics" who believed that the world was round. But because the "Earth is flat" was the dominant paradigm, the adherents to the round Earth view were seen as rebels and idiots, often ridiculed as such. However, eventually, a ship sailed off to the horizon and returned! That singular event casts serious doubt on the "Earth is flat" view and strong support for the alternative. Subsequent round-trip sailings overthrew the the old paradigm and the new one now becomes the dominant paradigm.

Notice the pattern of change here. It was not evolutionary but revolutionary. In fact, the cumulative addition of information under a dominant paradigm tends to support the paradigm rather than provide an objective report on phenomena. It takes an anomaly to challenge the dominant paradigm and lead to its eventual overthrow.

Application of Kuhn's View to Accounting   The authors of SATTA saw three elements in the accounting literature that supported their view that Kuhn's approach was more relevant to accounting than the evolutionary approach: (1) The main paradigm of accounting, "matching," was losing its appeal and importance; (2) many old ideas in accounting theory seemed to be irresolvable and consistently recycled into new theories; and (3) no new main paradigm had been found to replace matching.

The committee perceived the widespread diversity in theory formulations as evidence that accounting theorists do not share a common paradigm. They noted the considerable debate over matching but found no agreement. No consensus was developing. Instead, accountants were involved in debates and arguments over the basics. Even the SATTA committee was unable to identify the factors that would lead to a consensus in accounting theory.

IMPLICATIONS OF SATTA

SATTA declared three implications for accounting theory.

1. ***Theory closure cannot be dictated.*** That is, no authoritative body, such as a standard setter, can impose theory closure through its pronouncements and statements.

2. *The scope of external financial theory is much wider than previously thought.* Because of the importance and role of accounting in capital markets and capital allocation, the scope of theory is wide.

3. *There are many areas of disagreement among theory formulations.* All theories and approaches to theory are flawed when viewed from the perspective of another approach or theory.

The central message that SATTA wanted to communicate to accounting policy makers was that the usefulness of accounting theory to standard setting was limited until accountants found agreement on the fundamental issues in accounting.

REACTION TO SATTA

As expected, this theory statement was not without criticism. The most comprehensive assessment of SATTA was a review published in 1978.[3] The reviewer noted that the committee was asked to create another ASOBAT but did not; however, SATTA did produce something that was an interesting contribution to the accounting theory literature: a statement about the process of accounting theory formulation and theory acceptance.

The reviewer questioned SATTA's reliance on Kuhn's theory of science to explain accounting theory acceptance. He questioned the applicability of Kuhn's view to accounting. The concern was that Kuhn's theory primarily related to science and accounting was not a science. (Kuhn himself indirectly excluded the nonsciences from his pattern.) There was a dispute over whether one can extend Kuhn's theory to a nonscience, such as accounting, as SATTA did. Accounting, at best, was a social science, so treating accounting as a science was a mistake. It was a service activity that was devoted to helping meet the economic needs of the users and thus fulfilled society's needs, like medicine or law.

Other commentators also questioned how well the Kuhn model applied to accounting. Some said it did not apply; others said that if it did apply, accounting would be in the very first stage, the preparadigm stage at which no dominant paradigm exists. A few said it applied fully. Cushing believed that accounting was progressing through the stages of Kuhn's pattern (see Exhibit 6.2).[4] He claimed that accounting went through the normal science stage from the 1600s to the end of the 1950s. The crisis stage started in the early 1960s and was still ongoing. Others applied Kuhn's ideas to accounting and pointed to historical cost as the currently dominant paradigm. Others believed that matching was the dominant one.

The three approaches to the formulation of an accounting theory listed in SATTA were also controversial. Some approaches had been left out, and critics questioned the inclusion and classification of the approaches that were included. SATTA based much of its conclusions on the apparent lack of agreement among the three approaches to theory. These different approaches may not have been as competitive as SATTA thought. Perhaps they were complementary rather than competitive. Theory formulations may just represent the dominant interests of the theory authors at a point in time. These may have helped accounting by widening the scope of accounting theory.

Although SATTA provided a useful source of data on the status of theory and theory formulation, it did not attempt to emphasize areas of agreement or common ground. Instead, the emphasis was on the areas of difference and disagreement. The major conclusion of

SATTA—that theory closure is not on the horizon—was viewed as realistic by some but pessimistic by others.

EVALUATION OF SATTA

Had SATTA completed the original charge of the committee, to update ASOBAT, the results would have been very important and relevant to the new standard-setting body, the FASB. To fully evaluate SATTA, the atmosphere and climate surrounding the timing of SATTA must be considered. The committee was asked to formulate a theory of accounting at a time when a new standard-setting body was recently commissioned and just getting under way. Given the importance of theory to a standard-setting body, nothing would have made the FASB happier than to have the AAA present them with a new theory of accounting as a "welcome to the neighborhood" gift. But that was not going to happen.

Instead of a theory, SATTA's conclusions were largely negative toward theory and theory formulation. Notice the headings under the section, "SATTA Conclusions": "No Single Theory," "User Differences," "No Dominant Approach," "No Consensus on Theory," and "No Closure on Theory." This was the worst possible message to send to the FASB as it began its search for a theory of accounting on which to base new standards. The pessimism in SATTA was discouraging. Very little in SATTA was positive, and as mentioned previously, SATTA emphasized areas of disagreement rather than areas of agreement.

Thus, the FASB and accounting theorists were deeply concerned about the status of theory as chronicled in SATTA. Parts of SATTA appeared to describe the literature (e.g., the disagreement of past theories and approaches), but the overwhelming tone was negative.

POSITIVE ACCOUNTING

In the late 1970s through the 1980s, a new type of theory emerged, based on the new type of research done by accountants associated with the Rochester School of Accounting. This new theory was called *positive accounting*.

THE POSITIVE THEORY

Positive accounting was broader and had a different focus than other accounting theories.[5] It maintained that the purpose of accounting theory was to explain and predict accounting practice. It focused on two functions for theory.

1. *Explanation.* This means providing reasons that explain observed accounting practice. For example, accounting theory should explain why some firms adopt accelerated depreciation methods while others use straight-line depreciation.
2. *Prediction.* Theory should be able to predict unobserved practice. Unobserved practice is not just future practice but includes phenomena that currently exist but are not observed or documented. As an example of the latter, accounting theory should provide a hypothesis about the attributes of firms that use accelerated depreciation compared to the attributes of firms using straight-line depreciation.

This view of theory is consistent with a large part of the empirical research in economics and finance. The theory of positive accounting attempted to explain the relationship between accounting methods and stock market values. This could not be explained by just observing the relationship of changes in market values and changes in accounting procedures.

The positive theory was distinctly different from normative-deductive theories, which were prescriptive and required the specification of an objective. But because the objective is usually subjective, the positive approach saw the specification of an objective as a major flaw in the normative-deductive approach. Thus, the positive approach focused on reality— what *was* rather than what should be.

The term *positive* was borrowed from science. In science, a positive theory is one that is not normative but describes the reality of what is. University of Chicago economist Milton Friedman popularized this concept in 1953. Positive theory is concerned with how the world works, leading to predictions that are consistent with the subsequent empirical evidence. The theory seeks to explain some real-world phenomena. The critical question for a positive accounting theorist is: Why is accounting practice like it is?

This approach to theory had utilitarian appeal; that is, it was seen as very useful. Properly applied, it would provide users (investors, creditors, and regulators), public accountants, and statement preparers (management)—those who make decisions based on accounting numbers—with predictions of and consequences for their decisions.

THE POSITIVE APPROACH TO ACCOUNTING

The positive approach to accounting strived to distinguish itself from the normative-deductive approach that had been traditionally followed in accounting. Remember that the normative-deductive approach emphasized how things should be or ought to be (see Chapter 1). In contrast, the positive approach focused on how things are. The adherents of positive accounting drew inspiration from the works of the leading scholars in empirical finance and economics, such as Milton Friedman and Michael Jensen. Positive accounting's roots can be traced back to research done in the late 1960s, which introduced empirical finance research methods into financial accounting. This research showed that the market price of a firm's stock was influenced by the net income reported on the income statement and other accounting numbers reported in the financial statements. The stock market was deemed efficient. This new avenue of research quickly became popular, and many leading scholars (and those who would become leading scholars) focused on this approach.

But something was missing. Nothing in that body of research explained how firms choose their accounting methods. Although the resulting accounting measures influenced the market price of a firm's stock, nothing was known about how firms selected the accounting methods that produced those measures. Positive accounting researchers claimed that they did not want to offer any methodological prescriptions or explanations of how things should be. Instead, they strived to do empirical investigations into the nature of things to see how they are in reality. The positive approach has much in common with the inductive approach (see description in Chapter 1), although the term *inductive* was never formally associated with it.

The purpose of positive accounting was threefold:

1. to explain current accounting practices
2. to determine why groups and individuals attempted to influence accounting practice (especially in the standard-setting process) and expend resources toward that end
3. to determine the impact of accounting practices on groups and individuals

These determinations were necessary to decide whether prescriptions of normative theory are feasible. The positive approach to theory seeks to explain and predict why accountants do what they do, why they make the accounting choices that they do, and what the effects of their choices are.

Although the positive accounting movement's start is traced to a seminal work by Watts and Zimmerman,[6] interest in it was started in 1976 by Jensen. Jensen maintained that a positive accounting theory was a prerequisite to answering the normative questions that accountants ask. He was a faculty member at the Rochester School of Accounting. His work was continued and expanded by Watts and Zimmerman, who were his colleagues at the school. Therefore, many advocates of the movement were collectively known as the *Rochester School*.

THE WATTS AND ZIMMERMAN 1978 STUDY

The work of Watts and Zimmerman in 1978 was the first major application of the positive approach to empirical accounting. Watts and Zimmerman believed that the management of the firm, the statement preparers, played a central role in the determination of the accounting standards that the firm used. Watts and Zimmerman believed that management acts in its own self-interest in making these choices, lobbying for accounting standards that increase their share of the wealth in terms of their salary and salary option plans, such as bonuses. Naturally, managers prefer accounting methods that maximize their salaries and bonuses; consequently, they oppose accounting methods that decrease them.

Watts and Zimmerman found five variables that influence a firm's accounting and are considerations when managers decide to adopt an accounting standard.

1. *Taxes.* Because accounting standards affect the future earnings of a firm, management will support those standards that result in lower taxes, because lower taxes generally mean higher income.
2. *Government regulations.* If firms are subject to government regulations of the rates they can charge, then managers will choose accounting methods that result in smaller net income so they can raise their rates and ensure higher incomes in the future.
3. *Political costs.* Firms that earn high profits are more visible and tend to attract public interest and government attention. These conditions can lead to government regulation and intervention. In addition, higher profits also elicit higher wage demands from labor unions. Thus management will favor standards that lead to lower earnings. This is especially true for large firms because they are the most visible.
4. *Information processing costs.* Because new accounting standards can cause significant data processing and employee training costs, both of which tend to lower earnings, managers will support accounting methods that do not require high compliance costs.
5. *Management incentive plans.* Because most management incentive plans use earnings as a determinant, managers will favor standards that increase earnings (and their bonuses) as long as the higher earnings do not hurt the market price of the stock.

Watts and Zimmerman tested their theory on the written submissions of fifty-three firms to the FASB discussion memorandum (DM) on general price-level accounting. They hypothesized that these five factors played a significant role in management's decision to adopt a view on general price-level accounting. Their methodology was to treat the hypothesized five factors as independent variables in a multiple regression model. The dependent variable was dichotomous and represented the firm's support or opposition to general price-level accounting in the DM. Watts and Zimmerman found that large firms supported a proposed accounting standard that would decrease earnings because of the tax and political factors. The size of the firm was the most significant factor in explaining the results.

The publication of this study resulted in copious empirical research utilizing the positive approach.

REACTION TO POSITIVE ACCOUNTING

The reception to positive accounting was mixed. On the one hand, it started a new school of accounting thought, and several prominent researchers subscribed to this new view and embraced it for their research programs. The Watts and Zimmerman study was cited frequently in subsequent accounting literature. On the other hand, several researchers questioned the methodology and philosophy of positive accounting, and it soon became controversial. Two of the more prominent critics were Christenson[7] and Williams.[8]

Christenson claimed that positive accounting was a misnomer, and he was concerned with Watts and Zimmerman's methodology. He believed that positive accounting is not a science of accounting but a sociology of accounting. That is, the focus of the studies were not on the field of accounting but on the behavior of accountants and managers.

Williams pointed out logical inconsistencies in the 1978 study. He viewed it as an exploratory study that suffered from logical and methodological flaws. For example, no single variable had been identified as significant across a number of studies.

EVALUATION OF POSITIVE ACCOUNTING

The positive approach introduced a new dimension of empirical research to accounting that can serve as a complement to the traditional normative-deductive approach. It made the following contributions to accounting:

1. Research found systematic patterns in accounting choice and provided specific explanations for the patterns. Over a decade, this research provided information on the behavior of managers in the following areas: Managers of firms with earnings-based compensation plans tend to choose accounting methods that increase earnings; the larger a firm's debt-equity ratio, the more likely the firm's management will select accounting methods that increase current earnings; and the larger the firm, the more likely that management will select accounting methods that decrease current earnings.
2. The positive accounting literature provided a new intuitive framework for understanding accounting. It explained why accounting existed and provided a framework for predicting accounting choices.
3. The emphasis on predicting and explaining accounting phenomena encouraged research that was relevant to accounting.
4. Empirical regularities were discovered about accounting choice, and explanations were made to explain those regularities.
5. Researchers' attention was drawn back to primarily accounting issues.

6. Positive accounting can serve as a guide for predicting and explaining accounting phenomena that could not be explained by the traditional normative-deductive approach.

Despite these contributions, the positive approach suffered from several methodological and philosophical limitations.

1. Even when the statistical tests showed that the variables in a particular positive accounting model were significant, the explanatory power of the whole model was usually quite low. This was a signal that perhaps the model had omitted variables or that some variables were misspecified.
2. Alternative theories may be able to adequately explain the choices explained by positive accounting.
3. The link between theory and empirical tests is weak in positive accounting. It needed to establish a stronger link between theory and observed phenomena; better proxies for certain variables needed to be specified.
4. The term *positive* may be a misnomer, and some other title, such as empirical, could be more suitable. Friedman, from the Chicago School of Economics, used the term in 1953 to distinguish positive (scientific) economics from normative economics. (In the nineteenth century, the concept of positive science—a study of the actual—was popular. Unfortunately, its popularity faded when it became apparent that established sciences did not study only actual events but also normative and theoretical issues.)
5. Positive theories are value-laden. The values of the researchers influenced their studies and results.
6. To serve as a viable explanatory theory, positive accounting must be able to explain the apparent anomalies in its results.

Despite these limitations, positive accounting has had an important and significant impact on accounting theory and standard setting. It brought a new approach to accounting and served as a solid foundation for many research projects, which added to the knowledge of how accounting affected statement preparers and how preparers affected the standard-setting process. It especially provided insights on what factors motivated management to lobby on specific accounting standards. This has helped in understanding participation in the due process mechanism of the FASB. Over all, the effect of positive accounting has been agreeable.

SUMMARY

This chapter returned to the focus on theory formulation and considered SATTA and positive accounting. Neither of these two formulations was similar to earlier theories (Moonitz and Sprouse's theory and ASOBAT) in that they were not comprehensive theories of accounting. However, each contributed to theory development.

SATTA began as an attempt to update ASOBAT but evolved into a statement of the current status of theory. Positive accounting focused on the topic of "what is" and provided an alternative to the normative-deductive way of thinking about accounting. It was closer in emphasis to the inductive approach.

An interesting element of both these formulations was the issue of timing. SATTA began just as the new standard-setting body, the FASB, began its efforts. Given the importance of theory to a standard-setting body, if SATTA had simply updated ASOBAT, then the FASB would have had a theory to utilize from the very beginning. But that was not to be, and SATTA, published in 1977, described the current status of theory with some negative implications for the current theory effort of the FASB, the Conceptual Framework project (the topic of the following chapter, Chapter 7).

But timing also affected positive accounting. Note that it became popular after the publication of the Watts and Zimmerman study in 1978, just after SATTA was published. So SATTA did not consider positive accounting when it commented on the current state of theory. It is unknown how SATTA would have viewed or categorized positive accounting, but it would have been interesting to have SATTA provide some perspective on it.

REVIEW QUESTIONS

1. In what way was the timing of the AAA theory formulation effort, which ended up as SATTA, beneficial for the FASB?
2. In what way was the approach in SATTA different from ASOBAT?
3. How did the SATTA committee accomplish its work? How would you evaluate the process?
4. How does the title of SATTA differ subtly from ASOBAT? What are the implications of that difference?
5. What were the major conclusions of SATTA, and how were they supported?
6. Which of the major conclusions of SATTA was the most discouraging to those who believed that theory was necessary for accounting to survive?
7. Do you accept or which reject the following conclusions about SATTA: (a) no single theory, (b) differences between users, (c) no dominant approach, (d) no consensus on theory, and (e) no closure on theory?
8. How did the authors of SATTA defend their application of Kuhn's patterns to accounting?
9. What was the overall tone of SATTA? How could the authors of SATTA have made their formulation more positive?
10. How did you react when you first read about SATTA?
11. How did the positive accounting approach differ from the normative-deductive approach?
12. What two functions of theory did the positive approach concentrate on?
13. What five factors were found by Watts and Zimmerman to affect the choice of an accounting method?
14. Where did the term *positive* in positive accounting come from? Is it appropriate for accounting in this case?
15. Discuss the timing of SATTA and positive accounting. What other events were also occurring?

DISCUSSION TOPICS

1. Do you believe accounting to be more of a science or more of an art? How does your answer effect whether or not you think that Kuhn's pattern applies to accounting?
2. List and discuss three major pros and cons for positive accounting. Which is stronger, in your opinion, the pros or the cons?
3. In what ways was the positive approach similar to the inductive approach to accounting theory? Discuss.
4. If SATTA had included positive accounting, how do you think it would have been viewed?
5. Do you think that the managers of firms actively favor accounting methods that result in higher net earnings? If so, how do they implement their preferences for these methods?

RESEARCH PROJECT

Research Project: Read one of the Watts and Zimmerman positive accounting research articles listed in the bibliography. Compare the results of that article with the general themes of positive accounting in the chapter. How would you compare them?

NOTES

1 Kuhn.
2 Ibid.
3 Peasnell.
4 Cushing.
5 Adapted from Watts and Zimmerman, Chapter 1, "The Role of Accounting Theory," in *Positive Accounting Theory.* pp. 1–14.
6 Watts and Zimmerman, *Toward a Positive Theory*.
7 Christenson.
8 Williams.

REFERENCES

Christenson, Charles. "The Methodology of Positive Accounting." *Accounting Review* (January 1983): 1–21.

Committee on Concepts and Standards for External Financial Reports. *Statement on Accounting Theory and Theory Acceptance.* Sarasota, FL: American Accounting Association, 1977.

Cushing, Barry E. (1989). "A Kuhnian Interpretation of the Historical Evolution of Accounting." *Accounting Historians Journal* (December 1989): 1–37.

Friedman, Milton. "The Methodology of Positive Economics," in *Essays in Positive Economics*. Chicago, IL: University of Chicago Press, 1953.

Jensen, M. C. (1976). "Reflections on the State of Accounting Research and the Regulation of Accounting," in *Stanford Lectures in Accounting 1976.* Stanford, CA: Stanford University Press, 1976, 11–19.

Kuhn, Thomas (1970). *The Structure of Scientific Revolutions*, Second Edition. Chicago, IL: University of Chicago Press, 1970.

Peasnell, K. V. "Statement of Accounting Theory and Theory Acceptance: A Review Article." *Accounting and Business Research* (Summer 1978): 217–225.

Watts, Ross L., and Jerold Zimmerman. "Toward a Positive Theory of the Determination of Accounting Standards." *Accounting Review* (January 1978): 112–134.

———. "The Demand for and Supply of Accounting Theories: The Market for Excuses." *Accounting Review* (January 1979): 273–305.

———. *Positive Accounting Theory*. Englewood Cliffs, NJ: Prentice-Hall, 1986.

———. "Positive Accounting Theory: A Ten Year Perspective." *Accounting Review* (January 1990): 131–156.

Wells, M. C. "A Revolution in Accounting Thought." *Accounting Review* (July 1976): 471–482.

Williams, Paul F. "The Logic of Positive Accounting Research." *Accounting Organizations and Society* 14(5–6, 1989): 455–468.

CHAPTER 7

FASB: THE CONCEPTUAL FRAMEWORK PROJECT

LEARNING OBJECTIVES

After studying this chapter, you should be able to

> Describe the content of the third major accounting theory formulation, the Conceptual Framework project.

> Understand how the new view of accounting is embodied in the Conceptual Framework.

> Trace the struggles that the FASB had in issuing the Conceptual Framework.

> Evaluate the Conceptual Framework project.

> Understand the accounting profession's difficulties with theory formulation.

STANDARD SETTING	1900	THEORY FORMULATION
CHAPTER 1		
STANDARD SETTING I		THEORY 1
PRE-CAP	1900-1938	NATURE OF THEORY
SEC	1934	
STANDARD SETTING II		
CAP I	1938	
STANDARD SETTING III		
CAP II	1938-1958	
CHAPTER 2		
STANDARD SETTING IV		THEORY II
APB	1959-1962	
	1961-1962	ARS #1 AND #3
CHAPTER 3		
STANDARD SETTING V		THEORY III
APB	1963-1966	
	1966	ASOBAT
STANDARD SETTING VI		
DEMISE OF APB	1970	
CHAPTER 4, 5		
STANDARD SETTING VII		
TRUEBLOOD	1973	
WHEAT	1972	
TRIPARTITE STRUCTURE	1973-2001	
CHAPTER 6		
		THEORY IV
	1977	SATTA
		POSITIVE ACCOUNTING 1980s
CHAPTER 7		**THEORY V**
	1973-2001	**CONCEPTUAL FRAMEWORK PROJECT**
CHAPTER 8		
STANDARD SETTING VIII		
FASB: PRESENT AND FUTURE STANDARD SETTING: DOMESTIC AND INTERNATIONAL	2001	
	2002	

This chapter continues with the same focus as the previous chapter but examines the last major theory formulation in accounting: the FASB's Conceptual Framework project (referred to in this chapter as the CF project). Currently, the CF is the reigning theory for accounting. The Project represents the effort of a great number of people over a long time. It is the most ambitious theory formulation ever undertaken in accounting and probably in any discipline. As some old movies boasted for publicity purposes, it had a "cast of thousands" and a "cost of thousands." Many consider the CF as the single most important project that the FASB has undertaken in its tenure. It is considered by some to be a revolution in accounting, and some believe that the FASB used the CF to introduce revolutionary changes and new ideas to accounting. The new view of accounting, emphasizing the role of accounting as a capital allocator in both national security markets and money markets is prominent in the Project. The CF quickly became controversial and remained that way for more than two decades. The process did not run smoothly; there were some surprise twists and turns.

To help keep the topic of this chapter in perspective, refer to Exhibit 7.1. The chapter's coverage is in bold type.

FASB CONCEPTUAL FRAMEWORK PROJECT THEORY V

BACKGROUND AND OVERVIEW

Because of the importance of a theory to accounting standard-setting bodies, it was no surprise that the FASB listed the CF project on its initial agenda in 1973. This listing is significant in three ways.

1. By including it in the list of the first projects to be undertaken by the new standard-setting body, it showed the importance that the FASB associated with the project.
2. It was an admission that accounting was currently without a theory.
3. It showed that the FASB was not interested in setting accounting standards in the same way as its predecessors, the Committee on Accounting Procedure (CAP) and the Accounting Principles Board (APB), which set accounting standards without theory. The FASB was not interested in perpetuating the political approach to standard setting; it wanted theory to guide standard setting.

It is important to note that the CF project did not have to start from scratch. That is, in 1973, the FASB had the recently published Trueblood report. That study focused on the objectives of accounting and was a good starting place for the FASB.

PURPOSE

The CF project had the three following purposes:

1. Establish objectives and concepts that the FASB could use in developing standards of financial accounting and reporting.
2. Provide guidance for resolving problems of financial accounting and reporting that are not addressed in the authoritative pronouncements or literature.

3. Enhance the ability of users to assess the content and limitations of information provided by financial accounting and reporting, thereby furthering users' ability to use that information effectively.

Notice the focus of the purposes. It appears that the primary beneficiary of the CF was the FASB itself. The FASB expected the project to help it develop standards that are consistent and effective in leading the accounting profession toward the proper goals and helping it to resolve current accounting problems. Users are the secondary beneficiaries; the CF should help them use accounting information effectively.

The FASB intended the CF to act as a constitution—a coherent system of interrelated objectives and fundamentals that leads to consistent standards and prescribes the nature, function, and limits of financial accounting and financial statements. The CF was intended to be a guide, that is, a frame of reference, to determine the boundary or scope of accounting, help users, and improve comparability.

The FASB acknowledged that every discipline is based on concepts. Financial accounting is based on concepts rooted in economic activity, which become the foundation for generally accepted accounting standards. The CF is based on observations about the environment in which financial statements are published and used.

The project was expected to lead to FASB pronouncements that addressed the following four questions:

1. What are the objectives of accounting?
2. What qualities make accounting information useful?
3. What are assets, liabilities, equity, revenues, expenses, and net income?
4. How should assets, liabilities, equity, revenues, expenses, and net income be measured?

CONTENT

The CF project is composed of a series of seven Statements of Financial Accounting Concepts (SFACs), No. 1 through No. 7, although SFAC No. 3 was superseded by SFAC No. 6.[1] Notice that these SFACs do not establish GAAP. They establish financial accounting concepts rather than financial accounting standards. The concepts are subject to amendment, supersession or cancellation.

In this section, we provide a summary of each of the SFACs that make up the CF and comment on its content. The components of the CF project are shown in Exhibit 7.2, and a time line of the components is shown in Exhibit 7.3. (A summary of the CF project is given in Exhibit 7.7. Although this exhibit is introduced in a later section of the chapter, it may be examined now in order to preview the content.)

SFAC NO. 1—OBJECTIVES, 1978

The first element of the CF project was published in 1978 by the FASB as SFAC No. 1, "The Objectives of Financial Reporting by Business Enterprises." It was based on the Trueblood report but was not issued until five years after the Trueblood report was published. The purpose of SFAC No. 1 was to state the highest-level concepts in the prescriptive structure. SFAC No. 1 states that the primary objective of accounting is to provide useful information

EXHIBIT 7.2
Components of the Conceptual Framework

The following is the series of SFACs that comprise the Conceptual Framework:
- No. 1, "Objectives of Financial Reporting by Business Enterprises," 1978
- No. 2, "Qualitative Characteristics of Accounting Information," 1980
- No. 3, "Elements of Financial Statements of Business Enterprises,"1980, superseded by No. 6
- No. 4, "Objectives of Financial Reporting by Nonbusiness Enterprises," 1980
- No. 5, "Recognition and Measurement in Financial Statements of Business Enterprises," 1984
- No. 6, "Elements of Financial Statements," 1985
- No. 7, "Using Cash Flow Information and Present Value in Accounting Measurements," 2000.

EXHIBIT 7.3
Conceptual Framework Time Line

to those with limited access to financial data. It singles out the external users, investors and creditors, as the primary audience of accounting information. It states that users are primarily interested in prospective cash flows.

Cash Flows Contradiction   Consistent with Trueblood, SFAC No. 1 emphasizes cash flows. It states that users are primarily interested in three aspects of prospective cash flows: the amount of the cash flows (their magnitude), the timing (the expected realization), and their uncertainty (the risk associated with them). With the emphasis on cash flow, one might wonder if the FASB was de-emphasizing the accrual basis of accounting. But the FASB reconciled this apparent contradiction of its emphasis on cash flows and the need for the accrual basis of accounting by stating the accrual basis of accounting provides better information for predicting cash flows than the cash basis. The FASB concluded that accrual accounting information, such as net income, is more informative than current cash flow information for those concerned with the cash flows of the firm.

Although the FASB believed that this reconciled the apparent contradiction between SFAC No. 1's emphasis on cash flows and the fact that GAAP is based primarily on accrual accounting, others did not. Some believed that the cash flow emphasis should have signaled a return to the cash basis of accounting, and they questioned the FASB's reconciliation. This criticism could be likened to the following example: How would you feel if you were hungry for a hamburger and someone offers you a hot dog because "hot dogs satisfy your desire for a hamburger better than hamburgers"? Most people normally wouldn't accept the hot dog in place of a hamburger. Similarly, some don't accept the logic in SFAC No. 1 that accrual accounting better serves the user's need for cash flow information than cash flow information itself.

New Role of Accounting   SFAC No. 1 clearly reflects the new view of accounting (see Chapter 4). The broad social objective of accounting, which emphasizes the role of accounting in security and money markets and in the economy as a whole in its role in assisting capital resource allocation, is evident. Investors (present and prospective) and creditors are identified as the prime users of accounting information. Consistent with the new role of accounting, SFAC No. 1 includes a number of statements about the environmental context of accounting; Exhibit 7.4 lists some of these.

EXHIBIT 7.4

Selected Environmental Descriptions in SFAC No. 1

- The United States has a highly developed exchange economy based on prices for goods and services (par. 10).
- Investment frequently occurs through a complex set of intermediaries (par. 11).
- Most productive activity is conducted through investor-owned enterprises (par. 12).
- Investor owners commonly delegate control over economic resources to professional managers (par. 12).
- Business enterprises acquire capital in highly developed security markets (par. 13).
- Productive resources are generally privately owned, and markets are significant factors in resource allocation (par. 14).
- The effectiveness and efficiency of resource allocation in markets among competing users depend on information about the relative position and performance of business enterprises (par. 16).

An examination of these descriptive statements brings to mind a word that the FASB would *never* have associated with these statements: postulates. But note that the descriptive statements in Exhibit 7.3 resemble the postulates in ARS #1 (see Chapter 2). However, after the disaster that accompanied ARS #1, the FASB did not want to begin its framework by identifying these statements as postulates.

Also worth noting is the topic of No. 1—objectives. The objectives of accounting are a logical place to start; remember that under the normative-deductive approach, the first step in formulating a theory is to develop a statement of the objectives of accounting. However, whether starting with objectives, as in the normative-deductive approach, was conscious or just a coincidence, we'll never know. After ARS #1 and ARS #3, a stigma was associated with the normative-deductive approach. It was believed that following that approach to theory formulation was doomed.

Evaluation   As the first element of the CF project, SFAC No. 1 was well received; however, serious questions were raised about the timing. It took the FASB five years to issue its first statement, regardless of its head start with the Trueblood report.

Because it was the first statement, there wasn't much to criticize. Without the other parts of the CF, it was impossible to put the first one in context. The only major criticism was offered by Ernst & Ernst (one of the Big 8 accounting firms), which questioned its narrow focus, that accounting was to benefit investors, although others questioned the idea that investors and creditors are primarily interested in cash flows.[2] Although this idea had intuitive appeal, some wondered if there was any support for this notion in the literature, such as a published survey of users.

But it must be noted that with the acceptance of SFAC No. 1 in 1978, accountants finally had some degree of agreement on the objectives of financial reporting. This agreement was an important step for the project.

SFAC NO. 2—QUALITATIVE CHARACTERISTICS, 1980

The second SFAC was issued in 1980, "Qualitative Characteristics of Accounting Information." This concept statement identifies qualities that make information useful, called qualitative characteristics, which are to be used to judge the usefulness of information. If these characteristics are present, then that information is considered as useful and should be reported. The quality that makes information an attractive commodity for decision making is its usefulness. Usefulness is the most important characteristic.

SFAC No. 2 establishes this hierarchy of qualities; it is shown in Exhibit 7. 5.

EXHIBIT 7.5
Qualitative Characteristics Hierarchy

Users of Accounting Information	Decision Makers
Pervasive Constraint	Benefits Exceed Costs
User-Specific Qualities	Understandability
	Decision Usefulness
Primary Decision-Specific Qualities	Relevance
	Reliability
Aspects of Qualities	Relevance: Timeliness, Predictive Value, and Feedback Value
	Reliability: Verifiability, Representational Faithfulness, and Neutrality
Secondary Qualities	Comparability and Consistency
Recognition Threshold	Materiality

For the first time since ASOBAT, users of accounting information, called decision makers, are at the top of the hierarchy. Users need to understand accounting. A realistic situation in which users need some knowledge of accounting and some time to process the information is specified in SFAC No. 2.

In terms of the qualities of accounting information, at the highest level is usefulness for making decisions. This is the primary objective according to SFAC No. 1. The two primary decision-specific qualities in SFAC No. 2 are relevance (defined as making a difference in a decision) and reliability (defined as free from error and the assurance that the measure is representationally faithful). Relevance is further subdivided into three "ingredients of the primary qualities": predictive value (confirming earlier expectations), feedback value (knowledge of the outcomes of actions), and timeliness (availability of information to influence decisions). Reliability is also subdivided into three ingredients: verifiability (resulting from a prominent degree of consensus among independent measurers), neutrality (free from bias), and representational faithfulness (agreement between a measure and the object it claims to represent). Below these two decision-specific qualities are the secondary qualities: comparability (showing similarities and differences) and consistency. Information must also exceed a materiality threshold for recognition and pass the pervasive constraint by producing benefits that exceed the costs.

Evaluation   The CF project continued the main theme of ASOBAT by promoting relevancy as a primary quality that made accounting information useful. Although reliability is a surrogate for objectivity, it is always listed as second, making it appear that relevancy is more important. This in turn can be interpreted as a decision to make objectivity a secondary concept in accounting, which was not accepted by some in accounting.

SFAC No. 2 is comprehensive in its recognition of some of the realities in the current environment of financial reporting. For users to employ accounting information, they need to become knowledgeable about accounting. Accounting is not simply applying common sense, nor is accounting intuitive. SFAC #2's formal recognition of materiality and benefits exceeding costs is also realistic and positive.

SFAC NO. 3 AND SFAC NO. 6— ELEMENTS, 1980 AND 1985

The third component of the CF was issued in 1980 and titled, "Elements of Financial Statements of Business Enterprises." It contains ten definitions of basic financial statements elements, such as assets and liabilities. However, this statement was superseded by SFAC No. 6, "Elements of Financial Statements," in 1985. SFAC No. 6 extends the definition of elements to not-for-profit enterprises, hence the name change. Business enterprises was dropped from the title to express the coverage of the concepts statement. In this text, SFAC No. 6 will be used to avoid confusion, but the concentration is on the for-profit aspects of this statement.

SFAC No. 6 contains descriptions of the ten basic building blocks of financial statements: assets, liabilities, equity, comprehensive income, revenues, expenses, gains, losses, investments by owners, and distributions to owners. It also describes the most important characteristics of each element. (Many of these characteristics are discussed in detail in Part II of this text.) The basic definitions of the ten elements of financial statements are given in Exhibit 7.6.

Evaluation   The ten elements included SFAC No. 6 are interesting. Note the primacy of assets and liabilities. The eight other definitions are based on assets and liabilities and defined in terms of assets and liabilities. This is significant in light of a controversy that existed in accounting at the time of the CF project. Although the topic will be more fully discussed in Chapter 9, the controversy will be briefly discussed here to explain why the primacy of the definition of assets and liabilities caused some concern.

The issue centered on the question of which approach to determining net income is better. In the 1970s, the dominant paradigm for accounting had long been the Income Statement approach, based on the matching concept. In this approach, net income is the difference between the total revenues and total expenses during a given period of time. However, because revenues are inflows of assets and expenses are outflows of assets, net

E X H I B I T   7 . 6
Ten Elements of Financial Statements

1. **Assets** are probable future economic benefits obtained or controlled by a particular entity as a result of past transactions or events (par. 25).
2. **Liabilities** are probable future sacrifices of economic benefits arising from present obligations of a particular entity to transfer assets or provide services to other entities in the future as a result of past transactions or events (par. 35).
3. **Equity** or net assets is the residual interest in the assets of an entity that remains after deducting the liabilities (par. 49).
4. **Comprehensive income** is the change in equity of a business enterprise during a period from transactions and other events and circumstances from nonowner sources. It includes all changes in equity during a period except from those resulting from investments by owners and distributions to owners (par. 70).
5. **Revenues** are inflows or other enhancements of assets of an entity or settlements of its liabilities (or a combination of both) from delivering goods, rendering services, or other activities that constitute the entity's ongoing major or central operations (par. 78).
6. **Expenses** are outflows of assets or other using up of assets or incurrences of liabilities (or a combination of both) from delivering or producing goods, rendering services, or carrying out other activities that constitute the entity's ongoing major or central operations (par. 80).
7. **Gains** are increases in equity (net assets) from peripheral or incidental transactions of an entity and from all other transactions and other events and circumstances affecting the entity except those that result from revenues or investments by owners (par. 82).
8. **Losses** are decreases in equity (net assets) from peripheral or incidental transactions of an entity and from all other transactions and other events and circumstances affecting the entity except those that result from revenues or investments by owners (par. 83).
9. **Investments by owners** are increases in equity of a particular business enterprise resulting from transfers to it from other entities or something valuable to obtain or increase ownership interests (or equity) in it (par. 66).
10. **Distributions to owners** are decreases in equity of a particular business enterprise resulting from transferring assets, rendering services, or incurring liabilities by the enterprise to owners (par. 67).

income can also be defined as the change in net assets as measured on the Balance Sheet. The Balance Sheet approach is seen as superior by some because it can easily accommodate current values. However, many are against the introduction of current values (and the corresponding abandonment of historical costs) into the mainstream of accounting. Critics of SFAC No. 6 were concerned that the prominence of assets and liabilities was the beginning of a change from an Income Statement emphasis.

Of all the definitions in the statement, the most controversial at the time of issuance was comprehensive income. First, the new name conveyed a broad, all-inclusive approach to income determination. Notice that it is defined not in terms of revenues and expenses but in terms of the change in equity (assets minus liabilities). Thus the definition raised further concerns that the FASB had abandoned matching and historical cost in the CF project, and it reinforced the notion that current values were being introduced into accounting through the CF project. Some believed that SFAC No. 6 was the vehicle for radical change in accounting. Remember that the issue of whether current values should be introduced into accounting was the major reason for the APB's rejection of ARS #1 and ARS #3 in 1962.

Comprehensive income is generated by transactions *and* other events and circumstances from nonowner sources. *Transactions* (defined as mutual exchanges of things of value) are discrete events that occur in time and space. This definition was controversial because accounting has traditionally been based only on transactions. Transactions have been the raw material of accounting and are relatively easy to audit. However, now the FASB added "other events" and "circumstances" to transactions as things that can be used as determinants of net income. This was a big change from matching based on transactions, and it was a shock to many in the accounting profession.

In further defining comprehensive income, SFAC No. 6 notes that it is a broad term; it represents a return on financial capital that results from:

1. Exchange transactions and other transfers between the firm and nonowners
2. The productive efforts of the firm
3. The effect of interactions between the firm and the economic, legal, social, political, and physical environment

It is the third source of comprehensive income that raised many concerns, especially whether current values were becoming the dominant idea of the CF.

To quiet these concerns, the FASB only needed to state that it was not changing accounting to be based on current values. But because the framework was being worked on one step at a time, the FASB could not commit to that. That is, any questions about how to measure comprehensive income, assets, and liabilities were met with the comment that those questions would be addressed in future elements of the CF. How (and if) current values would affect financial statements could not be specified because answers would not be available until future statements were published. However, that approach did little to comfort or calm those who were concerned that massive change was being introduced to accounting practice through the CF project.

SFAC NO. 4—NOT-FOR-PROFIT, 1980

SFAC No. 4, "Objectives of Financial Reporting by Nonbusiness Enterprises," was issued in 1980. (Note that 1980 was a busy year for the FASB: three concepts statements were issued.) Although not-for-profit firms are a significant part of our economy, the focus of this text is on business enterprises; therefore, the discussion of the CF will not include this statement.

SFAC NO. 5—RECOGNITION AND MEASUREMENT, 1984

The fifth element of the CF project, SFAC No. 5, "Recognition and Measurement in Financial Statements of Business Enterprises," was issued in 1984. It had two related goals: to identify the basic set of five financial statements and to describe recognition criteria to be used to decide when and where to include items in the set of statements. As part of the recognition criteria, SFAC No. 5 addresses measurement criteria and at what dollar amount items should be recorded.

The issuance of this statement was the long-awaited part of the CF project for two reasons: (1) It dealt with the most important issues, recognition and measurement; and (2) questions about statements No. 1 through No. 3 had been deferred until it was issued. Now that it was issued, it was time to examine the answers to these questions.

To answer the question of what comprised the basic set of financial statements, SFAC No. 5 lists five statements:

1. *The financial position at the end of the period (Balance Sheet).* This provides information on a firm's assets, liabilities, and owners' equity at a point in time.
2. *Earnings for the period (Income Statement).* This reports on the profitability of the ongoing activities of the firm during a specific period of time.
3. *Comprehensive income for the period.* This provides a broader measure of the changes in the equity of the firm from sources other than transactions by owners.
4. *Cash flows during the period (Cash Flow Statement).* This reflects the sources of the firm's cash receipts and the disbursements of cash (by major uses) during a period of time.
5. *Owners' investments and distributions during the period.* This reports on transactions of owners during a period of time.

All statements, except for the first, are concerned with flows, covering events for a period of time. Note that two new statements are listed: comprehensive income and cash flows. At the time SFAC No. 5 was issued, GAAP only required an Income Statement, Balance Sheet, and Statement of Changes in Owners' Equity (or a more limited Statement of Changes in Retained Earnings). According to SFAC No. 5, a full set of financial statements would include these five.

The second major goal of SFAC No. 5 was to describe the fundamental recognition criteria to be used to decide when and where something was recognized in the five financial statements. SFAC No. 5 listed four recognition criteria.

1. *Element.* To be recognized, the item must satisfy the definition of an element in SFAC No. 3 (remember that SFAC No. 6 was issued after 5).
2. *Measurable.* The item must also have a relevant attribute that can be measured with reliability.
3. *Relevant.* The item is relevant for decision making (decision-relevant).
4. *Reliable.* It is representationally faithful, verifiable, and neutral.

Notice how the four recognition criteria are based on the earlier parts of the CF project; for example, *element* is based on the definitions of the ten basic elements in SFAC No. 6; *measurable* depends on SFAC No. 2, as does *relevant* and *reliable*.

SFAC No. 5 also listed the following five measurement values:

1. *Historical cost*—the amount of cash or its equivalent that was paid to obtain the item
2. *Current cost*—the amount of cash or its equivalent that would have to be paid now if the item is obtained
3. *Current market value*—the amount of cash or its equivalent that would be obtained if the item is sold in an orderly liquidation now
4. *Net realizable value*—the nondiscounted amount of cash or its equivalent that the asset is expected to be converted into minus any direct costs of that conversion

5. *Present value*—the discounted value of future cash flows into which an asset is to be converted in the normal course of business minus the present value of any cash outflows necessary to obtain the inflows

However, SFAC No. 5 did not express a general preference for any of these values. Each is noted as appropriate in certain instances. Therefore, for those who had been concerned that the CF project would replace historical cost–based financial statements with current value–based statements, they could now relax because the FASB did not select current market value and current cost as the only two measurements for accounting.

SFAC NO. 7—CASH FLOW AND PRESENT VALUE INFORMATION, 2000

After SFAC No. 6, which was unexpected, many thought that the CF project was completed. Certainly, the FASB endured a long period of criticism over the CF project on a number of fronts, which is discussed in the next section. One would think that formulating a theory of accounting over a twelve-year period (1973 through 1985) was long enough, and that it was time to close the project. However, the FASB surprised everyone again by first proposing and then issuing SFAC No. 7, "Using Cash Flow Information and Present Value in Accounting Measurements," in February 2000.

This new concepts statement is different from the others. It provides a framework for using future cash flows and present value as a basis for accounting measurements. It provides general principles governing the use of present values in accounting, especially when uncertainty is present, as well as a common understanding of the objective of using present value as an accounting measurement. It attempted to increase the understanding of present values and thus their use as a measure.

The objective of using present values is to capture the economic difference between sets of estimated future cash flows. The concepts statement advocates present value measures as superior to nondiscounted measures. But the present value must represent some observable attribute of the asset or liability, such as its fair value or firm-specific value. The goal is to capture the factors that would comprise a market price for the item.

SFAC No. 7 is the first concepts statement to address specific measurement issues. The FASB is careful to state that its intent is not to apply present values to all accounting measures. However, it was not an easy concepts statement to issue. Its gestation period was long. The project was first added to the FASB's agenda in 1988, a discussion memorandum was issued in 1990, and an exposure draft was issued in June 1997.

Before moving to a discussion of the major themes of the CF project, Exhibit 7.7 provides a summary of the major points of five of the seven concepts statements of the CF project.

THE FUNDAMENTAL NATURE OF THE CONCEPTUAL FRAMEWORK PROJECT

Given the content of the CF, what important themes or characteristics emerge? A number do, and they help explain why the CF is so controversial in its formulation and also help prepare you for the evaluation of the CF that follows.

EXHIBIT 7.7
Summary of the Conceptual Framework Project

SFAC No. 1
- Decision useful
- About cash flows, resources, claims to resources, and changes in cash flows, resources, or claims

SFAC No. 2
- Relevance
- Reliability
- Comparability and consistency
- Materiality
- Benefits exceed costs

SFAC No. 6 (supersedes SFAC No. 3)
- Ten elements: assets, liabilities, equity, investment by owners, distribution to owners, comprehensive income, revenues, expenses, gains, and losses.

SFAC No. 5
- Five financial statements
- Four recognition criteria
- Five measurement options

SFAC No. 7
- Present value

One theme that is emphasized in the CF is the new view of accounting, which emphasizes accounting in its broad, social, macroeconomic role in the economy and in capital markets. Accounting is a major resource allocator in security and money markets. As is discussed in Chapter 4, that view is quite far from the older view of accounting.

Another theme is the emphasis on relevance and subjectivity as compared to the previous emphasis on objectivity and verifiable data. A third theme is the emphasis on the asset and liability approach to net income. This is in sharp contrast to the matching and historical cost approaches. In the newer view of income, asset measurement is the key to income determination and is the basis behind the comprehensive income approach in the CF.

The CF flirted with current values and the extended use of market values to measure assets. Although there is no distinctive movement toward the adoption of market values as some expected (see the discussion in the next section), the orientation is there and is evident to many accountants.

REFORMATION VERSUS COUNTERREFORMATION IN SFAC NO. 5

In many respects, people saw the CF project as a vehicle for radical change in accounting. Certainly, the early SFACs contained some ideas that could cause radical change in accounting, depending on how the measurement and recognition issues were decided, which were the topics of SFAC No. 5. Miller described this aspect of the CF.[3]

During the formulation of the CF, many questioned whether the FASB was in the process of developing an accounting theory or engaging in political reform. That is, was the CF a legitimate effort at formulating a theory of accounting or was the project being used by some elements in accounting to promote radical change in accounting by declaration. Because the CF was developed by the FASB to be used in the issuance of its SFASs, it would be the most strategic place for reformers or revolutionaries in accounting to strike.

Some groups were deeply concerned that radical change was the emphasis of the CF. For example, auditors were concerned that the emphasis on decision usefulness and comprehensive income would greatly increase audit risk. Because decision usefulness is rather subjective and comprehensive income is so broad (including transactions, events, and circumstances), there were concerns that the auditors would have some major problems in auditing the compliance with the standards that attempted to achieve these goals.

Additionally, many preparers, the largest segment of the FASB constituency, were not oriented toward market values. They were content with historical cost as an asset measurement scheme and generally opposed the adoption of market values, which would introduce a degree of volatility into the accounting measures.

A part of the formulation of the CF involved resolving the differences between three political philosophies, all of which had accounting devotees who were involved in the CF project. The three philosophies were: (1) *reformation*, which advocates significant change within the system but without abandoning the current structure or goals; (2) *revolution*, which advocates radical change, involving the rejection of the current system and its goals and its replacement with another system and goals; and (3) *counterreformation*, which advocates keeping the current structure and principles, that is, maintaining the status quo.

The different philosophies and concerns regarding the project came to a head in SFAC No. 5. There was a reported deadlock, or stalemate, over the statement in October 1982. A prominent member of the academic community was brought to the FASB to attempt to break the stalemate but was not successful. The ultimate solution was to issue SFAC No. 5 without any major changes to current practice. In effect, a default to maintain the status quo resulted. The Board ultimately decided that accounting change would occur in an evolutionary and gradual manner, in contrast to the Kuhnian model.

EVALUATION OF THE CONCEPTUAL FRAMEWORK

In light of the importance of the CF and its prominence, it's not surprising that a number of groups, for example, the accounting profession, academic accountants, and statement preparers, closely watched the progress the FASB made. Each group had a vested interest in the outcome; all had a stake in the framework.

CONCERNS

As noted in earlier chapters, when any accounting theory formulation is completed, criticisms are sure to follow. The CF project is no exception. In fact, because the CF is the premier theory formulation by the FASB, it garnered the largest amount of criticism. The following sections select the most important criticisms and briefly describe each.

Cost   Although the project was not costed by the FASB, it is reasonable to estimate, based on the time involved and the number of staff devoted to the project, that it cost millions. That's a lot of money for a theory of accounting. Certainly, neither the AICPA nor the AAA paid anything close to that for ARS #1 and ARS #3 or ASOBAT, respectively. But the FASB devoted a lot of their resources to the CF project, and the project represented a large financial commitment.

Time   A related concern focused on the time it took the Board to complete the project: from 1973 when the project was started to 1985 when SFAC No. 6 was issued (or twenty-seven years if SFAC No. 7 is included). Although the Board never had the luxury of being able to devote its full energies to the CF project, many expected the project to be completed earlier. That expectation of earlier completion was reasonable because the Board had a head start on the project due to the existence of the Trueblood report about the objectives of financial accounting. In other words, the FASB did not have to start from scratch. By comparison, ARS #1 and ARS #3 and ASOBAT were each completed in only two years.

One factor influencing this excessive time is the FASB's due process procedure. The CF project was not exempt from this procedure. So each new part of the project was assigned to a task force, had a discussion memorandum prepared, had open hearings, and an exposure draft prepared. All these steps took time. And it took even longer for the due process for a concepts statement than an SFAS because it was more difficult and more time-consuming to process the feedback. SFACs by nature are subjective, so the feedback was more difficult to process, categorize, and summarize than standard statements.

Expectations Gap   As the CF project continued, a number of different opinions about what would eventually result emerged. Those who favored the project believed that it would be like a philosophers' stone (a way to turn base metals into gold); it would solve all problems and lead to accounting standards that met the objectives specified in SFAC No. 1. Others were less optimistic and believed that it would help the FASB to issue standards that would solve *most* accounting problems. Still others believed that it was not worth the cost in terms and time and money and should have been abandoned before its completion. Some questioned how the FASB could issue standards during the time the CF project was under way.

Use   Was the CF project practical? Did it have any utility for anyone other than the FASB? Although the CF project was designed primarily to help the FASB set standards, some authors believed that the project could be used to solve practice problems. For example, Rubin showed that although the primary beneficiaries of the framework are Board members, practitioners could be secondary users.[4] He used the definition of a liability in SFAC No. 6 to solve three practice problems.

Hudack and McAllister studied the content of the first 117 SFASs and discovered that the FASB emphasized almost evenly the qualitative characteristics of relevance and reliability from SFAC No. 2 in them.[5]

Controversy: The Myths   As an example of some other concerns about the CF project and as an insight into the "flavor" of the times, Miller listed eight myths about the CF project that existed and needed refuting.[6] These myths were subscribed to by accountants at the time and therefore reveal how people viewed the CF project as it was under way.

1. The APB failed because it didn't have a conceptual framework. Miller refuted this with the observation that the APB failed because it had a structural bias and did not obtain the clear support of the SEC.
2. The FASB can't succeed unless it has a conceptual framework. Miller refuted this with the observation that the FASB will succeed if the SEC continues to support it.
3. A conceptual framework will lead to consistent standards. Miller countered this with the argument that standards are generated through a political process and due process, not through the CF. Inconsistencies will occur.
4. The framework will eliminate the problem of "standard overload." Miller argued that the demand for standards will continue to cause the issuance of more standards.
5. The FASB's Conceptual Framework captures only the status quo of accounting practice. Miller contends that the framework is revolutionary in many respects.
6. The framework project cost more than it should have. Miller argued that no one knew how much the project would cost. Cost-benefit analysis cannot be applied to the CF project.
7. The FASB will revise existing standards to make them consistent with the conceptual framework. Miller contended that change would not be widespread. But if standards needed changing, then the FASB would change them.
8. The FASB has abandoned the CF project. Miller countered that although the Board abandoned some of the goals of the project, it had not abandoned the project.

Miller concluded that the framework should be understood as a political document rather than a purely conceptual effort. He noted that as of 1985, the framework was still in its "infancy" and that difficulties in its future use and application are inevitable.

FASB CONCEPTUAL FRAMEWORK DIFFICULTIES

To be sure, no theory formulation in accounting ever went smoothly. And some features of the FASB and its processes caused some of the criticisms listed above, which are discussed next.[7]

PEOPLE

From 1973 to 2000, the staff working on the CF project changed considerably as did the mix of Board members and the mix of people working directly on the CF project. With these changes came problems: The earlier work by others was changed, and new ideas changed the direction of elements of the project, which made producing the CF more difficult.

PROCESS

As noted earlier, the CF project followed the same due process procedure that SFASs followed. This took time and was difficult in light of the subjective nature of many of the elements of the CF project.[8]

STAKEHOLDERS

The constituents of the FASB were not interested in the CF project; that is, it was not seen as a high need by the following stakeholder groups.

1. Statement preparers were more concerned with the impact of proposed SFASs on their firms' reported earnings and on implementation issues associated with SFASs than with theory.
2. Users, such as investors and creditors, were primarily interested in the impact of reported earnings on the market price of the firm's stock or the ability of the firm to repay its loans. Accounting theory was not high on their list of priorities.
3. Auditors were concerned with auditing standards, the competition among firms for audit work, and SEC regulation of the auditing.

Academics were the only stakeholder group that watched the theory project with some interest. As discussed earlier, the primary beneficiary of the CF project was the FASB itself.

BALANCE OF POWER

During the CF project, the mix of stakeholders also changed. When the project began, the AICPA and the auditing profession were the dominant forces to deal with. However, as time passed, the AICPA and auditors retreated from standard setting and were replaced by statement preparers. The role of the SEC changed from an interested party to a very interested party with some concerns. All these shifts in the relative importance of stakeholder groups caused difficulty for the CF project.

THEORY WRAP-UP

Following the often difficult path that accounting theory formulation has taken, one might wonder, "What makes formulating an accounting theory so hard?" It looks relatively simple to accomplish, but it has been full of failures and difficulty. Is it really that difficult to formulate a theory of accounting? If it is, what makes it so challenging? Actually, there are four factors that answer that question. The coverage of theory formulation concludes with a discussion of the four factors.

COMPLEXITY

The business world that accountants try to financially document is complicated and getting more complex as time passes. Theories are simplified models of reality, developed to help one cope with the reality, but to formulate a theory, one must make a number of simplifying assumptions. However, one cannot do that in accounting and end up with a theory that is relevant. The inherent complexity of accounting makes formulating an accounting theory difficult.

OBJECTIVES

A related factor in the difficulty with formulating theory is that accountants have not been very successful in agreeing on what the objectives of accounting are. As noted in this chapter, there wasn't a consensus until 1978, and even then there was some disagreement. One of the consequences of the complexity described in the previous section is that it makes it more difficult for accountants to agree on a particular objective, which has been a limitation on developing an accounting theory.

PRAGMATISM

Accounting is utilitarian. It places a lot of emphasis on pragmatism and usefulness. In that atmosphere, theory is of limited value. Theory often ignores practice and practical implications, which are very important to the accounting profession.

SOCIAL SCIENCE

Although accounting would appear to be a science because it involves math and precision in measuring transactions, it is not. It is not like the physical sciences and, in fact, is more akin to a social science. Because of this, some believe that accounting cannot develop a meaningful theory because meaningful theories can only be formulated for the physical sciences.

In conclusion, although formulating a conceptual framework is difficult, this has been accomplished by the FASB. Accounting standard setters in Canada, Australia, New Zealand, and the United Kingdom also have conceptual frameworks, as does the IASC.

REVIEW QUESTIONS

1. What was the significance of the FASB's inclusion of the CF project on their initial agenda? Cite three implications of the FASB's action.
2. In what way was the CF project to act as a constitution in accounting?
3. What was a concern about the timing of the first element of the CF project, SFAC No. 1, especially in light of the completion of the Trueblood report?
4. Describe the cash flow contradiction in SFAC No. 1. How did the FASB reconcile it? Do you accept its reconciliation? Why or why not?
5. Describe the hierarchy of qualitative qualities in SFAC No. 2.
6. Contrast relevance and reliability. How are they related?
7. In what two ways was SFAC No. 2 directly related to ASOBAT?
8. What were the major differences between SFAC No. 3 and SFAC No. 6?
9. What are the dominant definitions in SFAC No. 6, and what controversy was associated with them?
10. What was controversial about the definition of comprehensive income in SFAC No. 6?
11. In what sense was SFAC No. 5 long-awaited?
12. What were the two goals of SFAC No. 5?
13. How was financial reporting changed by SFAC No. 5?
14. How could SFAC No. 5 have been a revolution in accounting? Describe how SFAC No. 5 represented a reformation and a counterreformation.
15. In what way was the issuance of SFAC No. 7 a surprise?
16. What is the major topic of SFAC No. 7, and how does this differ from the major themes of the other parts of the CF project?
17. What was the "flavor" of the CF project?
18. According to Miller, what eight myths about the CF project existed,?
19. What difficulties did the FASB face in completing the CF project?
20. Why is theory formulation in accounting so difficult?

DISCUSSION TOPICS

1. In your opinion, of the three purposes of theory, which does the CF seem to fulfill the best? Which purpose is fulfilled the least?

2. Do you believe that investors and creditors are primarily interested in cash flows? Support your position.

3. In the 1880s and early 1890s, the Balance Sheet was dominant over the Income Statement. From the 1930s to the 1960s, the Income Statement was dominant. The FASB then changed it back to make the Balance Sheet predominant in the 1970s. Why do you think these changes occurred? Where do you think this will go in the future?

4. In SFAC No. 5, the FASB decided that accounting would change in an evolutionary manner. How does this compare to Kuhn's view? Which view do you think is more appropriate for accounting?

5. Which of Miller's eight myths about the CF project seems to be the most important? Support your position.

6. In general, how can you trace aspects of the CF project back to ARS #1 and ARS #3, ASOBAT, and the Trueblood report?

7. How would you assess CF's major contribution to theory formulation compared to Moonitz and Sprouse's theory, ASOBAT, the Trueblood report, SATTA? Did the CF contribute more or less? Explain.

8. Which concern about the CF project seems the most important to you? Why?

9. Which does the accounting profession value more highly: the continued use of a particular accounting procedure (consistency) or the switch to another accounting method to be more in line with other companies in the same industry (comparability)?

10. The FASB really has a choice in formulating standards of accounting. It could formulate very specific standards that are very detailed and result in rigid uniformity and limit the professional judgment of accountants. Alternatively, the FASB could issue broad, general standards that discuss the issues and identify the relevant circumstances but leave some reporting alternatives to the discretion of practicing accountants. Assuming you just got appointed to the FASB, which approach would you favor and why?

RESEARCH PROJECT

Research Project: Read SFAC No. 1 and compare paragraphs 10 through 16 to the postulates of accounting given in Chapter 2 of this text. How are they similar? How they are different?

NOTES

1 FASB (1978), (1980a), (1980b), (1980c), (1984), (1985), and (2000); see bibliography.

2 Flegm, p. 213.

3 Miller, "The Conceptual Framework as Reformation and Counterreformation."

4 Rubin.

5 Hudack and McAllister.

6 Miller.

7 The section "FASB CF Difficulties" is based on Miller, Redding, and Bahnson, pp. 101–104.

8 It should be noted that the FASB also proposed a change to the definition of a liability in 2000. So the board continues to fine tune the CF.

REFERENCES

Brown, Victor. "Accounting Standards: Their Economic and Social Consequences." *Accounting Horizons* (September 1990): 89–97.

Dopuch, Nicholas, and Shyam Sunder. "FASB's Statement on Objectives and Elements of Financial Accounting: A Review," *Accounting Review* (January 1980): 1–21.

Financial Accounting Standards Board. FASB Discussion Memorandum: *"Conceptual Framework for Financial Accounting and Reporting: Elements of Financial Statements and Their Measurement."* Norwalk, CT: Financial Accounting Standards Board, 1976a.

———. "Scope and Implications of the Conceptual Framework Project." Norwalk, CT: Financial Accounting Standards Board, 1976b.

———. "Tentative Conclusions on Objectives of Financial Statements of Business Enterprises." Norwalk, CT: Financial Accounting Standards Board, 1976c.

———. "Objectives of Financial Reporting by Business Enterprises." *Statement of Financial Accounting Concepts No. 1.* Norwalk, CT: Financial Accounting Standards Board, 1978.

———. "Qualitative Characteristics of Accounting Information," *Statement of Financial Accounting Concepts No. 2.* Norwalk, CT: Financial Accounting Standards Board, 1980a.

———. "Elements of Financial Statements of Business Enterprises," *Statement of Financial Accounting Concepts No. 3.* Norwalk, CT: Financial Accounting Standards Board, 1980b.

———. "Objectives of Financial Reporting by Nonbusiness Enterprises," *Statement of Financial Accounting Concepts No. 4.* Norwalk, CT: Financial Accounting Standards Board, 1980c.

———. "Recognition and Measurement in Financial Statements of Business Enterprises," *Statement of Financial Accounting Concepts No. 5.* Norwalk, CT: Financial Accounting Standards Board, 1984.

———. "Elements of Financial Statements": *Statement of Financial Accounting Concepts No. 6.* Norwalk, CT: Financial Accounting Standards Board, 1985.

———. "Using Cash Flow Information and Present Value in Accounting Measurements," *Statement of Financial Accounting Concepts No. 7.* Norwalk, CT: Financial Accounting Standards Board, 2000.

Flegm, E. *How to Meet the Challenges of Relevance and Regulation.* New York: Wiley, 1984.

Gerboth, Dale. "The Conceptual Framework: Not Definitions, But Professional Values." *Accounting Horizons* (September 1987): 1–8.

Hudack, Lawrence, and J. P. McAllister. "An Investigation of the FASB's Application of Its Decision Usefulness Criteria." *Accounting Horizons* (September 1994): 1–18.

Keoppen, David. "Using the FASB's Conceptual Framework: Fitting the Pieces Together." *Accounting Horizons* (June 1988):18–26.

Miller, Paul. "The Conceptual Framework: Myths and Realities." *Journal of Accountancy* (March 1985): 62–71.

———. "The Conceptual Framework as Reformation and Counterreformation." *Accounting Horizons* (June 1990): 23–32.

Miller, P., R. Redding, and P. Bahnson. *The FASB, the People, the Process, and the Politics,* Fourth Edition. Boston, Irwin McGraw Hill, 1998.

Pacter, Paul. "The Conceptual Framework: Make No Mystique About It." *Journal of Accountancy* (July 1983): 76–88.

Pate, Gwen, and K. Stanga. "A Guide to the FASB's Concepts Statements." *Journal of Accountancy* (August 1989): 28–31.

Rubin, S. "How Concepts Statements Can Solve Practice Problems." *Journal of Accountancy* (October 1988): 123–125.

Solomons, David. "The FASB's Conceptual Framework: An Evaluation." *Journal of Accountancy* (June 1986), 114–124.

CHAPTER 8

FASB: PRESENT AND FUTURE

LEARNING OBJECTIVES

After studying this chapter, you should be able to

> Understand the current situation of the FASB.

> Describe the international and domestic competition to the FASB.

> Understand the issues and developments in the search for international GAAP.

> Debate whether accounting standard setting belongs in the public or private sector.

STANDARD SETTING	1900	THEORY FORMULATION
CHAPTER 1		
STANDARD SETTING I		THEORY 1
PRE-CAP	1900-1938	NATURE OF THEORY
SEC	1934	
STANDARD SETTING II		
CAP I	1938	
STANDARD SETTING III		
CAP II	1938-1958	
CHAPTER 2		
STANDARD SETTING IV		THEORY II
APB	1959-1962	
	1961-1962	ARS #1 AND #3
CHAPTER 3		
STANDARD SETTING V		THEORY III
APB	1963-1966	
	1966	ASOBAT
STANDARD SETTING VI		
DEMISE OF APB	1970	
CHAPTER 4, 5		
STANDARD SETTING VII		
TRUEBLOOD	1973	
WHEAT	1972	
TRIPARTITE STRUCTURE	1973-2001	
CHAPTER 6		
		THEORY IV
	1977	SATTA
		POSITIVE ACCOUNTING 1980s
CHAPTER 7		THEORY V
	1973-2001	CONCEPTUAL FRAMEWORK PROJECT
CHAPTER 8		
STANDARD SETTING VIII		
FASB: PRESENT AND FUTURE STANDARD SETTING: DOMESTIC AND INTERNATIONAL	2001	

2002

This chapter concludes the first part of this text. It focuses on the topic of standard setting, examines the current situation of the FASB, and makes some observations about what the future may hold. Chapter 7 examines the theory formulation efforts of the FASB, concluding that the current theory formulation, the Conceptual Framework (CF), has been criticized and is not as widely accepted as it could be. But there is certainly nothing on the horizon to compete with the FASB's framework as the theory of accounting.

Unfortunately, as examined in later sections of this chapter, that isn't the case for the FASB, as the accounting standard-setting body for the United States. Instead, the FASB has both domestic and international competition. It is possible that the International Accounting Standards Board (IASB) could become the world's accounting standard-setting body. In fact, this possibility is so serious that some would consider the FASB an endangered standard-setting body.

This chapter reviews some relatively new and significant national and international developments and trends that have important implications for the future for accountants and accounting. Many of these trends and developments are a result of a continuing stream of changes in domestic and international economic and financial markets. Although this chapter concludes Part 1, it contains some of the most interesting topics currently in accounting.

Exhibit 8.1 helps keep the topics of this chapter in perspective with the rest of Part 1. This chapter's coverage is in bold.

FASB: PRESENT

No accounting standard-setting body has been exempt from criticism. In fact, one could argue that if it is not criticized, then the standard-setting body isn't doing its job properly. Any form of regulation is bound to make someone unhappy. The FASB has not been exempt from criticism. In the next section, some of these recent criticisms and some current developments that appear to have significant effects on the future of the FASB we discussed. Some developments relate directly to the accounting profession and other aspects of accounting rather than to only the FASB. But the spillover effect is real, and the developments should be considered. Although presented individually, when taken together, these developments show the conditions under which the FASB must operate when setting accounting standards in the twenty-first century.

CRITICISM IN THE FINANCIAL MEDIA, 1997–2001

A key factor in the new economy is the availability of and access to financial information. The financial media (or press) are an important source of that information. Because accounting plays an important role in the capital market resource allocation process, the FASB is a valid focus for financial reporting. Reports on the FASB can have a positive or negative impact. The results are positive when the reports help users understand financial accounting and reporting so that they can better use accounting information in their decision models. Whereas the results are negative when the emphasis of the reports is not on education but criticism. A negative impact of this media attention is that very often the reports influence the views of the readers, creating a negative climate. This has been the outcome lately. In fact, it has become common to see articles in the financial media that severely criticize the FASB.

Here are the titles of some articles that have appeared in the financial media in the past, along with the date of publication, to illustrate this point:[1]

- SEC List of Accounting—Fraud Probes Grows (2001)
- It's Time to Simplify Accounting Standards (1999)
- The Auditors Are Always Last to Know (1998)
- Corporate America Bullies FASB (1997)
- Corporate America Is Fed Up With FASB (1997)
- Stand Back, the SEC Is Going to Fix Accounting (1996)
- Can the FASB Be Considered Antibusiness? (1996)

CREATION OF INDEPENDENCE STANDARDS BOARD

In 1997, the SEC and the AICPA announced the creation of a new private-sector body, the Independence Standards Board (ISB) to establish independence standards for the auditors of public companies. *Independence standards* are a group of rules and regulations to preserve and enhance the independence of auditors of public companies. They define the circumstances under which the auditors of public companies are able to both be free and appear free of any interest, financial and otherwise, that might be incompatible with integrity and objectivity. Independence is considered a keystone of the auditing profession.

The ISB is composed of eight members—four are practicing CPAs and four are public members. The ISB elects its chair from the public members. The ISB was established in response to a growing problem of addressing difficult independence issues in auditing firms as the firms enter into new service areas. Many of the existing independence regulations in the AICPA and the SEC do not provide guidance for today's business climate. This is especially true as public accounting firms expand into nonaccounting consulting areas, merge with other firms, and restructure their operations.

The SEC considers the ISB's principles, standards, interpretations, and practices as having substantial authoritative support (SAS). It is significant that the SEC was the primary factor in the creation of the ISB. Under new leadership in the 1990s, the SEC took a more activist role in accounting issues. The creation of the ISB signaled concerns that public accounting and the AICPA may not be doing enough in this area and thus required the intervention of the government. There may be implications in this situation for the FASB and accounting standard setting. If the SEC can react to problems of independence by creating a new body to address the issue, they could do the same for accounting standards.

This issue of the potential involvement of the SEC is covered in more detail in the section, "SEC Activism," later in this chapter.

FAF CONTRIBUTIONS, 1995–1999

One way to measure of the level of satisfaction or dissatisfaction with the FASB is to look at how contributions are flowing into the Financial Accounting Foundation (FAF). The FASB depends on contributions to the FAF for its funding. From 1992 through 1997, contributions to the FAF from statement preparers (industry) dropped by $500,000. In 1998, the amount rose slightly. In 1999, the FAF had an operating deficit of $1 million.[2] Contributions were down 2.6 percent from 1998, mainly due to a 9 percent decline from the industry sector. In light of these events, the Trustees are taking new initiatives to raise funds.

There has been concern in the FAF over this drop in contributions. Certainly, economic conditions and corporate mergers and restructurings have had an impact, but so have unpopular SFASs issued by the FASB.

GENERAL ACCOUNTING OFFICE STUDY, 1996

In September 1996, the General Accounting Office (GAO) released a report titled, *"The Accounting Profession, Major Issues: Progress and Concerns,"* that suggested a more active role for the SEC in supporting improvements in accounting standard setting. The report was sponsored by Representative John Dingell (D, Mich.).

The study concluded that although the accounting profession has responded to changes in the business world by making changes to improve financial reporting and auditing, those actions have not been totally effective in solving major problems. The report noted that the FASB made major efforts to increase user involvement in the standard-setting process, however, the representation and participation of user groups are lower than other groups. This makes it difficult to promulgate standards that have a balanced perspective in meeting users' needs. The report suggested that the SEC could play an important role in working with the FASB to resolve questions about the Board's efficiency and timeliness. Results like these further strengthen the critics of the FASB and those who believe that the SEC should take a more active role in setting accounting standards.

CONGRESSIONAL INTERFERENCE

As described in the section "FASB Politics" in Chapter 5, the first major national political experience of the FASB occurred in the mid-1970s and involved congressional subcommittees. But that experience did not result in congressional interference with the FASB.

However, more recent developments show that Congress apparently has overcome its reluctance to directly interfere with the FASB. In response to some controversial SFASs (on topics such as stock options, derivatives, and mergers and acquisitions), Congress has introduced a number of proposed pieces of legislation that would affect the authority or operations of the FASB. This interference directly threatens the existence of the FASB as a private-sector body and therefore is significant.

One situation occurred in 1994 and concerned the proposed SFAS on stock options. During one of the most contentious periods of time for the FASB, from 1993 to 1995, the business, public accounting, and political communities put intense pressure on the FASB to change its position on accounting for employee stock options. As part of the political pressure, members of Congress introduced the Accounting Standards Reform Act of 1994. This proposed law would require that each new accounting standard or principle (including FASB SFASs, interpretations, and technical bulletins; AICPA [AcSEC] pronouncements; and Emerging Issues Task Force [EITF] consensuses or any amendment to an existing pronouncement) be approved by the SEC. The effect of the legislation would be to severely limit the authority of the FASB. It would make the SEC an accounting appellate court.

More recent examples emerge from the controversy over the FASB's standard on accounting for derivatives. As a result of the pressure on the FASB to change its views, two bills were introduced into Congress in 1997 and 1998 to stop the FASB. Senator Lauch Faircloth (R, N.C.), chair of the Senate Subcommittee on Financial Institutions and Regulatory Relief, introduced S. 1560, "The Accurate Accounting Standards Certification Act of 1997," which would require federal banking agencies, such as the Federal Reserve, to approve any accounting standard on derivatives. House Banking Committee member and chair of the Subcommittee on Capital Markets, Representative Richard Baker (R, La.) introduced H.R. 3165, "The Financial Fairness Act of 1998," which would require the SEC to formally review and approve new SFASs. It would also give public companies the right to sue the SEC in federal court over new rules issued by the FASB.

From 1999 to 2001, the FASB dealt with the controversial subject of accounting for mergers and acquisitions. As part of its project, it proposed the elimination of the practice of pooling of interests. The proposal met with strong opposition from industry stakeholders (especially high-tech firms), who believe that pooling-of-interest accounting facilitates merger activity that would not otherwise occur. As part of the pressure on the FASB in this situation, in October 2000, thirteen members of the Senate (including a candidate for the vice presidency of the United States) signed a letter to the FASB, asking that it delay issuing the proposed standard. At the same time, legislation was introduced into the House of Representatives that would impose a one-year moratorium on the FASB proposal. This bill was cosponsored by four representatives, including the chair of the House Commerce Committee. In light of these concerns, the FASB redeliberated the issue of whether to retain the pooling-of-interests method in January 2001. In May 2001, it voted unanimously in favor of reconfirming its prior decision to eliminate pooling-of-interest accounting for business combinations. The new SFAS requires the use of the purchase method of accounting for all business combinations started after June 30, 2001; the use of the pooling-of-interest method is eliminated. This is an important change to the accounting for business combinations.

These efforts represent a serious threat to the authority of the FASB and its existence as a private-sector body. Many have risen to the defense of the FASB, including members of the Board and stakeholders, such as the Financial Executives International (FEI). In fact, the response of the FEI is interesting because it has been one of the strongest critics of the FASB in the past. However, in letters to Congress, the FEI quickly acknowledged that although the FEI has been dissatisfied with specific FASB processes and pronouncements, it wanted to preserve the standard-setting process in the private sector. That defense reflects the seriousness of the threat from Congress.

SEC ACTIVISM

When considering the subject of accounting standard setting, one must always keep in mind that the legal authority for FASB standard setting rests with the SEC. It was the SEC's decision in the 1930s to delegate this authority to the accounting profession and private sector. But that hasn't stopped the SEC from exercising authority by both influencing the FASB and overruling it.

The views of the chief accountant of the SEC and the chairman of the SEC are important factors that influence how the SEC will relate to the FASB and the accounting profession. If one, or both, believe a more active role in either standard setting or related issues is needed, the SEC becomes more of an activist for accounting standard setting. This has happened in the past and will happen in the future. The 1990s was one of the most intensive activist periods of the SEC.

The primary driver for this time of SEC activism was SEC chair Arthur Levitt (he stepped down in 2001). His dissatisfaction with auditor independence led to the creation of the ISB. He had been very outspoken about other accounting concerns. For example, in the summer of 1998, the SEC quietly held meetings with members of the FEI, FASB, and Big 5 accounting firms about accounting problems that surfaced at some prominent companies, such as Livent, Cedent, and Sunbeam. In a speech in September 1998, Levitt made some significant comments on what he characterized as "a game of nods and winks" and "hocus-pocus." He conveyed his deep concern with financial reporting and the ability of statements preparers to smooth earnings, meet earnings forecasts, and otherwise deceive users. He listed five areas in which he was concerned that management was deceiving users: big bath charges, creative acquisition accounting, miscellaneous cookie-jar reserves, materiality, and revenue recognition. He claimed the game of nods and winks was played by corporate managers, auditors, and financial analysts. He called for improved transparency of financial statements and presented a nine-point plan to achieve that result. His plan involved the SEC and the AICPA.[3]

Levitt expressed similar concerns later in the journal, *Strategic Finance.*[4] In his article, he attacked "numbers gamesmanship," an emphasis on short-term numbers rather than long term-performance designed to bend to the desires and pressures of financial analysts and boost stock prices. As part of this strategy, auditors are pressured not to "rock the boat" and to accept what's going on without complaint.

This increased SEC activism is important because it signaled that circumstances in financial accounting were serious enough to have the SEC step in. Generally, the SEC had been reluctant to do this unless absolutely necessary. Another aspect of the SEC's involvement is that it strengthened the case of those who wanted the SEC to take back the authority to set accounting standards. This issue will be revisited later in this chapter.

INTERNATIONAL COMPETITION

Rather than the SEC, perhaps the greatest threat to the FASB is from international competition.[5] Changing conditions have increased the need for an international accounting standard-setting body. The next section describes these changing conditions and discusses several trends and then focuses on standard setting at the international level by the International Accounting Standards Committee (IASC).

GLOBAL ECONOMY

The global economy has been defined as "an end to economic geography: a single unified marketplace for all goods, services, people, skills and ideas—and complete equality of treatment for all economic agents."[6] This global economy does not currently exist, but great progress toward its realization has been made. We live in a world characterized by increased international economic interdependence. That interconnectedness was proved in late October 1997. The speed at which currency market collapses and then stock market collapses spread from Asia to Europe to the United States was startling, proving that world currency and stock markets were tightly linked.

By 2000, world trade exceeded $7 trillion and is still growing rapidly despite the downturn that started in 2001. For example, through 1993, world trade generally expanded at an annual rate of 2 percent. World trade is expected to expand at an average rate of more than 3.0 percent per year in the period of 2001 to 2011. At the current rate of growth, the world production of goods and services will double by 2020.

A number of factors are coming together to produce this "golden age" of world economic growth: expanding economic freedom and property rights in the world (coupled with a reduction in the scope of government), soaring increases in trade and private investments, and the quickening pace of technological advances and other innovations.[7]

This world expansion has implications for accounting. This expansion of economic output will be processed through domestic and multinational firms in the world economy. Firms' accountants play an important role in all this. Transactions will be recorded; their impact on the firm and its resources will be measured and analyzed, and the overall results will be analyzed and reported to management and outside stakeholders (such as investors and creditors) by accountants. Other accountants will audit this activity. Thus, on the micro level, the growth in international economic activity will translate into much more accounting activity.

A question to be answered is, Will these economic developments evolve into a world composed of trading and monetary blocs? A factor to be considered is the recent development of world and regional trading agreements and their importance. These are discussed next.

WORLD TRADING PACTS

At the global level, there is only one trading pact, the General Agreement on Tariffs and Trade (GATT). GATT was established in 1948 with the goal of expanding the economic growth and development of the world economy by liberalizing world trade. In 1994, the Uruguay Round (so called because it started in Uruguay in 1986) of GATT was signed by 117 nations. GATT was seen as a step forward in a worldwide agreement among trading nations and showed that the nations of the world could cooperate on a global basis.

EVENT

The 1994 global trade agreement would lower world tariffs for goods, services, and trade. For the first time, services and information technologies were included in the agreement. The agreement also reduces agricultural subsidies and extends copyright and patent protections. The agreement created a World Trade Organization (WTO) arbitration panel to settle trade disputes between nations.

The WTO pact signed in December 1997 by 102 nations represented a landmark pact and opened the banks and financial services firms in these nations to foreign interests. This agreement covered almost 95 percent of the world's financial services market and gave banks and insurers freer access to these markets, estimated at over $20 trillion. This agreement will facilitate the financing of trade and foreign investment.

REGIONAL TRADING BLOCS

At the next level are regional trading blocs. These blocs involve a number of nations from a given region of the world, however defined. The number of these has been growing. A discussion of the major blocs follows.

ORGANIZATION **European Union** The oldest and most powerful regional trading bloc is the European Union (EU). It traces its heritage back to 1948 when the Organization for European Economic Cooperation was created to administer the Marshall Plan. The success of this cooperative effort led to the creation of the Common Market in 1957 with the signing of the treaties of Rome by France, West Germany, Italy, Belgium, The Netherlands, and Luxembourg. In 1973, Great Britain, Denmark, and Ireland also entered the EU; Greece joined in 1981; Spain and Portugal joined in 1986.

The Common Market pursued the integration of the European countries on three levels.

1. *Customs union*, the abolition of national import tariffs and restrictions
2. *Economic union*, the harmonization of national economic, fiscal, and monetary policies
3. *Political union*, leading to a united Europe

The Common Market countries have made remarkable progress on all three levels, with special emphasis on customs and economic union. The European Single Act of 1986 provided for the creation of the Single European Market and established the goal of monetary union. This single market began in 1994, guaranteeing free movement of people, goods, capital, and services (the Four Freedoms).

In March 1997, the Common Market celebrated its fortieth birthday. At that time the EU had fifteen members (Austria, Belgium, Denmark, Finland, France, Germany, Greece, Ireland, Italy, Luxembourg, The Netherlands, Portugal, Spain, Sweden, and the United Kingdom) and two groups of proposed members, including many nations in central Europe.

Then the whole world watched the most remarkable accomplishment of European integration: European monetary union, "monetary matrimony." In 1999, the currencies of eleven of the major European nations were integrated into a single system along with a new currency, the euro. By 2002, it replaced national currencies such as francs, deutsche marks, and guilders. To many, this is the biggest event to happen in world financial markets since the Bretton Woods Agreement in 1944, and if successful, it will mark the emergence of the EU as a global economic and political power. Members hope that currency union will cement political union and produce the benefits of a true single market.

The stakes are high for Europe and other nations. For example, Europe buys nearly 25 percent of U.S. exports. Many of the emerging economies of central and eastern Europe and Russia rely on a strong European economy.

In terms of accounting and accounting services, the European accounting profession is making significant strides toward unity and a single market for accounting services. European integration will increase the demand for accounting services and also change the structure of the European accounting profession. However, this will require the dismantling of twelve different sets of national regulations. The Fédération des Experts Comptables Européens has proposed legislation to enable temporary cross-border accounting services to resolve this problem. Under this legislation, providers of these services will not be required to obtain local qualifications as long as they are already appropriately authorized in another EU member state. In terms of financial statements, although there are many differences in national accounting regulations within the EU, financial statements prepared in one state must be accepted in all member states.

North American Free Trade Agreement (NAFTA)   NAFTA was signed in August 1992 and approved in the United States in 1994. This free trade pact is between the United States, Canada, and Mexico and is designed to effectively link these three economies into the world's largest free trade zone—from the Yukon to the Yucatan, 6,000 miles. In 2000, that free trade zone market was composed of approximately 400 million people, had a $7 trillion gross domestic product (GDP), and $300 billion in combined annual trade. NAFTA was designed to eliminate tariffs among the United States, Canada, and Mexico over fifteen years and to protect investments in those countries. It is expected that goods, capital, and services will flow freely between the three nations as they do now between the individual states in the United States.

In late 1994, Chile was invited to join NAFTA. Some planners hope to eventually include all Western Hemisphere nations in NAFTA.

Although both NAFTA and the European Union are regional trade pacts, NAFTA's objectives are significantly more limited than those of the EU. NAFTA is clearly concerned with economic factors, whereas the EU is concerned with political and other factors as well. It is fair to say that the EU structure has been greatly influenced by those who seek the formation of one European nation, while no such tendencies are currently present between countries in the NAFTA agreement.[8]

Professional Accounting Under NAFTA   In the first decade of the twenty-first century, it is generally believed that NAFTA will generate billions of dollars of additional trade, investment, and economic growth in the three member nations. Firms involved in these investments, mergers and acquisitions, new ventures, trade, and other transactions will rely on the advice of CPAs and other accountants. To engage in this type of activity, accountants must be knowledgeable about the financial practices, legal requirements, and business cultures throughout the region and be able to deliver their services anywhere in the region.

Under the Canada–United States Free Trade Agreement and NAFTA, many of the barriers and restrictions on accountants have been lifted. For example, in terms of general business barriers, Canadian and U.S. investors can now make direct investments in Mexican accounting firms; accounting professionals can freely sell their services across borders without establishing a local presence; and extensive property rules now protect proprietary technology and information. In terms of professional barriers, the free trade agreement stipulates that licensing requirements must be objective, and citizenship and residency requirements for certification will eventually be phased out.[9]

Below is a list of a broad range of services that accounting firms can provide to their clients throughout the NAFTA region:[10]

1. Gaining access to capital markets and financial reporting and disclosure requirements.
2. Managing foreign currency transactions and hedging programs
3. Solving international taxation problems
4. Providing a NAFTA certificate of origin to products to comply with NASTA tariff reductions
5. Designing and implementing multicultural information systems and internal control systems
6. Providing cultural advice and local contacts; helping form strategic alliances

Accounting Reciprocity   Reciprocity refers to mutual professional recognition. It generally arises when two or more bodies license a profession. Many nations see the licensing of professionals as part of their national sovereignty. However, under trade pacts, some procedure must be established to recognize those licensed in other countries so they can practice their profession throughout the region.

In 1991, the AICPA, the Canadian Institute of Chartered Accountants (CICA), and the National Association of State Boards of Accountancy (NASBA) approved the Principles of Reciprocity agreement. This agreement addressed three reciprocity issues:[11]

1. *Education*: All three groups agreed that each other's educational requirements will be reciprocal.
2. *Experience*: Each reciprocity candidate must meet the experience requirements of the jurisdiction granting the reciprocity designation.
3. *Examination*: Candidates who pass either the Canadian Uniform Final Examination or the U.S. Uniform CPA Examination are not required to take the other's exam to obtain reciprocity. But all candidates must pass a qualifying exam to be sure that they have satisfactory knowledge of relevant local and national legislation, standards, and practices.

NAFTA provides for the extension of similar provisions with the Mexican Institute of Public Accountants. Thus NAFTA will make it easier for accountants to extend their services to wherever their clients need them. This should offer new practice opportunities for professional accountants throughout the three countries.

Other Trading Pacts   In addition to GATT, the EU, and NAFTA, a number of other trading blocs emerged during the 1990s and continue to grow and flourish. Although they are important, especially in the region where they reign, the text will not cover them in detail. The following list gives you some idea of how extensive they are: Trans Atlantic Free Trade Agreement (TAFTA), Free Trade Area of the Americas (FTAA), Southern Cone Common Market (Mercosur), and Asia-Pacific Economic Cooperation (APEC).

THE FUTURE: TRADING AND MONETARY BLOCS?

The recent development of these regional trading agreements coupled with the progress that the EU has achieved in its drive for monetary union may be strong signals about the structure of the future of the world economy. Although there are many competing trading blocs now, some of these might merge and produce a world composed of a few large and powerful blocs. As nations combine into trading blocs, it will be quite natural for them to consider unifying behind one common currency, as Europe has, which could produce advantages to nations whose currencies are not strong. As they join trading blocs, they could adopt the currency of the strongest nation in the bloc as their currency and avoid some of the problems of having to defend their own currency.

Thus the future economic order of the world may well be a world composed of a few large and powerful trading blocs, each with one dominant currency, for example, the U.S. dollar for NAFTA, the Japanese yen for APEC, and the euro for Europe.

CROSS-BORDER CAPITAL FLOWS AND INVESTMENTS

International investing has been around for a long time as the following quote indicates:

There seems to be a lot of money in Genoa, so you shouldn't send our funds there. You can get a better price in Venice or Florence or here [in Bruges] or in Paris or Montpelier.[12]

The quote is from a note sent to Italian financier Francesco Datini by his partner in Bruges, Belgium, on April 26, 1399, nearly a century before Columbus set sail for America. The note was sent by courier—not faxed, cabled, emailed, or downloaded.

But obviously, since then, the size and pace of international investment have changed. With the fall of communism and the adoption of more open economies, two to three billion people were added into the free market economy of the world in the twentieth century. Developing nations seek capital to grow, and many nations are privatizing formerly state-owned firms. Advances in telecommunications and computerization make cross-border investing fast and easy. Therefore, the following three conclusions can be drawn:

- More investors seek investment opportunities in other countries.
- More securities are sold internationally.
- More capital is flowing internationally.

Some figures will demonstrate the size of these capital flows. Total cross-border investing, when investors in one country purchase stocks of firms in another, reached $2.75 trillion in 1995 and was expected to grow to $4 trillion by 2000.[13] The net new money invested by foreigners in U.S. financial assets (U.S. Treasurys, corporate stocks, and bonds) averaged $25 billion a month in 1999, $37 billion in 2000, and $44 billion for the first two-thirds of 2001.[14] Total foreign direct investments (investments in establishing active operations in other countries rather than passive portfolio investing) was expected to reach $1 trillion in 2000. To put this in perspective, foreign direct investment worldwide totaled only $40 billion in 1980.

In the United States, there have been three waves of foreign direct investment. The first wave involved the recycling of petrodollars by OPEC nations in the mid-1970s. The second involved the Japanese car makers' investments in U.S. assembly plants in the 1980s to avoid import restrictions. The third wave began in the late 1990s as foreign investors made record direct investments in American manufacturing affiliates. Also, the number and size of international mergers has increased since the second wave.

ACCOUNTING IMPLICATIONS: INTERNATIONAL GAAP

The growth of cross-border investing causes two accounting implications: the developing of international accounting standards and the relevancy of those standards for national and international capital markets. Both issues are controversial.

Our focus here is on the broader question of the need for developing a set of international accounting standards to facilitate cross-border capital flows. This need for such standards is even open to question. It would appear logical that given the growth of international investing, any barriers to the international flow of capital should be dismantled. Because of accounting nationalism, each nation has established its own set of accounting standards (national GAAP) that cover the disclosure of financial information in accounting reports for the firms that are domiciled within that nation's borders. The lack of uniformity and comparability of national GAAP would appear to be a problem for cross-border investment. That is, financial markets would be better able to allocate capital resources on the basis of financial statements prepared according to some uniform or harmonized international GAAP. Thus the growth of cross-border investment would pressure accountants to work toward a set of international GAAP or, at a minimum, to work for greater harmonization of national GAAP.

But the counterargument is that historically the lack of uniformity in national GAAP has not posed much of a problem. This viewpoint is based on the recent growth of cross-border investing, which occurred in a world without international GAAP. That is, the recent growth in international investment has happened without the benefit of international GAAP, and thus, to some, that indicates that there is no problem. The absence of international GAAP has not prevented the explosive growth in international investment.

There is no easy answer to this dilemma. Certainly, international investment has occurred in the absence of international GAAP. But would the level of international investment be even greater with some of the increased comparability that international GAAP would provide? And would better investment decisions be made (lower risks, greater rewards) if comparability were improved? These are important considerations in the debate.

THE INTERNATIONAL ACCOUNTING STANDARDS COMMITTEE

The International Accounting Standards Committee (IASC) was founded in 1973 by the leading professional accounting bodies in nine nations (Australia, Canada, France, Germany, Japan, Mexico, The Netherlands, the United Kingdom, including Ireland, and the United States). It is important to realize that nations are not members of the IASC; instead, professional accounting organizations, such as the AICPA, are members. No nation has surrendered its accounting sovereignty to the IASC.

ORGANIZATION

The IASC was established to issue international accounting standards to be followed in the preparation of audited financial statements. Currently, there are more than 125 accounting bodies from over 90 different nations who are members of IASC. The IASC has

EXHIBIT 8.2
IASC Time Line

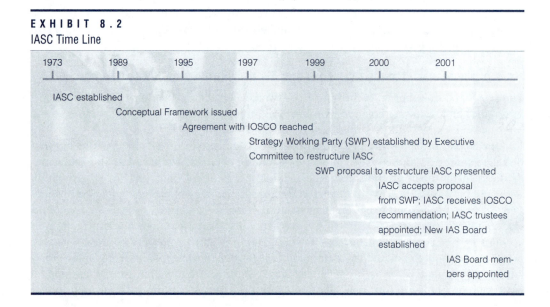

1973	1989	1995	1997	1999	2000	2001

IASC established

Conceptual Framework issued

Agreement with IOSCO reached

Strategy Working Party (SWP) established by Executive Committee to restructure IASC

SWP proposal to restructure IASC presented

IASC accepts proposal from SWP; IASC receives IOSCO recommendation; IASC trustees appointed; New IAS Board established

IAS Board members appointed

issued over thirty-five International Accounting Standards (IASs). They issued a Conceptual Framework for the Preparation of Financial Statements in 1989.

During the late 1990s and early 2000s, the IASC was active on three fronts: (1) issuing IASs, (2) restructuring operations, and (3) obtaining an endorsement from the International Organization of Security Commissions (IOSCO). The latter two are covered in the next sections. A time line for the IASC is shown in Exhibit 8.2.

Restructuring IASC Operations   A Strategy Working Party was formed in 1997 to consider changes in the way the IASC operates. Their proposal led to the massive changes, which were adopted by the IASC in May 2000. A new constitution with a completely changed structure was adopted. The new organization is governed by a group of nineteen trustees who appoint the IAS Board (IASB) members, exercise administrative oversight, and raise funds. The original group of fourteen board members was appointed in May 2000 and included some well-known financial figures (the chair was Paul Volcker, former chair of the U.S. Federal Reserve Board). The trustees then began their task of securing funding for the newly structured IASC (it was expected to cost approximately $82.5 million) from private sources and finding fourteen IAS Board members to serve on the IASB.

The IASB consists of fourteen individuals, twelve of whom serve full-time. The members possess the following: technical competence in financial accounting and reporting, analytical ability, communication and teamwork skills, awareness of financial reporting issues, integrity and objectivity, commitment to the IASC, and judicial decision-making skills. The first group of twelve full-time members was named in March 2001; two previous members of the FASB were included: James J. Leisenring and Anthony T. Cope.

A Standards Advisory Council of thirty members was created to provide a forum for those interested in financial reporting. A Standing Interpretations Committee of twelve members is also part of the new structure. This committee is designed to interpret the application of IASs.

It is obvious that the new IASC structure was patterned after the FASB in order to set international accounting standards. The new structure also reveals that the IASC is gearing up for that responsibility.

Endorsement From the International Organization of Security Commissions   The IOSCO is an international nonprofit association of security regulatory agencies. It was founded in 1974 as an Inter-American regional organization, but its membership has increased to more than one hundred members, representing almost all of the world's security regulators, from developed countries to emerging economies. The IASC has been working diligently on a set of worldwide accounting standards for global capital markets. In 1995, after nine years of negotiations, the IASC and the IOSCO agreed to endorse a core set of international accounting standards for cross-border offerings and listings on the stock exchanges of all member nations by 1999. This was conditional on the IASC's successful development or revision of fifteen of its standards. If the IASC was successful and the core set endorsed, IOSCO member regulators (which includes the U.S. SEC) agreed to consider replacing the use of national GAAP with the IASC-based financial statements for cross-border offerings and listings.

In March 1996, the IASC accelerated its work on the core set of standards and updated the timetable, promising that it would be ready by mid-1998. The IASC's determination is evident in the following quote of Stig Enevoldsen, incoming IASC chair, 1998:

The effectiveness of modern telecommunications has made global capital markets a reality; it is now easy for an investor sitting in Detroit or Seoul to invest in shares all over the world. Because of this, it is critical that we rise above our present accounting Tower of Babel, where we not only speak different accounting languages, but also report the same economic events and transactions differently. We need and should have one global accounting language throughout the world."[15]

The IASC also received endorsement from the European Accounting Commission, which decided to support IASC standards rather than setting separate European standards, and from the WTO.

The long-awaited decision from IOSCO came in May 2000. In what can be considered a landmark decision, IOSCO voted to recommend that all members allow multinational issuers to use IASC standards to prepare their financial statements for cross-border offerings and listings. Individual regulators were permitted to require certain supplementary treatments (the reconciliation of certain items) and additional disclosures, and to be able to specify choices between accepted alternatives in IASC standards.[16] Some see the addition of these qualifications as limiting the endorsement.

ACCOUNTING IMPLICATIONS: INTERNATIONAL LISTINGS ON THE NEW YORK STOCK EXCHANGE

The New York Stock Exchange (NYSE) is the world's largest stock market, with total capitalization of $17.2 trillion as of May 31, 2001. given the breadth and depth of this market, it is not surprising that many foreign firms want to be listed on the NYSE to access American capital. (This is fine with the NYSE, which wants foreign firms to list because it wants to remain the world's leading capital market.) Currently, about 325 foreign firms are listed on the NYSE, and 430 are listed on NASDAQ. Although the number for the NYSE represents a big increase from 1990 when only ninety-six were listed, there are still about two thousand other major foreign firms that could be listed. So the stakes involved are tremendous. The NYSE faces competition from capital markets in London, Tokyo, and Hong Kong and has viewed foreign listings as an important potential source of growth. For example, if another two hundred large foreign firms listed on the NYSE, the capitalization of the NYSE could be doubled.

However, a big obstacle to the satisfaction of both of these "wants" (the desire of foreign firms to list on the NYSE and the desire of the NYSE to have more foreign firms listed) is the requirement that firms listing on the NYSE must be in compliance with U.S. GAAP. Foreign firms do not want to comply with the more rigid and stringent U.S. GAAP; instead, they prefer to report financial results and other information using their own accounting standards. However, many U.S. regulators and investors fear relying on foreign accounting standards for investment decisions. And U.S. firms are concerned that a two-tier reporting system will develop: foreign registrants will follow their GAAP or IASC standards, yet domestic firms will be required to follow the more stringent U.S. standards, yet both firms will compete for the same capital.

One issue concerns the differences between U.S. GAAP, the national GAAP of other countries, and IASC standards. In February 1997, the FASB issued a comparative study of U.S. and international accounting standards.[17] This study reported many important differences between U.S. GAAP and IASC standards, for example, recognition differences, measurement differences, differences in alternatives, and lack of requirements or guidance.

Examples of accounting topics in which the report showed differences between international standards and U.S. GAAP included lease accounting, income tax accounting, stock options, depreciation, and business combinations. Thus in the eyes of the FASB, the IASC has many issues it must address before its standards can be used in the United States.

The extent of differences between national accounting standards was revealed in the results of a study published in Spring 2001, conducted by the International Forum for Accountancy Development.[18] It was a survey of the accounting rules in fifty-three nations, which represents 95 percent of the world's gross domestic product. The results showed that existing discrepancies among national accounting standards were extensive enough to prevent investors in one country from accurately interpreting the financial statements of firms from another country.

The SEC has been drawn into this debate. In general, the NYSE has been favorable toward the adoption of foreign GAAP or IASC standards as a way to increase its foreign listings. However, the FASB has resisted this move because it believes its standards are more rigid than foreign GAAP or IASC standards. The SEC is the watchdog of American capital markets and is responsible for protecting the stock market and setting and enforcing reporting standards. It has been sensitive to the potential risks to investors, the market, and the U.S. economy of allowing foreign firms to offer their stocks on the NYSE. But the SEC has also tried to ease the burden on foreign registrants by accepting several procedures from international accounting standards (such as reporting cash flow statements in accordance with IAS No. 7). Although the SEC has been supportive of the IASC's efforts, it is concerned that international accounting standards have as high-quality standards as the United States. In fact, in 1997, the SEC chair, Arthur Levitt, repeated his previously stated concerns "that international standards must produce financial reporting with the same credibility and integrity produced by U.S. standards" and did not endorse the notion of allowing world-class firms to list in the U.S. exchanges without reconciling their home-country accounting and reporting to U.S. GAAP.[19]

This issue first surfaced in 1993 when Daimler-Benz, a German firm, decided to list on the NYSE. A critical issue that arose in the negotiation was whose accounting standards to follow, German or U.S. GAAP? After extensive discussions between Daimler-Benz and the SEC staff, Daimler-Benz agreed to file a separate set of books that adhered to U.S. GAAP. When Daimler-Benz reconciled their German income to U.S. GAAP, the results were interesting. Under German GAAP, Daimler-Benz reported a 1993 net income of $100 million; under U.S. GAAP, that net income became a net loss of $1 billion![20]

Another large European firm interested in listing on the NYSE is Nestlé SA, with $50 billion in sales. Nestlé is 15 percent owned by Americans. The major roadblock appears to be the demand that it conform to U.S. GAAP.

An interesting development occurred in early 2000 when the SEC released a plan to ask U.S. firms whether the SEC should allow foreign firms to list on the NYSE under the IASC standards.[21] The plan was issued as an SEC Concept Release (No. 33-7801) in February 2000. Although the SEC doesn't need the approval of U.S. firms, this move was seen as a way of gauging the response of U.S. firms. By Fall 2001, the SEC was still in the process of analyzing the responses. Details about the proposal and the comment letters received by the SEC can be viewed at http://www.sec.gov/rules/concept.shtml by scrolling down to Release No. 33-7801. It was uncertain if the SEC also planned on allowing U.S. firms to follow IASC standards when they list.

THE FINAL QUESTION: WHOSE STANDARDS?

Harmonization Pressures   The developments described earlier all exert strong pressure on U.S. accountants and accounting to move in the direction of international harmonization. As a new world order is established on the basis of economic power and as the world economy expands, pressures will build to simplify the differences between national and regional GAAPs and improve access to world capital markets. The FASB has been aware of these pressures and has responded, as the next section explains.

International Activities of the FASB   The FASB is still implementing its strategic plan for international activities.[22] This plan was started in 1992 and updated in 1995. The FASB is pursuing a more supportive and active role in the arena of international standard setting. This role has six parts:

1. Considering more intensely IASC standards in all domestic FASB projects
2. Working with the IASC on international standard-setting projects on selected topics
3. Considering the adoption of IASC standards that are judged to be superior to U.S. GAAP
4. Influencing the IASC to adopt U.S. standards that are judged to be superior to IASC standards
5. Agreeing on a choice of standards where U.S., IASC, or other standards are considered equal
6. Continuing efforts to encourage financial statement requirement equality for domestic and non-U.S. firms in U.S. capital markets

As examples of greater international involvement, in 1991, the FASB initiated a joint project with Canada and Mexico to monitor each other's accounting practices. The FASB also worked with the IASC in revising nearly identical standards on earnings per share (EPS), and the FASB and IASC both issued nearly identical standards on EPS in 1997. Additionally the FASB worked closely with the Canadian Institute of Chartered Accountants (CICA) on a new pronouncement on segment reporting. As a result, the FASB and CICA issued nearly identical standards on segment reporting in 1997.

In December 2000, the FASB published a special report, "Financial Instruments and Similar Items," which was prepared for another international group of standard setters, the Financial Instruments Joint Working Group. This group was formed in 1997 for the purpose of developing a coherent framework for reporting financial instruments at fair value. The Joint Working Group is made up of accounting representatives from Australia, Canada, France, Germany, Japan, New Zealand, five Nordic countries, the United Kingdom, the United States, and the IASC.

As these developments show, the FASB has been active in pursuing its international plan. In fact as the following statement from Edmund L. Jenkings, chair of the FASB, commenting on the formal implementation of the IAS Board (IASB) shows, the FASB is very supportive of the recent changes in the IASC:

> *It is a critical and welcome event in establishing an independent global standard setter to provide high-quality financial reporting standards to serve our global financial markets. For several years the FASB has had a vision of an environment that could accomplish that result and has worked hard to assist in the*

restructuring of the former International Accounting Standards Committee. The FASB anticipates a close, constructive, and active relationship with the IASB and its members named in January (2001) and with other national standard setters in achieving convergence of high-quality financial reporting standards around the world.[23]

The Final Question: Conclusion   Many accountants who are aware of the pressure for international standardization may question the future of U.S. accounting standards. Certainly, if cross-border investment continues to grow and both foreign firms and the NYSE favor the listing of foreign firms through compliance with national GAAP or IASC standards, will U.S. GAAP be viable in that world? One can easily foresee the potential demise of U.S. GAAP, given the need for more flexible standards that are compatible with international investments. That process was hastened in 2000 after IOSCO endorsed the core set of IASC standards. If IOSCO member regulators replace the use of national GAAP with the IASC-based financial statements for cross-border offerings and listings, another important step toward recognizing IASC standards and GAAP will occur. However, the IOSCO decision serves only as a recommendation to member regulators, each of whom must decide for themselves. If these pressures cause the SEC to acquiesce and allow foreign firms to be listed on the NYSE following foreign GAAP or IASC standards, some see dire consequences for both the FASB and U.S. capital markets.

> *If the SEC were to accede to this irrational but powerful political pressure to permit international standards to be used in the United States, two negative effects would be created. First, the quality of public information would decline while the quantity of private information would increase. . . . Second . . . the FASB would become redundant.*[24]

Unfortunately, there still appears to be no consensus to the question of which accounting standards to use.

EVALUATION OF INTERNATIONAL COMPETITION

In the future, the solidly established global financial markets will channel more money internationally and to more investors than ever before. Modern nations currently regard their capital markets as vital components of their national economies. Strong competition has developed among the capital markets of the world for investment flows and offerings of securities. Accounting and accountants are involved in these activities. For example, in response to the global economy, the AICPA launched in 2001 a proposal to issue a global business credential. Upon the official establishment of the credential, a new global professional accounting body, separate from the AICPA, was to be formed to provide support for the credential. A section of the September 2001 Journal of Accountancy was devoted to details on the global business credential proposal. However, in January 2002, the AICPA made the decision to withdraw this proposal.

As the language of business, accounting disclosures are an important source of information about a firm and its securities. Nations differ in the strictness and stringency of their accounting rules and listing requirements. These differences may have to change as pressure for greater harmonization builds and as security markets begin to see that accounting rules are part of their competitive advantage, or disadvantage, in attracting capital and securities to sell. Additionally, the increased emphasis on regional trade blocs and pacts will work to harmonize accounting rules on a regional basis. Professional reciprocity agreements for the accountants of partner countries (such as those in NAFTA) will have to be negotiated. These will be a positive step forward toward greater worldwide harmonization.

DOMESTIC COMPETITION

In addition to international competition from the IASC, two private-sector bodies and one public-sector body compete with the FASB. It should be noted that the Wheat Committee did not want any domestic rivals for the FASB; it wanted accounting standard setting centralized in one body. The two private-sector bodies are discussed next.

EMERGING ISSUES TASK FORCE

The first of these bodies is the Emerging Issues Task Force (EITF). It was created by the FASB in 1984 and is composed of sixteen senior technical partners of public accounting firms (national and smaller) and statement preparers, the FASB's director of research (as chair), and the SEC's chief accountant as an observer. All serve part-time, and no users are represented. The EITF was created to assist the FASB in the early identification of emerging accounting issues, hopefully to solve the problem of timely guidance in accounting matters.

The EITF works by consensus. On a particular issue, if no more than two members disagree, then the solution is adopted. The SEC accepts the solution as substantial authoritative support for the practice for SEC registrants.

The EITF works well. It issues GAAP in a much quicker manner than the FASB, and its pronouncements have gained substantial public support. This may represent more than the original intent of the FASB. Instead of acting in a supporting role to the FASB, the EITF may have developed into a standard-setting body. A criticism of the EITF is that no users are on the task force.

ACCOUNTING STANDARDS EXECUTIVE COMMITTEE

The second competitor is the AICPA Accounting Standards Executive Committee (AcSEC). This was formed by the AICPA in 1973 to serve as its voice on accounting and reporting issues. It is composed of fifteen members (all CPAs) who serve part-time. Some members are partners of large pubic accounting firms, others are from smaller firms, some are representatives of industry, and one member is an academic. No users are represented. AcSEC is considered the senior technical committee and represents the AICPA in matters of financial reporting. The committee issues Statements of Position (SOPs).

In 1977 to 1978, a turf battle broke out between the AcSEC and the FASB over the authority of SOPs. Some members of AcSEC wondered about the authority of SOPs, and members of the FEI had the same question. The central question was whether the AcSEC had become an accounting standard-setting body. In general, SOPs were quite specialized and were recognized as supplementary guidance on accounting and reporting matters. The issue was resolved in January 1992 when the AICPA issued Statement on Auditing Standards No. 69, "The Meaning of 'Present Fairly in Conformity With Generally Accepted Accounting Principles' in the Independent Auditor's Report," which identified AICPA SOPs as a source of GAAP. A due process procedure was installed, and the FASB must approve all new SOPs. The result was cooperation between the FASB and AcSEC rather than conflict.

THE PRIVATE-SECTOR VERSUS PUBLIC-SECTOR DEBATE

The last issue this chapter discusses represents the logical conclusion of many of the topics in the chapter. Should accounting standard setting be continued in the private sector or should it be returned to the public sector?[25] This question has arisen a number times in the topics discussed earlier. The answer to this question depends on one's view of the role of financial reporting. There are at least three different views on the objectives of financial reporting, and they often seem to conflict.

1. *Corporate reporting.* Permit the reporting firm to present financial information most conducive to its purposes.
2. *Investor evaluation.* Provide investors (present and potential) with information that allows them to compare two or more firms.
3. *Government reporting.* Provide the national government with basis for macroeconomic decision for economy.

Which objective you view as most important will influence your view on the private–public debate. Some would say that the first objective is dominant today. In fact, most would agree that Arthur Levitt's statement reported earlier is an appropriate reaction to such an objective. Others would choose the second objective of financial reporting as the most important. Still others would select the third. Those selecting either the second or third objective are making the case for standard setting in the public sector. Only the first objective fits squarely with private-sector standard setting.

In the United States, as shown in Exhibit 8.3 on the following page, there are three levels of authority in standard setting, private and public. These three levels are discussed next.

AUTHORITY LEVEL ONE

At the highest level of authority are all the branches of the national government: executive, legislative, and judicial. Currently, the U.S. Congress has led the way in this area by establishing the SEC in the 1930s and giving it legal authority to set accounting standards. Notice that at this level, the authority is not exercised but rather delegated to the next level.

EXHIBIT 8.3
Three Levels of Standard-Setting Authority

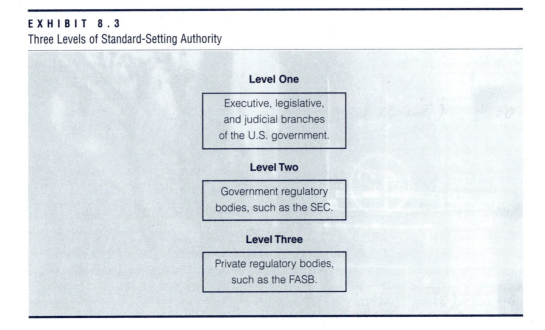

Level One

Executive, legislative,
and judicial branches
of the U.S. government.

Level Two

Government regulatory
bodies, such as the SEC.

Level Three

Private regulatory bodies,
such as the FASB.

AUTHORITY LEVEL TWO

At the next level are all the governmental regulatory bodies, such as the SEC. These receive the delegated authority from level one and either exercise it or delegate it to the third level. The SEC took that approach with regard to accounting standard setting.

AUTHORITY LEVEL THREE

The third level consists of private regulatory bodies that operate as public bodies, such as the FASB. The FASB issues accounting standards under the authority delegated to it by the SEC. Thus although we frequently hear people speak as though the FASB is the only accounting standard-setting body in the United States, this is not true. Congress has the ultimate authority, which it has delegated to the SEC. The SEC then delegated that authority to the FASB. But Congress can withdraw that authority from the SEC and from the FASB. If Congress wishes, it could be the sole source of accounting standards in the United States.

ARGUMENTS FOR PUBLIC-SECTOR STANDARD SETTING

There are a number of arguments that support the idea that accounting standard setting rightfully belongs in the public sector. In this section, a number of major arguments to support this view are summarized.

Congressional Intent.   One argument is that Congress intended this outcome when it issued the laws that established the SEC in the early 1930s. It was Congress's intent that this activity be delegated to the public sector, not the private sector.

Public Stake.   Another major argument is that too much is at stake to trust this significant area to the private sector. The public interest in financial reporting and capital markets is too significant to trust to anyone other than the public sector. With more than half of all Americans owning stock in 2001, this is a powerful argument.

More Impartial.   An important argument is that a public-sector body would not have conflict of interest and would be more impartial than a private-sector group. It would not become a tool of business interests and could maintain its objectivity better than a private-sector body.

Wider Views.   This argues that a public-sector body could obtain the views and participation of a wide variety of people from more intellectual disciplines, such as from economics and law, to standard setting than the private sector could.

More Responsive.   Another dispute is that the private-sector approach is not responsive to the needs of the national government. A public-sector body would be more responsive to the government on national issues.

Stronger Compliance.   An interesting argument is that a public-sector body would issue accounting standards that would have the force of law behind them. Compliance could be enforced better when accounting standards are laws.

ARGUMENTS FOR PRIVATE-SECTOR STANDARD SETTING

As you might expect, a number of arguments also support the idea that accounting standard setting should be kept in the private sector; these are summarized next.

Access to Personnel.   The private-sector body has access to highly qualified personnel who would not want to work for a public-sector body at government wages. These individuals prefer the private sector, which is free of government bureaucracy and rules.

Operational Flexibility   The private sector is not saddled with rules and regulations and can be more responsive to changes in the business world than the public sector.

Neutral.   The private-sector body could avoid political influence and not be influenced by presidential administrations. And it could avoid lobbying efforts by special interest groups.

Funding.   This argument emphasizes that the private-sector body, privately funded, does not add to the cost of government or increase the size of the federal deficit.

Greater Accessibility.   This argues that a private-sector body has greater access to business leaders than public-sector agencies. Certainly, a private-sector body could be located away from Washington, D.C., and therefore be closer to the major money markets, such as in New York City or Chicago.

Whether standard setting should be a public- or private-sector activity is a very controversial issue; there is validity in the arguments for both sides. Many of the arguments listed above have become reality in the chronological development of standard setting covered in this section of the text.

Whatever your personal opinion, the conclusion many people reach is that the current situation, in which a private-sector body operates with public-sector body oversight is a good compromise. The next section focuses on the relationship between the FASB and the SEC.

ADVANTAGES OF THE FASB FOR THE SEC

Whatever your views on the private-public debate, you should recognize that the current arrangement provides some excellent advantages for the SEC. From its standpoint, little is to be gained by eliminating the FASB and consolidating accounting standard setting within the SEC. Five arguments to support the current arrangement follow:

The FASB Works.   The FASB issues SFASs; it is successful in setting accounting standards.

SEC Control.   Although the FASB issues accounting standards, the SEC is still in control. It can easily influence the agenda of the FASB and get any issue that the SEC considers as important on that agenda. It also can participate in the due process procedure of the FASB and influence the standard-setting process. It can override any SFAS that is issued.

Heat Shield.   The FASB acts like a shield for the SEC. Many of the controversies that focused on the FASB would have been focused on the SEC if there were no FASB. The FASB draws controversy away from the SEC.

Frugal.   The SEC does not have to fund a set of accounting standards. The FASB is funded by the private sector at no cost to the government.

Expert Advice.   Through the FASB, the SEC has access to advice that it could not afford to obtain elsewhere.

As you can see, there are a number of advantages for the SEC to having the FASB. It's unlikely that the SEC, if given a choice, would opt to eliminate the FASB and take over the job of setting accounting standards. The SEC appears to have the best of both worlds. But conditions are changing, and what has worked well in the past may not work well in the future.

SUMMARY

The accounting landscape has certainly changed from 1973 to 2001. Major international and domestic developments have changed the face of accounting standard setting. In 1973, there was the newly emerging FASB, part of the newly developed tripartite structure. Importantly, the IASC had also recently been created, although with little fanfare and notice.

As a result of the changes and developments, the FASB is currently facing a number of domestic rivals, from both the private and public sectors, and a major international rival. The restructured and newly endorsed IASC is a potentially powerful force in the world of international standard setting, which maybe expanded to include U.S. standard setting. The problems that have plagued the FASB recently, if continued, might lead to its demise. No other U.S. accounting standard-setting body has lasted twenty-seven years as the FASB has.

REVIEW QUESTIONS

1. What are some of the relatively new and significant national and international developments and trends that have important implications for accounting and accountants?
2. What are some of the negative consequences of "FASB bashing" in the financial media?
3. Describe the formation of the ISB. What implications does its creation have for the FASB?
4. How did Congress try to interfere with standard setting during 1990 to 2000? How was this different from the congressional involvement in the mid-1970s and 1985 (see Chapter 5)?
5. What factor drives the SEC's activism? What major change in this factor which occurred in 2001 may change the intensity of this activism?
6. What international economic conditions changed to make the need for international accounting standards greater in the twenty-first century?
7. What are the accounting implications of an increase in the growth of world trade and business?
8. Describe professional accounting and accounting reciprocity under NAFTA. How could these be a model for other trade pacts?
9. How does the growth of cross-border investment activity affect accounting?
10. Describe the IOSCO. What influence does it have on international accounting standards?
11. How has the NYSE become involved in the debate over international accounting standards? What are the SEC's concerns about this issue?
12. What organization has been the international accounting standard setter in the past? What changes have been made in that organization recently to position it as a rival to the FASB?
13. What two private-sector bodies represent the domestic competition to the FASB? Which is the more serious threat?
14. In the private-public debate, which side you do favor and why?
15. What are the advantages of the FASB for the SEC?

DISCUSSION TOPICS

1. Assess the current situation of the FASB. Are you optimistic or pessimistic about its future as a standard-setting body? Support your position.
2. Do you think the financial media should consider the positive or negative impact of their reports on the FASB and private-sector accounting standard setting when reporting the financial news?
3. Should the SEC be "activist"? Discuss the pros and cons.
4. Do you agree with Arthur Levitt's 1998 comments on the current state of financial reporting? Cite recent examples to support your position.
5. What are the implications of international reciprocity for domestic reciprocity of CPAs? That is, within the United States, many states do not recognize the certification from another state. Will this change with the growth of international reciprocity?

6. Throughout the period of time covered in Part I of the text, accounting standard setting has gone through some changes. Describe the major events and which organizations were involved and indicate whether it was positive and negative for standard setting in general.

7. What advantages does the IASC have for becoming the world's accounting standard setter. Do you think this will happen?

8. Discuss the prospect of the replacement of U.S. GAAP with IAS from the perspective of:
   (a) United States financial statement preparers
   (b) financial statement users in the United States
   (c) U. S. auditors
   (d) accounting regulators in the United States

9. How do the FASB, the SEC, and the NYSE differ in their views of foreign firms listing on the NYSE? Whose view do you agree with?

RESEARCH PROJECT

Visit the FASB's web site (http://www.fasb.org) and consider the recent trend in contributions to the Financial Accounting Foundation. Has the trend over the past five years been up or down? What are the implications of this trend for the FASB?

NOTES

1 Beresford, Greenberg, Lowenstein, Zweig and Foust, Jenkins, Schroeder, and Lowenstein, respectively.
2 FAF, p. 7.
3 "Arthur Levitt Addresses 'Illusions.'"
4 Williams.
5 Much of this section is based on Evans, M Taylor, and Rolfe.
6 Gyllenhammar, p. 61.
7 Zachary.
8 Feldstein.
9 Heeter.
10 Cornell and Weatherholt.
11 Heeter, p. 72.
12 Sesit.
13 Ibid.
14 Phillips, et al.
15 Bitton and Goligoski, p. 26.
16 Chairman's Review.
17 Financial Accounting Standards Board, *A Report on the Similarities and Differences*.
18 Strategic Finance. The report is also available at www.ifad.net.
19 Barlas, p. 10.
20 Burton.
21 MacDonald.
22 Adapted from Evans, Taylor, and Rolfe, p. 13.
23 "FASB Supports IASB Efforts," p. 1.
24 Miller, Redding, and Bahnson, p. 176.
25 Based on Foster, pp. 25–26, 52–53.

REFERENCES

"Arthur Levitt Addresses 'Illusions.'" *Journal of Accountancy* (December 1998), 12–13.
Barlas, S. "Levitt on International Standards," *Management Accounting* (February 1997): 10.

Beresford, Dennis. "Frustrations of a Standards Setter." *Accounting Horizons* (December 1993): 70–76.

———. "How Should the FASB Be Judged?" *Accounting Horizons* (June 1995): 56–61.

———. "It's Time to Simplify Accounting Standards." *Journal of Accountancy* (March 1999): 65–67.

Bitton, V. and R. Goligoski. "Breaking the Language Barrier to Cross-Border Capital Formation." *Perspectives on Business 1997* (Deliotte & Touche, LLP, 1997): 26.

Burton, L. "All Accountants Soon May Speak the Same Language," *The Wall Street Journal* (August 29, 1995): A15.

Chairman's Review. "A Very Happy Moment for IASC," *Insight* (The Newsletter of the International Accounting Standards Committee) (June 2000): 1–2.

Cornell, D. and N. Weatherholt. "Making the Most of NAFTA." *Journal of Accountancy* (January 1995): 53–58.

Evans, T., M. Taylor, and R. Rolfe. *International Accounting and Reporting*, Third Edition. Houston, TX: Dame Publications. 1999.

Feldstein, Martin. "Europe's Monetary Union: The Case Against the EMU." *The Economist* (June 13, 1992): 19.

Financial Accounting Foundation. *1999 Annual Report of the Financial Accounting Foundation*. Norwalk, CT: Financial Accounting Foundation, 2000.

Financial Accounting Standards Board. *A Report on the Similarities and Differences between IASC Standards and U.S. GAAP.* Norwalk, CT: Financial Accounting Standards Board, 1997.

———. "FASB Supports IASB Efforts." *Financial Accounting Series No. 217-B* (February 28, 2001): 1.

Foster, George. *Financial Statement Analysis*, Second Edition. Englewood Cliffs, NJ: Prentice Hall, 1986.

Greenberg, Herb. "The Auditors Are Always Last to Know." *Fortune* (August 17, 1998): 228–229.

Gyllenhammar, P. "The Global Economy: Who Will Lead Next?" *Journal of Accountancy* (January 1993): 61.

Heeter, C. "NAFTA Opens New Markets for CPA's." *Journal of Accountancy* (March 1994): 69–72.

Jenkins, Holman Jr. "Stand Back, the SEC Is Going to Fix Accounting." *The Wall Street Journal* (May 28, 1996): A19.

Kulish, Nicholas. "Foreign Direct Investment Saw Slowed Growth in '99." *The Wall Street Journal* (October 4, 2000): A23.

Lowenstein, Roger. "Can FASB Be Considered Antibusiness?" *The Wall Street Journal* (March 21, 1996): C1.

———. "Corporate America Bullies FASB, Part II." *The Wall Street Journal* (September 11, 1997): C1.

MacDonald, Elizabeth. "U.S. Firms Likely to Balk at SEC Move to Ease Listing of Foreign Companies." *The Wall Street Journal* (February 18, 2000): A3, A4.

Miller, P., R. Redding, and P. Bahnson. *The FASB, the People, the Process, and the Politics,* Fourth Edition. Boston: Irwin McGraw Hill, 1998.

Phillips, M., M. Sesit, and S. Ascarelli, "Foreign Investors Jittery Over Holidays, Begin Pulling Some Funds from the U.S.," *The Wall Street Journal* (September 26, 2001): B14.

Schroeder, M. "SEC List of Accounting—Fraud Probes Grows," *The Wall Street Journal* (July 6, 2001): C1.

Sesit, M. "Going Global." *The Wall Street Journal* (May 28, 1996): R23, R24.

Williams, Kathy. "SEC's Levitt Renews Call for Quality Financial Reporting." *Strategic Finance* (November 1999): 27.

"World Accounting Rules." *Strategic Finance* (March 2001): 67.

Zachary, G. P. "Global Growth Attains a New, Higher Level That Could Be Lasting." *The Wall Street Journal* (March 31, 1997): A1, A8.

Zeff, Stephen A. "A Perspective on the U.S. Public/Private-Sector Approach to the Regulation of Financial Reporting." *Accounting Horizons* (March 1995): 52–70.

Zweig, Philip and Foust, Dean. "Corporate America Is Fed Up With FASB." *Business Week* (April 12, 1997): 108–109.

INTRODUCTION

In the second part of this text, the attention is shifted to contemporary accounting topics; however, Part 2 is based on Part 1. That is, after studying the chronological development of standard setting and theory formulation, a better understanding of how much difficulty accountants have encountered in making progress in both theory formulation and standard setting has developed. The text has shown that, unfortunately, both processes have been troublesome and somewhat flawed. (That is not being critical; it is just stating the facts.)

In light of this, it is understandable that many of the current accounting standards are similarly flawed. This part contains a critical examination of selected areas to find those flaws and understand what remains to be done to improve GAAP and financial reporting.

The topics are not approached from the technical level; there is no emphasis on debits and credits or journal entries, for example. Instead, the approach is from the standpoint of theory, especially the FASB's Conceptual Framework. The theoretical concepts studied in Part 1 are applied, especially the definition of the ten elements in SFAC No. 6, to current accounting practices.

Recall from Part 1 that theory has three major purposes:

(1) to explain current practice;
(2) to evaluate current practice; and
(3) to facilitate the development of future practice.

In Part 2, we focus on the second and third purposes of theory. This section begins with Chapter 9, which deals with a historically important area—accounting for income. This area has been controversial and is currently undergoing massive changes.

CHAPTER 9

ACCOUNTING FOR INCOME

LEARNING OBJECTIVES

After studying this chapter, you should be able to

> Understand the nature of income.

> Appreciate the difficulty in measuring income.

> Distinguish between the matching and asset-liability approaches to accounting income.

> Describe comprehensive income.

> Understand the controversy over revenue recognition.

Historically, the determination of net income has been the hallmark of accounting. It has been the central core of accounting since the 1930s. If anything "marks" the accountant, the procedure for calculating net income certainly does. Accounting for income has been controversial. In the past, accounting for net income was dominated by the ideas of matching, periodicity, and the related concept, historical cost. But all that is expected to change because of the FASB's Conceptual Framework project and a series of recent SFASs that challenge two concepts, matching and historical cost, as the cornerstone of income determination.

Before accounting for a given phenomenon, accountants should first attempt to understand that phenomenon. Surely, the better accountants understand what they are trying to account for, the better will be their accounting. Unless it is understood what net income is, it cannot be accurately accounted for. To obtain information about the nature of income, we must turn outside accounting to economics and related fields.

To prepare you for some difficulty ahead, two aspects of income should be noted. First, income is an artificial concept. That is, it was invented by accountants and economists but does not really exist. It is an artifact, something created by man; it does not exist in nature. Second, as a concept, it does not refer to anything specific in the existing world. If we talk about accounting for a piece of machinery or delivery truck, these exist in the world and the concept of a delivery truck as an asset can be referenced to the actual vehicle. But that is not the case with net income. Because of these reasons, you should be warned that understanding the nature of income can be a little difficult.

INCOME CONCEPTS

BASIC NATURE

Let's begin with the basic notion of income. In its most basic form, income (or net income) is anything that satisfies our needs or wants. Because people are motivated by wants and needs, the satisfaction of these wants and needs produces a sense of well-being, and income is the result of these actions to satisfy wants and needs.

This definition is obviously very broad and all-inclusive and therefore income becomes very personal and subjective. But we must understand that this basic definition of income is what income really boils down to. Many things qualify as income under this definition that would not be monetary or considered as income in a traditional sense.

To help you understand this definition better, take a minute to think about the following question:

> *Assuming that you are currently employed, what one change in your job would make you the happiest in the next six-month period?*

Your answer to this question can take many forms: a different boss, a parking space that's closer to your building, a faster computer, a window for your office, better relations with colleagues, a higher salary, better fringe benefits, a bonus. Notice that not all of the answers are monetary, although some are. Instead, they refer to conditions about the nature of your job or the people you work with. This simple exercise shows that the basic definition shown above is true. Income is whatever meets your needs or satisfies your wants. For some people, that is money—more money means greater happiness. But for others, other things count more than money. They all represent income. This is the nature of income in its broadest sense.

BASIC DEFINITIONS

Using this very subjective and broad definition of income, you can image how difficult it would be to measure the income for individuals or, even more, for business entities. So much of what meets our needs are economic goods and services. These economic goods and services can be measured or expressed in dollars and cents. Very early in the economic history of man, economists became interested in the issues of income and measuring income. As a result, the economic idea of wealth (a stock of economic resources at a point in time) plays a major role in the definition and measurement of income.

One of the first definitions of income was founded on this idea of wealth. Adam Smith, in *The Wealth of Nations* published in 1776, defined income as an "increase in wealth." Income was seen as a flow of economic resources (changing over time) that made the wealth (a stock of economic resources) larger.

A later and often-cited definition of income is that of economist Sir John R. Hicks in *Value and Capital* published in 1939. His definition of income was

> *"a person's income is the maximum amount that he can consume during a week and still expect to be as well off at the end of the week as he was at the beginning."*[1]

Hicks's simple definition has many elements. Notice that income represents a flow of resources that can be consumed without affecting the stock of resources, or wealth. That wealth is undisturbed by the consumption of resources that represent the income. Two examples will illustrate how this definition works.

In simple terms, if you began the week with $100 and received another $200 during the week, then your income for the week would be $200—the maximum you could spend without diminishing the $100. If you spent $250, you would end the week with $50, which is less than when you started the week. Note that you don't have to spend the $200 to make it income; you could only spend $80, and end the week with $220. The $220 becomes your new wealth measure, which is used to define your income for the next week.

Suppose you start off a month with a portfolio of investments of $100,000, and the dividends from that portfolio total $6,500 during the month. Market prices are steady, and your portfolio is worth $100,000 at month's end. According to Hicks's definition, your income is $6,500. If you spend it, your portfolio stays at $100,000. If you spend $7,500, then your portfolio would decline to $99,000.

In financial terms, the aspect of Hicks's definition of income that doesn't allow the reduction of the beginning wealth measure is called *capital maintenance*. That is, you do not erode the beginning measure of wealth. Income, as defined by Hicks, doesn't emerge until the capital is maintained ($100 and $100,000 in our two examples). In this way, income is a return *on* capital, not a return *of* capital.

Hicks's definition of income is often considered the basis for the definition of accounting income. But this definition is not friendly to accounting nor is it compatible with the methods accountants use to determine net income. The process accountants use is much more subjective than most people think. Notice that the whole definition hinges on expectations: ". . . and still expect. . . ." Expectations do not easily subject themselves to measurement. In addition, note how subjective another element of the definition is: ". . . as well off. . . ." Exactly how do you measure "well off-ness"? Although Hicks's definition shows the essential character of income, it is not easily applied and measured. The following example helps to illustrate the problems:

Jon and Jeff Example   The subjective nature of income and the difficulties of measuring it can be illustrated with the following example.

> *Suppose there are two baseball card collectors, Jon and Jeff. In baseball card collecting you must understand the difference between: (1) A complete set—a collection of cards that contains all the players for all major league teams during a season. Often a complete set is factory-sealed; it has not been opened, which makes it the most valuable. (2) An incomplete set—a collection of cards that has one or more missing elements. (3) Commons—cards (often duplicates) that are easily traded and of little value by themselves.*

> *Suppose that Jeff has been collecting cards longer than Jon and has 1,000 complete sets, 100 incomplete sets, and 1,500 commons. Jon has 20 complete sets, 4 incomplete sets, and 500 commons. While trading with each other, each trades a common card that, in turn, completes an incomplete set. Jeff now has 1,001 complete sets, and Jon has 21 complete sets.*

Based on this scenario, our basic question concerns the measurement of income in the transaction: As a result of the trade, did Jon have income? Did Jeff have income? If both had income, what was the relationship between the two net incomes? Were they equal, or was one greater than the other?

This is a simple situation involving the basic definition of income. Using it, the conclusion is that both have income because both agreed to trade and both came out of the trade ahead, as reflected in a larger number of completed sets.

Consider the relationship of their incomes. Were both incomes equal, or did one have more income than the other? This is more difficult to answer. Some would say that the increase from 1,000 to 1,001 completed sets for Jeff was less satisfying than the increase from 20 to 21 completed sets for Jon. Others would argue that Jeff's increase was more satisfying. Some might believe that without any dollar amount associated with the trade, you can't really measure net income or determine the relationship of their incomes.

So, let's add more details to the situation and further complicate it by adding numbers to satisfy the accountants.

> *Suppose that the common card that Jon traded to Jeff had a market value of $4.50 and the common card that Jeff traded to Jon was worth $3.00.*

Now, reconsider the questions: Who had income, and what was the relationship of their incomes? Notice the effect on this example that the introduction of numbers causes. From a strict accounting standpoint, Jon had a $1.50 loss on the trade ($4.50 card given up for $3.00 card received) and Jeff had a gain of $1.00. The introduction of numbers changes the scenario in which both Jeff and Jon had income, as well as changes the answers to the earlier questions. Notice the impact that the introduction of numbers had on Jon's situation: Jon had a loss, even though he voluntarily made the trade and it increased his number of completed sets. Another complication is discussed next.

> *Suppose additionally that the newly completed set for Jeff has a market value of $30 more than the market value of the incomplete set, whereas Jon's newly completed set has increased in market value $45 more than the incomplete set.*

Reconsider the original questions: Who had net income, and what was the relationship of their incomes? Notice how introducing the market values for the completed sets affected this example. Using the market values given, both Jeff and Jon had income; Jon had more income because his set's market value ($45) was higher than Jeff's ($30).[2] The introduction of market values produces results that are the opposite to the results from the introduction of market values for the individual cards traded. This example shows how the determination of net income can become complicated and controversial.

This example also illustrates an important point. Accountants must be very careful that their measurement of net income does not change the underlying phenomenon that they are attempting to measure. This is often an issue with many measurement systems.

Range of Income Concepts   In an important article, Philips explained the trade-off between the true definition of income and the need to measure it.[3] He believed that almost all of the major controversies in accounting could be traced back to differences in what should be considered income and that progress in accounting theory must begin with income concepts. Philips stated that it would be better to have a single rather than a variety of concepts of income. He proposed *accretion income* as that single concept. He viewed it as an all-purpose income concept that applied equally well to accounting and taxation. Philips believed that a general acceptance of the accretion concept of income would have significant effects on accounting practice as well as theory.

Income under the accretion concept was defined as an increase in economic power based on market values. To support his points, Philips described five different income concepts.

1. *Psychic income.* This is purely subjective income; income is what you think it is. It is based on utility and personal well-being and is inseparable from consumption. One person's income would not necessarily be the same type as another's. It is very personal and subjective. But Philips believed that only psychic income could claim to represent true income.

2. *Economic present value income.* This income is measured by taking the discounted present value of future receipts. To accomplish this, you need to know the future cash receipts and the appropriate discount rate. Noneconomic factors are not included. Present value income suffers from problems of uncertainty about the future.

3. *Accretion income.* This income is an increase in economic power, measured by the change in the market values of assets. Income is the difference in market values over time. Accretion income recognizes income if the increase in value is reasonably measurable.

4. *Accrual income.* Based on a market transaction, accrual income relies on outside exchanges. It recognizes revenue when earned and expenses when incurred. Matching represents this type of income.

5. *Cash income.* This income is strictly objective. It is based on cash inflows and outflows. Cash realization is the only trigger for recognition of income.

Philips considered these income concepts as on a continuum. As you moved from psychic to cash income, the objectivity of the measurement increased; however, as you moved from psychic to cash, the conceptual reasonableness decreased. So there is a trade-off.

If the emphasis is theory, the most conceptual approach to income is psychic, which is consistent with the basic definition given previously. However, if the main objective is to measure income and do so with objectivity (reliability or verifiability), then cash income is the best.

Given those conditions, the adoption of a particular income concept involves sacrificing either some support or justification from theory or the ability to objectively measure the income. The presence of a trade-off illustrates why measuring income is almost always controversial.

Philips concluded that accounting should move from using accrual income to accretion income, which would lessen the objectivity of income measurement but increase the conceptual reasonableness of the measure. He believed that because the accretion concept defines income as an increase in economic power, which can be measured with reasonable objectivity, it is superior to accrual accounting. The accretion concept is a realization-based concept in the sense that a change in economic power is recognized (realized) whenever it can be reasonably measured. As the accretion concept emphasizes market values as measures, Philips believed it is the best all-purpose income concept for accountants to use.

IMPORTANCE OF INCOME

To complicate matters, consider the role in and importance of income to society and the economy. It has been the central measure of accounting for more than sixty years. For example, income is important to society and our economy as a basis for taxation, in formulating broad social programs, and determining stock prices; to appraise the operating performance of a business entity; to determine creditworthiness and measure the efficiency of the firm; and as a guide to prudent investment and the firm's dividend policy. Income measures permeate almost all society; hardly any areas exist where income is not important for decision making.

APPROACHES TO ACCOUNTING FOR INCOME

As important as income is to society, and to accounting, it's very important to understand the two approaches to the measurement of income that have been developed by accountants. These two approaches, matching and asset-liability, are discussed in the following sections.

THE MATCHING APPROACH

Historically, the matching approach has been accountants' methodology for determining net income. Matching involves selecting a time period, bringing together the revenues earned during a period of time, and matching them against the expenses incurred to produce those revenues. In a sense, using time as a boundary, matching attempts to bring together effort (expenses) and the resulting accomplishments (revenues) to determine net income. It uses cause (expense) and effect (revenue) and calculates net income as the algebraic difference.

The Venture Basis   Matching can be traced back to the *venture basis* of business that was popular during the Renaissance. At that time, much business was conducted on a venture-by-venture basis. Instead of having business firms that lasted a long time, business firms were created to complete a single particular project or task and then disbanded when the task was done. It was easy to measure the net income of each venture because the venture had a beginning and an end.

For example, suppose a number of business entrepreneurs in Italy get together to form a particular venture. They pool their capital resources (1,000 gold coins), buy a ship (200), hire a captain and crew, buy Italian leather goods (800), put them aboard the ship, and sail the ship to England. In England, they sell the Italian leather goods (for 900), buy English wool cloth (for 900), and sail back to Italy. In Italy they sell the English wool cloth (for 1,300), sell the ship (250), pay off the captain and crew (100), and divide the remaining capital proceeds (1,450). The investors are then free to invest in other ventures.

In this example, it's fairly straightforward to calculate net income of 450 gold coins (1,450 proceeds – 1,000 investment) because there is a finite beginning and an end. All the costs that were incurred were directly related to the venture and paid off in cash at its conclusion. It was neat and tidy from an accounting viewpoint.

However, applying the venture basis idea to a business firm today is more difficult due to a number of factors. First, business firms, especially corporations, are not disbanded after a single venture; instead, they operate continuously over a number of time periods. Second, many costs are common costs, which cannot be directly related to a particular function of the business. Third, at any point in time, some costs have been paid and others have not.

Matching attempts to overcome these difficulties and still provide a solid basis for determining net income using measures of revenues and expenses. Revenues are measures of what the firm accomplished, and expenses are measures of what the firm expended to produce the revenues.

Paton and Littleton   The greatest proponent of matching was written by Paton and Littleton, *An Introduction to Corporate Accounting Standards*, in 1940.[4] This important work in accounting can be characterized as "the gospel of matching." According to Paton and Littleton, the primary purpose of accounting is the measurement of period net income through the systematic process of matching costs and revenues. Although business is continuous and income is a stream, the stream must be broken up into convenient time sections for measurement purposes. Matching is the crucial phase of accounting, and the Income Statement is the primary financial statement. Paton and Littleton believed that matching was objective because it was based on recorded costs, which represented objectively determined data, based on evidence. Revenue and expenses were events that really happened.

Evaluation of the Matching Approach   Matching dominated accounting from 1930 until the late 1990s. Matching measured net income as revenue minus expenses. To be counted, the revenue must be realized or realizable and the expenses incurred. Cash inflows and outflows were unnecessary.

Matching has five characteristics.

1. It is based on transactions, outside exchanges of things of value.
2. It focuses on a period of time and measured net income for that particular period.
3. To be used in matching, revenue has to be realized or realizable. An asset must have resulted.
4. The expenses are based on historical cost, the amount expended for the item.
5. Matching appears logical.

This method had advantages, which is why it survived for about sixty years. It appeared to be objective and verifiable. It was thought to be conservative. And matching was consistent with the stewardship basis of accounting.

However, there were also disadvantages. Matching did not recognize unrealized increases in assets. The net income figure was not comparable across firms due to alternative cost computations. Its emphasis was on objectivity, not relevance. It put primacy on the Income Statement, and relegated the Balance Sheet to a place for items that were not yet ready to be matched on the Income Statement. Revenues and expenses were enigmatic.

In matching, the two components were vague. Often, revenue was defined as "something" that resulted from the sales of products or rendering of services. But the "something" was not precisely defined. Similarly, expenses were often described as the cost expended to create the revenue or as costs expired in the production of revenue, nothing precise. Notice how expense was defined circularly with revenue. Because revenue was vaguely defined, the definition of expenses was vague too.

Under matching, net income resulted from the matching process. Revenues and expenses are the primary measures, and assets and liabilities are derived as the consequences of revenues and expenses. As shown in Exhibit 9.1, the independent factors are revenues and expenses, whereas the dependent factors are assets and liabilities. The Balance Sheet contains assets and liabilities and other things that are necessary for matching, but the Income Statement is primary.

EXHIBIT 9.1

Comparison of the Matching and Asset-Liability Approaches

Approach	Independent Factors	Dependent Factors
Matching	Revenues and expenses	Assets and liabilities
Asset-Liability	Assets and liabilities	Revenues and expenses

Concerns with matching appeared in the mid-1970s. These concerns were summarized in an article written by Most.[5] He noted that evidence was building that accounting was relying less and less on matching as a concept. He foresaw the shift from matching to the asset-liability approach described in the following section.

The Asset-Liability Approach   The second approach to income determination is the asset-liability approach. It was developed after the matching approach. Using this approach, net income is determined by measuring the change in the net assets of the firm (assets minus liabilities) over time. Therefore, it calculates net income based on Balance Sheet measures rather than the Income Statement measures as matching does.

In this approach, earnings result as a consequence of changes in assets and liabilities, and revenues and expenses occur as a result. Note in Exhibit 9.1, that with this approach, the assets and liabilities are independent and the revenues and expenses, dependent. Assets are viewed as economic resources of the firm that represent future economic benefits to the firm. Assets are the primary measure under the asset-liability method.

The asset-liability approach views revenues as inflows of assets into the firm from the sale of its product or rendering of its service. Expenses are outflows of assets expended to produce revenues. Net income is, therefore, the change in net assets over time.

You can see how this works by recalling what you learned in your first financial accounting course, Principles of Financial Accounting. Early in the course, as you learned about transactions and how to prepare financial statements from them, you probably encountered a homework assignment that presented you with a trial balance and then asked you to prepare a Balance Sheet and Income Statement. Because the Balance Sheet was listed first, you probably tried to prepare that statement first. But it wouldn't balance because it was off by the amount of the net income, which we normally determine first on the Income Statement and then add to Retained Earnings so the Balance Sheet balances. But why doesn't it balance before we add net income? Because net income is already there, reflected in the increased balances of the net assets of the firm. By adding the net income to Retained Earnings, all you are doing is recognizing the increase in the net assets as part of the owners' equity account and balancing the statement.

For example, suppose the following is the trial balance of the Becky Corporation at the end of the current year:

	Dr.	Cr.
Cash	10	
Accounts Receivable	15	
Merchandise Inventory	20	
Prepaid Expenses	5	
Plant Assets	30	
Accumulated Depreciation		10
Accounts Payable		10
Long-Term Debt		25
Common Stock		20
Retained Earnings		10
Revenue		90
Depreciation Expense	15	
Wages Expense	40	
Supplies Expense	30	
Totals	165	165

If you attempted to prepare the Balance Sheet for Becky Corporation from this trial balance, it would not balance. The net assets total $70 ($10 + 15 + 20 + 5 + 30 – 10), whereas the liabilities total $35 ($10 + 25) and the owners' equity, $30 ($20 + 10). The Balance

Sheet is off by $5. That $5 is exactly equal to the net income of the firm ($90 − 15 − 40 − 30). When the net income of $5 is added to Retained Earnings, the Balance Sheet will balance. This simple example shows that net income already exists in the assets of the firm before net income is calculated on the Income Statement.

Evaluation of Asset-Liability Approach   This approach is seen as conceptually superior to matching. Under this approach, assets and liabilities are primary, and they are real. Revenues and expenses are not real; they do not have a real-world counterpart. Revenues and expenses are an accounting construct or artifact, developed to facilitate matching. But assets and liabilities do exist and thus are a better basis for determining net income.

The asset-liability approach is seen as more flexible and accommodating than matching. Assets and liabilities can be measured at values other than historical cost. This allows accounting to use fair market values for assets and liabilities and to measure the change in assets in the period in which they occurred rather than waiting for an outside transaction to occur as with matching. This makes the asset-liability approach more adaptive.

The asset-liability approach is also more consistent with the new view of accounting. It reflects the new economy better than matching. (In fact, matching was a key component of the old view of accounting.) The asset-liability approach appears more consistent with the emphasis on macroeconomics. This consistency is discussed more fully in a later section.

Another reason for the importance of the asset-liability approach is that the FASB adopted it for the Conceptual Framework project, which is consistent with the FASB's emphasis on the new view of accounting. This is reflected in SFAC No. 6, as is explained next.

SFAC NO. 6: COMPREHENSIVE INCOME

In SFAC No. 6 (1985), the ten elements of financial statements are listed. The FASB adopted the asset-liability approach for its definition of income, called comprehensive income. *Comprehensive income* is the change in equity (net assets, defined as assets minus liabilities) of a business enterprise during a period of time from transactions and other events and circumstances from nonowner sources. Comprehensive income is a broad concept of income; income represents a return on financial capital. It results from exchange transactions and other transfers between the firm and other entities that are not its owners; from the productive efforts of the firm; and from price changes, casualties, and other effects of interactions between the firm and its economic, legal, social, political, and physical environment. (Matching was included in SFAC No. 6 as one a means of recognizing expenses.)

SFAS No. 6 represented a major switch from matching to the asset-liability approach and from the Income Statement to the Balance Sheet as the primary financial statement. The Balance Sheet becomes more important because its focus is on the measurement of the net assets of the firm.

Recall that comprehensive income was the most controversial aspect of the FASB's definitions of the ten elements when it first appeared in 1980 as part of SFAC No. 3. Concerns were raised about the following aspects:

•   It represented a major departure from matching.

- It was a broad concept of income, inclusive of many components that were not a part of income before.
- It was based on the primacy of assets and liabilities not revenues and expenses.
- It included events and circumstances in addition to transactions. Events and circumstances were broadly defined and were viewed with alarm by both auditors and statement preparers. The auditors saw them as causing greater audit risk and more opportunity for management to "smooth" net income. Statement preparers were concerned that these new elements would introduce more variability into net income.
- It was seen as a way of introducing current market values into accounting.

REPORTING COMPREHENSIVE INCOME

The FASB showed their support for comprehensive income by issuing SFAS No. 130, "Reporting Comprehensive Income" (1997).[6] This SFAS requires firms with certain gains and losses (such as unrealized holding gains and losses on available-for-sale securities and foreign currency translation adjustments) to measure comprehensive income in addition to the traditional income measure (using matching). Comprehensive income may be reported in three ways, but the FASB preferred that it be reported in a combined statement of financial performance that would show net income followed by other comprehensive income. An example of this is shown in Exhibit 9.2, highlighting comprehensive income.

EXHIBIT 9.2
Combined Statement of Comprehensive Income

The Vince Company Combined Statement of Comprehensive Income For the Year Ended December 31, 20XX	
Revenue From Sales	$400,000
Cost of Goods Sold	300,000
Gross Margin	$100,000
Selling and Administrative Expenses	45,000
Net Income	$ 55,000
Currency Translation Adjustment (debit)	10,000
Unrealized Holding Gain, net of tax	5,000
Comprehensive Income	$ 50,000

The FASB was encouraged by many, including the Association for Investment Management and Research (AIMR), to develop a standard that required the disclosure of comprehensive income. As one of the largest and most influential group of users, AIMR believes firms should report more information on the changes in the market value of their assets, and comprehensive income is the best way to accomplish that objective. In a number of SFASs issued in the late 1990s, the FASB has required the disclosure of market values and changes in those values; the Comprehensive Income Statement is a convenient place to present those disclosures. Prior to the development of the Comprehensive Income Statement, such market value changes were reported in equity in an unorganized way. With the new statement, they are presented in an organized manner that allows users to focus on them.

Although SFAS No. 130 showed strong support for the asset-liability approach and comprehensive income and increased the visibility of comprehensive income, the flexibility in reporting comprehensive income allowed by SFAS No. 130 is a concern. Such flexibility could produce a lack of comparability as firms choose among the three alternatives. This lack of comparability might create confusion on the part of statement users and thus reduce the impact and importance of comprehensive income. Whether alternative formats produce confusion is an issue that should be tested in empirical research on this standard.

ELLIOTT'S THIRD WAVE OF ACCOUNTING

The consistency of the asset-liability approach with the new view of accounting is more clearly seen when we consider the article, "The Third Wave Breaks on the Shores of Accounting," by Elliott in 1992.[7] In this forward-looking article, Elliott applied the three-wave model of author Alvin Toffler in his book, *The Third Wave* (1991). Elliott saw three successive (and somewhat overlapping) periods of wealth creation in the world of business. The first wave was agricultural, the second industrial, and the third informational. Elliott believes that the world of business is now in the midst of its third wave and that the main change element is information technology (IT). Elliott believes that IT is changing everything in business—the way business is conducted and changing decisions that must be made—and accounting must adapt to this change or become obsolete. Because accounting information is an input factor for decision making, accounting must also change. This change affects accounting information both within and outside the firm. Changes in accounting will lead to changes in public accounting, accounting education, and accounting research.

Elliott is concerned that accounting is trying to supply information to third-wave firms (those managing in the IT environment) using accounting methods that were developed to meet the information needs of second-wave firms. In the second wave, manufacturing was dominant, the supply side of firms was the focus, firms had a hierarchical and rigid organization structure, decisions were made in a hierarchical manner strictly following the organization chart, tangible assets were dominant, and the emphasis was on past events.

In contrast, third-wave firms are characterized by the following:

- The emphasis is on information, processes, and resources.
- The focus is on soft assets, such as human capacity or research and development.
- The important measures are demand-related, such as value to the customer.
- Measures are in real-time, with immediate access to information.
- Organization structures are networked or matrix-based.
- Firms will use IT to get closer to their customers, to determine their needs and wants, and to satisfy such demand quickly.

In this environment and for these types of firms, second-wave accounting won't work. Elliott is concerned that accountants are not developing new methods consistent with the third wave.

In terms of income determination, Elliot saw wealth (defined as a stock of assets) as a first-wave concept. The determination of net income (which calculates the change in wealth) is a second-wave procedure. He believes that the third-wave income measure should focus on transformation, the rate of change in resources and processes. For income, it will be the rate of change in net income. That is more consistent with the asset-liability approach to net income. He challenged accountants to develop new methods of accounting to meet the informational needs of the third wave.

REVENUE REALIZATION AND RECOGNITION

One of the most difficult aspects of revenue measurement is the determination of when the firm earned it and when it can recognize revenue in the accounting records (accompanied by the receipt of an asset). The general principle that accountants use is that revenue is recognized when earned. But earning is a complicated process. For some firms, revenue is earned continuously; for others, it's earned when the firm accomplishes the major task (the critical event) it is in business to do. A major task can be the delivering of a product or the providing of a service or both.

To guide this revenue measurement process, four simple models of revenue recognition that accountants apply to the recognition of revenue have been developed.

1. *During production.* In some cases, firms earn revenue as they produce a product or prepare it for the customer. This applies to firms with long-term contracts. They use the percentage-of-completion method to recognize revenue. Many accruals are also in this category such as interest revenue, which is earned as time passes.
2. *At the end of production.* If the firm has a ready market for its product and that market cannot be influenced by the seller's product, then revenue can be recognized when production is completed. In general, the costs to complete the sale are minimal in these cases. Basically, the firm's major task is to produce the product. When that's complete, the revenue is earned. This approach applies to agricultural firms and firms in the extractive industry, for example.
3. *At the time of sale.* This is the traditional point of revenue recognition for firms that sell a product. At the point of sale, title passes to the customer and the sale is complete.
4. *After the sale is completed.* In rare cases, firms may delay recognizing revenue until it is collected in cash. This is especially true for situations in which there is significant risk associated with collection or the claim against the customer is of dubious validity.

REVENUE CONTROVERSY

Revenues were dominant component under matching. Recall that revenues are earned continuously by the firm but recognized when they have been earned through the accomplishment of the major task with a corresponding realization of an asset.

Revenues are an independent factor compared to expenses, which are dependent. This occurs because the matching procedure specified the following sequence of steps to calculate net income: First, you select a time period; second, you measure the revenues that were earned during that period; third, you measure the expenses that were incurred to produce those revenues; and finally, you match the revenues and expenses to determine the net income. This process demonstrates how dominant revenue is under the matching approach.

Given the importance of revenue to matching, it's significant to note that revenue recognition continues to be a controversial accounting topic, especially for the new high-tech firms of the new economy such as Internet firms. For example, each year the FASB surveys its board members, the FASB's director of research, members of FaSAC, and others to order its priorities and determine which topics should be on its agenda. Revenue recognition was the hot topic for 1999, as it was in previous years. This emphasis on revenue recognition was supported by the SEC. In fact, the SEC has been greatly concerned with revenue recognition in the past five years.

One factor that makes revenue recognition controversial is its importance. As important as income is, it's surprising to note the following observation about revenue recognition was made by SEC's chief accountant, Lynn Turner: "while revenue recognition represents the biggest item on the financial statement, it has the smallest amount of accounting rules governing it."[8] This comment shows the contrast between the importance of revenue recognition and the absence of guidance in that recognition. This contrast has been highlighted in recent years because of the accounting practices of a number of Internet firms.

As new forms of business, many Internet firms have encountered unusual revenue recognition situations. Because their financial results are so visible and the level of competition severe, many of these firms have overstated their revenues. And their methodologies have been criticized. Below are six examples of revenue recognition problems at Internet or high-tech companies. The first five were suggested by Kessler;[9] the sixth by Thurm and Weil:[10]

1. *Empty Cost of Goods Sold.* When Internet firms offer customers a discount on future purchases, they consider that discount as a marketing expense rather than an addition to the cost of goods sold of the next purchase or a reduction of revenue. If the discounts had been added to the cost of goods sold, gross margin would dramatically decrease. Similarly, if discounts had been treated as a reduction in revenue, gross margins would decrease. The treatment of future discounts as a market expense protects the gross margin from these effects.

2. *Logrolling.* Some Internet firms have turned the cash they received from their initial public offering (IPO) into sales by providing that cash to other firms (who need cash), which then agreed to buy the Internet firm's services in the future. As a result of this practice, the Internet firm trades the cash for revenue.

3. *Tweaking Knobs.* This occurred when Internet firms sold customers three years worth of service or software and reported all the revenue immediately. These long-term deals should be accounted for on a year-by-year basis, not counting all the revenue up front.

4. *Inflated Revenues.* Some Internet firms "juice up" their revenue numbers by including the total revenues from sales even when they are merely distributing products on behalf of other firms. The more proper treatment would be to report only the distribution fees they earned as revenue.

5. *Play Money.* This refers to the practice of some firms that trade banner advertising with other firms. Both firms count as revenue the value of the advertising and also record

that amount as an expense. Although the sum of the two is zero, by recording the revenue, the firm boosts its total revenue amount, which makes it appear that its market share is higher than it actually is.

6. *Inventory Charges.* Some high-tech firms wrote down the value of inventories of equipment because of a sharp slowdown of sales and did not include those write-down charges in pro forma net income. Pro forma net income is released to investors and analysts. Once written down, if demand rebounds and the inventory is sold, profits would show an increase.

These and other practices are bringing revenue recognition to the forefront of accounting again. The SEC, AICPA, and Emerging Issues Task Force (EITF) are all involved in trying to find solutions to these problems.

TWENTY-FIVE YEAR PERSPECTIVE ON INCOME

In light of the controversy over accounting for income, it is interesting to consider the perspective provided by Solomons, who wrote an article on the economic and accounting concepts of income in 1961.[11] In the article he contrasted the two concepts and examined proposals for their reconciliation. In general, economic income is based on concepts such as Hicks's and focuses on future receipts. Economic income is broad, encompassing unrealized changes in assets. Accounting income is narrower, based on matching, and focuses on the past. Matching relied heavily on realization. Solomons was unable to reconcile the differences between accounting and economic incomes satisfactorily. He concluded that the measurement of periodic income was not an effective tool. He stated that the periodic income measurement has already been superseded by other measures of performance, and he predicted that the next twenty-five years would see the twilight of income measurement.

His second article was written twenty-five years later as a follow-up to that prediction.[12] He concluded that nothing substantial had changed in regard to accounting for income during that period. Some minor changes were noted, such as the greater emphasis on components of income and segmented income statements. But these were changes in details; the fundamental nature of accounting income had not changed as he predicted. He noted the debate in 1987 between the "Balance Sheet school" of income and the "Income Statement school," but he did not predict how that would be resolved. He did suggest, however, that one bad call in twenty-five years stopped him from making any more predictions.

SUMMARY

Accounting for income has always been controversial. Income as a concept had its beginning in a subjective notion and was made more measurable by economists. Finally, accountants, through matching and historical cost, attempted to measure it precisely. The old matching approach has been replaced by the asset-liability approach. This approach appears to be more consistent with the new view of accounting and the third wave, as described by Elliott.

The change in income measurement is the result of the new view of accounting and the Conceptual Framework project of the FASB. Of course, no one expected accounting for income to be cast in concrete. Change has occurred in many areas of accounting, and accounting for income is not an exception.

But where that change is headed is uncertain. The movement toward some third-wave measure of income is unclear. But whatever the future for accounting for income, as Solomons concluded, predictions are risky.

REVIEW QUESTIONS

1. What two aspects of income make it a difficult topic to understand and account for?
2. What is the basic notion of income? What are the characteristics of the basic notion of income?
3. How did economists get involved in defining income?
4. What was Hicks's 1939 definition of income? What are some of the measurement problems associated with this definition?
5. What are the five income concepts that Philips listed?
6. How would you rank the ways that income is important to society and our economy mentioned in this chapter? Which do you think is the most important? The least important?
7. What are the two approaches to accounting income? How do the two approaches differ?
8. What are the advantages of the matching approach? The disadvantages?
9. Why did Paton and Littleton support matching?
10. What are the advantages of the asset-liability approach? The disadvantages?
11. Which do you prefer—the matching or the asset-liability approach? Why?
12. How did the FASB define comprehensive income in SFAC No. 6?
13. What concerns were raised about the definition of comprehensive income in SFAC No. 6?
14. How did the issuance of SFAS No. 130 support comprehensive income?
15. Do you agree with Elliott's conclusion that accounting is providing second-wave information to firms in the third wave? How can that be changed?
16. What four different models of revenue recognition have been used by accountants?
17. What are some of the revenue recognition problems of Internet and high-tech firms?
18. What are some of the SEC's concerns about revenue recognition issues in business firms today?
19. Do you agree with the change in emphasis from the Income Statement to the Balance Sheet?
20. Where do you picture accounting for income going in the future? What prediction would you make for the next twenty-five years?

DISCUSSION TOPICS

1. Do you agree with Philips that accounting should accept one concept of income rather than allow the use of a variety of concepts? Do you think this would improve accounting? Why or why not?

2. In Philip's range of income concepts, which income concept do you think accounting should adopt? Do you agree with Philips that the accretion concept is superior to accrual because it measures economic power based on market prices?

3. For each of the following situations, discuss the proper accounting treatment for revenue recognition:

   a. DottyKom Company gives each customer a $5 coupon that can be used on the next purchase from DottyKom if used within one week. When customers use their coupons, DottyKom considers the $5 as a marketing expense.

   b. Webb Company received $2 million from their IPO. They lent half of that to Buyer Company that then entered into a short-term purchase agreement with Webb for $1 million. Webb considered the $1 million as revenue.

   c. The Juice Company signed an agreement with Provider Company to distribute Provider's products through Juice's web site. As Juice distributes Provider's products, it recognizes the amount it receives as revenue.

   d. Banner Company signed an agreement with Streaming Company. Each agreed to display advertising from the other on its web site. They exchanged $10 million for the service. Banner considered the $10 million as revenue.

4. Rooms Gone is a new mega–furniture store located near a major metropolitan university, The University of Middle Florida (UMF). UMF is a junior and senior and graduate university. It admits no freshmen or sophomores. The vast majority of its students are transfers from junior colleges who start at UMF as juniors. Almost all the junior college students complete their bachelor's degrees in two years. The university has only a small number of living communities on campus, so almost all the students who attend the university must either live at home or rent unfurnished apartments that surround the university. Rooms Gone provides a complete apartment furniture package and allows the students to delay paying for two calendar years. In fall 2002, their business has been booming, with almost all their sales to UMF students.

   Discuss whether Rooms Gone should consider the furniture sales made to UMF students in August 2002 that are not to be collected until August 2004 as revenue in 2002.

5. Marilyn and Karen are avid coin collectors. Both have large collections. They frequently get together to trade coins. At a recent meeting and after much haggling, Marilyn traded a 1960 quarter to Karen for a 1950 dime.

   a. Based on the nature of income, did Marilyn and/or Karen have income as a result of this trade? What was the relationship between their incomes?

   b. Using the nominal values of the coins ($0.25 and $0.10) to measure the trade, does that change your answers?

   c. Suppose also that the market value of Marilyn's quarter was $4.00 and Karen's dime was $5.00. Does that change your answers?

6. Consider the quote of the SEC's chief accountant, Lynn Turner, presented in the chapter: "while revenue recognition represents the biggest item on the financial statement, it has the smallest amount of accounting rules governing it." Why do you think that the most significant item on the Income Statement has the fewest rules associated with it?

7. Consider the following situation: A. Deb is a super salesperson in a women's clothing shop. She keeps detailed records of all her customers on index cards, and feels she really knows the clothing tastes of her clients. When new merchandise comes in, she is

always the first salesperson to look over the new stock. Then she gets right on the phone to call her clients to tell them about the new arrivals. If she is successful in reaching one of her clients, she then describes a particular garment to the client and invites her customer into the store to try it on. A. Deb believes that the sale is made when her client answers the phone, not when they come into the store to try on the garment and agree to buy it. She maintains that she's such a good salesperson and knows her customers tastes so well that once the customer answers the phone, the sale is made. She knows that traditional revenue recognition in accounting occurs when the sale is actually made, but she disagrees. Do you agree or disagree with A. Deb's view as to the time of revenue recognition from the sale? Defend your position.

8. Consider the example of baseball card collectors Jeff and Jon in the chapter. Using the market values given to individual cards to determine net income, Jeff had a $1.00 gain and Jon had a $1.50 loss. But using the market values associated with the completed sets, Jeff had a gain of $30, whereas Jon had a gain of $45. Which sets of accounting income measures do you think is better: the measures based on market values for individual cards traded or the market values of the complete sets? Defend your choice.

9. **Application Problem.** Ready Manufacturing Company produces and sells product X to consumers. It generally maintains a showroom and inventory of product X at all times. The following information is about product X during October 20XX and the few days after:

Beginning inventory	$ 20,000	(10,000 units at $2.00 per unit)
October 20XX production costs	$600,600	(273,000 units at $2.20 per unit)
Ending Inventory	$????	(22,000 units)

The replacement cost of the inventory on October 1, 20XX, was $2.00 per unit. Ready values its inventory at cost (because it is always less than replacement value anyway). FIFO is the cost flow assumption for its GAAP financial statements.

   Revenues for October equaled $1,000,000. The replacement cost of the inventory on October 31 was $2.40 per unit. On November 7, 20XX, Ready sold the entire inventory of product X (all 22,000 units) for $70,000 cash. No other replacement activity took place during this time period. The inventory had a replacement cost of $2.42 on November 7, 20XX, however.

   What was the income for Ready for October 20XX and for the first seven days of November 20XX using the

   a. Accrual income concept (present GAAP).
   b. Accretion (market value) income concept.

10. **Application Problem.** For each of the following, discuss whether it is proper for Ace Electronics Company to record the particular amount of revenue according to GAAP:

   a. A customer purchased a television set from Ace in July 20XX for $600 (cash). However, since the customer was going on an extended vacation to another country, she asked Ace not to deliver the TV until August. Ace immediately recorded the $600 cash received as revenue in July.

   b. Ace sold a customer a computer and software for $3,000 in December 20XX. The customer paid a down payment of $1,800 and agreed to pay the balance by monthly installments beginning in January of the next year. The customer's credit rating is very good. Ace recorded only $1,800 as revenue for the year ended December 31, 20XX.

c. Ace repaired a customer's copy machine on December 28, 20XX. The customer was called on December 28 and told that the machine was ready for immediate pickup. However, the customer did not pick up the machine until January of the next year. Ace recorded the revenue from the repair in January when the customer picked up the machine and paid the $700 repair bill.

11. **Application Problem.** The Mountain Bike King Company, located in Boulder, Colorado, operates a training ground and exercise program for mountain bikers. Mountain Bike King owns 150 acres of land near the base of the Rocky Mountains on which it has constructed numerous mountain-bike trails. These trails are suited for bikers of all skills, ranging from beginners with limited stamina and skills to treacherous trails for the most experienced mountain bikers. Mountain Bike King sells two-year memberships for $300. The membership entitles bikers to an initial fitness assessment and individual program analysis and to unlimited use of the trails for the two-year membership period. Mountain Bike King employs a sales force of three people who operate on a straight 20 percent commission for each membership sold. The initial fitness assessment and individual program analysis is handled by the same individuals who maintain and operate the trail facility. Mountain Bike King typically sells many more memberships than the capacity of the trails because members frequently lose interest after the first three months and seldom use the trail facility thereafter.

Determine how Mountain Bike King should recognize revenue from a typical membership sale of $300. Your answer should include a discussion of the possible revenue recognition alternatives and a determination of which alternative is most appropriate for Mountain Bike King.

12. **Application Problem.** The City of Taintsville has recently repossessed a parcel of land and properties belonging to the Ace Chemical Company. Due to Ace's past activities, the city suspects there may be some hazardous waste contamination (both in the buildings and on the property) present. The city wants the buildings removed and the contamination cleaned up for a new public sports and recreation site; however, it does not want to pay for the unlimited cleanup costs. Consequently, with the help of the We Will Sue law firm, the city draws up a proposal that solicits contractors to bid on the demolition and contamination restoration project. The contractor will only receive the contract amount; therefore, the city has effectively shifted the potential sizable cleanup costs to the successful bidder. Act Contractors, with complete knowledge of the possible contamination, was the low bidder at $1,200,000. The contract is expected to take three years to complete. As an accountant for Act, how would you recommend that they account for this contract?

13. **Application Problem.** Act Builders is a small publicly traded construction company that specializes in disaster relief-type work. The firm has been especially successful, primary due to the efforts of Joe Workaholic, the office manager and principal bidder on most jobs. Joe has the ability to obtain the lowest bid without leaving too many profit dollars on the table. As one would anticipate, Joe has received some very attractive offers from Act's competitors. Consequently, Act, on January 2, 20X1, gave Joe 10,000 stock options with an option price of $45 per share and 6,000 stock appreciation rights,

which are payable in cash for the difference between the current market price and a $40 per share predetermined price. Both the stock options and the stock appreciation rights become exercisable on December 31, 20X4. In addition, Act has offered, in writing, to give Joe $60,000 cash on December 31, 20X4, if Joe is still in the employ of Act on that date. Act Builders's stock was trading at $50 on January 2, 20X1; $53 on December 31, 20X1; $55 on December 31, 20X2; $68 on December 31, 20X3; and $59 on December 31, 20X4.

In 20X3, Joe really messed up on a major bid for a large disaster relief project. Joe forgot some major items that needed to be covered and consequently bid extremely low. The bid was so low that the job resulted in a huge loss for Act and created a severe cash drain on the company. Joe continued in Act's employ, exercised his stock options and stock appreciation rights on December 31, 20X4, and promptly resigned on January 3, 20X5. No retirement party has yet been scheduled for Joe (nor is the prospect of a party very likely).

Determine what effects the above events with Joe would have had on the Income Statements for each of the calendar years 20X1 through 20X4 for Act Builders.

14. **Application Problem.** The Duece Company has had extremely good fortunes in its operations and has developed a significant cash balance. Because the present cash balance is in excess of its internal demands, it made the following investments during the current fiscal year:

a. It purchased some vacant land close to a growing retail area of the city. Duece paid $500,000 for the land but has received several offers from potential buyers already. The offers have ranged from $800,000 to $1,200,000. The property is appraised at $820,000.

b. Duece paid $300,000 for shares of stock in General Motors Corporation, and the shares' market value at year-end was $390,000. Duece has classified these shares as current assets, securities available for-sale.

c. It invested in the bonds payable of Ford Motor Company. The Ford bonds will mature in ten years, but Duece has no intention of keeping the bonds that long. Duece probably will keep the bonds for two or three years. Duece paid $500,000 for the bonds, but because of an interest rate fluctuation in the market, they are presently (at the end of the current fiscal year) only worth $460,000.

d. Duece purchased 40 percent of the outstanding shares of Johns Company for $400,000. Since that acquisition, Johns Company has declared and paid cash dividends totaling $20,000 and reported income of $60,000. The market value of the shares of stock in Johns Company at fiscal year-end was $410,000.

e. Land containing timber was purchased for $600,000. The land was valued at only $350,000, and $250,000 of the purchase price was attributable to the timber to be harvested. During the current year, the trees increased in size, and by year-end, the value of the future timber increased to $270,000. The land value remained fairly constant at $350,000.

How much income (on its Income Statement as a component of net income) should Duece recognize for the fiscal year just ended related to the above investments?

NOTES

1 Hicks, p. 172
2 It is recognized that the market values for individual cards and completed sets are arbitrary. Choosing different individual card and completed set market values could change the results. But the point of the example remains: Determining net income is complex and controversial.
3 Philips.
4 Paton and Littleton.
5 Most.
6 Financial Accounting Standards Board.
7 Elliott; see also R. Elliott and Peter Jacobson.
8 As quoted in MacDonald.
9 Kessler.
10 Thurm and Weil.
11 Solomons (1961).
12 Solomons (1987).

REFERENCES

American Accounting Association, 1964 Concepts and Standards Research Committee. "The Matching Concept." *Accounting Review* (April 1965): 368–372.

Beaver, William, and Joel S. Demski. "The Nature of Income Measurement." *Accounting Review* (January 1979): 38–45.

Beresford, Dennis, L. Todd Johnson, and Cheri Reither. "Is a Second Income Statement Needed?" *Journal of Accountancy* (April 1996): 69–72.

Elliott, Robert K. "The Third Wave Breaks on the Shores of Accounting." *Accounting Horizons* (June 1992): 61–85.

Elliott, Robert K. and Peter D. Jacobson. "U.S. Accounting: A National Emergency." *Journal of Accountancy* (November 1991): 54–58.

Financial Accounting Standards Board. "Reporting Comprehensive Income," *Statement of Financial Accounting Standards No. 130*. Norwalk, CT: FASB, 1997.

Hicks, J. R. *Value and Capital*. Oxford: Oxford University Press, 1939.

Johannes, Laura. "No Accounting for the Net? Profit Issue Sparks Conflict." *The Wall Street Journal* (May 19, 2000): C1.

Johnson, L. Todd, Cheri L. Reither, and Robert J. Swieringa. "Toward Reporting Comprehensive Income." *Accounting Horizons* (December 1995): 128–137.

Kessler, Andy. "Creative Accounting.com." *The Wall Street Journal* (July 24, 2000): A24.

MacDonald, Elizabeth. "Concerns on Internet Firms' Accounting Prompt SEC to Tighten Standards." *The Wall Street Journal* (November 18, 1999): A4.

Most, Kenneth. "The Rise and Fall of the Matching Principle." *Accounting and Business Research* (Autumn 1977): 286–290.

Paton, W. A., and A. C. Littleton. *An Introduction to Corporate Accounting Standards*. Sarasota, FL: American Accounting Association, 1940.

Philips, G. Edward. "The Accretion Concept of Income." *Accounting Review* (January 1963): 14–23.

Shwayder, Keith. "A Critique of Economic Income as an Accounting Concept." *Abacus* (August 1967): 23–35.

Smith, Pamela and Cheri Reither. "Comprehensive Income and the Effects of Reporting It." *Financial Analysts Journal* (November–December 1996): 14–19.

Solomons, David. "Economic and Accounting Concepts of Income." The *Accounting Review* (July 1961): 374–383.

_____. "The Twilight of Income Measurement: Twenty-Five Years On." *Accounting Historians Journal* (Spring 1987): 1–6.

———. "Criteria for Choosing an Accounting Model." *Accounting Horizons* (March 1995): 42–51.

Sprouse, Robert. "The Importance of Earnings in the Conceptual Framework." *Journal of Accountancy* (January 1978): 64–71.

Thurm, Scott, and Jonathan Weil. "Tech Companies Charge Now, May Profit Later." *The Wall Street Journal* (April 27, 2001): C1.

CHAPTER 10
ACCOUNTING FOR ASSETS

LEARNING OBJECTIVES

After studying this chapter, you should be able to

> Understand the importance of assets in the new view of accounting.

> Define an asset and describe its important characteristics.

> Compare and contrast the different values associated with assets.

> Identify concerns that have been raised about the definition of assets.

> Describe different ways of reporting assets on the Balance Sheet.

Part 2 focuses on issues associated with the assets, liabilities, and owners' equity reported on the Balance Sheet. The Balance Sheet is important for two reasons. First, even though the Income Statement was the most important statement to accounting in the past, most of the past accounting controversies were rooted in the Balance Sheet. Second, the FASB has adopted a Balance Sheet emphasis in issuing accounting standards. So it is an important focus for the rest of the book.

We begin with the basic definition of an asset, explore the implications and ramifications of that definition and then examine the controversies associated with assets.

THE NATURE OF ASSETS

Assets are centrally important to business entities. One view of the business firm is that it really can be defined as a collection of assets brought together for a purpose. Firms acquire assets from resource providers (investors and creditors) and transform them individually and in combination into products or services, which are then exchanged with other entities for other assets. This process is the central activity that produces worth, or utility, to the firm.

Similarly, assets are an important basic element of accounting. But it is usually easier to think of specific examples of assets rather than to think of a good basic definition. Accordingly, the definition of an asset should convey the basic nature of an asset.

Unfortunately, the chronological development of defining an asset in accounting was a difficult, but interesting, process. This process reveals the changes in the definition until the one that accountants now follow, which was set forth in the FASB's Conceptual Framework project in Statement of Financial Accounting Concepts (SFAC) No. 6, "Elements of Financial Statements." A time line listing the various definitions is shown in Exhibit 10.1.

EXHIBIT 10.1
Asset Definition Time Line

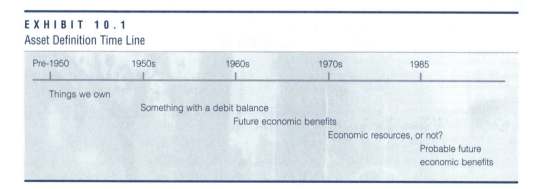

NEW IMPORTANCE

Before considering the definitions of asset described in subsequent sections, first you need to be aware of the special significance of assets. Because the FASB has adopted a Balance Sheet emphasis in issuing standards, this also means that the FASB has been changing the way accountants measure income, moving from the matching approach to the asset-liability approach. Under matching, the balance sheet was a holdover, a juncture between two Income Statements. Assets were placed there, awaiting future manifestation on the Income Statement via matching.

Now this has changed. The definition of assets has become of primary importance. No longer are assets just "leftovers" from the matching process; instead, assets are now in the forefront and are the prime determinants of net income. In the asset-liability approach to income measurement, net income is measured by the change in net assets (assets minus liabilities) during a time period after adjusting for transactions with owners and other comprehensive income items. In light of assets' primacy in determining net income, assets have a much higher status now under the new FASB approach compared to their role under matching.

In addition, one view of the definition of the ten elements in SFAC No. 6 considers assets being the most fundamental element.[1] This view considers assets as the primary element. All of the other definitions of elements are based on the definition of assets. For example, liabilities are negative assets, equities are defined as net assets (assets minus negative assets), and comprehensive income and its components (revenues, expenses, gains, and losses) are defined as changes in equity or net assets. Because all of the other elements are derived from the concept of assets, defining assets properly is a high priority in accounting theory. Thus it is vitally important that we define assets carefully. We need to carefully explore the implications of the following definitions of assets, keeping in mind their importance.

THINGS WE OWN

In its most fundamental form, the most frequent notion of assets is "things we own." Although this simple definition expresses the basic idea, it is seriously flawed, and we can build toward our understanding of the definition of an asset by examining those flaws. First, assets are not necessarily things; they can be intangible. The word "things" connotes something that has physical substance or form. Because it is normal for firms to have both tangible and intangible assets (surprisingly, the most common intangible asset is Accounts Receivable), a definition of assets that limits them to the tangible ones is incomplete.

Secondly, assets are not necessarily owned. As long as the firm has control, leased items can be considered assets. Legal ownership is not a correct requirement of the definition of an asset. All a firm needs to be able to do is control the item and have exclusive access to it. Given the flaws in the original simple definition, accountants progressed to other definitions.

DEBIT BALANCE "SOMETHINGS"

In an effort to improve over this basic notion of an asset, one of the earliest official definitions by the AICPA appeared in 1953 in its *Accounting Terminology Bulletin No. 1*:

> *Something represented by a debit balance that is or would be properly carried forward upon a closing of books of account. . . . on the basis that it represents either a property right or value acquired or expenditure made which . . . is applicable to the future.*[2]

On the positive side, this definition stated that assets represented property rights or values that apply to the future.

However, this definition has some major flaws: (1) the reliance on the technology of accounting to define an asset, as shown by the primacy of the phrase, "Something represented by a debit balance," (2) the vagueness of the components of value that make up an asset, "on the basis that it represents either a property right or value acquired or expenditure," and (3) the projection into the future with little guidance on how the future value benefits the firm. These limitations cause the definition to be not too helpful as stated.

FUTURE ECONOMIC BENEFITS

In 1962, Moonitz and Sprouse defined assets in Accounting Research Study (ARS) #3 as follows:

> *Assets represent expected future economic benefits, rights to which have been acquired by the enterprise as a result of some current or past transaction.*[3]

Moonitz and Sprouse further explained in ARS #3 that the benefit of an asset is expected, or in the future, conveying the idea that some degree of uncertainty is involved with assets. The benefits are economic in the sense that they are scarce and have value. The event that brought the asset into existence for the firm is a transaction—one that happens currently or happened in the past.

This definition combines the best of the previous definitions and therefore represents an improvement. It correctly put the emphasis on the economic benefits of assets and specified that assets represent future economic benefits. It also stopped the previous practice of including deferred charges and unexpired costs as assets. The essence of an asset is the benefit it produces or confers on its owner. Those economic benefits are in the future. The firm has a right to those benefits but does not necessarily have to own them. The right has been acquired by the firm in a transaction, past or present.

Unfortunately, when the Accounting Principles Board (APB) rejected ARS #1 and ARS #3 as too radical, it caused accountants to generally ignore this definition of assets.

ECONOMIC RESOURCES, OR NOT?

The next official definition of assets appeared in 1970 by the APB in Statement No. 4, "Basic Concepts and Accounting Principles Underlying Financial Statements of Business Enterprises."

> *Economic resources of an enterprise that are recognized and measured in conformity with generally accepted accounting principles. . . . Assets also include certain deferred charges that are not resources. . .*[4]

Notice that this definition is an improvement in the sense that assets are now elevated from "something" to economic resources, which is a broader concept. The notion of economic resources, which are scarce factors with economic value or worth, is closer to the real nature of assets.

But once again, the definition relies on the accounting measure of an asset to define the asset, and it concludes by contradicting itself. Based on this definition, you must conclude that assets are either economic resources or not economic resources! Although this definition represents an improvement over the previous ones, because of these flaws, this definition is still not too helpful in defining an asset.

SFAC NO. 6 DEFINITION AND REQUIRED ELEMENTS

Fortunately, the FASB's definition of assets in the Conceptual Framework in SFAC No. 6 reflects the best aspects of the past definitions. (Note the similarities in this definition of assets with ARS #3).

> *Assets are probable future economic benefits obtained or controlled by a particular entity as a result of past transactions or events.*[5]

The Conceptual Framework's definition of an asset has three important characteristics (other features of assets exist, but these three are the primary ones). All three must be present for an asset to be recognized:

1. *Probable future economic benefits in cash flows.* The essence of an asset is the existence of future economic benefits or service potentials that accrue to the firm. The specific benefit will contribute either directly or indirectly to the cash inflows of the entity and either individually or in combination with other assets.

   A key part of this definition is what is meant by "probable." This word was used to convey the notion of uncertainty that is associated with the benefits. The FASB, citing the standard dictionary definition, concluded that probable is what is "reasonably expected or believed on the basis of available evidence or logic but is neither certain nor proved."[6] A more precise meaning was not provided; this choice is a controversial aspect of the definition.

2. *Controlled by the firm.* The entity in question has obtained the benefit and can control others' access to it. The firm must have a claim on those rights or services and can exclude others from using the asset or share the benefit with others. The entity does not need to legally own the item to control it.

3. *Past transaction or event has created the benefit.* The asset must have been created by a past transaction or event. This event must have already happened. Occurrence of an event or transactions is the trigger to the recognition of the asset.

Of these three essential characteristics, the first, the existence of future economic benefits, is the most important, and it leads to a further consideration of the nature of the benefit. Where did it come from and in what form does it exist? How can we be sure the benefit is real?

SOURCE AND EVIDENCE OF THE BENEFIT

To amplify the meaning of future economic benefit, the source of that benefit must be considered. According to SFAC No. 6, the future economic benefit of an asset can be embodied in the following three values:[7]

1. *Exchange value*—the firm can receive something in exchange for the asset.
2. *Production value*—the firm can use the asset to produce something else of value.
3. *Acceptance value*—the firm can use the asset to settle a liability.

What evidence of the benefit can be found? According to SFAC No. 6, evidence of the existence of the benefit can be based on three factors.[8]

1. *Market value*—the asset is commonly bought and sold in a market. The item can be

bought and sold individually or in combination with other assets, commonly called a *basket* purchase or sale.

2. *Acceptability*—the asset can be used to settle a liability or debt; it would be commonly accepted by a creditor or lender to discharge a debt.

3. *Productivity*—the asset can be used to produce tangible or intangible goods and services with market value or common acceptability.

SFAC No. 6 also noted that the incurrence of cost (economic sacrifice) may also be evidence of the acquisition or enhancement of future economic benefits associated with an asset.

To help apply the concepts about the characteristics of an asset, consider the following situation.

ASSET DISCUSSION CASE: THE LOTTERY TICKET

Taking a Long Shot . . .[9]   To supplement donations collected from its general community solicitation, Tri-Cities United Charities holds an Annual Lottery Sweepstakes. In this year's sweepstakes, United Charities is offering a grand prize of $1,000,000 to the 1 winning ticket holder. A total of 10,000 tickets have been printed, and United Charities plans to sell all the tickets at a price of $150 each.

Since its inception, the Sweepstakes has attracted area-wide interest, and United Charities has always been able to meet its sales target. However, in the unlikely event hat it might fail to sell a sufficient number of tickets to cover the grand prize, United Charities has reserved the right to cancel the Sweepstakes and to refund the price of tickets to holders.

In recent years, a fairly active secondary market for tickets has developed. This year, buying-selling prices have varied between $75 and $95 before stabilizing at about $90.

When the tickets first went on sale this year, multimillionaire Phil N. Tropic, well-known in Tri-Cities civic circles as a generous but sometimes eccentric donor, bought one of the tickets from United Charities, paying $150 cash.

We will consider three issues based on this case.

Lottery Ticket Case: First Issue   The first issue to consider in this situation is whether Phil's purchase of a sweepstakes ticket represents an asset.

To resolve this question, ask, "Does the ticket satisfy the definition of an asset?" To answer that question, consider the three required elements for an asset from SFAC No. 6, and then apply them to the lottery ticket.

1. Probable future economic benefit in cash flows
2. Controlled by the firm
3. Resulting from a past transaction or event

The easiest part of this case is to recognize that the second and third required elements are present. By buying the ticket, Phil controls the ticket (he has sole possession of it), and the purchase of the ticket was the transaction that gave him control. It is the first required element of an asset, the probable future economic benefit in cash flows, that is the central issue in this case.

Whether the ticket embodies probable future economic benefits depends on how the rights associated with the ticket are interpreted. There are three different views of that right. The first position views the right as consisting of the right to receive $1 million. The second position is that the right consists of the right to participate in the drawing; this event may result in the right to receive $1 million. The third position views the right as depending on Phil's intent in buying the ticket: Did he buy the ticket to hold until the drawing is held, or will he sell the ticket to someone else before the drawing? It is possible to know his intent when he purchased the ticket but impossible to know whether that intent will change over time.

FIRST ISSUE SOLUTION

The ticket would not be recognized as an asset because the future economic benefits were not probable. Based on the number of tickets sold, ten thousand, Phil has a 1 in 10,000, or 0.0001, chance of winning the lottery. That is not high enough to warrant that winning the $1 million will occur.

　　This solution does not take into account the possibility of his selling the ticket in the secondary market. Because that question involves the topic of asset valuation, it is be addressed after the following section.

ASSET VALUATION

Once accountants ascertain that they have an asset according to the definition cited in SFAC No. 6, the next issue is how to value the asset. Accountants have agreed that accounting should measure the assets of the firm. Moonitz stated in ARS #1 that one of the functions of accounting is "to measure the resources held by specific entities."[10]

　　Remember that when accountants use the word value in accounting, they don't report the asset at its market or fair value. Instead, the word *value* means to measure assets by quantifying the asset in terms of monetary units, that is, to associate monetary units with the asset.

　　Valuation has always played a vital role in accounting. Asset valuation is used both in determining net income and presenting the financial position of the firm on the Balance Sheet. Investors, creditors, and management all have a stake in the valuation of assets. Asset valuation has been controversial, not the process of valuation, but what approach should be taken to arrive at the monetary amount.

MEASUREMENT OF ASSETS

The measurement of assets was a controversial aspect in ARS #3, which presented the valuation of an asset as a three-step process.[11]

1. A determination is made to see if the future benefit or service does in fact exist.
2. An estimate of the quantity of the benefit or service is prepared.
3. A choice of method for valuing the quantity of the benefit or service determined in step 2 is made.

In general, three different exchange prices were available to value the asset.

1. *Past exchange price* (e.g., acquisition or historical cost)
2. *Current exchange price* (e.g., current replacement cost)
3. *Future exchange price* (e.g., anticipated selling price)

The valuation of an asset in ARS #3 was viewed as uncertain because it was dependent on estimates. The proper valuation of an asset is dependent on estimates of the existence of future benefits or services regardless of the choice of exchange price used to value the asset. Although the need for estimates is unavoidable, the resulting estimates are considered as uncertain.

VALUATION MODELS

Over time, two different models, or schools of thought, about what value should be associated with an asset have developed: the input model and the output model. Both schools advocate different exchange, or conversion, values for the asset.

INPUT MODEL

The input model advocates asset valuations that reflect some measure of the amount of consideration used or necessary to acquire the asset (i.e., to reflect input or acquisition prices). Two possible input valuations are historical cost and replacement cost (also called current cost). A third input valuation, lower of cost or market, is a hybrid valuation that reflects accountants' conservative bias and uses either historical cost or replacement cost. The three approaches to implementing the input model are described below, including advantages and disadvantages for each.

- *Historical cost.* The asset is valued at the original cost that the firm paid to acquire the asset in an arm's-length transaction or exchange. Generally, the initial value associated with the asset is not changed until the asset is disposed of or somehow removed from the firm. That is, once recorded, historical cost is maintained in the records until the asset is disposed of in some way. The main advantages to this approach are that it's objective, verifiable, and represents the asset's value to the firm. A primary disadvantage of the historical cost approach is that the cost may become outdated with changes in the market for the asset.
- *Replacement cost or current cost.* The asset is valued at what it would require today to obtain the asset or its services. The advantage of this approach is that it represents the best measure of the current value of the asset to the firm and for matching. It also allows the measurement of holding gains and losses. The disadvantages are the loss of objectivity and the fact that the current asset's value may not represent the asset's value to the firm.
- *Lower of cost or market.* This approach compares the historical cost of the asset to its current replacement cost (market cost) and values the asset at the lower of the two. It's advantageous when the cost of an item has fallen in the market. This method allows the firm to record the decline when it occurs. A disadvantage is that it is internally inconsistent because it does not treat increases in the replacement cost of an asset similarly. Only declines are recognized; increases are ignored.

OUTPUT MODEL

The output model advocates valuation concepts based on exchange or conversion values that reflect some measure of the consideration to be received in the future from the asset. This approach focuses on the benefit associated with the asset. The four approaches to its implementation are described below, with advantages and disadvantages cited where appropriate.

- *Present value.* This approach values the asset at the present value of future cash receipts associated with it. It represents a useful abstraction, but it is often not practical for many assets. However, the usefulness of present values in accounting was given a boost in 2000, when the FASB issued SFAC No. 7, "Using Cash Flow Information and Present Value in Accounting Measurements." SFAC No. 7 provides general principles governing the use of present values in accounting, especially when uncertainty is present, and a common understanding of the objective for using present value as an accounting measurement.
- *Current selling price.* This approach values the asset at the price at which it is currently offered in a market. If the selling price is reduced for the cost of completing the sale, it is called the *current net realizable value.* Unfortunately, current selling prices only apply to assets held for resale or offered in a market. It is beneficial because it has a future focus.
- *Liquidation value.* This approach measures the asset based on what the firm can receive for it from a forced sale at reduced prices. It may not be relevant for firms that are going concerns.
- *Expected value.* Johnson and colleagues suggested that the use of expected values in accounting could satisfy the objective of providing useful information about the amounts, timing, and uncertainty of prospective net cash flows in some situations.[12] Expected value considers all possible outcomes associated with an event and weights them by their probability of occurrence. This approach has not been used very often in accounting, but the authors believe it shows promise for meeting users' information needs.

CONSISTENT WITH DEFINITION

It is interesting to view these seven different approaches to the valuation of an asset and consider their use in accounting during the past seventy years. Certainly, the historical cost approach has the distinction of being the dominant approach. Yet, if we compare the input and output models to the current definition of an asset, we must conclude that the output model is more consistent with that definition. The Conceptual Framework's definition clearly has a "future focus," which is more consistent with the output model. (This helps to explain why the FASB has emphasized market values in many of its recent SFASs, and it may mean that the FASB will continue to emphasize market values in future SFASs.)

LOTTERY TICKET CASE: SECOND ISSUE

Refer to the lottery ticket case presented previously and consider the second issue: If an asset were to be recognized, at what value should it be recorded? The second issue assumes that the lottery ticket is an asset and asks at what value it should be recognized. There are four options.

1. Historical cost, $150.
2. Current selling price in the secondary market (fair market value), $90.

3. Expected value, $100.
4. No value, zero.

Perhaps the simplest approach to take in valuing this asset is to use the acquisition cost of $150. This is the traditional approach to valuing this asset and is reliable and objective, because Phil paid $150 for it. It represents the sacrifice that Phil made, and if the lottery were canceled (which it probably won't be), it would be the amount that is refunded to Phil by United Charities.

A second approach to valuing this asset is the use the current selling price of $90. It represents the immediate cash flow if Phil decides to sell the ticket rather than hold it until the drawing. However, the current selling price is only relevant if Phil does not hold the ticket until the drawing.

The third approach is one that is not often seen in practice. It requires the calculation of the expected value as: $1,000,000 \times 0.0001$ (the chance of winning) = $100.00, and it uses that amount to value the asset.

The last option is no value, or zero. If all the tickets are sold and Phil intends to hold the ticket until the drawing, he has a 0.001 percent chance of winning the $1 million. This probability can be considered to be so low as to make it inappropriate to value the asset at anything other than zero.

SECOND ISSUE SOLUTION

The solution in this case is difficult. All four of the alternative values considered so far ($150, $100, $90, and zero) are not indicative of the amount he could win. The current selling price is not relevant if Phil intends to hold the ticket. The historical cost, while objective, does not indicate the potential cash flow from winning or the current market price on the secondary market and is the least relevant amount. Assuming that Phil holds the ticket until the drawing, he will actually get $1 million or zero.

Given these factors, the expected value, $100, appears to be the best choice because the expected amounts of cash flow outcome and the probability of each outcome can be measured precisely.

LOTTERY TICKET CASE: THIRD ISSUE

A third issue in this case involves combining the first two issues and asking, "Does the existence of the secondary market, including a market value for the ticket, change your answer to the first issue?" Is the ticket an asset because of the secondary market value of $90?

Third Issue Solution   Can we consider the secondary market value of $90 as the future economic benefit for the ticket and recognize it as an asset at that value? Although this is tempting, the answer is no. Unless Phil purchased the ticket to resell in the secondary market, the $90 is irrelevant to the situation because his intent is not to resell. If we override his intent and recognize the asset at $90, we are not sending the correct signal to financial statement users. So the existence of a market value does not necessarily make something an asset.

ISSUES ABOUT ASSETS

ISSUES ABOUT ASSETS

SCHUETZE'S CONCERNS

Because of the importance of the definition of an asset, it is not surprising that it has been evaluated and criticized. One of the more interesting of those criticisms is the controversy created in 1993 by W. Schuetze, then chief accountant of the SEC. He was deeply concerned about features of the asset definition in SFAC No. 6. Specifically, he cited the statement in paragraph 6: "that is, assets may be acquired without cost, they may be intangible, and although not exchangeable they may be usable by the entity in producing or distribution other goods or services."[13] Because of this and accountants who testified before the SEC, he concluded that the definition of an asset in SFAC 6 is "so complex, abstract, so open-ended, so all-inclusive, and so vague that we cannot use it to solve problems."[14] Further, he characterizes the definition as "an empty box. A large empty box. A large empty box with sideboards. Almost everything or anything can fit into it."[15] As such, he finds the definition not to be usable.

Schuetze's criticism that the definition is vague is a serious charge that focuses on one of the most important aspects of a definition, which is to clearly distinguish between items that satisfy the definition and those that do not. A definition should help you identify something and also recognize other things that are not the same. A definition that is vague cannot distinguish between items and, as such, is seriously flawed and not usable

Schuetze seriously questioned the Conceptual Framework statements that an asset may be without cost and may not be exchangeable. In his colorful article, he also described his experience in the SEC with having teams of practicing accounts swearing under oath that the Conceptual Framework definition of an asset supports their position even when the testifying teams appear to have different positions. He was concerned that the definition did not clearly distinguish between assets and expenses, which allows the recognition of items as assets that were considered expenses according to others. He wondered how a single definition could be used as justification to support two opposing positions. Additionally, the failure of the definition to distinguish between assets and expenses would cause problems for those who wished to assess the financial position of the firm by examining the assets of the firm. As some of the listed assets may in reality be expenses, they would not be relevant to an assessment of the firm's financial position.

A second issue Schuetze questioned related to the "heart" of an asset: future economic benefits. He accepted this as the most important aspect of an asset, but he questioned the idea that the cost of an asset reflects the future economic benefit to the firm. Instead, he believed that the cost is not the same as the future economic benefit, and therefore, assets should not be reported at cost. He stated: "The cost of many assets does not represent anything close to the 'probable future economic benefit' to be derived from the asset."[16] Simply put, the emphasis on future economic benefits in the definition of assets is not consistent with historical cost accounting.

Schuetze suggested an alternative definition for assets, a simple one: "Cash, contractual claims to cash or services, and items that can be sold separately for cash."[17] In contrast to the FASB's emphasis on future economic benefits, he believed that his definition was real, not an abstraction. It included as assets things that are real, such as things that could be sold, pledged as collateral, and contributed to charity, and emphasized the exchangeability of an asset. That is, to be considered an asset, the item should be able to be sold by the firm.

Schuetze considered his definition to have two main advantages over the FASB's definition: It included real things as assets and emphasized the importance of exchangeability. He concluded his article with a request that the FASB reconsider its definition of an asset; apparently that never happened.

SAMUELSON'S CONCERNS

Another extensive critique of the FASB's definition of assets was written in 1996 by accounting professor Richard Samuelson.[18] He reiterated the concerns of Schuetze and added some new ones. He also provided an alternative definition of assets that is more useful and better supported by theory. He believed that SFAC No. 6's definition needed revision because of two factors: (1) the definition of assets plays a critically important role in accounting theory and setting accounting standards, and (2) the definition was too complex and ambiguous and thus allowed too many things to be considered as assets when they were not.

Samuelson viewed the main use of the definition of an asset in practice to be the classification of expenditures as assets or expenses. This ability to distinguish between assets and expenses is an important part of many accounting standards. He agreed with Schuetze that the definition did not clearly distinguish assets from expenses and thus allowed the recognition of thing as assets that had little relevance to an assessment of the financial position of an enterprise.

The definition of assets has two fundamental components, according to Samuelson: (1) the **economic component**, which recognizes assets' economic or technical characteristics, and (2) the **legal component**, which identifies the legal or proprietary characteristics. In the FASB's definition of assets, both components, are present, but the economic component is more prominent. This leads to three weaknesses in the definition that limit its usefulness in accounting standard setting.

1. The definition confuses the definition of assets with the measurement of assets.
2. The definition confounds the idea of time by defining assets, which are stocks, as future economic benefits, which are really flows. Generally, stocks are in the present, whereas flows occur in the future. Both are included in the FASB's definition of assets. In addition, because the FASB definition emphasis future events, these are not observable and thus cannot be confirmed empirically.
3. The definition emphasizes the economic component over the legal component.

To remedy these concerns, Samuelson recommended defining assets as "property rights or rights to future services of wealth." He believed this definition would improve the relevance, reliability, and comparability of financial statements and make the definition more consistent with the qualitative characteristics of SFAC No. 2. He viewed this definition—which emphasized property rights—as more relevant because property rights are exchangeable for other assets and because the wealth that underlies property rights can be used to produce other assets. So he believed that this was a better definition. But like the definition proposed by Schuetze, no apparent action has been taken by the FASB on Samuelson's proposal.

OTHER ASSET CONCERNS

Other concerns have been raised about the definition of an asset in SFAC No. 6. Some find the vagueness of the word *probable* troubling. The lack of a more complete specification creates the situation in which individual probability views govern the recognition of an asset. For example, Amer and colleagues found that in a sample of professional auditors, most interpreted the word probable to mean a probability of .79 (mean) or .80 (median).[19] Many would have preferred the FASB to more clearly specify what it meant by probable, for example, by stating that it means at least a 65 percent chance of happening.

Instead, the FASB's definition of probable is "that which can be reasonably be expected or believed on the basis of available evidence or logic but is neither certain nor proved."[20]

Other criticisms of the definition focus on its requiring the need for a past transaction or event. Some believe that this requirement is unnecessary because if the firm has control over probable future economic benefits, the benefits must have come from somewhere, that is, as the result of a transaction or event; therefore, they question the need for specifying this aspect in the definition.

However, others are concerned with this aspect of the definition in the opposite way. They believe that the requirement for a transaction in the definition limits the firm from recognizing assets that have developed over time without a specific transaction. For example, the Nike logo has increased in value due to Nike's products and advertising, and Mickey Mouse and Donald Duck are now universally recognized symbols of Disney. However, no specific transaction has occurred in either case; therefore, neither asset is reported on either firm's Balance Sheet. In many other firms, major economic resources are not shown as assets.

In addition, some wonder why this element of the definition has not been recognized in past accounting practice. For example, accountants are reluctant to recognize executory contracts in accounting, which are defined as the exchange of promises (e.g. purchase commitments, leases, the hiring of a new executive). But usually, this exchange is accompanied by a written agreement and a transaction, the signing of a contract. However, accountants generally ignore the transaction and wait until some performance occurs to validate the promise. Some view this reluctance to recognize executory contracts as inconsistent with the definition of an asset because a transaction has occurred but has not been recognized.

REPORTING ASSETS ON THE BALANCE SHEET

Assets are reported on the Statement of Financial Position, often called the Balance Sheet. Once recognized and recorded in the accounting records, assets eventually are presented to stockholders, creditors, and other outside stakeholders on the Balance Sheet. (It's interesting to note that there are two different explanations for the name Balance Sheet: The most popular view is that because it has two sides that are supposed to balance [assets = liabilities + owners' equity], the Balance Sheet is named after that feature. The second view is that because the Balance Sheet is simply a list of the balances of the trial balance, the name was shortened from "A List of Trial Balance Balances" to "Balance Sheet." Both explanations are plausible, but the first explanation is more common.)

CLASSIFICATION OF ASSETS

Assets and their valuation are presented on the Statement of Financial Position in a certain way (classified) and in a specific order. The processes of classification and ordering are aimed at helping financial statement users better comprehend the information. Classification is a way of summarizing the information into categories to make it more comprehensible than if it were presented as raw data.

Accountants readily assume responsibility for the classification scheme to absolve statement users from that task; accountants are considered to be more knowledgeable about the underlying data and thus better able to perform the classification. The alternative would be to provide a list of assets and their values and allow users to perform their own classification and groupings. However, some accountants favor doing just that. They believe accountants should not assume the responsibility for categorizing assets. They recognize that by performing these classifications, accountants are inadvertently biasing the information toward some statement users and away from others. One cannot classify raw data without assuming some objective, which will be more important than alternative objectives, and thus the process of classifying assets involves arbitrary choice that necessarily favors some users and disfavors other users.

Historically, accountants have favored creditors in developing a classification scheme. The scheme emphasized solvency, which is of primary importance to the creditor user group, and favored classifying assets by the speed at which they could be converted into cash, their liquidity. This emphasis eventually leads to a classification scheme that distinguishes between current and noncurrent assets and emphasizes *working capital* (defined as current assets minus current liabilities).

Current and Noncurrent Classifications   The traditional classification scheme for assets is two categories, current and noncurrent assets, based on their liquidity. Liquidity was originally defined in terms of one year. A current asset is one that is expected to be converted into cash or used up within one year. Later, the operating cycle of the firm was taken into consideration, and the time period used in determining current status was revised to include operating cycles that are longer than one year.

The *operating cycle* of a firm is the time it takes a firm to complete its primary purpose for being in business and cycle its assets into cash. For example, for a retail firm, the operating cycle will be the time period it takes for the firm to acquire inventory, sell the product to customers, collect the cash from the customer, and replenish its inventory. For most firms, the calendar year is their reporting period. Some firms have operating cycles longer than a twelve-month year. A current asset is one which is expected to be converted into cash within one year or the current operating cycle, whichever is longer.

Although universally used to categorize assets on the Balance Sheet today, the current and noncurrent classification scheme is widely criticized. Many argue that it does not accomplish its goals and should be abandoned. Some of the reasons follow:

1. Other financial statements, such as the Cash Flow Statement, do a better job of providing information on the liquidity of the firm and its ability to pay its debts.
2. Financial reports are more useful to present and potential investors than creditors, who often obtain information about the debt-paying ability of the firm through supplementary reports.

3. The current and noncurrent classification scheme produces a measure called working capital, the ability of the firm to pay its debts. This measure is defective because working capital is a static measure, whereas the ability to pay debts is dynamic and based primarily on the cash flow provided by operations. At best, working capital may signal the protection or buffer in the current assets for short-term creditors. But otherwise, the working capital measure implies that debts are paid by the liquidation of current assets. The Cash Flow Statement provides a better measure of the firm's ability to pay its debts, called *cash flow from operations*.

4. Current assets are a heterogeneous group, not a homogeneous group. Included as current are different assets, such as cash, short-term investments, receivables, inventory, and prepaid expenses. Some current assets are monetary (defined in currency units) and others are nonmonetary. Therefore, these assets are valued using different valuations. These items have less in common than originally thought and should not be reported in the same class. Adding their values together does not produce a meaningful sum. In simple terms, apples and oranges are in this category.

5. Firms are able to easily manage or manipulate the working capital measure.

6. The current and noncurrent scheme is more appropriate for retail and manufacturing firms than service firms. Yet our economy today is composed of more service firms, and this scheme is not as relevant to their operations.

Many critics of the current scheme believe that a better classification scheme is one that would permit financial statement users to predict cash inflows.

CASH FLOW PREDICTION

Based on SFAC No. 1, the objective of reporting assets on the Balance Sheet is to help users predict the amount, timing, and uncertainty of future cash inflows. The current and noncurrent scheme and working capital do not accomplish that objective. One scheme that may better accomplish that objective is grouping assets by their underlying valuations, which is similar to the proposal in ARS #3.

1. *Assets valued at a future exchange price—the anticipated selling price.* For example, agricultural products that can be sold in a ready market with minor selling costs.

2. *Assets valued at a current exchange price—the current replacement cost.* For example, the replacement costs of productive assets such as plant, property, and equipment.

3. *Assets valued at a past exchange price—the acquisition or historical cost.* For example, the price land purchased in the past.

Using the underlying valuation method to classify assets would provide information about the likely timing of their conversion into cash (their availability for conversion) and the timing of the payment of the firm's obligations, which some consider an improvement over the current and noncurrent asset scheme.

SUMMARY

In general, one of the first steps accomplished in the formulation of a theory in most disciplines is the definition of the basic terms, called *primitive terms*. Accountants have had difficulty in accomplishing this step, especially defining assets. The latest definition was completed in the 1980s with the publication of SFAC No. 3. But even that definition has been found defective by some theoreticians.

The asset definition process did not take place in a vacuum; instead, as accountants grappled with the definition of assets, the assets themselves became much more important to accounting as the FASB moved to a Balance Sheet emphasis and the asset and liability approach to determining net income.

In light of these factors, accountants must agree on the definition of assets before they can make progress in the definition of other elements.

REVIEW QUESTIONS

1. Why are assets centrally important to business entities?
2. Why are assets centrally important to accounting?
3. What factors created the new importance of assets in accounting?
4. Critically evaluate the definitions of assets prior to the definition in the Conceptual Framework (SFAC No. 6). What advantages and disadvantages were associated with the definitions?
5. What are the three essential characteristics of assets according to SFAC No. 6?
6. A key part of the definition of assets in SFAC No. 6 is the word probable. What was this word intended to convey according to the definition in SFAC No. 6?
7. What are three sources of the future economic benefit of assets?
8. In what way are the ten definitions of elements in SFAC No. 6 derived from the definition of assets?
9. How does the definition of assets in SFAC No. 6 reflect the previous definitions of assets presented in this chapter? What characteristics of the previous definitions are embodied in the SFAC No. 6 definition? Was any previous definition more of an influence on the FASB than the others?
10. What are the two valuation models accountants have used for assets? Which model is more consistent with the SFAC No. 6 definition?
11. What were some concerns with the asset definition in SFAC No. 6 expressed by Schuetze?
12. What were some concerns with the asset definition in SFAC No. 6 expressed by Samuelson?
13. How have assets traditionally been reported on the Balance Sheet?
14. What are some concerns about the current and noncurrent asset classification scheme?
15. How could assets be reported on the Balance Sheet to help users predict future cash flows?

DISCUSSION TOPICS

1. One of the first tasks of any discipline formulating a theory is to define the basic elements of that discipline. These are called primitive terms. Why do you think accountants have had so much trouble formulating a definition of assets?

2. Consider the following: **The Lottery Ticket Case (part 2): "Tilting the Odds . . ."**[21]

   In order to generate increased enthusiasm about the next year's lottery, United Charities decided that the single grand prize of $1,000,000 would be replaced by a number of smaller prizes. The following schedule of prizes was established:

Number of Prizes	Prize and Amount	Total Amount
1	Grand prize of $100,000	$ 100,000
10	Gold prizes of $10,000 each	100,000
100	Silver prizes of $1,000 each	100,000
1,000	Bronze prizes of $300 each	300,000
4,000	Tin prizes of $100 each	400,000
5,111		$1,000,000

   The total number of tickets to be issued remained at 10,000 at a price of $150 per ticket.

   Because of the increased chances of getting a winning ticket, sales of tickets this year have been exceptionally brisk, with United Charities selling out its entire stock of 10,000 tickets in the first week the tickets were offered for sale. As in previous years, a secondary market for tickets again developed with prices settling at about $110 per ticket.

   Once again among the purchasers was Phil N. Tropic, who, like last year, purchased on ticket for himself.

   Should Phil N. Tropic recognize this lottery ticket as an asset and, if so, at what amount?

3. Both Schuetze and Samuelson proposed new definitions of assets as an improvement over the definition in SFAC No. 6. Which of the two proposed new definitions do you prefer? Support your answer.

4. Consider the following: **The "See-Through" Office Building Case: "What Goes Down Must Come Back Up"**[22]

   Dauntless Development Company owns what is referred to as a "see-through" office building, as the glass-walled structure is largely unoccupied and most floors are unfinished internally. The building cost Dauntless $10 million to build and was the last building completed during the downtown building boom. It is now 5 years old and has a carrying amount of $9 million.

   Although the building is less than 30% occupied, management believes there is no reason that its carrying amount will not be recovered over the remainder of the building's expected 50-year life. Current vacancy rates are such that there is a 15-year supply of equivalent vacant space available in the area.

Should the building that Dauntless owns continue to be reported as an asset at its carrying value of $9 million or be regarded as an "impaired asset" and its carrying amount be written down? If so, to what amount should it be written down?

5. **Application problem.** The Smith Construction Company holds numerous land holdings as investments. Smith frequently purchases large tracts of land and subsequently develops those tracts into subdivisions of either single- or multiple-family (condominiums) homes. The potential value of multifamily home properties is approximately 75 percent higher than single-family home properties. During January of the current year (20X1), Smith purchased a tract of land for $400,000. The price is considerably more than the current value of land to be used for single-family homes, which would be around $300,000. The land is currently zoned for single-family homes exclusively. Believing that the land could be rezoned for multifamily homes, Smith paid more than the market price. However, what appeared as a routine rezoning change (from single- to multiple-family) has turned into a nightmare. Stiff neighborhood resistance was mounted against the rezoning proposal, and the local rezoning board has, after three lengthy meetings, refused to rezone the property. Smith has appealed the decision to the township board. The board has until next July (20X2) to render an opinion and appears to be taking its time to decide this hot zoning issue. Although it is clearly difficult for Smith to obtain multiple-family rezoning, Smith is optimistic and does not think it is totally impossible.

At what amount should Smith Construction Company record this land investment on its books at the end of the current fiscal year, December 20X1?

6. **Application Problem.** During September and October 20X4, the Lohman Company purchased some common shares of three different companies. None of these stock purchases represented 20 percent or more of the respective corporation's outstanding common shares and are appropriately classified as securities available-for-sale. The Lohman Company's year-end is December 31. In the preparation of its classified Balance Sheet for the year ending December 31, 20X4, you inquire of management as to their intent regarding these three common stock investments. They respond with the following statement, "Since we believe these investments to be in sound companies with consistent dividend payouts and that represent some potential for growth in stock prices. However, should cash needs arise, we will first sell these investments rather than borrow funds from a bank." How should these investments be classified on the December 31, 20X4, Balance Sheet of the Lohman Company?

7. **Application Problem.** The Sweetwater Company gave $100,000 cash on January 2, 20X4, to the Mr. Dough Company, which is owned and operated by some distant cousins of the Sweetwater family, and received in exchange a four-year, 3 percent note receivable. Assuming Sweetwater Company's incremental borrowing rate at the time was 12 percent, how should the note receivable be recorded by the Sweetwater Company on January 2, 20X4?

8. **Application Problem.** The Adams Company is actively involved in an expansion of its business operations to minimize seasonal and weather-related cycles. Accordingly, Adams recently purchased a fast-food restaurant on a busy intersection in San Diego, California. Adams paid $800,000 for the property, which included 2 acres of land, a building, and numerous items of equipment. An appraisal costing $5,000 indicated fair

market values for the land, building, and equipment of $300,000, $450,000, and $250,000, respectively. Because the restaurant had been closed for several years, the equipment needed significant improvements to meet current OSHA requirements. Adams contracted with Equipment Renewals to upgrade the equipment. The upgrading process was extensive, lasting from June 7, 2014, through March 31, 2015. Adams paid Equipment Renewals $100,000 on July 31, 2014; $80,000 on November 1, 2014; and $70,000 on February 1, 2015. To finance the equipment upgrade, Adams specifically borrowed $100,000 on July 31, 2014, by signing a 10 percent three-year note payable. In addition, Adams had the following borrowings outstanding (during the entire construction period):

$500,000, 12 percent, ten-year note payable, dated June 2010
$800,000, 6 percent, twenty-year bond payable, dated April 2012

The building was structurally sound, requiring only a new roof costing $40,000. Adams held its grand opening of the new restaurant on April 12, 2015.

Determine at what amounts the land, building, and equipment would be reported on the April 12, 2015, Balance Sheet of Adams Company.

NOTES

1 Samuelson.
2 AICPA, par. 26.
3 Sprouse and Moonitz, p. 20.
4 APB, par 132.
5 FASB, par. 25.
6 FASB, par. 26.
7 FASB, par. 172.
8 FASB, par. 173.
9 Johnson and Petrone, p. 32.
10 Moonitz, p. 23.
11 Sprouse and Moonitz, pp. 23–24.
12 Johnson et al.
13 Schuetze, p. 67.
14 Ibid., p. 67.
15 Ibid., p. 67.
16 Ibid., p. 69.
17 Ibid., p. 69.
18 Samuelson.
19 Amer et al., as quoted in Johnson et al., p. 85.
20 FASB, par. 25.
21 Johnson and Petron, p. 33.
22 Ibid., p. 51.

REFERENCES

American Institute of Certified Public Accountants. *Accounting Terminology Bulletin No. 1.* New York: AICPA, 1953.

Accounting Principles Board. *Statement No. 4, Basic Concepts and Accounting Principles Underlying Financial Statements of Business Enterprises.* New York: AICPA, 1970.

Dieter, R., and Arthur Wyatt. "Get It Off the Balance Sheet." *Financial Executive* (January 1980): 42–28.

Financial Accounting Standards Board. *Statement of Financial Accounting Concepts No. 6, "Elements of Financial Statements."* Norwalk, CT: Financial Accounting Standards Board, 1985.

Heath, Loyd. "Is Working Capital Really Working?" *Journal of Accountancy* (August 1980): 55–62.

Johnson, T., and Kimberly Petrone. *The FASB Cases on Recognition and Measurement, Second Edition*. Norwalk, CT: Financial Accounting Standards Board, 1995.

Johnson, T., Barry Robbins, Robert Swieringa, and Roman Weil. "Expected Values in Financial Reporting." *Accounting Horizons* (December 1993): 77–90.

Kirk, Donald J. "On Future Events: When Incorporated Into Today's Measurement?" *Accounting Horizons* (June 1990): 86–92.

Moonitz, Maurice. *The Basic Postulates of Accounting*. New York: AICPA, 1961.

Samuelson, Richard. "The Concept of Assets in Accounting Theory." *Accounting Horizons* (September 1996): 147–157.

Schuetze, W. "What Is an Asset?" *Accounting Horizons* (September 1993): 66–70.

Sprouse, Robert and Maurice Moonitz. *A Tentative Set of Broad Accounting Principles for Business Enterprises*. New York: AICPA, 1962.

CHAPTER 11

CASH AND CASH FLOWS

LEARNING OBJECTIVES

After studying this chapter, you should be able to

> Understand the reasons for the renewed emphasis on cash flows.

> Explain the importance of cash to a firm.

> Describe the three activities reported in the Statement of Cash Flows under SFAS No. 95.

> List five ways that supplementary cash flow information helps users.

> Analyze the Statement of Cash Flows using ratios.

In this chapter, we focus on cash and cash flows. Although in the past, cash and cash flows have been seen as primitive concepts when compared to the more sophisticated accrual concept, this view of cash has been changing. This change has been caused by the renewed emphasis on cash flows in accounting theory formulations and standard setting. The process of change started by the Trueblood report and continued through to two aspects of the FASB's Conceptual Framework (SFAC No. 1 and SFAC No. 5) to the final outcome, a new FASB accounting standard requiring the reporting of a statement of cash flows, SFAS No. 95, "Statement of Cash Flows," issued in 1987. As such, the attention on cash is a good example of how theory identifies a need in financial accounting and points the way for standard setting to address that need. In this case, the process worked effectively.

Cash will be examined first, beginning with applying the definition of an asset from SFAC No. 6. In this chapter, we concentrate on six specific important accounting events and discuss the general development of accounting for cash flows:

1. Pre cash flow and funds flow reporting.
2. APB Opinion #3 (1963), "The Application and Source of Funds"
3. APB Opinion #19 (1970), "Reporting Changes in Financial Position"
4. SFAC No. 1 (1978), "The Objectives of Financial Reporting by Business Enterprises"
5. SFAC No. 5 (1984), "Recognition and Measurement in Financial Statements of Business Enterprises"
6. SFAS No. 95 (1987), "Statement of Cash Flows"

A time line of these developments is presented in Exhibit 11.1.

APPLYING THE ASSET DEFINITION

The focus here is on the cash held by a firm at a point in time. To start, let's examine how well cash fits the definition of an asset. As you might expect, it fits it well. Recall from Chapter 10, according to SFAC No. 6, the three required elements of assets are

1. Probable future economic benefit in cash flows
2. Controlled by the firm
3. A past transaction or event created the benefit

EXHIBIT 11.1
Time Line

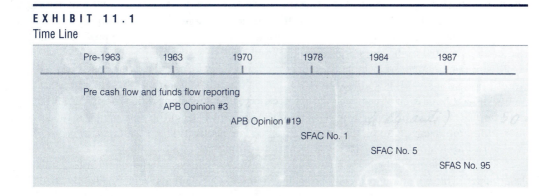

The cash possessed by the firm at a point in time meets these three requirements. It has future economic benefit, primarily through its exchange value and acceptance value. Because the firm's cash is in its accounts and subject to the will of the firm, the entity has control over the asset. And finally, some underlying transactions have created the cash balance, so the third requirement is also met. Therefore, the conclusion is that cash is an asset; the examination of the importance of cash to the firm follows.

Cash and Cash Flows Importance   There are many important positives about cash and cash flows. The most fundamental underlying economic events and transactions in a firm are the cash inflows and outflows. All accounting measurements are based directly or indirectly on these cash flows. Ultimately, all transactions end up as cash flows. Cash flows are free from the arbitrary allocations that characterize much of accrual accounting. Whereas accounting net income is an abstraction, cash flows are real.

The importance of cash and cash flows centers around their role in the survival of the firm. To illustrate this point, we'll use the format of a popular TV game show started in the 1970s, *Family Feud*, to examine the importance of cash to a firm. Following the format of *Family Feud*, if you asked one hundred people what caused a firm to fail or go bankrupt, what answer would you get most frequently? The most popular answer (or "good answer," as the host would say) is "no profit." And that's what most people think will destroy a firm, the absence of profits or presence of losses. But accountants and most businesspeople know that's not correct. Although the absence of profit isn't good, the primary cause of a firm's bankruptcy is the absence of cash. The truth of this is demonstrated in the observation that even profitable firms can fail from the loss of cash.

Despite the truth of this, for a long time, accountants tended to regard cash and the cash basis of accounting as being too primitive or elementary to be highly regarded. They believed that the accrual basis of accounting was superior conceptually, and cash was relegated to a place of secondary importance. Unfortunately, that situation was contradicted in the actual business world in the 1970s and 1980s by the development of a number of existing firms going out of business from a lack of cash or liquidity. The accrual basis masked this from investors and creditors.

The classic case of this was the W. T. Grant Company. This firm was one of the leading retailers in the United States. Grant's Income Statement reported rising profits through 1974. But to the surprise of many, W. T. Grant filed for bankruptcy in 1976 because of cash flow problems. It was a profitable firm without enough cash to pay its bills, so it failed. This occurred before firms provided a Statement of Cash Flows so financial statement users were not warned about Grant's problems. If cash flow statements had been prepared by Grant, they would have showed the true situation of the firm. Exhibit 11.2 shows summarized reconstructed cash flow statements for Grant for two years.

As the statements show, in both years, the cash flow from operations was negative. Grant's operations were not able to provide enough cash to support it. In fact, the statements show that in each of the two years, the cash receipts from customers ($1,579,320 in 19X5 and $1,317,218 in 19X4) were less than the amount of cash the firm paid out to suppliers and employees ($1,683,760 and $1,336,428, respectively). Two sequential years of this represented a bad sign for the cash situation of the firm.

Because of the need for cash flow information, cash and cash flows came into a new prominence. This chapter chronicles those developments. In some respects, it is summarized

EXHIBIT 11.2
W. T. Grant Company

RECONSTRUCTED CASH FLOW STATEMENTS
(in actual dollars)

Cash Flows	19x5	19x4
Cash Flow from Operations:		
Cash Receipts from Customers	$ 1,579,320	$ 1,317,218
Cash Receipts from other Revenues	10,057	8,924
Cash Payments to Suppliers and Employees	(1,683,760)	(1,336,428)
Cash Payments for Interest	(21,127)	(16,452)
Cash Payments for Taxes	(8,459)	(8,143)
Other, net	9,704	7,964
Cash Flow from operations	$ (114,265)	$ (26,917)
Cash Flow from investing activities	$ (26,141)	$ (31,915)
Cash Flow from financing activities	$ 121,498	$ 74,674
Increase (decrease) in cash	$ (18,908)	$ 15,842

Source: Based on Harrison and Horngren, p. 538.

in the statement shouted often by the character, Rod Tidwell, in the popular 1996 Tom Cruise movie *Jerry Maguire:* "Show me the money!"

But as the following section shows, accountants began the process of providing more information by emphasizing a broader measure—funds—rather than cash.

REPORTING FUNDS FLOWS

BACKGROUND

The first statements to address users' needs for information on cash mandated by accountants did not focus on cash; rather, they dealt with a broader concept, funds flows. The reason for this was the belief that a focus on only cash flows was too narrow. Initially, the concept of funds was defined in a variety of ways. In fact, a number of the following alternative definitions of funds had some support:

1. *Short-term monetary asset flows* (monetary assets were those defined in a fixed number of currency units).
2. *Net short-term monetary asset flows* (short-term monetary assets minus short-term monetary liabilities).
3. *Net working capital* (current assets minus current liabilities).
4. *All financial resources flows* (these flows would include net working capital and other significant long-term acquisition of assets and financing activities).

5. *The all significant events approach* (which gives greater detail on changes in current assets and liabilities and shows all material changes in the Balance Sheet accounts).

Among these five alternatives, the net working capital definition of funds had the most support.

THE NET WORKING CAPITAL CONCEPT

One use for the classification of assets and liabilities into current and noncurrent is to provide a measure of the short-term solvency of the firm, called *net working capital*. Working capital was defined as resources that would be consumed, sold, or converted into cash within a year minus obligations that would be discharged or settled within one year. The linking of these two elements, current assets and current liabilities, appeared natural. The expected excess of current assets over current liabilities was viewed as the net investment required in the firm to maintain day-to-day operations, hence the other name for net working capital, *circulating capital*.

Historically, net working capital was used as a measure of a debtor's ability to meet its obligations in the case of liquidation. Over time, the use changed to become a measure of the ability of a firm to pay its maturing obligations as they came due from the funds generated by current operations.

EVALUATION OF WORKING CAPITAL

As described in Chapter 10, working capital now is viewed as an incomplete concept. It is considered flawed because working capital is a static measure, whereas the ability to pay debts is dynamic and based primarily on the cash flow provided by operations. At best, working capital may signal the protection or "buffer" in the current assets for short-term creditors. But otherwise, the working capital measure implies that debts are paid by the liquidation of current assets. A Statement of Cash Flows provides a better measure of the firm's ability to pay its debts through a measure of the cash flows from operations.

In addition to these concerns, Fess pointed out some other problems with funds defined as net working capital.[1]

1. Because the length of the operating cycle differs from firm to firm and industry to industry, financial statement users may not be able to compare the net working capital of two firms if either had a different operating cycle length.
2. The classification between current and noncurrent assets is not really sound. Some current assets have more in common with noncurrent assets. For example, if a firm prepays its insurance for three years, that prepayment will be classified as a current asset. But machinery with a three-year economic life is classified as noncurrent. In both cases, the cost incurred would be expensed over a three-year period.
3. Some of the assets classified as current are really permanent assets and have many characteristics of noncurrent assets. For example, firms may maintain a rather constant amount of accounts receivable or merchandise inventory. Thus although individual receivables are collected, the dollar level of receivables may be relatively permanent.
4. Net working capital is not a proper measure of the resources provided by operations.
5. Many of the current assets are valued inconsistently, for example, some at cost, some at market value, and some at retail. This inconsistency prevents calculating a meaningful sum of these assets.

FUNDS FLOW PRONOUNCEMENTS

The first pronouncement to deal with funds flow was issued by the Accounting Principles Board in 1963 as APB Opinion #3, "The Application and Source of Funds." This opinion recommended that a firm publish a funds flow statement as supplementary information along with its Balance Sheet and Income Statement. However, that was only a recommendation; it was not mandated. The funds flow statement was intended to bridge the gap between a firm's two consecutive years' balance sheets and summarize the firm's financing and investing activities.

In 1970, the SEC required firms to prepare a funds flow statement, and some firms were voluntarily including funds flow statements in their annual reports. That motivated the APB in 1971 to issue APB Opinion #19, "Reporting Changes in Financial Position," which required firms to publish a funds flow statement titled, Statement of Changes in Financial Position. Under APB Opinion #19 statement preparers had flexibility in the definition of funds and latitude in the method of presenting changes in financial position. Firms were given latitude in the preparation of the statement and could define funds as cash, cash and temporary assets, quick assets, or working capital. This flexibility and latitude limited the ability of users to understand the information presented in the funds flow statement and to use it to compare firms. Firms followed APB Opinion #19 through the late 1980s.

REPORTING CASH FLOWS

The funds flow approach dominated accounting thinking until 1978 when SFAC No. 1, "Objectives of Financial Reporting by Business Enterprises," in the Conceptual Framework was issued and cash flows were elevated in importance. This event was heralded by the issuance of the Trueblood report in 1973, which listed the following as one of the twelve objectives of financial accounting: "to provide information useful to investors and creditors for predicting, comparing, and evaluating potential cash flows to them in terms of amount, timing, and related uncertainty."[2] Trueblood was the first official modern theory formulation to emphasize cash flows.

ROLE OF CASH FLOWS IN SFAC NO. 1

Recall from Chapter 7 that SFAC No. 1, "The Objectives of Financial Reporting by Business Enterprises," was the first element of the Conceptual Framework project. The purpose of SFAC No. 1 was to state the highest-level concepts in the prescriptive structure. According to SFAC No. 1, the primary objective of accounting was to provide decision useful information to those with limited access to financial data. It singled out the external users—investors and creditors—as the primary audience of accounting, and it emphasized cash flows. SFAC No. 1 stated that investors and creditors were primarily interested in prospective cash flows.

Users were interested in three aspects of these cash flows: the amounts of the cash flows (their magnitude), the timing (the expected realization), and their uncertainty (the risks associated with them). This cash flow emphasis eventually led to the issuance of a new accounting standard that abandoned the previous reliance on net working capital and adopted a new approach, which emphasized cash flows and was consistent with SFAC No. 1.

STATEMENT OF CASH FLOWS IN SFAC NO. 5

The movement toward a Statement of Cash Flows was given additional momentum by the issuance of SFAC No. 5, "Recognition and Measurement in Financial Statements of Business Enterprises," in 1984. In this part of the Conceptual Framework project, a Statement of Cash Flows was included in the full set of financial statements that should be prepared by firms. The statement was designed to provide information to help assess a firm's liquidity, financial flexibility, profitability, and risk.

After issuing SFACs No. 1 and No. 5, it was clear that the FASB would eventually issue a financial accounting standard that would replace the funds flow pronouncements of the APB. That standard was issued in 1987 and is discussed in the following section.

SFAS NO. 95, STATEMENT OF CASH FLOWS

In 1987, the FASB issued a standard on cash flows, "Statement of Cash Flows," which was the first direct result from the Conceptual Framework project. This statement is designed to report the firm's cash flows during the period. It fills the information gap between the Balance Sheet and Income Statement. The Balance Sheet reports the current cash balance, and the Income Statement reports the period's revenues, expenses, and net income. But neither statement explains how the cash balance changed from last year to this year or what caused the change. You can determine the change in cash balance by obtaining two balance sheets and calculating the difference in cash. But that still doesn't tell you what caused the change.

The Statement of Cash Flows explains the causes of the change in the balance of cash from the end of the previous period to the end of the current period. It discloses the firm's cash receipts and disbursements for the year.

CASH DEFINITION

In SFAS No. 95, the FASB recommended that cash be defined more broadly than the firm's cash in the bank. The FASB recommended that the statement include cash on hand, cash in the bank, and cash equivalents. Cash equivalents are short-term, highly liquid investments made by the firm. The investments are part of the firm's efforts to manage its cash. Firms park idle funds temporarily in investments to earn a greater return than in the corporate checking account. Cash equivalents can be quickly converted back into cash (within 90 days); so they are considered as "near cash" and should be included. Throughout the rest of this chapter, the term cash is used interchangeably with cash equivalents.

STATEMENT OF CASH FLOWS CONTENTS

The cash flow statement according to SFAS No. 95 contains information about cash flows from three activities: operating activities, investing activities, and financing activities. It also discloses the overall change in cash during the period and may additionally include a supplementary schedule of noncash investing and financing activities. These latter activities are long-term investments or financing transactions that actually did not directly involve cash. For example, a firm may acquire a tract of land for a new plant site by issuing stock directly to the owner of the land. Normally, the firm would engage in two transactions: issue stock for cash and use the cash to buy the land. So although the actual transaction did not involve cash, it could be reported in a supplementary schedule at the bottom of the cash flow statement or in a separate schedule. The effect of reporting these noncash transactions is providing additional information on the investing and financing activities of the firm.

THREE ACTIVITIES

The Statement of Cash Flows is organized into three categories that mirror the major activities of the firm: operating activities, investing activities, and financing activities. Refer to Exhibit 11.3 for an example of these sections.

EXHIBIT 11.3
Statement of Cash Flows

LEE ENTERPRISES INC.
STATEMENT OF CASH FLOWS
FOR YEAR ENDED DECEMBER 31, 20XX
(in millions)

Cash Flows from Operating Activities	
Receipts:	
Collections from customers	$ 250
Dividends received on investment	10
Total cash receipts	$ 360
Payments:	
To suppliers	$(110)
To employees	(50)
For interest	(5)
For income tax	(5)
Total cash payments	$(170)
Net Cash Inflow from Operating Activities	$ 190
Cash Flows from Investing Activities	
Acquisition of plant assets	$(100)
Proceeds from sale of land	15
Net Cash Outflow from Investing Activities	$ (85)
Cash Flows from Financing Activities	
Proceeds from issuance of common stock	$ 30
Payment of long-term bonds	(10)
Dividends paid	(5)
Net Cash Inflow from Financing Activities	$ 15
Net Increase in Cash	$ 120
Beginning Cash Balance	$ 30
Ending Cash Balance	$ 150
Supplementary Schedule of Noncash Investing and Financing Activities	
Acquisition of land by issuing note payable	$ 40

The operating activities represent the day-by-day activities of the firm. These are the most important activities of the firm. Operating cash flows are the largest and most important source of cash for the firm and are listed first on the statement. Operating activities create revenues, expenses, gains, and losses, which are normally reported on the Income Statement. But the accrual concept is used to report these items on the Income Statement, whereas they are reported on the Statement of Cash Flows in terms of their impact on the firm's cash flow. This category typically includes cash inflows in the form of receipts from customers, interest received on notes receivable, and dividends received on investments in stock. The cash outflows are payments to suppliers, to employees, for interest, and for income taxes. The largest cash inflow in this category should be from the collections from customers from cash sales or collections of accounts receivable. For the typical firm, the net cash flow from operations should be an inflow. The normal operations of the firm should be the main source of cash (or the firm would be better off by not operating).

One of the most controversial aspects of SFAS No. 95 focuses on the classification of cash receipts from interest and dividends. Although these transactions arise from what are normally considered as investing activities, the FASB decided to include them in the operating category. Similarly, the payment of interest, normally considered as a financing activity, is included as an operating activity. The FASB's reasoning was that these items normally are included in the computation of net income and thus should be included in the same category. However, cash payments of dividends are included in the financing activities because they represent cash transfers to the owners of the firm and are not used in the computation of net income.

The second category of activities on the statement is investing activities. This category involves increases and decreases in the long-term assets of the firm. Examples of these activities are the purchase and sale of plant assets, buying and selling the stock of another firm, purchasing land for a plant site, and so on. The acquisitions of these assets represent cash outflows; the sales of them represent cash inflows. In general, the overall cash flow for this category is outward, because the firm should be expanding by investing in assets.

The third category reports cash flows from financing activities. These activities refer to the firm's obtaining cash from investors and creditors. The sale and repurchase of stock, borrowing by selling long-term debt, paying off debt, and paying dividends are all examples of transactions that belong in this category. In general, the overall balance of this category should be a cash inflow. However, some firms will generate large amounts of cash and will pay off long-term debt, pay dividends, and repurchase stock, all of which will produce a net cash outflow in the financing activities section.

Cash Flow Patterns   Dugan and coauthors noted that the relationship between the three cash flow categories (operating, investing, and financing) is important.[3] Eight interesting possible patterns of cash flows emerge from these three categories, according to the authors. By characterizing cash inflows as "+" and cash outflows as "–", the eight possible patterns are shown in Exhibit 11.4. The first four patterns are based on net cash inflows from operations, and the last four patterns are based on net cash outflows from operating activities.

The first firm pattern represents the situation in which the firm has net cash inflows from all three activities, operating, investing, and financing, which means the firm is producing positive cash flows from operations, selling its long-term assets, and raising additional capital from financial markets. That is a very unusual combination of activities.

In the firm pattern #2, the firm is producing such a strong cash inflow from operating activities that it can use this cash to expand by investing in long-term assets and also pay down it debt or pay dividends to investors. This pattern reflects a mature and successful firm.

The third firm pattern shows that both operating and investing are cash inflows. These two positive cash flows are being used to repay investors or debt holders or both. This pattern represents a firm that is downsizing or has been restructured. The firm is not investing in additional resources; instead, it is using its cash inflows to service debt or shareholders.

EXHIBIT 11.4
Cash Flow Patterns

Firm Pattern	Cash Flows from Operating Activities*	Cash Flows from Investing Activities*	Cash Flows from Financing Activities*
#1	+	+	+
#2	+	–	–
#3	+	+	–
#4	+	–	+
#5	–	+	+
#6	–	–	+
#7	–	+	–
#8	–	–	–

*+ = cash inflow; – = cash outflow

Source: From Dugan et al., p. 36.

Firm pattern #4 is typical for a high-growth company. The firm has cash inflows from operating and financing activities. That cash flow is being used to expand (invest in additional assets).

In firm pattern five, the operating cash outflow is made up from the positive cash flows from the sale of long-term assets and financing from shareholders or debt holders. Thus it appears that the firm is either selling off assets or raising capital to stay in business.

The sixth firm pattern is typical of a young, fast-growing company. In this pattern, the firm has an operating cash outflow, yet it is expanding by investing in additional long-term assets. Both of these cash outflows, operating and investing, are financed through borrowings or the issuance of stock.

In firm pattern #7, the firm has cash outflows in its operating and financing activities, and a cash inflow in investing activities. It appears that this firm is shrinking or downsizing by selling off its long-term assets and using that cash to make up for the negative cash flow from operations and to pay off debt holders or pay dividends to shareholders. This is not a healthy situation for a firm.

The eighth firm pattern shows a firm with cash outflows in all three activities. This unusual situation can only occur if the firm has previously accumulated cash to meet these cash outflows. The outflow of cash cannot continue for long, however. It will eventually lead to the firm's bankruptcy.

According to Dugan and coauthors, the ability of a firm to generate positive cash flows from operations is vital. If a firm produces a cash inflow from operating activities, it means that the firm is able, through its sales, to pay its bills. Any cash excess can then be invested in additional assets or distributed to shareholders or long-term creditor. Dugan et al. noted that in addition to the direciton of the cash flow, the relative magnitude of the cash flows should be considered.

Format of the Statement of Cash Flows   The FASB allowed two formats to present the operating activities section of the Statement of Cash Flows: direct and indirect. The direct method lists the cash receipts from each specific operating activity and cash payments for each major operating area. It clearly shows the major sources and uses of cash for each operating activity. The FASB expressed a clear preference for the direct method in SFAS No. 95. The direct method was used in preparing the statement shown in Exhibit 11.3.

The indirect method begins with net income from the Income Statement, computed under accrual accounting, and reconciles the net income to the cash flow from operating activities. The reconciliation involves a number of adjustments, such as depreciation expense, gains and losses on the sales of assets, and increases and decreases in current assets and current liabilities. It concludes with the overall net cash flow from operations. The indirect method is also known as the *reconciliation method*. It shows the link between accrual accounting net income and cash flow from operations better than the direct method. Exhibit 11.5 shows an example of a Statement of Cash Flows preapred with the indirect method for the same firm as shown in Exhibit 11.3. Comparing the operating section of Exhibit 11.3 to Exhibit 11.5 shows the major difference between the direct and indirect approaches.

EXHIBIT 11.5
Indirect Method Example

LEE ENTERPRISES INC.
STATEMENT OF CASH FLOWS
FOR YEAR ENDED DECEMBER 31, 20XX
(in millions)

Cash Flows from Operating Activities		
Net income		$180
Add (Subtract) items that affect net income and cash flow differently		
Depreciation	$20	
Gain on sale of plant assets	(10)	
Increase in accounts receivable	(15)	
Increase in interest receivable	(15)	
Decrease in merchandise inventory	5	
Increase in prepaid expenses	(10)	
Increase in accounts payable	40	
Decrease in accrued liabilities	(5)	10
Net Cash Inflow from Operating Activities		$190

Although it preferred the direct method, the FASB allowed the indirect method because it was often easier for firm's accounting systems (under the accrual method) to compute cash flows from operations. When using the indirect method, firms start with a reconciliation of net income to generate cash flows from operations. The indirect method is interesting because it clearly shows the relationship between accounting net income and the cash flows created by operations. Because of this, firms that used the direct method were required to prepare this net income reconciliation also. Thus the FASB ended up, by default, seeming to favor the method it did not favor. Because firms using the direct method had to complete the indirect method of net income reconciliation anyway, they simply changed to the indirect method. An alternative explanation of the preference of firms for the indirect method is that they did not want to use the direct method.

Remember that these two methods involve only the format of the cash flow from operations section. The difference is confined to that section. No other differences between these two methods affect the financing and investing activities sections. Both methods also produce the same subtotals for all three activity categories and for the net change in cash.

IMPORTANCE OF CASH FLOW INFORMATION

The liquidity crisis during the 1980s showed the need for cash flow information. This information could be used to assess aspects of the firm's performance. These aspects were not available from either the accrual approach or the statement of funds prepared using the working capital definition of funds. Cash flow information was seen as useful supplementary disclosures, helping users in the following five ways. (Note: each points out a limitation of accrual accounting.)

1. *Quality of income.* Investors and others have created a concept, quality of income (or quality of earnings), to describe the net income reported under the accrual basis. If a firm's net income is closely related to the cash flows from those operations, then that firm's net income is "high-quality earnings." If the opposite is true, then the firm has "low-quality earnings." Notice that the criterion used to judge the quality of earnings is earnings closeness to cash flows. That is, how closely does the net income represent the cash flows from operations?

2. *Cash flow from operations.* An important component of the Statement of Cash Flows is the amount of cash flow from operations. This figure should be positive. If not, it signals a very poor situation for the firm from a liquidity standpoint. If the firm's normal operations don't provide an excess of cash for investing and financing activities, then the firm would be better off (from a cash standpoint) to cease operations, which would stop the "hemorrhage" of cash.

3. *Future cash flows.* According to SFAC No. 1, investors and creditors are interested in the amount, timing, and uncertainty of future cash flows from the firm. The best predictor of future cash flows is past cash flows. Certainly, future cash flows will more closely follow past cash flows rather than working capital flows or accrual net income.

4. *Flexibility and liquidity.* Cash flow information should help users assess the ability of the firm to adapt to new situations and opportunities in their markets (*flexibility*). Due to the rapidly changing conditions in business today, this flexibility is highly desired.

Firms with excess cash are better able to react and take advantage of opportunities as they arise, whereas firms with cash deficiencies may lose opportunities because they can't act swiftly. *Liquidity* refers to the ability of a firm to convert its assets into cash. This is important for debt-paying calculations and is of special interest to creditors.

5. *Comparability.* Cash flow information is more uniform from firm to firm and thus allows better comparisons than accrual accounting.

USING CASH FLOW INFORMATION

The Statement of Cash Flows meets the described needs of investors delineated in SFAC No. 1. The statement discloses the effects of net income on the cash resources of the firm, how the firm acquired its assets, and how these operations and assets were financed. This information should permit investors and creditors to predict the amount of cash to be disbursed to them in the form of dividends and interest and allow investors and creditors to assess the risk associated with those predictions. Empirical research on this process concludes that cash flow information is supplementary to accrual net income information and superior to information on changes in working capital.[4] The evidence supports the FASB's desire to provide information that helps investors and creditors make financial decisions. Cash flow information does help investors and creditors make better predictions of future cash flows and risk assessments.

Carslaw and Mills noted the support for the Statement of Cash Flows since it was proposed in 1986.[5] But they also noted that by 1990, few new financial ratios had been developed that could be used in the analysis of the statement. To remedy that lack of new ratios, Carslaw and Mills proposed four groups of ratios. Analysts have traditionally used financial ratios to evaluate financial statements. Carslaw and Mills suggested these new ratios, which should be used with the other traditional Balance Sheet and Income Statement ratios, to provide a better understanding of the financial strengths and weaknesses of firms. The new ratios are shown in Exhibit 11.6 and described in the next paragraph.

SFAS No. 95 was designed to provide information that allows an assessment of the firm's ability to meet its obligations and pay dividends. Carslaw and Mills suggest three cash flow ratios that analyze the firm's ability to meet its obligations:

1. Cash interest coverage ratio, which shows the number of times cash outflows for interest are covered by the cash flows from operations
2. Cash debt coverage ratio, which reveals the relationship of retained operating cash flow (cash flow from operations less dividends) to the debt principal
3. Cash dividend coverage ratios, which provide evidence of the ability to meet current dividends from normal operating cash flows.

Two quality of income ratios, which compare net income and associated cash receipts and payments, are suggested by Carslaw and Mills: (1) quality of sales ratio shows the relationship between cash flows from sales and sales, and (2) quality of income ratio (measured in two ways) indicates the variation between cash flow from operations and income. Two capital expenditure ratios are suggested that attempt to measure the firm's ability to finance capital expenditures: (1) capital acquisition ratio shows the ability of the firm to meet its capital expenditure needs, and (2) investment/finance ratio (measured in two ways) indicates how investments are financed.

Carslaw and Mills suggest two cash flow returns ratios, which reflect the return on investments: (1) cash flow per share ratio indicates the operating cash flow attributable to each common share, and (2) return on investment ratios (cash return on assets, cash return on debt and equity, and cash return on stockholders' equity) measure the ability of the firm to generate cash flows from invested funds.

EXHIBIT 11.6
Cash Flow Statement Ratios

Cash Coverage Ratios

Cash interest coverage:	CFFO* before interest and tax/interest
Cash debt coverage:	CFFO – total dividends/debt
Cash dividend coverage:	CFFO – preferred dividends/common stock dividends
	CFFO/total dividends

Quality of Income Ratios

Quality of sales:	Cash from sales/sales
Quality of income:	CFFO/operating income
	CFFO before interest and tax/income before interest, taxes, and depreciation

Capital Expenditures Ratios

Capital acquisitions:	CFFO – total dividends/cash paid for acquisitions
Investment/finance:	Net cash flows for investing/net cash flows from financing
	Net cash flows for investing/net cash flows from operating and financing

Cash Flow Returns

Cash flow per share:	CFFO – preferred dividends/weighted common stock
Cash return on assets:	CFFO before interest and tax/total assets
Cash return on debt and equity:	CFFO/stockholders' equity and debt
Cash return on stockholders' equity:	CFFO/stockholders' equity

*Cash flow from operations.

Source: From Carslaw and Mills, pp. 67–69.

EVALUATION OF CASH FLOWS

By and large, the reaction to SFAS No. 95 has been overwhelmingly positive. It was seen as an important standard that made the reporting of cash flow information mandatory. Investors and creditors were viewed as benefiting greatly from this standard.

However, there were some concerns expressed about SFAS No. 95. Nurnberg is concerned with the three-way (operating, investing, and financing) classification scheme in SFAS No. 95.[6] Although this scheme was generally based on the finance literature, he compares the distinctions in SFAS No. 95 with those in the literature and found several inconsistencies. He also believes that some of the decisions made about the components of the categories resulted in the misclassification of some cash flows and the inconsistent treatment of others; both would detract from the statement's usefulness and hinder comparability between firms. Another concern expressed by Nurnberg relates to the inclusion of interest and dividend receipts and interest payments in the cash flow from operations. He believes that this contaminated that amount by including elements that are really investing and financing in nature. He also expresses a similar reservation about including income taxes in operating cash flows. Nurnberg concludes that SFAS No. 95 was internally inconsistent and ambiguous in some important aspects. His purpose was to inform readers so they would become more aware of the limitations of the Statement of Cash Flows prepared under SFAS No. 95 and make the appropriate adjustments in their financial decisions.

SUMMARY

After developing and using concepts of fund flows that did not meet the real need of investors and creditors, accountants eventually accepted that cash flows are needed information. Historically, starting with the Trueblood report and then the Conceptual Framework with the issuance of SFAC No. 1 and SFAC No. 5, the attention turned to cash flows. This process culminated in the issuance of SFAS No. 95 in 1987, which mandated the publication of a Statement of Cash Flows by statement preparers. This statement reported four major aspects of the firm: (1) Its ability to generate future positive cash flows; (2) its ability to meet its obligations, pay dividends, and meet its needs for external financing; (3) the reasons for differences between net income and cash receipts and payments; and (4) the effects of cash and noncash investing and financing activities on the firm's financial position. This information was viewed as meeting the needs of investors and creditors for their financial decisions.

The chapter provides an example of how theory formulation and standard setting can work together to advance financial accounting, beginning with a description of funds flows and the weaknesses and limitations of this approach. Accounting theory formulations identified an alternative approach, which was followed by the standard-setting process. Theoretical concerns came first, followed by standard setting. This represents a good example of how the process should work.

REVIEW QUESTIONS

1. Why have accountants in the past regarded the cash basis of accounting as inferior to the accrual basis?
2. What key change factors caused the Statement of Cash Flows to become more prominent in accounting?
3. What alternative definitions of funds were used by accountants?
4. What are some limitations of the concept of working capital?
5. What definition of funds did APB Opinion #3 and Opinion #19 employ?
6. What emphasis was placed on cash flows by the Trueblood report?
7. Trace the development of the Statement of Cash Flows of SFAS No. 95, including SFACs No. 1 and No. 5.

8. How is cash defined in SFAS No. 95?

9. Do you agree with the arbitrary conclusion in SFAS No. 95 that cash receipts of dividends and interest and cash payments of interest should be included in the operating activities section of the Statement of Cash Flows?

10. Compare and contrast the direct and indirect methods to cash flow from operations. Which do you prefer and why?

11. List five ways that cash flow information helps investors and creditors.

12. How do the positives about the cash flow statement represent negatives about accrual accounting?

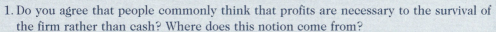

DISCUSSION TOPICS

1. Do you agree that people commonly think that profits are necessary to the survival of the firm rather than cash? Where does this notion come from?

2. One concern raised about the Trueblood report's emphasis on cash was that it was never proved that investors and creditors are primarily interested in cash. Do you accept this idea on face value or would you prefer to have it proved?

3. Historically, one reason frequently cited for preferring the accrual basis over the cash basis is the idea that cash flows can be easily manipulated. However, as accrual accounting has become more complicated, the counterargument can be made that accrual accounting now lends itself to much manipulation. Take either side, cash or accrual, and argue that it's more easily manipulated.

4. **Application Problem.** Joe, the owner of Joe's Rug Store, enjoys going to work and watching the traffic in front of his store. He had, in earlier years, carried an extensive inventory of rugs in his store. Now, however, he has only one rug in inventory. Joe paid $100 for the rug several years ago and has a sales tag on the bottom corner, with a price of $250. One nice summer day, a couple from Chicago visited Joe's Rug Store and desired his rug. Joe was quite taken back but quickly agreed to sell them the rug for $250. But rather than go out of business, Joe promptly purchased a similar rug for $160 and put a sales tag of $250 in the bottom corner.

   What was the impact on income for Joe's Rug Store from the above transactions? How was the cash flow statement for Joe's Rug affected by these transactions?

5. **Application Problem.** Joe, from Joe's Rug Store, had a blue 2001 Ford 150-ton truck that was owned by the company. Joe bought the truck new from the local Ford dealership for $18,000. The net book value of the truck as of December 27, 2002, was $12,000. Joe liked the truck, but deep down inside he really wished he would have purchased a red truck. He knew he could have the truck painted red, but it really would not have been quite the same as owning an original red truck.

   On December 28, 2002, Joe was going down Stadium Drive and saw a red 2001 Ford 150-ton truck with a for sale sign in the back window parked at the local donut shop. Joe quickly pulled into the parking lot, observed that the truck had been driven 12,200 miles and was in good shape. He offered the owner $15,000 (cash) for the red truck. The sale was finalized for that amount. Joe put an ad in the local paper the next day and promptly sold his blue truck on December 31, 2002, for $15,000 cash.

Joe is now extremely happy and is often seen driving around town in his red truck. On nice days, he even has his one rug strapped on the back.

Determine the effect on income for Joe's Rug Shop resulting from the truck purchase and the truck sale during 2002. What effect did these transactions have on his cash flow, as reported in the Statement of Cash Flows for Joe's Rug Store?

6. **Application Problem.** Evaluate Lee Enterprise using the Carslaw and Mills cash flow ratios in Exhibit 11.6. Use the direct and indirect cash flow statements of Lee Enterprise in Exhibits 11.3 and 11.5 and the following additional information (in millions of dollars except were noted otherwise) for 20XX:

Long-term debt, 12/31/20XX	100
Preferred dividends	3
Common dividends	2
Earnings before interest and taxes	115
Weighted shares of common stock	250
Total assets	900
Stockholders' equity	650
Sales	300

7. **Project:** Go on the Internet and select a major corporation (*Fortune* 500), and obtain its Statement of Cash Flows. Analyze the firm's cash flow pattern using the patterns of Dugan et al. in Exhibit 11.4.

8. **Project:** Go online and select a major corporation (*Fortune* 500), and obtain the financial statements of the firm (Balance Sheet, Income Statement, Statement of Stockholders' Equity, and Statement of Cash Flows), and analyze the firm using the cash flow ratios of Carslaw and Mills in Exhibit 11.6.

NOTES

1 Fess.

2 American Institute of Certified Public Accountants, p. 62.

3 Dugan.

4 Bowen.

5 Carslaw and Mills.

6 Nurnburg.

REFERENCES

Accounting Principles Board. "The Application and Source of Funds," *APB Opinion #3.* New York: American Institute of Certified Public Accountants, 1963.

———. "Reporting Changes in Financial Position." *APB Opinion #19.* New York: American Institute of Certified Public Accountants, 1971

American Institute of Certified Public Accountants. *Objectives of Financial Statements.* New York: American Institute of Certified Public Accountants, 1973.

Bowen, R., David Burgstahler, and Lane A. Daley. "The Incremental Information Content of Accruals Versus Cash Flows." *Accounting Review* (October 1987): 723–747.

Carslaw, C., and John R. Mills. "Developing Ratios for Effective Cash Flow Statement Analysis." *Journal of Accountancy* (November 1991): 63–70.

Dugan, Michael T., Benton E. Gup, and William D. Samson. "Teaching the Statement of Cash Flows." *Journal of Accounting Education* (Spring 1991): 33–52.

Fess, Philip. "The Working Capital Concept." *Accounting Review* (April 1966): 243–256.

Financial Accounting Standards Board. "Objectives of Financial Reporting by Business Enterprises." *Statement of Financial Accounting Concepts No. 1.* Norwalk, CT: Financial Accounting Standards Board, 1978.

———. "Statement of Cash Flows." *Statement of Financial Accounting Standards #95,* Norwalk, CT.: Financial Accounting Standards Board, 1987.

Harrison, W., and C. Horngren. *Financial Accounting,* Fourth Edition. Upper Saddle River, N.J.: Prentice Hall.

Heath, Loyd C. "Let's Scrap the 'Funds' Statement," *Journal of Accountancy* (October 1978): 94–103.

Ketz, E., and James A. Largay III. "Reporting Income and Cash Flows from Operations." *Accounting Horizons* (June 1987): 9–17.

Largay, James A., III. and Clyde Stickney. "Cash Flows, Ratio Analysis and the W. T. Grant Company Bankruptcy." *Financial Analysts Journal* (July–August 1980): 51–54.

Mazhin, R. "A Spreadsheet Template for the Statement of Cash Flows." *Journal of Accountancy* (March 1989): 110–113.

Nurnberg, H. "Inconsistencies and Ambiguities in Cash Flow Statements Under FASB Statement No. 95." *Accounting Horizons* (June 1993): 60–75.

Securities and Exchange Commission. "Adoption of Article 11A of Regulation S-X." *Accounting Series Release No. 117.* Washington, DC: Securities and Exchange Commission.

CHAPTER 12

THE NATURE OF LIABILITIES

LEARNING OBJECTIVES

After studying this chapter, you should be able to

> Understand why the process of defining liabilities is more difficult and controversial than expected.

> Appreciate how the changed importance of liabilities has increased the importance of properly defining them.

> Identify the important components in the FASB's definition of a liability.

> Apply the definition of liabilities to accounting situations.

> Evaluate the FASB's definition of liabilities.

In this chapter, we examine the basic nature of liabilities. This issue becomes the foundation for the following chapters, which apply the definition to a number of topical areas, such as accounting for income taxes, pensions, and other postemployment benefits. We concentrate on the definition of a liability in SFAC No. 6 and the events that led up to that definition.

"SNAKE PIT" OF FINANCIAL REPORTING

The definition of a liability and its application to accounting problems have been an area of difficulty for accounting standard-setting bodies, and its definition resulted in some of the most controversial accounting standards.

Because of this, defining and measuring liabilities can be regarded as the snake pit of financial reporting. That is, accounting standard-setting bodies could not approach this area without encountering great controversy when proposing that firms recognize some new liability. It appeared that whenever an accounting standard-setting body addressed an issue related to liabilities, its members ended up feeling like they had walked into a snake pit and never should have started the process. In general, the process of defining particular liabilities was more difficult and caused more controversy than expected.

This has been especially true for the FASB, as defining liabilities has been the source of much criticism and controversy. As the following chapters show, many liability topical areas and SFASs were issued by the FASB, such as accounting for income taxes (SFAS No. 109), pensions (SFAS No. 87), and OPEBS (SFAS No. 106), that have become controversial in financial reporting.

A major reason for the difficulty in this area relates to the role of liabilities in the asset-liability approach to income measurement. No longer are liabilities simply the result of credit decisions and borrowing by management. Instead, now they are an important independent determinant of net income. Liabilities have been given a separate identity and detached from a necessary linkage with expenses. This change is explained in the following section.

IMPORTANCE: DEPENDENT VERSUS INDEPENDENT

The asset-liability approach to determining net income has transformed the nature of liabilities. Under the matching approach to measuring net income, liabilities were a dependent element of financial reporting, created as the other side of an entry that emphasized expense recognition (the debit). Under matching, expenses were the primary concern, and when recording them, the liability was the other, often secondary, side of the entry (the credit).

This emphasis was dramatically changed by the move to the asset-liability approach to net income measurement: Liabilities became an independent element. Their role became primary, not secondary. This change also made the proper reporting of liabilities much more important than it was under matching. Liabilities have a higher profile now.

Another problem for the new emphasis on liabilities is that management does not especially welcome the recording of liabilities (especially when compared to the recording of assets). Management's reluctance is understandable because most firms operate under the provisions of debt covenants; therefore, recognizing more liabilities increases the risk that firms are in violation of those covenants. So management is not willing to recognize more liabilities than absolutely necessary. Additionally, recognized liabilities must eventually be paid. Because the payment of liabilities has the general effect of reducing the level of cash available in the firm, liabilities are unpopular with management.

Thus the definition of a liability, and the characteristics of that definition, is vitally important in financial reporting today and a troubling area for statement preparers and auditors.

DEFINITIONS OF LIABILITIES

The first question about liabilities is, What are they? The answer to this question leads to the definition of a liability. A number of definitions have been developed and are covered in this section. The development of the definitions is traced to the current definition in SFAC No. 6.

What We Owe   The simplest answer to the question, What is a liability? is, "things we owe." This simple definition has functioned as the basic definition of liabilities for a long time in accounting. But in our complex world, simple definitions are usually inadequate, and that's true for liabilities. The main problem with this definition is that it emphasizes the legal obligation—what we owe. Although, as shall be shown later, the legal side of liabilities is very important, accountants have generally not been willing to abdicate their authority to define liabilities to allow the courts and lawyers to take charge. Thus accountants have sought a better definition of a liability.

Credit Balance "Something"   In the chronological development of the definition, a second definition (an official one) appeared in 1953 in Accounting Terminology Bulletin (ATB) No. 1. ATB No. 1 defined a liability as *"Something represented by a credit balance that is or would be properly carried forward upon a closing of books of account."*[1] The definition states additionally that liabilities arise from debts or obligations. This definition emphasizes the legal nature of liabilities, and although it is a good starting point, it lacks the precision accountants needed.

Economic Obligations, or Not   A third definition was stated in APB Statement No. 4: *"Economic obligations of an enterprise. . . . Liabilities also include certain deferred credits that are not obligations."*[2] Notice that this definition contradicts itself and, therefore, does not serve accountants well. To its credit, it does add the idea that liabilities are not only legal obligations but also economic obligations, thus broadening the concept of liabilities. This expansion of the definition is more consistent with accountants' notion of a liability and is a step in that direction.

DEFINITION OF LIABILITIES IN SFAC NO. 6

The most recent official definition of a liability was set forth in 1980 in SFAC No. 3 (now SFAC No. 6).

> *Liabilities are probable future sacrifices of economic benefits arising from present obligations of a particular entity to transfer assets or provide services to other entities in the future as a result of past transactions or events.*[3]

First, note the close relationship between the definition of liabilities and assets. Each appears to be one side of a coin. Assets are probable future economic benefits; liabilities are the probable future sacrifices of those benefits.

Let's examine this definition further. The following are the elements of a liability according to SFAC No. 6:

- *Probable.* In a world of uncertainty, similar to the definition of an asset, the FASB decided to use the concept of probable to describe an important component of a liability. Because nothing is certain, this emphasis is appropriate. However, because the FASB did not precisely define what it meant by probable, problems of interpretation accrue to this term when used to define a liability, as they did in the case of assets.
- *Future sacrifice of economic benefits.* As a corollary to the definition of assets, liabilities represent the outflow of those economic benefits. Whereas assets represent the inflow of economic benefits, liabilities are the outflow.
- *Present obligation.* The entity in question must be currently responsible for settling the obligation as well as unable to avoid this obligation.
- *Transfer assets or services.* The settlement of the obligation requires the use of assets or services.
- *Past transaction or event.* The cause of the liability is some occurrence in the past, either a transaction or an event. A transaction or event is the trigger that causes the liability to emerge and thus be recognized in the records.

In summary, a liability involves an existing duty that requires the future settlement in assets or services that is unavoidable to the entity as a result of an event that already occurred.

SOURCES OF LIABILITY

It should be noted that liabilities are directly based on a human invention: credit. Credit is the delayed payment of an obligation. Credit, as a major source of resources, has facilitated expanded economic activity and is responsible for the growth of many enterprises. The invention of credit led to the existence of liabilities.

But specifically, there are three general areas where liabilities are created and should be recorded:

1. *Normal operations.* These are the natural transactions that a firm undertakes to conduct its normal business. Transactions that involve acquiring resources and capital or activities that use resources to produce the product or service of the firm create liabilities. Examples of liabilities that arise under these circumstances are accounts payable, wages or payroll payable and interest payable.
2. *Courts and government.* A number of liabilities arise from the actions of courts and the government. In general, these actions result in the imposition of liabilities on the firm. That is, either a court or the government obligates the firm to pay something or puts the firm in the position of an intermediary in the government process, for example, the tendency of the U.S. government to use firms as collectors of a number of payroll taxes and sales taxes. The firms are then also obligated to remit those collections to the government. Payroll taxes and sales taxes should be collected by the government, but that is deemed impractical, so business firms or economic entities are used as collectors.

The firms are generally unwilling to perform this role and must be compelled by law. Firms are not unpatriotic; but they would rather expend resources to produce their product or sell their service rather than act as an agent of the U.S. government with no compensation for their service.

3. *Ethical and moral obligations.* Ethical and moral obligations are a third source of liabilities to the firm. These arise from a variety of sources and often are not recognized formally in the records. One reason for the lack of recognition of ethical and moral obligations is their subjective nature. As an example, assume that a U.S. multinational has a subsidiary located in a developing country and local firms are economically dependent on that subsidiary. If the U.S. parent company decides to close down the subsidiary, it may have a moral obligation to provide materials to the local firms for a while to ease the transition rather than just cut off the resources and drive the local firms into bankruptcy.

TYPES OF LIABILITIES

In this section, we discuss how firms become obligated with liabilities. What are the underlying circumstances that cause the obligations? What's the basis or nature of the obligations? These are related to the sources of liabilities.

1. *Contractual.* In many cases, the liability arises from a contract, either expressly or implicitly. These contracts can be written or oral. All legal elements (such as competent parties, and consideration) must be present.

2. *Constructive.* In some cases, firms can be obligated on the basis of past actions even in the absence of a written or oral contract. If a firm consistently continues the action, it may set a precedent that will serve as an implicit contract. For example, suppose that a firm, without any contract to do so, provides each of its employees with a turkey at Thanksgiving for a number of years. After doing this consistently for ten years, as a cost-cutting move, the firm decides to stop. The past action may imply a contract, and thus, the firm might be compelled to continue to provide the turkey.

3. *Ethical.* These are obligations due to ethical considerations, such as fairness or moral grounds. In general, these obligations are not currently recorded in financial statements. But this has changed recently. During the 1990s, revelations about the sources of clothing and other products created situations in which ethical obligations were recognized and reflected in the accounting records. For example, many high-fashion houses have subcontractors located in underdeveloped countries. These subcontractors often do not pay workers a minimum wage (by U.S. standards) or provide benefits that are commonly provided workers in the United States. Sometimes, after receiving funds from the high-fashion house, the subcontractor skips out before paying the workers. Bear in mind that the final products of the high-fashion house are sold in the United States at premium prices. On a few occasions in the 1990s, when these circumstances were exposed by the media, the high-fashion houses assumed the liability for livable wages and a minimum level of benefits to the workers. In other cases, similar situations became issues on some college and university campuses; students rallied and protested to lobby the administration to stop buying athletic gear and clothing from U.S. firms that were accused of outsourcing their products to "sweatshop" facilities in the

underdeveloped world. Rather than lose the university market, these firms willingly recognized the obligation to its workers for a livable wage.

This feature of U.S. firm multinational operations in which upscale or highly visible products for developed nation markets are produced in underdeveloped or developing countries is commonplace and may become the springboard for the increased recognition of ethical and moral obligations by U.S. firms in the future. The recognition of ethical and moral liabilities may become more commonplace.

APPLICATION SITUATIONS

To see how the SFAC No. 6 definition of a liability and the nature of a liability can be used in a specific situation, two cases follow.

DISCUSSION CASE 12.1
SilVall Tech, Inc.[4]

Suppose an established and industry-leading high-tech firm, SilVall Tech, Inc. in Silicon Valley, California, has had a defined contribution pension plan; that is, the type of plan in which the firm agrees to contribute a certain amount (usually based on an employee's term of employment and salary) to a pension fund. The size of the fund when the employees retire determines the benefits received. The size of the fund is a function of the firm's total contributions to the fund over time and performance of the fund and its investments.

As a relatively new firm, the first group of employees retired two years ago. These were the employees who originally formed the firm, got it launched through its IPO and initial years, and then loyally remained with the firm throughout its full history (the past twenty-five years). However, due to stock market declines and other factors, such as the cost of living in the area around the firm where most retirees live, these employees are not able to live on their retirement benefits. Some local news people have done a number of stories on their plight, and this situation has been reported to the firm. The daughter of the founder of the firm (who died five years ago) is very upset about the situation of this first group of retirees. She knows many of them personally and feels they are part of her family. She individually knew many of them as "aunts and uncles" because when she was a child and accompanied her dad to the office, they would often babysit her. Many of her fondest memories of her father are associated with these employees, and a number of these employees are in the photos of her dad that decorate her office. She also knows that the news stories reflect badly on the firm and that this could damage the morale of current employees as well as make recruiting new employees much more difficult.

As the majority stockholder, she met with the board of directors about the situation and then called a news conference to announce the firm's new program, which would immediately triple the retirement benefits for this first group of retirees for the rest of their lives (approximately fifteen years). In making the announcement, she emphasized the past contributions of these people to the success of the firm and their importance to the firm now and in its future. The total cost of the plan enhancement was $10 million (the actuarial present value), with annual payments of $1,000,000 per year.

Question: How should SilVall Tech account for this new program?

Analysis

The Obligation   Initially, this case would appear to involve a complex pension question, the topic covered in another chapter. But it really is not. This situation is an example of applying the basic definition of a liability.

The first consideration is whether the firm is even liable for this new program. From a strictly legal standpoint, this announcement lacks a central element of a contract: receiving consideration. The firm promises to triple retirement benefits for these people without any returned promise from them. The retired employees did not agree to return to the firm or perform any future services for the firm. Because the original pension payments were based on the employees' services to the firm and these are past services, strictly speaking, the firm is not legally obligated to fulfill its promise. The firm's board of directors could change its mind and not be held legally liable. The firm could completely avoid the liability. With the media spotlight on the situation, however, such a move would have negative consequences for the firm from a public relations standpoint. But one must conclude, from a legal standpoint, that because of a lack of consideration, the firm is not legally liable to follow through on this promise. No contractual obligation exists.

However, one set of circumstances could change this and create the possibility that the firm would be legally obligated even without consideration: If any of the retirees, relying on the announcement, incurred any costs, such as fixing up a home or buying a new car, the firm could be legally obligated to fulfill its promise to that extent. That is, if relying on this announcement one of the retired employees went ahead and incurred some cost, such as buying a new car for $50,000, then the firm would be obligated to repay him or her the $50,000 and any additional damages that a lawsuit could obtain. (In fact, if successfully sued, the firm could be liable for as much as three times the damages, $150,000 in this case.) The key to these changed circumstances is that the firm's promise, although without consideration, did cause another party to incur some cost or make some sacrifice. This legal concept is called the *concept of promissory estoppel*.

But even though one could argue that no legal liability exists here, it was noted earlier that firms may be obligated under contracts or under moral or ethical obligations. The latter aspect of a liability would apply here. The firm fully intends to follow through on this program due to the concerns (corporate and personal) of the president, and thus, this promise can be considered a liability—an ethical or moral one. It should be recorded as a liability on this basis.

Liability Definition   Given that this event qualifies as a liability, the three following elements in the definition of a liability apply:

1. *The probable future sacrifice of economic benefits.* This element of the definition is satisfied because the firm will pay $1,000,000 a year to its retirees.
2. *A present obligation of a particular entity to transfer assets or provide services.* The obligation is likely to be unavoidable because the firm committed to it.
3. *As a result of a past transaction or event.* The event that triggered the program was the meeting of the board of directors, at which it agreed to provide the funding for this enhancement of the pension.

We conclude that the firm has a liability; following the pension accounting procedures under SFAS No. 87, it should recognize a liability for the present value of the $10 million. But the question asked how should SilVall Tech account for this; so far, the concentration has been on just part of the question, the liability. To completely answer the question, the other side of the journal entry, the debit, must be considered.

The Debit   To fully answer the question of how to account for the transaction, we must also consider the debit side of the analysis. First, we must ask, "What does SilVall Tech get for its expenditure?" Initially, it would appear that a simple solution is to conclude that SilVall Tech gets nothing of future benefit from its payment to the retired employees, which leads to a debit to Pension Expense for the $10 million. But that solution doesn't fully consider the situation. The amount paid to the retirees is not really a pension. Pensions are defined as payments to employees after they no longer work for the firm based on their past employment. One could easily argue that the $1,000,000 doesn't reflect the past employment of the work-ers—it reflects the present charity of the board. So the expenditure really doesn't represent a pension expense in accordance with the definition of a pension.

Another aspect of solving this with a debit to Pension Expense is troubling. In exchange for the pay-ment, the firm will obtain some benefit. We've already concluded that the firm doesn't get more service from the retired employees. But other benefits accrue to SilVall Tech from this expenditure. The case notes that by paying $1,000,000 per year, SilVall Tech avoids some negative publicity and recruits future workers easier. Therefore, some future benefits accrue to the firm from this payment. Expensing the $10 million appears to deny the existence of these future benefits.

In light of the future benefits to SilVall Tech, a better solution is to debit an asset account for $10 mil-lion. Which asset account is another question. Some would consider using an intangible asset, such as a form of Goodwill, whereas others would consider using an account such as Public Relations. Whatever account, it should be an asset account. However, this leads to a third question. What future treatment should be accorded to this account? Should the account remain an asset in perpetuity or be written off or amortized over time? Because the payments will continue as long as the current retirees are alive, that time period (or a shorter period that would correspond to the benefit to the firm from solving the economic problems of the first group of retirees) would appear to measure the future economic benefits to SilVall Tech. In this transaction, the account should be written off over the fifteen years that the employees are expected to live. This treatment is consistent with the objectives of the program and the credit side of the journal entry.

A second case follows that focuses on other aspects of the definition of a liability that are interesting.

DISCUSSION CASE 12.2
The Lottery Ticket Case (Part 3)[5]

"EXTRA! EXTRA!—MILLIONAIRE DRAWING."   United Charities has just completed the sale of all the lottery tickets that it had printed for this year's annual fund-raising sweepstakes. United Charities decided to have only a single grand prize of $1 million as it had in earlier years. In total, United Charities sold 10,000 tickets at $150 each, thereby swelling its bank account by $1.5 million. All tickets are identified only by number.

The drawing is to be held in thirty days, at which time the one winning ticket will be drawn. The holder of the winning ticket is entitled to the sweepstakes prize of $1 million. If the holder of the winning ticket does not come forward at the drawing to claim the prize, the terms of the lottery (as printed on each ticket) call for United Charities to publish the number of the winning ticket in the next day's edition of the local newspaper. The holder then has ninety days to claim the prize. If no winner comes forward by the end of that time, United Charities is entitled to keep the $1 million prize money to apply to its charitable activities.

Questions:

1. Should United Charities recognize a liability prior to the drawing? If so, what is the amount of that liability?
2. If United Charities recognized a liability prior to the drawing and no one came forward at the drawing to claim the prize, should the amount of the liability be adjusted?
3. Suppose no one comes forward to claim the prize by the seventy-fifth day following the drawing. Should United Charities adjust the liability?

Analysis

To begin to answer the three questions above, consider the three essential elements of a liability according to SFAC No. 6: (1) a present duty that requires the future settlement with assets or services; (2) the present duty is unavoidable and thus obligates an entity; and (3) the obligation has been caused by a past transaction or event.

Apply these to the general situation of United Charities and its sweepstakes. First, United Charities has agreed to pay $1 million to the holder of a winning ticket, provided that person comes forward within a ninety-day period following the drawing. Second, United Charities cannot avoid the obligation, and the sale of the tickets constitutes the past transaction. Third, the payment of the $1 million is probable under the terms of the sweepstakes. Although the possibility exists that the holder of the winning ticket cannot be found or has lost the ticket, the chance of those circumstances is less than 50 percent. So, in general, we conclude that United Charities should recognize a liability under the terms of the sweepstakes lottery for $1 million. This answers the first question.

It's interesting to compare this answer with the answer to the Lottery Ticket Case (Part 1) in Chapter 10. In general, the solution to that case was that no holder of the ticket could consider it as an asset because of the low probability that an individual ticket was the winning ticket. But if all the ticket holders followed that solution, we'd end up with United Charities recognizing a $1 million liability with no asset counterpart. That is, the liability would not be balanced by the recognition of $1 million in assets. This raises an interesting question about whether a counterbalancing asset is needed before recognizing a liability. It makes sense that if someone owes, then someone else is owed and has an asset.

The second question asks whether United Charities should adjust the $1 million liability if no winning ticket holder comes forward at the drawing. In general, the question refers to a possible change in the probable nature of the payment. But although there are a number of plausible reasons for someone not publicly coming forward and as they have ninety days to claim the prize, it appears a $1 million liability is warranted because that payment is probable.

The third question pushes the time limit back to seventy-five days. It raises the issue of the possibility that no winning ticket holder exists. Although the winning ticket holder has ninety days to claim his or her prize, some would begin to think that the probability that United Charities would have to pay out the $1 million is lower than it was on the day of the drawing. However, there are some plausible reasons as to why someone would wait at least seventy-five days to claim the prize. She or he may be involved in complex legal actions to change a will or to shelter the winnings from taxes. However, as the clock ticks, some would begin to wonder if that person exists. But in general, as long as time still allows that person to claim the prize, most accountants would not adjust the liability on the seventy-fifth day.

CONCERNS WITH LIABILITIES

An important part of the FASB's Conceptual Framework Project is the definition of the elements of financial reporting (assets, liabilities, equities, etc.). These elements were defined initially in SFAC No. 3 in 1980 and then later (1985) in its replacement, SFAC No. 6.

The definitions are given an important role in the Conceptual Framework. Gerboth concluded that of all the FASB's concepts, "the definitions in Statement No. 6 are the most robust," and that when the FASB seriously tries to use the conceptual framework to structure debate on accounting issues, it turns to the definitions."[6] Pacter calls the elements "the basic building blocks" with which financial statements are assembled. He also states, "Concepts Statement No. 3 provides a frame of reference within which the FASB can question recognition or nonrecognition practices. The asset and liability definitions themselves are likely to have a direct and ongoing impact on accounting practice."[7]

These definitions of elements have played a major role in the issuance of statements of financial accounting standards by the FASB. Some believe that the FASB is using the element definitions in SFAC No. 6 to restructure financial accounting. Groves stated that the FASB has adopted a view of financial reporting that differs fundamentally from that of the APB. He believed that the FASB view emphasizes the Balance Sheet and is a "balance sheet tilt."[8] He also believed that this involves not only a shift in emphasis from the Income Statement to the Balance Sheet but also a shift from off the Balance Sheet to onto the Balance Sheet. This view sharply contrasts with the Income Statement emphasis of the FASB's predecessor, the Accounting Principles Board (APB).

The definition of a liability has been used extensively by the FASB to justify some of its more controversial pronouncements, such as SFAS No. 87, Pensions; SFAS No. 96, Income Taxes; SFAS No. 109, Income Taxes; and SFAS No. 106, Other Post-Employment Benefits. In addition, articles in popular practitioner journals have promoted the application of the element definitions as the most user-friendly aspects of the Conceptual Framework.[9]

The potential significant impact of the new liability definition on deferred income tax accounting was heralded in SFAC No. 6. In this document, the FASB clearly applied the new definition to deferred tax credits and concluded, "Only the deferred method that is prescribed by APB Opinion 11, Accounting for Income Taxes, does not fit the definitions."[10] Because of this, the FASB embarked on a twelve-year project to revise accounting for income taxes, which resulted in the issuance of SFAS No. 96 in 1987 and SFAS No. 109 in 1992.

The definition of a liability has not been criticized directly as has the related definition of an asset. For example, Schuetze criticized the FASB's definition of an asset as "so complex, so abstract, so open-ended, so all-inclusive, and so vague that we cannot use it to solve problems."[11] No similar criticism of the FASB's definition of a liability has been published.

Although the definition of a liability has had a major effect on financial reporting through its use by the FASB in issuing accounting standards and others have found the definition to be useful to practitioners in resolving practice problems, some troublesome aspects of the definition need to be addressed, especially in terms of recent developments in financial instruments.

Recall that SFAC No. 6 identifies three essential characteristics of liabilities: (1) a present duty or responsibility to one or more other entities that entails settlement by probable future transfer or use of assets at a specific date, (2) the duty obligates the firm, leaving little or no discretion to avoid the future sacrifice, and (3) the transaction or other event obligating the firm has already happened.[12] In the following sections, issues and concerns about this definition are discussed. The first concern focuses on the first characteristic and its insistence on settlement of the liability with assets or services.

SETTLE ONLY WITH ASSETS OR SERVICES

The aspect of the definition of concern here focuses on the FASB's requirement that a liability must involve a future sacrifice of assets to be settled. In further explaining its definition, the FASB emphasized this requirement in SFAC No. 6:

> *The essence of a liability is a duty or requirement to sacrifice assets in the future. A liability requires an entity to transfer assets, provide services, or otherwise expend assets to satisfy a responsibility to one or more entities that it has incurred or that has been imposed on it.*[13]

In practice, although most of the obligations of an entity are settled with the assets of the entity, situations arise when a firm enters into a legal obligation and the settlement is not with assets. How does the FASB definition in SFAC No. 6 apply in those circumstances? Although the FASB did foresee some situations that they considered to fall into this category, such as deposits and prepayments, they concluded that these situations would eventually be settled with the assets or services of the firm.

But our concern is with situations that do not involve settlement with assets. Are such obligations liabilities? This issue becomes more important in this age of rapid developments in the design and implementation of hybrid financial securities and complex financial instruments.

MLC CORPORATION EXAMPLE[14]

For example, how should you account for the following situation? Suppose Jose Gonzales, a venture-investor, was approached at the beginning of a year by a recently organized firm—MLC Corporation—that was in the process of developing a new software product. The investor recognized the risky nature of the business and was willing to invest $1,000 as a one-year loan, with annual interest at 12 percent. The loan is made, and the firm signs a note payable. However, the note states that the loan will be settled not with cash but by the issuance of 1,120 shares of the firm's own authorized but unissued $1.00 par value common stock (the market value of the stock at the beginning of the year was $1.00).

This situation is analyzed using the following issues:

1. *Recognition.* Is the "loan" a creditor or owner claim against the firm? Does the end-of-year payment represent interest expense or distribution to owners?
2. *Measurement.* How should the transaction be measured?
3. *Disclosure (display).* Should the result of this transaction be reported on the Balance Sheet or the Income Statement?

The analysis is presented in two parts: The first emphasizes the economics and facts of the situation. The second emphasizes the GAAP approach.

1. Economic Recognition and Measurement

How does SFAC No. 6 apply in this situation involving borrowing with the promise to repay in the stock of the firm? In this case, the lender is not initially interested in becoming a stockholder in the firm; because of the risk associated with MLC, Gonzales wants to wait to see how the firm does on its software project and what effect that has on its stock. To compensate him for such risks, the loan carries an interest rate. The question arises: Does the firm have a liability in this situation? Most would agree that the firm is legally, morally, and ethically obligated to issue the stock to repay the loan and interest.

Thus the following entries would appear to properly reflect the events (assuming that the market value of the firm's common stock remains at $1.00 at year's end and that there are no valuation problems initially because 12 percent is a "fair" rate of interest):

Jan. 1, 20XX		
Cash	$1,000	
Notes Payable		$1,000
December 31, 20XX		
Notes Payable	$1,000	
Interest Expense	120	
Common Stock		$1,120

Economic Disclosure   The primary impact of this transaction is reported on the Balance Sheet. During the period, the obligation would be reported as a liability, Notes Payable. The Interest Expense would be reported on the Income Statement at year-end.

2. GAAP Recognition and Measurement

However, does the application of the FASB's definition reach the same conclusion? No. With the FASB's emphasis on the requirement that a liability be settled with assets or services, the conclusion is that there is no liability, because no asset is involved (only the unissued, authorized common stock of MLC Corporation).

Following SFAC No. 6, the following entries are suggested:

Jan. 1, 200X		
Cash	$1,000	
Common Stock Distributable		$1,000
December 31, 200X		
Common Stock Distributable	$1,000	
Additional Paid-In Capital—Common	120	
Common Stock		$1,120

GAAP Disclosure   According to GAAP, this transaction will only affect the Balance Sheet. The obligation to repay the loan will be reported as an element of owners' equity on interim statements. Because no liability exists under SFAC No. 6, no interest is recognized. The interest is charged against Additional Paid-in Capital—Common (or Paid-in Capital in Excess of Par—Common). However, it is probable that the lender, Gonzales, will recognize this transaction as an asset in his books (Loan Receivable) and report an asset on his Balance Sheet. He would also recognize the interest income ($120) at the end of the year.

Analysis   Although inconsistent with the facts in the situation, the GAAP treatment is consistent with procedures for similar transactions. For example, when a firm declares a cash dividend, a liability is recognized for the future payment of the dividend. However, when a firm declares a stock dividend, their obligation is not recognized as a liability but as an owners' equity item. Similarly, when a firm issues stock by subscription, its obligation to issue stock is not recognized as a liability, but as an owners' equity item.

It could be argued, however, that the situation described above is not really a loan but an investment in the firm. When someone gives a firm cash in return for stock in the future, it is generally considered an investment. But what investment involves interest, a note, and repayment at a specific date? Those factors are inconsistent with the typical investment situation. The underlying motivation of the lender is to consider this as a loan and the interest as revenue.

To help analyze this transaction, Exhibit 12.1 contains a list of thirteen factors that are used to help classify securities as debt or equity. Except for one factor, conversion feature, all the other factors would classify the current note as a debt (creditor claim). However, under GAAP, that would be inconsistent with the definition of a liability.

This concern with the definition of a liability does not appear to have been adequately addressed in the literature. Kam mentioned it and suggested a case in which a company borrows money from a bank and repays with its own common stock.[15] He concluded that no liability existed in this situation because the stock of the firm is neither assets nor services.

Rubin applied the SFAC No. 6 definition to a situation in which a firm made an agreement with its employees under which it had an option to issue stock or pay cash to employees early in the next year if target sales for the current year were achieved.[16] If the target sales were achieved, the question posed in the article was whether the firm should recognize a liability at year-end. Rubin concluded that no liability should be recognized because the firm had the option to avoid the future sacrifice of assets. So he concluded that no liability existed. The fact that the obligation could have taken the form of stock was not specifically addressed.

FOCUS TENSION

A second issue or concern with SFAC No. 6's definition of a liability focuses on the tension between the various time periods mentioned in that definition. For example, the definition states that a liability is "a probable future sacrifice . . . arising from a present obligation . . . as a result of a past transaction." The definition encompasses all three time periods: past, present, and future. The concern arises when these are different for a particular item. In that case, which prevails?

For example, suppose a firm has a present obligation to do something that also involves a future obligation to do something else and the two obligations differ. According to SFAS No. 6, the firm has a liability. But which is the liability, the present obligation or the future sacrifice? The definition does not indicate which to choose when they differ.

A typical area where this becomes important deals with employee compensation and pensions. This topic is the focus of Chapter 14 but is relevant to the current discussion. In a pension, an employee is paid a postemployment salary based on past employment periods. Under most pensions, the pension is earned (after vesting) as the employee works for

EXHIBIT 12.1
Factors to Help Classify Securities on the Right Side of the Balance Sheet
Is It Debt or Equity?

Classification Factors	Debt (creditor claim)	Equity (owner claim)
Maturity date	Fixed maturity date	Does not mature
Claim on assets	Priority interest	Residual interest in net assets
Claim on income	Fixed, cumulative	Not fixed, subordinated, participatory
Voice in management	None	Voting right
Maturity value	Fixed maturity value	No maturity value
Intent of parties (investor attitude and investment character)	Safety first	Opportunity for capital growth
Preemptive right	No preemptive right	Includes preemptive right
Name of security	Bond, note, etc.	Stock
Conversion feature	No conversion feature	May be converted into common stock
Potential dilution of earnings per share	None	Potential to dilute earnings per share
Right to enforce payment	Periodic interest payments and payment at maturity are legally enforceable	Not legally enforceable
Good business reason for issuing (alternatives and capitalization)	High level of capitalization	Financial difficulties or a low level of capitalization
Who invests in security	Different individuals hold debt securities and equity securities	Same individuals hold debt and equity securities

Source: Adapted from Schroeder and Clark (1991), p. 105.

the firm. So at any point in time, the firm owes that employee a pension, the value of which can be measured using the employee's work record so far. But the amount that the employee ultimately receives from the pension may differ from that amount because the amount of the final pension is also based on the future employment of that person and the amount of interest that the pension fund can earn. That means that the future sacrifice of the firm is larger than the current obligation to that employee. For example, suppose that based on the employee's work record so far, the firm is obligated to her for a pension of $20,000, but if she continue to work for the firm for the rest of the employment period and if the pension plan earns its expected returns, the firm will be obligated to pay her a pension of $50,000.

Which of the two amounts, $20,000 or $50,000, is the firm's liability to her now? To some, the answer is clear: She has earned a pension benefit of $20,000, and that's what the firm owes her; it is the present obligation of the firm. But if we assume a going concern, others would argue that the future sacrifice of the firm, $50,000, is the real obligation to her and that $50,000 should be recognized as the liability by the firm. In cases where the FASB has addressed this focus tension (i.e., present obligation and future sacrifice don't agree), it has tended toward recognizing the future sacrifice (measured by the present value of the expected future sacrifice) as the liability. Accounting for pensions (SFAS No. 87) and other postemployment benefits (SFAS No. 106) are examples of this.

LEGAL ENFORCEABILITY

A third issue associated with the definition of a liability in SFAC No. 6 concerns the importance of legal enforceability in the definition. Recall that prior definitions of liabilities relied heavily on legal enforceability as a mainstay in the definition. In the past, if the liability would not hold up in court, then it wasn't really a liability. In some sense, the past reliance on legal enforceability was similar to using the courts as a screening mechanism for the definition of a liability. It simplified the issue by declaring that liabilities were legal claims against the firm.

However, the FASB did not put legal enforceability into its definition of a liability. Instead, it adopted a broader definition that allowed firms to recognize liabilities for items that may or may not be legally defendable in court. In general, the FASB was not willing to allow courts to decide the final definition of a liability. Although many accountants viewed that as a wise step, others were concerned that by omitting legal enforceability from the definition, the FASB was expanding the definition to include items that were not really liabilities. Those concerned saw the issue as the FASB's opening a door, and they were not sure what would be coming through that open door in the future to be recognized on the firm's Balance Sheet as liabilities.

INSUBSTANCE DEBT DEFEASANCE

As an example of the type of situation that can arise with regard to liabilities when the legal issues are minimized, consider insubstance debt defeasance. This situation occurs when a firm with long-term debt on their books considers covering the debt (making an investment that provides interest revenue that matches the interest expense on the debt and a cash inflow that could be used to repay the principal of the debt). Because of changed market conditions, the market value of the long-term debt is lower than the book value. The changed market conditions allow the firm to invest in long-term debt of the U.S. government or other corporations to exactly match the principal and interest payments of its own long-term debt. It is able to make this investment at less than the current book value of its own debt. The investment is then placed in an irrevocable trust for the sole purpose of servicing its own debt. Exxon Corporation is credited with pioneering this effort, and in 1982, it had long-term debt with a book value of $515 million. Exxon was able to invest in U.S. government debt for $312 million that exactly matched the principal and interest payments on Exxon's debt. Because the cost of the U.S. government debt was less than the book value of Exxon's debt, Exxon recorded a $203 million gain (before taxes) on the transaction. Once this became known, many other firms followed Exxon's example. The popularity of this type of financial transaction raised questions about how it should be recorded.

The FASB added this topic to its technical agenda in 1982, and fifteen months it later issued SFAS No. 76. This standard allowed a firm to consider the original obligation satisfied when it entered into an insubstance debt defeasance. The majority of the Board believed that the firm made the sacrifice to settle the obligation even though the firm still had the legal obligation to pay the debt. The Board concluded that the original obligation was settled by the procedure, and firms were allowed to remove the debt from the Balance Sheet even though the firm still legally owed the debt.

It should be noted that the FASB later recanted on this issue. In 1996, to remedy this situation, SFAS No. 125 was issued, and in paragraphs 218 to 225, SFAS No. 76 was superseded. As part of the discussion, the FASB noted that several concerns and criticisms were aimed at SFAS No. 76. On reconsideration, the FASB concluded that the "de-recognition" of a liability in an insubstance debt defeasance was not appropriate for a number of reasons: For example, the firm is not released from its original debt in the situation, and the "de-recognition" of the debt was not representationally faithful. So SFAS No. 76 was superseded.

This example illustrates the danger of minimizing the legal enforceability aspect of liabilities. Although the FASB corrected the situation created by SFAS No. 76, that accounting standard was GAAP for more than thirteen years.

WHICH PAST EVENT?

A fourth concern about the SFAC No. 6 definition of a liability deals with the lack of precision as to *which* past event is the source of the liability when there are multiple past events.

Under the FASB's definition, a liability is launched, or created, by a past event or circumstance. Although some would argue that this goes without saying, others were concerned that some transactions have multiple events and that the liability definition does not tell you which of those is the past event.

A related question refers to the lack of agreement on *what* is the past event. Can a liability be recognized if there is no agreement on what past event caused it? And can you have a liability when the other party doesn't recognize it as such, as in the case of deferred taxes? When a firm reports deferred taxes, the Internal Revenue Service (IRS) does not recognize the firm either as owing additional taxes (deferred tax liability) or as prepaying its taxes in advance (deferred tax asset). These issues will be covered in detail in a future chapter, but they represent important questions to consider when you think about the definition of a liability.

REVISION OF LIABILITY DEFINITION

Due to these and other concerns about the definition of a liability, the FASB proposed an amendment to the liability definition in October 2000.[17] The FASB cited its work in the financial instruments project and other projects as the reason for a reconsideration of the definition of a liability. In an exposure draft, "Accounting for Financial Instruments with

Characteristics of Liabilities, Equity, or Both," the FASB decided that certain financial instrument elements included obligations that would be settled by the issuance of equity shares. These should be considered as liabilities.

The FASB concluded that certain obligations that require settlement by issuance of the issuer's equity shares should be classified as liabilities. As we noted before, these situations would be not considered as liabilities under SFAC No. 6. The proposed amendment to SFAC No. 6, paragraph 35, also includes as liabilities certain obligations that require or permit settlement by issuance of the issuer's equity shares and that do not establish an ownership relationship. The proposed amendment would add a footnote to paragraph 35 including:

> *Certain obligations, primarily financial instruments or components of compound financial instruments, require or permit settlement by the issuance of equity shares. If those financial instrument components establish a relationship between the issuer and the holder that is not an ownership relationship, they are liabilities.*[18]

SUMMARY

Given the importance of the definition of elements in the Conceptual Framework and the FASB's reliance on these definitions to issue accounting standards, it appears significant that the definition of the liability is flawed. The flaws were not immediately apparent; the flaws emerged as the definition was applied to a number of accounting topics. That is as expected. One cannot fully appreciate a definition until it is applied or used to distinguish items.

The move by the FASB to amend the definition is positive. It shows that the FASB is demonstrating the flexibility that is needed to keep the definition current and contemporarily relevant. In addition, the decision of the FASB to correct the flawed application of the definition of a liability in SFAS No. 76 with SFAS No. 125 is a positive development. As long as the FASB is willing to correct standards that are not optimal and amend definitions—as is currently proposed—it is ensuring that the definition will be current and relevant.

REVIEW QUESTIONS

1. In what way is the area of liabilities a "snake pit" for standard setters?
2. How has the change to net income from the matching to the asset-liability approach impacted liabilities? Is this a positive change in your opinion?
3. What are the advantages and disadvantages of the simple definition of liabilities as "things we owe"?
4. How was the SFAC No. 6 definition of a liability related to the three other definitions presented in the chapter. Trace the development of the definitions to SFAC No. 6's definition.
5. What are the typical sources of liabilities?
6. What types of liabilities are there? Give an example of each type.

7. How have the sources and types of liabilities been changing over time? Which source or type was dominant in the past, and which will be more dominant in the future?

8. What are the five components of the definition of a liability according to SFAC No. 6?

9. The requirement that a liability must be settled with assets or services limits the definition of a liability in what ways?

10. What is the "focus tension" associated with some liabilities?

11. Which of the four concerns about the definition of a liability presented in the chapter do you think is the most serious? Why?

12. How has the FASB proposed changing the definition of a liability? In your opinion, would the change represent an improvement to the definition?

DISCUSSION TOPICS

1. Discuss the role of legal enforceability in the definition of a liability. Do you regard it as primary or secondary element of the definition? Discuss and support your position.

2. Do you think business firms should recognize more ethical or moral liabilities than they currently recognize? Should this type of liability be considered as fundamentally different from the other two types? In what ways?

3. What is your view of the original position taken by the FASB on insubstance debt defeasance in SFAS No. 76? Do you agree with the FASB's change?

4. What position do you take on the proposed amendment to SFAC No. 6 for liabilities?

5. In the Lottery Ticket Case (Part 3), what is your opinion of the significance of recognizing a liability when there is no corresponding asset recognized? Should the existence of an asset be a requirement for the recognition of a liability in double-entry accounting?

6. In the Lottery Ticket Case (Part 3), is there any point in time during the ninety-day period when you would seriously consider adjusting the liability of United Charities if no winning ticket holder came forward? Support your position.

7. **Application Problem.** The Jones Company and the Smith Company have been sued. The probability of those companies losing the suit is set at 83 percent (by an advisor in the finance/law department who speaks only in terms of numbers and says very few words). The suit is seeking joint and several liability, which means that if the Smith Company is unable to pay, then Jones will have to pay the entire amount. The advisor also indicates that the amount of the eventual loss could range from a low of $800,000 to a high of $2,200,000. No amount in that range is any more likely than any other amount. The advisor, after completing a financial analysis of the Smith Company, indicates that there is only a 45 percent probability that Smith can contribute its share of the loss (which is assessed at one-half of the total assessment). At year-end, how should Jones Company report in regards to this situation?

8. **Application Problem.** Willis Star has just signed with the Bithlo Bumpers of the Junkyard International Semi-Pro Basketball League. Because the league is newly established and team field houses are being built, most players have agreed to deferred compensation contracts, including Willis Star. Willis is guaranteed to receive $1,000,000 at the end of five years. In addition, assuming Willis averages 20 points or greater per game over the entire five-year contract period, Willis will receive a bonus at the end of the fifth year totaling $200,000. It is now at the end of the first year of Willis's contract, and

Willis finished the season with an average of 22 points per game. (He had to shoot numerous times per game to arrive at that total, and his team mates are beginning to call him "gunner"; appropriately so, since Willis averaged only one assist per game).

How should the Bithlo Bumpers account for Willis Star's deferred compensation contract at the end of the first year? Would your answer have been different if Willis had averaged only 18 points per game in the first year of his five-year contract? Suppose he averaged only 10 points per game?

9. **Application Problem.** The Silver Dollar Store, located in Silver Springs, Florida, has been in operation for seventy years. However, the changes have not gone very well. Silver Dollar currently has a $680,000 loan, which includes $80,000 of accrued interest, that is due and payable. Silver Dollar cannot pay the loan currently. The Silver Springs Bank and Trust Company has agreed to grant Silver Dollar Store the following concessions: The bank will accept equipment valued at $200,000 (which has an original cost and net book value on Silver Dollar Store's books of $500,000 and $280,000, respectively) and 3,000 shares of Silver Dollar Store restricted common stock with a par value of $10 and an imputed market value of $25. In addition, the bank will forgive $50,000 of accrued interest due in one year and reduce the interest rate to either 4 percent or 6 percent (from the original interest rate of 9 percent), depending on whether the company can complete a restructuring with the previous owner. The previous owner is a relative; therefore, the chance of obtaining the needed restructuring is quite good. How should Silver Dollar Store account for the agreement with the bank?

10. **Internet Project.** Search the web for a *Fortune* 100 firm that has financial instruments that will be settled by the issuance of equity shares. Examine the disclosures associated with the financial instruments. How has the firm explained this obligation?

NOTES

1 AICPA Committee on Terminology, par. 27

2 Accounting Principles Board, par. 132.

3 Financial Accounting Standards Board (1985), par. 35.

4 Based loosely on "The Pension Enhancement Case," in Johnson and Petrone, p. 40.

5 Johnson and Petrone, p. 34.

6 Gerboth, p. 2.

7 Pacter, p. 87.

8 Groves.

9 See Rubin, for example.

10 Financial Accounting Standards Board (1985), par. 241.

11 Schuetze, p. 68.

12 FASB (1985), par. 197.

13 FASB (1985), par. 193.

14 Based on the unpublished paper by T. Evans and C. Kelliher, "The Flaw in the Definition of a Liability," presented on July 23, 1998, at the annual meeting of the International Society of Systems Sciences, Atlanta, Georgia.

15 Kam, p. 113.

16 Rubin, p. 124.

17 FASB (1985), par. 35.

18 FASB (2000).

19 FASB (2000), p. 2.

REFERENCES

Accounting Principles Board. "Basic Concepts and Accounting Principles Underlying Financial Statements of Business Enterprises." *Statement No. 4.* (New York: AICPA), 1970.

American Institute of Certified Public Accountants, Committee on Terminology (1953). *Accounting Terminology Bulletin No. 1,* "Review and Resume," (New York: AICPA).

Financial Accounting Standards Board. "Elements of Financial Reporting." *Statement of Financial Accounting Standards No. 6.* Stamford, CT: Financial Accounting Standards Board, 1985.

———. "Proposed Amendment to FASB Concepts Statement No. 6 to Revise the Definition of Liabilities." Norwalk, CT: Financial Accounting Standards Board, 2000.

Gerboth, Dale. "The Conceptual Framework: Not Definitions, But Professional Values." *Accounting Horizons* (September 1987): 1–8.

Groves, R. "What Today's Balance Sheet Tilt Means." *Financial Executive* (September/October 1989): 26–30.

Henderson, M. S. "Nature of Liabilities." *Australian Accountant* (July 1974): 328–334.

Hughes, John S. "Toward a Contract Basis of Valuation in Accounting." *Accounting Review* (October 1978): 882–894.

Johnson, L. Todd, and Kimberley R. Petrone. *The FASB Cases on Recognition and Measurement,* Second Edition. New York: John Wiley & Sons, 1995.

Kam, V. *Accounting Theory,* Second Edition. New York: John Wiley & Sons, 1990.

Ma, Ronald, and Malcolm Miller. "Conceptualizing the Liability." *Accounting and Business Research* (Autumn 1978): 258–265.

Pacter, Paul. "The Conceptual Framework: Make No Mystique About It." *Journal of Accountancy* (July 1983): 76–88.

Rubin, S. "How Concepts Statements Can Solve Practice Problems." *Journal of Accountancy* (October 1988): 123–125.

Schuetze, W. "What Is an Asset?" *Accounting Horizons* (September 1993): 66–70.

Schroeder, R., and M. Clark. *Accounting Theory, Text and Readings.* New York: John Wiley & Sons, 1991.

CHAPTER 13
ACCOUNTING
FOR INCOME TAXES

LEARNING OBJECTIVES

After studying this chapter, you should be able to

> Understand the purposes of income and other taxes.

> Contrast the purposes of income taxes and the purposes of financial reporting.

> Distinguish between the cash and allocation approaches to income taxes.

> Appreciate the difficulty the accounting profession has had in settling accounting standards for allocating income taxes.

In this first chapter devoted to the application of the SFAC No. 6 definition of a liability to an accounting topical area, we consider accounting for income taxes. A "taxing" subject if ever there was one—in the sense that it has been and continues to be a source of controversy and difficulty for accounting standard-setting bodies, especially the FASB. So in the introduction to this subject, the basics and the nature of income taxes are covered, to provide you with the background that you need to understand the controversy and difficulty associated with accounting for income taxes.

In this chapter, six specific important accounting events and the general development of accounting for income taxes are discussed:

1. Pre-1913, no income tax law
2. Sixteenth Amendment (1913)
3. ARBs #2, #43, and #44
4. APB Opinion #11
5. SFAC No. 3 (now No. 6)
6. SFASs No. 96 and No. 109

A time line of these developments is presented in Exhibit 13.1.

To provide some humor to this otherwise serious topic, recall comedian Jerry Seinfeld's opening monologue about taxes on one of his shows. He complained that the government's income tax system treated adults like children. To prove what he meant, he compared paying income taxes to the classic *Leave It to Beaver* television show of the late 1950s and early 1960s.[1] Seinfeld said that income taxes made children out of adults. In his monologue, the government and the IRS were given the role of the parents, Ward and June Cleaver, and taxpayers were the children, Wally and the Beaver. The tax accountant was the neighbor's child, Eddie Haskell, who always got the Beaver or Wally into trouble in the show. When Wally and the Beaver got into trouble, they were sent to their room by their parents. As the tax accountant, Eddie shows taxpayers how to get around the rules and gets them into trouble with the IRS, their parents. As a consequence, they have to go to their room! Of course, in reality, if taxpayers try to "get around" the tax laws or break them, they might be sent to jail, not their room.

EXHIBIT 13.1
Time Line

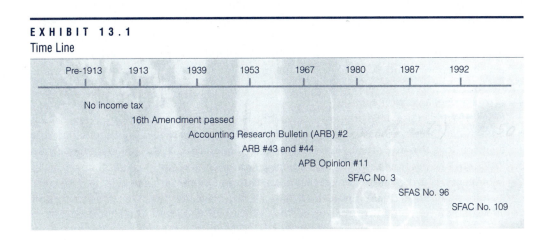

As the accounting issues and standards about income taxes are examined, three difficult questions about taxes will be considered:

1. Are income taxes a valid expense of the firm?
2. Can a liability exist when it is not recognized by the other party to it?
3. Can you have a liability without a triggering event or transaction to cause it?

As you can see, accounting for income taxes raises some interesting questions. To prepare you to deal with these difficult questions, in the next section some of the basics of taxation are presented.

PURPOSES OF INCOME AND OTHER TAXES

The first issue concerns the reasons for having income taxes and other taxes. Why have income taxes? What motivates the government to impose these taxes on individuals and firms? Remember the source of all federal taxes. Federal income taxes are based on the Sixteenth Amendment to the U.S. Constitution, which was passed in 1913. Other federal taxes are gift, estate, and payroll. Federal income taxes are based on tax laws that are passed by Congress and published in the Tax Code. The Internal Revenue Service (IRS) administers the federal tax law. Federal tax laws are the dominant form of taxation in the United States and have a far-reaching effect on all financial decisions.

There are a number of motivating reasons for having taxation, especially income taxes.

1. *To fund the government.* Taxes are the major source of revenue to support the vast array of government services on which all citizens rely. In fact, the largest single source of federal revenue comes from individual income taxes.
2. *To redistribute wealth.* Income taxes tend to even out the distribution of wealth in society. In general, income tax rates are progressive, which means that the rate increases with increased income. Those who earn more pay higher income taxes, and that tends to even out the distribution of income. As a result, the rich are less rich and poor are less poor; therefore, after-tax incomes are closer and the gap between the rich and poor has been narrowed. Taxes act sort of like a modern Robin Hood, who robbed the rich and gave to the poor. But income taxes tax the rich more and the poor less. This notion of redistributing wealth has been traditionally popular in American society.
3. *To accomplish macroeconomic objectives, such as to spur the economy.* Taxation is an effective macroeconomic tool within the economists' fiscal policy toolbox. By adjusting income taxes rates, the government can inject funds into the economy to make the economy grow or shrink. In general, cuts in the income tax rates are seen as helping the economy grow, and tax rate increases have the opposite effect.
4. *To accomplish certain social objectives.* Certain preferences of individuals, such as for cigarettes or alcoholic beverages, are discouraged by heavy taxes on those items, which tend to make them more expensive and less affordable. The deductibility of charitable contributions is a way of encouraging individuals to contribute to such organizations.
5. *To stimulate particular industries and sectors of the economy.* Sometimes, special tax incentives are given to firms to encourage them to enter a particular industry that is important to national interests. Common examples of these are the depletion allowances given to oil firms or tax credits for firms that increase their exports.

It is important to understand the purposes and sources of income and other taxes to contrast them with the purpose and source of financial accounting. Taxation does include many accounting measures and concepts but is not really based on accounting. Federal taxation is designed to accomplish at least the five objectives listed above and is based on tax laws promulgated by Congress. Sometimes those objectives conflict, and sometimes certain objectives are given a priority over others. What results is a U.S. Tax Code and regulations of about 50,000 pages.

But financial accounting is vastly different. The purpose of financial accounting is to provide external parties—shareholders and creditors—with financial information relevant to financial decision making. The standards that govern financial accounting are issued by the Financial (not federal) Accounting Standards Board (FASB), which is a private-sector body. This comparison reveals that although financial accounting standards and the Tax Code share some common ideas and measures, taxation and financial accounting are vastly different in terms of their purposes and sources. This conclusion is important for understanding the next section, how this difference affects the Income Statement.

INCOME STATEMENT ELEMENTS

Exhibit 13.2 contains a model Income Statement for a firm. Consider the source of each of the listed items (the lines are numbered to facilitate discussion), that is, where the rules for recording or reporting the item originate and which agency or standard-setting body has jurisdiction or authority over the recording and reporting of that particular item.

EXHIBIT 13.2
Model Income Statement

Line	Account	Subtotals	Totals
1	Revenue from sales		$10,000
2	Cost of goods sold		5,000
3	Gross margin		$ 5,000
4	General and administrative expenses:		
5	General expenses	$1,500	
6	Administrative expenses	1,500	
7	Total expenses		3,000
8	Earnings before taxes		$ 2,000
9	Income taxes		1,000
10	Income after taxes		$ 1,000

Line 1 reports the revenue from sales and is governed by generally accepted accounting principles (GAAP). That is also true for line 2 and, by computation, line 3, gross margin. General and administrative expenses, shown on lines 4 through 7, are also reported in accordance with GAAP. So, too, is the subtotal, earnings before taxes, listed on line 8. But with line 9, things change. That's because line 9 reports the income taxes on the income reported on line 8; yet the amount of income taxes is governed by the Tax Code, which is written by Congress. So line 9 has a different origin and basis, or authority, source than the rest of the items on the Income Statement. Line 9 is the only line whose source is different.[2]

This fundamental difference is part of the controversy and difficulty with accounting for income taxes. By its nature, the amount of the income taxes on the Income Statement is independent of GAAP and determined by the Tax Code as applied to that particular firm, not by GAAP. This inconsistency could lead to a situation in which the amount of the income tax is inconsistent (much larger or smaller) than appears to be appropriate from the rest of the statement. This inconsistency has troubled accountants and led to steps to rectify the situation.

ACCOUNTING OPTIONS FOR TAXES

Accountants have developed two alternative approaches to accounting for income taxes; the cash method and the allocation method. Both are described in this section.

CASH METHOD

In the cash method of accounting for income taxes, a simple and direct approach is taken. This method reports on the Income Statement the amount of income taxes actually paid (or owed) by the firm for that year. That amount is taken from the firm's income tax return and not adjusted in any way. Of course, given the current state of the tax code and the expertise of tax accountants, the amount of tax a firm pays in a given year can vary considerably from year to year. However, the cash approach treats income taxes as most other expenditures: The amount you pay is the same amount you report.

The cash method is relatively easy to apply. The firm's actual transaction to record its income tax liability (based on that year's tax return) is the basis for the amount of income tax expense reported on the Income Statement. And that's it. For example, if the firm's tax on its return is $100 million for a particular year, then the income tax expense on that year's Income Statement is also $100 million.

ALLOCATION METHOD

The allocation method is different than the cash method. Following it, the actual amount of tax paid by the firm in the year is basically ignored when it comes to reporting income tax expense on the Income Statement. Instead, the amount of income tax expense reported on the Income Statement is based on the income tax rate that the firm pays, applied to the amount of pretax income (earnings before taxes). What results is an amount of income tax that is perfectly appropriate for the before-tax earnings, given the firm's tax rate. The income tax expense reported on the Income Statement is therefore perfectly consistent with the before-tax income. If allocation is used, it looks like all items on the Income Statement are based on the same method. But the amount of income tax expense doesn't necessarily relate to the amount of tax on the firm's tax return.

Because the firm also records a transaction for the actual income tax liability, the allocation approach becomes complicated. To record the actual tax liability but report income tax expense differently requires some difficult accounting. Because the income tax liability is determined by the tax return and the income tax expense is determined by the tax rate applied to the before-tax earnings, an offsetting amount is necessary to balance the entry. The balancing amount is either a debit or a credit, depending on the relationship between the actual tax paid and the amount of income tax on the Income Statement.

For example, if the firm's tax return shows income taxes of $100 million but the pretax earnings are $300 million and the tax rate is 35 percent, then the income tax expense reported on the Income Statement would be $105 million. In a very general form, the following entry would necessary:

Income Tax Expense ($300 × 0.35)	$105	
Income Taxes Payable		$100
Balancing Credit		5

At this stage of the discussion, the balancing credit of $5 million is not being labeled; it simply shows that under the allocation method, although the Income Statement shows income tax expense perfectly consistent with pretax earnings, the recording of the actual income tax transaction will not balance without some balancing credit or debit. Its nature is discussed next.

The allocation basis produces an interesting element, the balancing credit or debt, which leads to a question about the nature of the balancing credit or debit. What does it represent? Is it an element of the actual liability for taxes? The answer is no, not for the current year because the liability for taxes is determined on the firm's tax return and is $100 million. Is it part of the expense? No, because the tax expense is correctly determined by applying the firm's tax rate of 35 percent to the pretax earnings of $300 million. So what is the balancing debit or credit? There is no clear answer to this question. Some consider it the current accounting recognition of the temporary difference between the accounting measure of the tax expense (the $105 million) and the actual tax liability ($100 million) that will somehow be taken care of in the future. If the $5 million is a credit, as it is in this example, it is the current accounting recognition of a potential future tax liability. If the $5 million were a debit balancing item, it would represent the current measure of a future potential tax prepayment. But not all accountants agree with this view. Answering the simple question, "What is that $5 million?" has caused much confusion and controversy in accounting. Despite this, tax allocation is the preferred method of accounting for income taxes.

TAX ALLOCATION AS PART OF GAAP

Given the indirect nature of the tax allocation approach, complications, and the nebulous balancing element of the allocation method of accounting for income taxes, why is this method a part of GAAP? A number of arguments support allocation, and a number take the opposite position. Both are discussed in the next sections.

Support for Allocation

1. Tax allocation is viewed as simply an extension of accrual accounting. Just as other items are recorded at an appropriate amount and reported as such, income taxes are no different. To report income tax expense at the firm's income tax rate multiplied by the before-tax income is consistent with other forms of accrual accounting and is similarly justified.

2. The allocation of income taxes is another example of the matching approach to income determination. Because the firm had a pretax income of a certain amount, the related tax should be matched against pretax income and be based on the same amount. Matching considers income tax as an expense and simply matches it against the related revenue.

3. Tax allocation avoids some of the wild swings in earnings after taxes that the cash basis produces. Earnings volatility is not easily understood by investors and not appreciated by management, who believe it signals that the firm is more risky than it really is. Tax allocation solves the problem of distortions of earnings after tax because by leveling the differences in the timing of tax expenses and revenues. Thus using the tax allocation approach has the effect of "smoothing" the reported earnings after tax and avoiding variability.

4. The balancing item produced by tax allocation eventually goes away. It will reverse and be canceled by the normal operations of the firm. So the problem with tax allocation is self-correcting in the future. An example supporting the argument that tax differences generally even out is shown in Exhibit 13.3.

EXHIBIT 13.3
Single-Asset Tax Allocation

Assume a firm, subject to a tax rate of 40 percent, invests in a $40,000 plant asset with a four-year life and no salvage value. The firm uses double-declining depreciation for taxes and straight-line for financial reporting. Below are the annual depreciation amounts under both methods, the excess tax depreciation, and the tax allocation balancing item.

Year	Tax Depreciation	Financial Reporting Depreciation	Excess Tax Depreciation	Balancing Item (credit)
1	$20,000	$10,000	$10,000	$4,000
2	10,000	10,000	0	0
3	5,000	10,000	(5,000)	(2,000)
4	5,000	10,000	(5,000)	(2,000)
	$40,000	$40,000	$ 0	$ 0

Notice that over the four-year life of the asset, although the annual depreciation amounts are different, the total depreciation is the same under both financial reporting and tax methods of depreciation. The last column shows that the balancing item, a credit, self-corrects and is zero by the end of year four.

Support Against Allocation

1. The first argument against allocation questions the consideration of income taxes as an expense. Although this issue will be discussed further in a following section, consider the similarities and differences of income tax with other expense items. Expenses of the firm have the following three things in common:

(a) All expenses are outflows of assets of the firm to produce revenue.

(b) Expenses are typically voluntary; it is up the discretion of the firm as to whether the expenditure will be made.

(c) Because the aim or objective of incurring expenses is to directly or indirectly produce revenues for the firm, often the size of the expense expenditure will be directly related to the amount of revenue produced.

Notice that except for (a), income taxes have nothing else in common with other expense items. The firm does not voluntarily incur income tax expense; it is legally required to pay it. The firm does not expect to receive, directly or indirectly, any specific revenue from the amount of the income tax expenditure, nor is the revenue produced directly related to the size of the tax expenditure.

2. Accounting methods should not be considered "smoothing" devices. Nothing in the objectives of financial accounting refers to the need to smooth income after taxes. The argument suggests that accountants are actually doing a disservice to outside users of financial statements if they disguise what really happened to after-tax net income by allocating taxes. Outside users will be better served if they see the actual tax payments of the firm on the Income Statement. This information is potentially useful as a measure of the performance of the management of the firm for that period. Some investors value the actions of management to minimize the income tax payments of the firm.

3. The argument that tax allocation does not produce a problem by using the balancing debit or credit because over time the difference will even out, assumes that the firm is static and invests in one asset at time and does not buy a new one until the old asset is done. Firms are dynamic. They invest in and divest assets every year as part of their normal operations. Over time, they expand their operations by investing more in assets than they divest.

Unfortunately, firms do not behave as the example shown in Exhibit 13.3 indicates. Instead, as firms grow, they invest continually. As that happens, the total amount of the balancing items (debit or credit) does not shrink or go away. In fact, the opposite happens: The amount of the balancing item tends to increase. So instead of eliminating the problem associated with the balancing item, tax allocation compounds it and makes it worse. A number of studies have shown that in the more realistic situation of firms that invest continually, the balancing item does increase over time.[3] This situation is shown in Exhibit 13.4, in which a second asset is added to the same firm used in Exhibit 13.3.

As revealed in Exhibit 13.4, the balancing item does not reverse and cancel out; instead, it grows. Notice that by adding one more asset in Year 2, the size of the balancing item increases for the next two years. Recall that in Exhibit 13.3, the balancing item decreased in Year 2. For this simple example, only one more asset was added. But for the typical firm that is investing in assets each year, the effect is much more dramatic.

4. Tax allocation introduces uncertainty into the Income Statement. Because tax allocation uses the firm's tax rate, which is determined by the Tax Code, changes in that code will affect the firm currently and in the future. It will also impact the firm's past, as tax allocation produces balancing debits and credit that are based on past tax rates. If these rates change, the amounts of the balancing debits and credits change. If accountants are serious about limiting the volatility that is introduced into financial statements, then tax allocation is the wrong procedure because it introduces a great deal of uncertainty. Uncertainty regarding future tax rates and new laws make tax allocation uncertain and complex.

EXHIBIT 13.4

Expanding Asset Tax Allocation

Assume the firm in Exhibit 13.3, subject to a tax rate of 40 percent, invests in a second $40,000 plant asset at the start of Year 2, with a four-year life and no salvage value. The firm uses double-declining depreciation for taxes and straight-line for financial reporting. Below are the annual depreciation amounts under both methods for both assets, the excess tax depreciation, and the tax allocation balancing item, shown here as the cumulative balancing item.

Year	Tax Depreciation	Financial Reporting Depreciation	Excess Tax Depreciation	Credit Balancing Item (cumulative)
1	$20,000	$10,000	$10,000	$ 4,000
2	30,000	20,000	10,000	8,000
3	15,000	20,000	5,000	10,000
4	10,000	20,000	(5,000)	8,000
	$75,000	$70,000	$20,000	

5. The last argument against tax allocation considered here is that it introduces fictional accounting into the accounting records. Tax allocation reports a tax expense that does not correspond to the actual taxes paid by the firm and thus is inconsistent with the tax return. The question is, Why are accountants justified in changing the amount of tax expense from what actually happened to a fictional amount that happens to be more consistent with the rest of the elements on the Income Statement? Is this a proper role for accounting, or is it inconsistent with the nature of accounting? Does it set a dangerous precedent for other areas of accounting?

As this section has shown, accounting for income taxes is troublesome. The next section chronicles the procedures that accountants have developed to deal with this area.

ACCOUNTING PRONOUNCEMENTS

The chronological development of accounting pronouncements for taxation clearly reveals the controversy and difficulty that standard-setting bodies have had with this topic. The discussion that follows will show what concepts dominated the thinking of accountants and standard-setting bodies across time. Accountants have struggled with formulating the appropriate rules for taxation for a long time. Accounting for income taxes was first officially mentioned in Accounting Research Bulletin (ARB) #2 in 1939, but ARBs #43 and #44 (1953) established tax allocation as a canon of financial accounting, although its application was voluntary.

This struggle to formulate appropriate GAAP for income taxes provides the background necessary to understand the current situation. Knowing how accountants got into the current situation enables you to understand the current standards and prepares you to make improvements in the future. Many believe that improvements in accounting standards are necessary because they are still not satisfied with the current accounting standard for taxation; it is not regarded as effective. The following sections provide a summary of the major pronouncements and analyze them from an accounting theory viewpoint.

APB OPINION #11, "ACCOUNTING FOR INCOME TAXES"

Although ARBs #43 and #44 established the concept of tax allocation in 1953, firms were not required to implement it. Some did; others did not. Some firms adopted comprehensive tax allocation; others applied it selectively; and still others used the cash method. It wasn't until 1967 in APB Opinion #11 that firms were required to adopt comprehensive tax allocation.

The procedures dictated in APB Opinion #11 involved complete and comprehensive tax allocation for timing differences. Under APB Opinion #11, when the accounting net income exceeded taxable net income, a balancing credit should be recognized; when the taxable net income exceeded the accounting, a balancing debit should be recognized. Opinion #11 considered the balancing credit a deferred credit and the balancing debit as a deferred charge.

Deferred charges and credits were a default classification. Deferred charges and credits were not actually defined in APB Opinion #11. They were placed on the Balance Sheet in the "no-man's land," or undefined region, between liabilities and owners' equity (for deferred credits) and between assets and liabilities (for deferred charges). The primary support for characterizing the balancing credits and debits as deferred items was the belief that that they would eventually reverse and cancel out, so the treatment as deferred items was seen as appropriate as a temporary measure. The other option was to consider deferred credits as liabilities and deferred debits as assets, but the APB didn't choose that treatment.

Few concerns were raised in the late 1960s over the procedures in APB Opinion #11. The movement to comprehensive tax allocation was viewed as progress in financial reporting standards. Remember, the APB was primarily concerned with reporting the appropriate income tax expense on the Income Statement; the corresponding debit or credit on the Balance Sheet was of lesser importance. Because the APB believed that the resulting deferred credits and charges would eventually reverse and then be canceled, APB Opinion #11 was widely regarded as a positive development.

For the period of 1967 through 1980, APB Opinion #11 ruled, and firms followed the comprehensive tax allocation procedures, reporting deferred charges and credits. APB Opinion #11 appeared to work well except for two aspects. First, over time, because of changes in tax rates (generally lower) and the dynamic nature of firms (continually expanding by investing in assets), firms usually reported deferred credits, and these grew instead of reversing and being canceled. The balance of deferred tax credits on firms' Balance Sheets began to grow in size, and some of them approached the size of the owners' equity in the firm. This result began to be a concern for some accountants.

Second, some accountants still questioned the nature of the balancing debits and credits that resulted from the application of APB Opinion #11. They questioned whether presenting the balancing debits and credits as deferred charges and credits on the Balance Sheet was the best way to present these elements. Their concern was soon addressed in the FASB's Conceptual Framework project.

SFAC NO. 3, "ELEMENTS OF FINANCIAL STATEMENTS OF BUSINESS ENTERPRISES"

The concern about the procedures in APB Opinion #11 was settled when the FASB issued the third pronouncement of the Conceptual Framework project, SFAC No. 3 in 1980 (now SFAC No. 6), which presented the definitions of the elements of financial statements.[4] Unfortunately for APB Opinion #11, deferred charges and credits were not on the list of ten financial statement elements. That meant they were no longer appropriate elements to be presented on the Balance Sheet. In fact, paragraph 241 in SFAC No. 6, unambiguously states that "only the deferred method that is prescribed by APB Opinion No. 11, Accounting for Income Taxes, does not fit the definitions."[5] You can't get more blunt than that.

The definitions of the elements in SFAC No. 6 clearly ruled out the deferred credits and charges that resulted from the comprehensive tax allocation procedures of APB Opinion #11. This was one of the first consequences that the Conceptual Framework and the definition of the elements had on existing accounting pronouncements. The process showed how elements that were not consistent with the definitions in SFAC No. 6 could be eliminated from the Balance Sheet.

Another consequence was that now the FASB had to pick up the pieces. That is, because the Conceptual Framework invalidated APB Opinion #11, the FASB became the appropriate standard-setting body to issue a standard for accounting for income taxes. Issuing that standard would turn out to be a ten-year process for the FASB.

SFAS NO. 96, "ACCOUNTING FOR INCOME TAXES"

In light of the impact of the definitions of element in SFAC No. 3, the FASB began in 1982 to consider a new standard on accounting for income taxes that would be consistent with the Conceptual Framework's definition of elements. The Board generally supported the notion of comprehensive tax allocation in APB Opinion #11, but it considered the balancing debits and credits as assets and liabilities. So the FASB essentially replaced the deferred debits and credits with assets and liabilities. The FASB followed their due process and issued a discussion memorandum in 1983, an exposure draft of a new standard in 1986, and the new standard, SFAS No. 96, in 1987 with a 4 to 3 vote.[6] Notice that it took five years to issue the replacement for APB Opinion #11, and the close vote shows that accounting for income taxes was still controversial among the Board members.

SFAS No. 96 required comprehensive tax allocation for timing differences, and it considered the balancing items as assets and liabilities. SFAS No. 96 attempted to measure the specific tax liability arising from the activities during the period and show this tax liability on the Balance Sheet. This accounting was consistent with the FASB's emphasis on measuring assets and liabilities more accurately. It also made accounting for income taxes consistent with the Conceptual Framework's definition of elements.

In SFAC No. 96, the resulting tax liability or asset is adjusted for the effect of changes in tax laws or rates. But SFAS No. 96 was asymmetrical in its recognition of tax assets and liabilities. Tax liabilities as balancing items were readily recognized, but tax assets received different treatment as balancing items. Firms could recognize tax assets only (1) to the extent of tax liabilities or (2) because they would be recovered if they could be carried back for a refund of taxes. This accounting was a very conservative and restrictive approach to the recognition of tax assets.

Because of the complications of tax allocation at the time due to tax reform and changes in tax rates, the FASB formed an implementation group for tax allocation in 1988 and deferred implementation of SFAS No. 96.[7] The FASB issued a special report on implementation issues in 1989. More implementation complications led to requests that the implementation of SFAS No. 96 be deferred further; SFAS No. 96 was deferred to the first quarter of 1992 and then to the third quarter of 1992. This series of major implementation problems and deferrals of the effective date show the difficulty of obtaining resolution on tax allocation issues.

SFAS NO. 109, "ACCOUNTING FOR INCOME TAXES"

Because of the complexities and difficulties that firms encountered in implementing SFAS No. 96, in 1991, the FASB issued an Exposure Draft of a new standard on income taxes that would supersede SFAS No. 96. The primary issues that motivated the new standard were concerns about the criteria for recognizing and measuring deferred tax assets. The AICPA Accounting Standards Executive Committee (AsSEC), Financial Executives International (FEI), the Institute of Management Accountants (IMA), and many public accounting firms expressed concerns that the criteria in SFAS No. 96 for recognizing tax assets were too restrictive.

The new standard on income taxes, SFAS No. 109, "Accounting for Income Taxes," was issued in 1992, again by a narrow vote, 4 to 3. In contrast to SFAS No. 96, it permitted the consideration of future events in determining whether tax benefits will be realized—and thus reported—as assets. A deferred tax asset must be recognized for all tax differences that lead to balancing debits if it is more likely than not that some portion or all of the deferred tax asset will be realized. Thus the FASB resolved the major problem with SFAS No. 96, asymmetrical treatment, and also stated some criteria for the definition of an asset when applying the definitions of the elements in SFAC No. 6. In the case of the recognition of a tax asset, the Board used the criterion of "more likely than not" to define *probable*, which implies that a level of likelihood of more than 50 percent qualifies for recognition as a tax asset. How this definition of probable applies to other assets is unknown.

THREE DIFFICULT QUESTIONS ABOUT INCOME TAXES

This chapter began with a warning that accounting for income taxes has been controversial and difficult, which is corroborated by the fact that between the APB and the FASB, three financial accounting standards all named the same, "Accounting for Income Taxes," were issued. This demonstrates that accountants have had to make multiple efforts to resolve this issue. Why all these problems? What makes accounting for income taxes so difficult? The following three questions help explain why it has been so difficult to achieve consensus on this topic.

QUESTION 1: ARE INCOME TAXES AN EXPENSE?

The first question refers to the appropriateness of reporting income taxes on the Income Statement as an expense. If tax expenditures were not an expense, then an alternative treatment could remove taxes from the Income Statement and report them on the Balance Sheet, Statement of Retained Earnings, or Statement of Comprehensive Income, but that represents only a potential solution to the problem.

So the question is, Are income taxes an expense? To answer the question, consider the definition of expenses in SFAC No. 6. paragraph 80:

> *Expenses are outflows or other using up of assets or incurrences of liabilities (or a combination of both) from delivering or producing goods, rendering services, or carrying out other activities that constitute the entity's ongoing major or central operations.*

To further explain expenses, SFAC No. 6 lists examples of typical expenses for the firm: units of product delivered or produced, employees' services used, kilowatt hours of electricity used, or taxes on current income.

Although SFAC No. 6 lists taxes as an expense, how well do income taxes fit the definition of an expense according to SFAC No. 6? First, income taxes certainly qualify as an outflow of assets or incurrence of a liability. The law accomplishes that outcome. But there is some question as to the motivation for paying taxes. Certainly, that is also explained by the need to obey the law. But is that the underlying motive for paying taxes? Notice that three purposes for expenses are listed in SFAC No. 6: (1) delivering or producing products or goods, (2) rendering services, or (3) carrying out other activities that are the entity's central operations. Taxes do not fit into any one of those three categories. So although the FASB listed taxes on current income as an example of an expense, the application of the criteria does not necessarily lead to the same conclusion.

QUESTION 2: ARE NONRECIPROCAL LIABILITIES VALID?

A second question about accounting for income taxes under the allocation method refers to the status of the balancing items, debits and credits. Under the FASB's approach, these are reported as deferred tax liabilities and deferred tax assets, respectively. If this is true, it would appear, for example, that if a firm reports a deferred tax liability, we could confirm that liability by contacting the other party to the liability, the IRS, that should have recognized a corresponding asset. But you won't be able to confirm it. Similarly, if a firm reports a deferred tax asset, presumably because it "prepaid" its taxes, you cannot contact the IRS to confirm it. So there are assets and liabilities that do not have the reciprocities that are expected for them. It is reasonable to expect that if one firm reports a liability, then the other party to that specific transaction will similarly report a corresponding asset. But not in the case deferred taxes. Does this nullify the procedure or seriously question its validity? Some think, yes, to both implications.

QUESTION 3: WHAT IS THE EVENT?

A third question about accounting for income taxes refers to the underlying transaction or event that triggers the transaction. Recall that according to the definition in SFAC No. 6, a liability must have a past transaction or triggering event that is the genesis of the transaction being recorded and reported.

Rosenfield questioned this very issue with regard to accounting for income taxes under the allocation method.[8] He regarded the concepts supporting SFAS No. 96 as "fatally flawed." Although the FASB explained that in its view the obligating event for deferred taxes was the origin of the temporary differences, Rosenfield disagreed. He questioned the FASB's view in two regards: (1) The FASB view did not take into account the last events that cause tax liabilities, and (2) the past event that the FASB referred to didn't cause the liability.

Rosenfield questioned the issue regarding which event was the last event to cause the tax liability and was that the appropriate event? He believed that the event causing deferred taxes is not a tax event but rather is an accounting one and therefore wasn't appropriate. He viewed deferred taxes as arising from accounting decisions, such as using straight-line depreciation for financial reporting and double-declining depreciation for income taxes, thus creating a balancing credit that is considered a deferred tax liability. Because the IRS was not involved in any of those decisions or in those circumstances, Rosenfield questioned whether an event really occurred that created the tax liability.

He questioned the whole issue of the allocation method by pointing out that tax allocation is really an Income Statement concept that doesn't fit well on the Balance Sheet. He noted that because the APB emphasized the Income Statement, tax allocation made sense. But because the FASB emphasized the Balance Sheet, tax allocation does not fit. He suggested that in using the liability approach to deferred taxes, the FASB "compounds an already doubtful measurement technique by misdefining 'liability' both in terms of the FASB's own conceptual framework and in terms of conventionally accepted practice.[9] Rosenfield's view was supported by Defilese, who concluded that "deferred taxes do not constitute liabilities—present or future."[10]

These three difficult questions raise doubts about the validity of tax allocation. The following case illustrates some of these issues in accounting for income taxes.

DISCUSSION CASE 13.1
The Income Tax Carryforward Case[11]

"Accounting 101"

The Rustbelt Manufacturing Company, a parts supplier for the Big 3 automakers, usually has managed to earn a profit until the past year when it incurred an operating loss of $1 million because of a business recession. Assume that the resulting net operating loss (NOL) carryforward of $1 million legally cannot be carried back to be applied against taxable income of prior periods for a refund of taxes previously paid. However, the company can use that carryforward to offset its future taxable income and thereby reduce its income taxes payable in future years.

The recession has not yet ended, and Rustbelt does not anticipate turning a profit for another two or three years. However, it does expect to have future taxable income in excess of $1 million within the twenty-year carryforward period allowed by law. Rustbelt's corporate income tax rate is 30 percent.

Rustbelt's accounting manager, Betty Bookit (also an accounting instructor at the local community college) views the NOL carryforward as a benefit. Bookit writes a journal entry to record an asset of $300,000 related to the income tax carryforward and hands it to Joe Greenshade, accounting clerk, the day the books are to be closed for the year. Greenshade, responsible for making all journal entries, hesitantly enters her office and asks, "What accounting class did I miss that allows us to turn a loss into an asset?"

Question: Should Rustbelt recognize the NOL carryforward as a $300,000 asset?

Analysis

This is a typical NOL situation: A firm has an NOL that it can use to offset future taxable income. The question is whether that NOL is an asset that should be recognized in the financial statements of the current year.

Using the definition of an asset from SFAC No. 6, consider whether the following three critical aspects of an asset are present in this situation:

1. A probable future economic benefit
2. Controlled by the firm
3. As a result of a past transaction or event

The second and third criteria are satisfied in this case. The NOL is controlled by Rustbelt and resulted from the operating loss sustained by Rustbelt.

But a serious question arises about the first criterion, the benefit. The question is, Does the loss generates a benefit or does the benefit occur only when the loss is applied to an operating profit in future years? Because profits are expected in the future, the benefit will not be realized until some future period. If you believe that the NOL itself generates the benefit, then you should recognize it as an asset. If you believe that the application of the NOL to future operating profit is the benefit, then no asset is recognized now.

Other issues complicate this analysis. If Rustbelt can sell or transfer the NOL to another firm, that would support the recognition of an asset because the benefit is independent of Rustbelt's earning a profit.

Another major question refers to the probable nature of the benefit. According to Rustbelt, it expects to earn a profit in the future. But no likelihood or probability is associated with that expectation. Does this constitute enough evidence to qualify as "probable" under the definition of an asset? Most would say no.

It should be noted that applying the principles of SFAS No. 109, Rustbelt would record a deferred tax asset of $300,000 for the NOL carryforward. Because Rustbelt does expect future profit (more likely than not), the benefit is there. If Rustbelt considered some of the carryforward as not realizable, a valuation allowance could be established.

Conclusion

The conclusion of the case from a theory standpoint differs from the GAAP conclusion. As noted in the previous paragraph, under SFAS No. 109, a deferred tax benefit would be properly recognized by Rustbelt in the current years financial statements.

But the theory conclusion is different. Using the definition of an asset in SFAC No. 6, one cannot conclude that the benefit of the NOL is probable enough to qualify as an asset. In general, more likely than not, or just in excess of 50 percent, is generally not high enough of a threshold for recognizing an asset. This is an example of a basic conflict between theory and GAAP in accounting for taxes. However, it should be noted that a variation of this result (no asset recognized) is exactly what was called for in SFAS No. 96.

SUMMARY

As this chapter demonstrates, accounting for income taxes has been a continuing controversy and has been difficult for accounting standard-setting bodies. Although income taxes have a very different purpose and source than the other elements on the Income Statement, accountants have traditionally considered taxes as an expense that belongs there. GAAP includes procedures to implement this view, and comprehensive tax allocation has become the dominant approach. But tax allocation has led to more complications, such as those related to accounting for the balancing debits or credits. Accounting standard setters have not been successful in formulating well-accepted accounting procedures for the balancing debit or credit. In light of those difficulties, it is a wonder (to some) that accountants have not turned to the cash approach to resolve these problems.

In a positive sense, accounting for taxes has demonstrated the power of the definitions of elements in the Conceptual Framework. In a negative sense, it also reveals how the FASB used a special definition of probable in formulating SFAS No. 109. This definition is not generally applicable to defining other assets, which results in inconsistency in asset definitions under the Conceptual Framework.

Looking at the chronology of events presented in this chapter, one cannot help but wonder when the FASB will be involved in another accounting standard called, "Accounting for Income Taxes."

REVIEW QUESTIONS

1. What are the five purposes of income and other taxes?
2. How would you prioritize (rank from high to low) the five different purposes of income and other taxes?
3. How does the cash method for income taxes work?
4. What are the advantages of the cash method for income taxes? The disadvantages?
5. How does the allocation method for income taxes work?
6. What are the arguments for allocation? What are the arguments against allocation? Which arguments are stronger, in your view?
7. Examine the time line for the accounting pronouncements for income taxes. What does it reveal in terms of the time period when accounting for income taxes became more important to accountants?
8. Why did the APB decide that the balancing debits and credits were deferred charges and credits? In retrospect, was this shortsighted?
9. Should the APB and accountants have accepted the argument that deferred tax credits and debts would reverse and cancel over time? Is Exhibit 13.3 or 13.4 more realistic in your opinion?
10. How did the issuance of SFAC No. 3 (No. 6) affect APB Opinion #11 and accounting for income taxes?
11. Compare and contrast SFAS No. 96 and SFAS No. 109. What was the major change made to accounting for income taxes in SFAS No. 109?
12. What are the three difficult questions about accounting for income taxes?

DISCUSSION TOPICS

1. Do you agree with comedian Seinfeld's view of the tax system treating adults like children? Do you feel that way about paying taxes?

2. Do you agree with the purpose of taxes to redistribute wealth? Do you think this idea is more or less accepted today than in the past?

3. What do you see as the nature of the balancing debit or credit under the tax allocation method?

4. Recall the three purposes of theory from Chapter 1. Do you think it was a good example of how theory should evaluate current practice when SFAC No. 3 invalidated APB Opinion #11?

5. Do you think the threshold of more likely than not used in SFAS No. 109 to decide when to recognize an asset should be generally accepted as the threshold for all assets?

6. Which of the three difficult questions about accounting for income taxes is most important, in your opinion?

7. How would you answer each of the three questions about income taxes discussed in the chapter?

8. Do you think accounting for income taxes should return to the cash method?

9. One could argue that all expenses necessary to generate revenue are "central activities of the firm" and that income taxes are simply one more item incurred to produce revenue. Do you agree or disagree with this statement? Support your position.

10. Do you agree or disagree with the following statement: Under the cash approach to income taxes, the ratio of income tax expense to pretax income varies greatly from period to period and accountants do not want that result. Support your position.

11. **Application Problem.** On January 1, 20X2, the Taintsville Manufacturing Corporation invested $80,000 in a plant asset with a four-year economic life and no salvage value. Taintsville is subject to an income tax rate of 40 percent. Assume they use straight-line depreciation for financial reporting and double-declining balance method for income taxes. Prepare a schedule similar to Exhibit 13.3 showing the tax depreciation, the financial reporting depreciation, and the cumulative balancing item over the four-year life.

12. **Application Problem.** Assume the Taintsville Corporation in Question 11 invests in a second plant asset on January 1, 20X3. The asset costs $80,000, has a four-year economic life, and has no salvage value. Taintsville continues to use straight-line depreciation for financial reporting purposes and double-declining balance for tax purposes. Prepare a schedule, similar to Exhibit 13.4, showing the tax depreciation, financial reporting depreciation, and cumulative balancing item.

13. **Application Problem.** Assume the Taintsville Corporation had net income before depreciation and taxes of $500,000 in 20X2 and that net income would grow 10 percent for each of the next three years. Using the information on Taintsville's plant asset investments in Questions 11 and 12, prepare a schedule of cash outflows for taxes for each of the four years (20X2 through 20X5) and compare the cash paid for taxes each year to the accounting income tax expense. Which set of numbers (cash paid for taxes or accounting tax expense) appears more reliable?

NOTES

1 In case you never saw *Leave It to Beaver,* it was a classic TV family comedy show of the late 1950s about the Cleaver family who lived at 485 maple Drive in Mayfield, USA. It started in October of 1957 and ran six seasons. In it, Theodore, nicknamed the Beaver (the "Beav"), and his older brother, Wally, frequently got into interesting family situaitons with their parents, Ward and June Cleaver. Ward and June were solid, dependable, and very loving parents. Often, the brothers got into trouble because of the influence of a neighbor kid, Eddie Haskell, who often had ideas that ended up getting all three kids into some difficulty because Eddie's plans didn't work out as he expected. Eddie was more streetwise than either Wally or the Beav and always had lots of "good ideas." In those days, getting into trouble took the form of breaking a window with a baseball or wrecking a new bicycle.

2 Technically, lines 5 and 6 could also include FICA and other taxes governed by tax laws.

3 See Livingstone (1967 and 1969).

4 FASB (1980).

5 FASB (1985), par. 241.

6 I recall attending a meeting in San Francisco on this issue in 1984 when I was a visiting professor of accounting at the University of California at Davis. The open hearing was composed of FASB staff and a number of financial executives and accountants from the Bay area. I remember that one of the biggest issues at that meeting was what to do with the very large balance of deferred taxes payable on the Balance Sheets of most of the firms. One option in the Discussion Memo was a return to the cash basis of accounting for income taxes. But that left unanswered the question as to how to treat the very large amount of deferred taxes payable (in some cases, the amount of deferred taxes payable was almost equal to the amount of owners' equity). Proposals were suggested to transfer that amount to owners' equity, recognize it as a tax gain on the Income Statement, or reclassify it as owners' equity from a contribution from the government. None was considered satisfactory. But without some satisfactory way to deal with the result of tax allocation (which remember should have automatically reversed and canceled), the financial executives and FASB staff realized that they had to continue tax allocation. The situation of the FASB on this issue was likened to "holding a tiger by the tail." This is, you don't have any good options: If you continue to hold on, you've got a tiger by the tail. If you let go, then you have a tiger to deal with. The FASB was in that dilemma over the issue of what to do with the large deferred taxes on most firms' balance sheets.

7 See Sheehy and Schlitt, for example.

8 Rosenfield.

9 Rosenfield, p. 100.

10 Defilese, p. 89.

11 Johnson and Petrone, p. 23.

REFERENCES

Accounting Principles Board. "Accounting for Income Taxes." *Accounting Principles Board Opinion #11.* New York: American Institute of Certified Public Accountants, 1967.

Behn, Bruce, Tim Eaton, and Jan Williams. "The Determinants of the Deferred Tax Allowance Under SFAS No. 109." *Accounting Horizons* (March 1998): 63–78.

Cheung, Joseph, G. Krishnan, and C. Min. "Does Interperiod Income Tax Allocation Enhance Prediction of Cash Flows?" *Accounting Horizons* (December 1997): 1–15.

Committee on Accounting Procedure. "Restatement and Revision of Accounting Research Bulletins." *Accounting Research Bulletin No. 43.* New York: American Institute of Certified Public Accountants, 1953.

Defilese, Philip. "Deferred Taxes—More Fatal Flaws." *Accounting Horizons* (March 1991): 88–91.

Financial Accounting Standards Board. "Elements of Financial Statements of Business Enterprises," *Statement of Financial Accounting Concepts No. 3.* Norwalk, CT: Financial Accounting Standards Board, 1980.

———. "Elements of Financial Statements." *Statement of Financial Accounting Concepts No. 6.* Norwalk, CT: Financial Accounting Standards Board, 1985.

———. "Accounting for Income Taxes." *Statement of Financial Accounting Standards No. 96.* Norwalk, CT: Financial Accounting Standards Board, 1987.

———. "Accounting for Income Taxes." *Statement of Financial Accounting Standards No. 109.* Norwalk, CT: Financial Accounting Standards Board, 1992.

Livingstone, John L. "A Behavioral Study of Tax Allocation in Electric Utility Regulation." *Accounting Review* (July 1967): 544–552.

———. "Accelerated Depreciation, Tax Allocation, and Cyclical Asset Expenditures of Large Manufacturing Firms." *Journal of Accounting Research* (Autumn 1969): 245–256.

Read, William J., and Robert A. J. Bartsch. "The FASB's Proposed Rules for Deferred Taxes." *Journal of Accountancy* (August 1991): 44–53.

Rosenfield, Paul. "The Fatal Flaw of FASB Statement No. 96." *Accounting Horizons* (September 1990): 98–100.

Sheehy, Janice, and Linda Schlitt. "SFAS No. 96: The New Age of Tax Accounting." *Management Accounting* (October 1991): 50–53.

CHAPTER 14

ACCOUNTING FOR POSTEMPLOYMENT COMPENSATION

LEARNING OBJECTIVES

After studying this chapter, you should be able to

> Contrast the cash and matching (accrual) methods of accounting for pensions.

> Understand the nature of pensions, the parties involved in pensions, and the two accounting issues associated with accounting for pensions.

> Appreciate the potential conflict between the present and future liability issue in pensions.

> Describe the similarities and differences between pensions and other postemployment benefits.

In this chapter, the theme of Chapter 13 continues with application of the definition of a liability in the FASB's Conceptual Framework project to the accounting for postemployment compensation. Two specific examine postemployment compensation topics are examined: accounting for pensions and accounting for other postemployment benefits.

The concentration is on four specific important accounting events as well as a discussion of the general development of accounting for postemployment compensation:

1. Pre-1966—cash basis for pensions.
2. 1966—APB Opinion #8.
3. 1985—SFAS No. 87.
4. 1990—SFAS No. 106.

A time line of these events and developments is presented in Exhibit 14.1.

EXHIBIT 14.1
Compensation Time Line

Pre-1966	1966	1985	1990
Cash Basis for Pensions			
	APB Opinion #8		
		SFAS No. 87	
			SFAS No. 106

The pattern used in Chapter 13 is followed here, that is, first looking at the background of the issues associated with accounting for pensions and other postemployment benefits. Then the accounting procedures for these two topics are examined from a theory viewpoint. The difficulty that the FASB has had in issuing standards on pensions and other postemployment benefits that would achieve a high degree of acceptance by both practitioners and statement preparers is explored. The chapter also applies the definition of a liability to the latter two topics.

THE MOST IMPORTANT ISSUE

To begin the chapter, a basic question should be addressed: Why do firms need a special way to account for postemployment compensation? Common sense would dictate that any payments to employees who are no longer employed are obviously expenses when paid. Isn't it that simple and, therefore, not worthy of any further concern?

This argument is support for what's known as the cash method, and it was generally accepted for some time. Firms following the cash method recognized expenses for compensation paid in the period when pension payments were paid. No attempt was made to link or match the expenditures with revenue.

The counterargument to the cash method is the matching concept, which provides for the recognition of all expenses incurred while producing the current period's revenue. One of those expenses deserving recognition is the delayed compensation that employees and executives will receive after they cease employment but earn now, during their current employment. Thus matching requires recognition in the current period of the total cost of employee and executive compensation, which is composed of two elements: current compensation and the future compensation in the form of pensions after retirement. That is, the current productive effort of employees and executives requires compensation now and in the future. Thus the current period's compensation expense must include an element representing this future compensation.

However logical and sensible that argument sounds, the actual implementation of it is not that simple. Part of the problem of accounting for postemployment compensation is that it involves future costs, which must be estimated and which depend on the occurrence of a number of future events, none of which are sure or certain. These difficulties are covered in future sections.

PENSIONS

DEFINITION

A pension plan is an arrangement between employees and their employers to pay postemployment compensation to employees after they retire from active service. Most plans contain provisions that each employee, on reaching a specified age, can retire and receive a pension during each year of his or her retirement. These plans became popular after World War II and since then are commonplace in employment contracts.

There are two types of pension plans: defined benefit plans and defined contribution plans. Defined contribution plans are simpler than defined benefit plans and do not pose difficult accounting problems. The employer (and sometimes the employee) contributes an amount to a pension plan. The terms of the plan usually indicate how much the employer is responsible for contributing annually to the plan. The sponsoring firm discharges its liability when it makes that contribution and usually recognizes an expense for its contribution to the plan. Upon retirement, the employee gets whatever benefits have been earned by the contributions to the plan and the return on the plan's investments.

The defined benefit plan is more complicated. The employee and employer each contribute an amount to the pension fund. The plan promises to pay retired employees specific retirement benefits, and the sponsoring firm is liable for those benefits. Those promised benefits are independent of the level of contributions. A number of factors make this type of plan more complicated. The sponsoring plan must continually recalculate its contribution as the size and composition of its workforce changes. In addition, the investment returns of the fund are also a variable that can affect the ability of the fund to pay the expected benefits.

An important concept involved in pensions is called *vesting*. Vesting determines when the employee or executive is legally entitled to some level of pension benefits. In general, vesting occurs after a probationary time period, and once an employee vests, the employee is entitled the benefits whether or not they remain employed by that firm. Pension benefits do not legally accumulate or increase in value with each year until the vesting requirements are met. Prior to vesting, the employee has no right to the benefits.

THE PARTIES INVOLVED

Four parties are involved in a pension arrangement: the sponsoring firm, the employee, the pension plan or fund, and the Pension Benefit Guarantee Corporation (PBGC).

1. *The sponsoring firm is the focus of accounting for pensions.* In general, it is responsible for the pension benefits and makes contributions to the fund during the term of the employees' service life.
2. *The employee is the person who receives the benefits after retirement.* Presumably, part of the motivation in working for the firm is based on the promise of a future retirement benefit.
3. *The pension plan or fund is a separate entity established to manage a firm's pension plan.* Firms that formulated pension plans and decided to manage them soon discovered that a great deal of work went into running the plan, accepting contributions, making investments, keeping track of employees and benefits, and paying the benefits. In response to this need, a number of firms, such as subsidiaries of insurance companies, were established to specialize in managing pension plans for sponsoring firms, for a fee. Most industrial corporations recognized the wisdom of outsourcing the management of their pension plans to a separate organization.
4. *The PBGC is a government-created organization to insure pension plans covered by the 1974 Employee Retirement Income Security Act (ERISA).* It acts as a form of national insurance for pension plans covered by ERISA. ERISA improved access to pension benefits and their security. It protected employees from discretionary funding clauses in plans and the termination of plans. In most pension plans, the payment of benefits is to be made solely from pension fund assets, not the assets of the sponsoring firm. The PGGC requires a minimum level of funding of pension plans by sponsoring firms and insures vested benefits. It funds its insurance function by collecting premiums from sponsoring firms and pension plans.

As you probably have begun to realize, the simple idea of paying an employee postemployment benefits has become complicated, as evidenced by the relationships of the four entities involved. When you consider the size of the workforce in U.S. firms, you can get some idea of the magnitude of this issue. The fact that Congress has issued a landmark act of social legislation in the last thirty years (ERISA), which also led to the creation of the PBGC, shows the importance of the issues but also makes them more complicated.

TWO ACCOUNTING ISSUES

Two major accounting issues are associated with pension plans. The first issue is the cost: What does the pension plan cost the firm? The answer leads to the recognition of pension expense. The second issue involves liability: What amount does the firm owe? The answer leads to the recognition and measurement of the firm's liability for pensions. The cost and liability issues are related.

Pension Expense   The cost side of pensions calculates the amount of pension expense to be recognized on the Income Statement as a part of employee and executive compensation. It is supported by the notion that the current compensation expense associated with current employees includes not only their current compensation (pay) but also their future compensation (pension benefits). So firms are not allowed to recognize the amounts they currently pay as retirement benefits as the pension expense of the current period. Of course, attempting to include in compensation expense some measure of the current expense associated with future pension benefits requires estimates and assumptions. Another element of the cost issue concerns the relationship of the annual expense for pensions compared to the cash contributed to the pension plan during the same year. What should be the relationship between these two amounts? Should the expense equal the cash contribution or be more or less than that amount? Is the actual expense more than just the cash contributed to the plan that year?

Pension Liability   The liability side of pensions involves the amount that should be shown on the Balance Sheet as the sponsoring firm's obligation for pensions. This is a little more difficult to visualize. During any year, the current employees earn present compensation as well as future compensation in the form of future pension payments. Attempting to measure the future pension benefits that the sponsoring firm is obligated to make becomes complicated when you consider the number of changes that occur in the workforce of a firm over a period of time: for example, employees quit or are terminated, employees are laid off or take new jobs within the firm, employees die, and employees retire. Such workforce changes greatly affect the firm's pension obligation.

Another factor must also be considered: the investment returns that the plan can earn. Actuaries are the professionals who are the specialists on such issues; they take all these actuarial factors into account and provide the firm with an estimate of its liability at a point in time, which the firm can adopt. This liability is also linked to the firm's contributions to the plan. If the firm does not contribute all that it is obligated to contribute in a year, it creates unfunded accumulated benefits. Do these unfunded benefits create a liability for the sponsoring firm? If so, how should these be measured and reported?

Over the life of the plan, the amount of pension expense must equal the total amounts paid to employees. Although the expense and liability sides of pensions are like two sides of a coin, accounting pronouncements have not always treated them as equals.

Instead, some past accounting pronouncements have tended to emphasize one side over the other, such as the expense over the liability side. The next section chronicles accounting pronouncements on pensions. When compared with the chronology of accounting for income taxes in the previous chapter, a similar pattern emerges. The first accounting approach was the cash basis. The APB issued a pronouncement that emphasized the accrual approach and matching, and the FASB's pronouncement changed the emphasis to a liability approach. The next section provides the details on these pronouncements.

PENSION ACCOUNTING PRONOUNCEMENTS

CASH METHOD

As discussed in other chapters, before the accrual method was adopted, the cash method was popular. It is a "pay-as-you-go" method; firms reported pension expense as they made pension payments either to their pension plan or directly to retired employees. No liability was ever recognized for amounts owed but not yet paid. This method was simple to use, but it did not accomplish matching nor did it report the firm's liability for pensions in the future (near and long term).

ACCRUAL METHOD: APB OPINION #8

In 1966, the APB issued Opinion #8, "Accounting for the Cost of Pension Plans," which mandated the replacement of the simple cash method of accounting for pensions with the accrual method (matching). It was an attempt to make pension expense recognition consistent between firms. Opinion #8 emphasized the legal form of the pension plan and the pension expense reported on the Income Statement. The accrual method was adopted because it achieved a rational and systematic recognition of pension expense over the working lives of the employees. The APB allowed flexibility in the choice of actuarial methods to be used.

According to Opinion #8, the annual provision for pension expense should be based on an accounting method that uses an accepted actuarial cost method and results in an annual expense that falls between a maximum and minimum. Two actuarial cost methods were allowed: the accrued benefit cost method and the projected benefit cost method.

Although the accrual method of Opinion #8 was an improvement over the cash method, the emphasis on the expense reported on the Income Statement caused some limitations. Four concerns arose, revealing these limitations:[1]

1. The annual pension cost was inappropriately measured in Opinion #8.
2. Significant assets and liabilities were ignored in the Statement of Financial Position.
3. Opinion #8 considered defined benefit and defined contribution plans as having the same economic effects on the sponsoring firm.
4. The defined benefit pension fund trust was considered a separate entity from the sponsoring firm.

The limitations showed the need for a new pension accounting standard.

FASB INTERPRETATION NO. 3 AND SFAS NO. 87, "ACCOUNTING FOR PENSIONS"

Sparked by the passage of ERISA, the FASB issued an interpretation in 1974 that reaffirmed APB Opinion #8. However, the FASB formally added the topic of accounting for pensions to its agenda in 1981, issuing a discussion memorandum (DM) on pensions. A second DM was issued in 1983. Public hearings were held in early 1984, and an exposure draft (ED) was issued in 1985. After four years of due process, the FASB issued its pronouncement on accounting for pensions, SFAS No. 87, in December 1985. SFAS No. 87 was very controversial (the vote was 4 to 3). Much of the opposition came from financial statement preparers, who preferred APB Opinion #8. SFAS No. 87 represented a big change from APB Opinion #8. It adopted a liability view of pensions, with the emphasis on correctly measuring and reporting the firm's liability for pensions on the Balance Sheet. Changes in this liability caused the related pension expense on the Income Statement.

SFAS No. 87 mandated one actuarial method. It emphasized the economic substance (rather than the legal form) of the pension plan. The following three concerns were raised about SFAS No. 87:

1. It made pension fund performance more prominent in the financial statements.
2. The provision that the pension fund be annually revalued at market value introduced volatility into the Income Statement.
3. It emphasized the short-term—rather than the long-term view of the pension fund.

TWO DIFFICULT PENSION ACCOUNTING QUESTIONS

Beyond the three concerns listed above and similar to accounting for income taxes, there are two difficult questions about accounting for pensions: (1) Whose liability is it and when is the company liable? (2) Which liability should be measured, the present or the future? These questions are addressed next.

WHOSE LIABILITY AND WHEN?

The first difficult question about accounting for pensions focuses on whose liability it is and at what point in time should that liability be reported.

The number of parties involved in a pension plan and the U.S. government's involvement through the PBGC and ERISA have complicated the relationships of the parties to a pension from a legal liability standpoint. This creates confusion with regard to exactly who is responsible for a pension and to what extent is their liability. Is the individual sponsoring firm or its pension fund or the PBGC responsible? The legal responsibility in defined contribution plans is clearer because the firm is basically liable for the annual amounts that are determined to be its contribution to the plan. However, the confusion is much more pronounced with regard to defined benefit plans.

The confusion is created by the somewhat overlapping responsibilities of the sponsoring firm, the pension fund, and the PBGC. By outsourcing their plans to pension funds, firms have established legal firewalls (called *exculpatory clauses*) that potentially shelter the firm from legal liability under certain conditions. But ERISA and the PBGC set minimum funding levels for sponsoring firms and legal obligations for vested benefits, for which the sponsoring firms are legally liable.[2] SFAS No. 87 recognizes the minimum liability, so it does properly apply the element of a liability from the Conceptual Framework definition: A firm is legally obligated because of an obligating event.[3]

A related question refers to the timing of the recognition of the liability. If there is confusion about the ownership of the liability, it certainly carries over into the timing of the recognition of that questionable liability. Should the firm recognize a liability in the period before vesting? Should the sponsoring firm recognize all of that liability upon vesting? In general, firms recognize the liability when vesting has occurred.

PRESENT OR FUTURE LIABILITY?

The second difficult question about accounting for pensions focuses on which of two potential liabilities should be measured, present or future? Unfortunately, the essence of a pension is that these two amounts generally are different. For most pensions, the amount currently owed to an individual will differ from the amount owed in the future. This creates a "pension tension" between the amount owned now and that owed in the future. More specifically, should the current pension liability be based on present salaries or future salaries? This tension is also present in the definition of a liability. According to SFAC No. 6, a liability is defined as a present obligation to pay a future amount. For most liabilities, there is not a problem because the present obligation and future amount are the same. But not when accounting for pensions. In fact, the amounts are almost sure to be different, which requires some solution.

For an example to demonstrate this, consider an employee who has worked for the same firm for ten years. Her pension benefits vest after four years of employment, and she is eligible for retirement after a total of thirty years. Actuarially, you can determine the firm's present pension obligation to her, based on her past ten-year employment. Assume that it is $10,000. But that's not necessarily the total amount of pension she will earn by the time of her retirement in twenty years. That amount will depend on her continued employment with the firm, her future salary and positions within the firm, and so forth. Assuming that we can estimate the final pension amount and that its present value is $15,000, you can see that it differs from the current pension obligation to her ($10,000) based on her past employment. So, which amount—$10,000 or $15,000—is the more accurate measure of the firm's present obligation to her and should be reported as its liability on the Balance Sheet?

If your answer is the future obligation, $15,000, that leads to another difficult aspect of this question: What's the past transaction? If the future obligation is what should be reported, then one can question whether there has been a past transaction to trigger this future obligation. If you select the present obligation as the more valid representation of the obligation to her, then you don't have a problem with the past transaction. It is the establishment of the pension and her past service to the firm that earned the pension benefits. That isn't the case with the future obligation; no future transaction exists to create that liability. The future obligation is based on a projected salary and projected events. *There is no past transaction.*

The future obligation approach does not appear consistent with the past transaction or event aspect of the definition of a liability stated in SFAC No. 6; therefore, the present obligation approach appears more consistent. To further explore the potential conflict between the present obligation and the future obligation, consider the following case.

DISCUSSION CASE 14.1
The Bonus Case[4]

"Cashing In"

Charles P. ("C.P.") Adams, an aspiring young CPA, has just joined the staff of Foote & Tick, a local public accounting firm. Located in a rapidly expanding suburban area, the firm has enjoyed double-digit annual growth in both clients and revenues.

Because of the area's growth, many opportunities are available to young professionals. The field is rich for "hanging out your own shingle," and many existing firms are "staff poor." As a consequence, Foote & Tick has suffered heavy staff turnover almost since its inception ten years ago. The typical staff member has left after only two or three years either to join a larger firm or to establish a practice on his or her own. Turnover is so high that clients are complaining about the lack of continuity in the staff servicing their accounts.

In order to entice staff members to stay with the firm, Foote & Tick has decided to implement a new "retention bonus" program. Its terms provide for a one-time cash bonus to be paid to each employee on the completion of five years of continuous employment. The amount of the bonus will be the sum of 10 percent of the salary paid in each of the first five years of employment. Due to the bonus, the partners anticipate that about half of the new hires will still be employed after five years.

C.P. is the first employee to be hired under the new bonus plan. His first year's salary is to be $45,000. The partners expect that his salary will be about $60,000 in the fifth year and will average about $53,000 over the five-year period.

Question: How should the firm recognize the bonus payable to C.P. Adams if he remains with the firm for five years?

Analysis

Recall that according to SFAC No. 6, a liability is a probable future sacrifice of economic benefits from a present obligation that resulted from a past transaction or event. The central question in this case is whether Foote & Tick has a liability to C.P. at the end of the first year. If it does, at what amount should that liability be reported?

The answer is not easy. Use the three elements in the definition of a liability to structure the analysis:

1. What is the past event that triggers this liability? This is debatable. Some could argue that hiring C.P. is the transaction that creates the liability. But others suggest that hiring C.P. does not obligate the firm to pay the bonus; instead, he must remain with the firm for five years to be eligible for the bonus. So the event that obligates Foote & Tick to pay a bonus to him is five years' continuous employment.

   Because the terms of the bonus plan clearly state that the bonus will be paid only if the individual remains with the firm for at least five years, one could argue that the firm owes C.P. nothing after the end of the first four years; he doesn't earn the bonus until after five years. If he were to leave before then, he gets no bonus. Similarly, if he is dismissed from the firm, he loses the bonus.

2. Is the future payment of the bonus probable? Another issue deals with the likelihood of the bonus payment. The case stated that the plan was designed to entice at least 50 percent of the new hires to remain with the firm for five years. So the likelihood of paying the bonus to C.P. is at least 50 percent. For some, this probability is not high enough to make the payment of the bonus probable; therefore, it would not be considered a liability.

3. Another issue in this case illustrates the "pension tension" mentioned earlier in the chapter: the difference between the present and future obligations. At the end of the first year, if we assume that C.P. is eligible to receive the bonus four years later, he would get $4,500 for the first year of his employment at Foote & Tick. But if his average salary is $53,000 over the five-year period, he will get a total bonus of $26,500 ($53,000 × 0.10 × 5 years) and one-fifth of that is $5,300. So if we decide to recognize a liability for C.P. at the end of Year 1, should it be the amount that this year contributed to his bonus, $4,500, or one-fifth of the future amount of the bonus, $5,300? Notice how this demonstrates the essence of the "pension tension" in the definition of a liability. At a point in time, for example, the end of Year 1, Foote & Tick potentially owes C.P. $4,500. But in five years, the slice of the total liability to him represented by the first year is $5,300. So which should Foote & Tick recognize now? Pension accounting under SFAS No. 87 would say $5,300.

Conclusion

The conclusion to the case is to not recognize a liability to C.P. until the end of Year 5. The timing issue is central. Because the purpose of the plan is to pay the bonus for five years of continuous employment, no earlier recognition of the obligation would be warranted. C.P. does not earn the bonus year by year; he could not get any portion of the bonus for less than five years' employment for Foote & Tick. For example, if he left the firm after two years, he would not be entitled to any of the bonus. Although the legal side of this plan is not central to the question of whether Foote & Tick should recognize a liability, it plays a role. It is unlikely that C.P. could successfully sue Foote & Tick for part of the bonus during the five-year probationary period.

A second issue relates to the likelihood that C.P. will work for five continuous years. The case suggests that the plan was devised to keep at least 50 percent of the new hires for five years. There are a number of factors which could cause C.P. to leave the firm before the end of the five-year period: unhappiness with the work, unhappiness with the firm, offers from competing firms, the desire to start his own firm, and unsatisfactory reviews of his performance at Foote & Tick. (One cannot avoid recognizing the possibility that the firm would dismiss him at the end of Year 5 to avoid paying the $26,500 bonus.)

This conclusion does create some additional problems. By waiting until the bonus has been earned by C.P., Foote & Tick will not be disclosing the potential cash outflow for the bonus plan over the first four years. Financial statement readers would consider the cash flow implications of the bonus plan as relevant. So at a minimum, Foote & Tick should mention the existence of the plan and the potential cash outflow of the plan in the notes to their financial statements to inform statement users.

Notice that the case was structured around one individual, Charles. If Foote & Tick hired a number of employees under the bonus plan, a group approach would present a better solution. The firm could apply the allowance method of accounting for doubtful accounts to group of new hires under their bonus plan. They could recognize a liability (and an expense) for 50 percent of the expected bonus associated with the total salary paid in the first year to the group of new hires. This approach could be continued for each year until the five-year period was concluded. This would be preferred to no recognition of the obligation of the bonus.

OTHER POSTEMPLOYMENT BENEFITS

INTRODUCTION

Other postemployment benefits are simply benefits other than pensions promised to employees after their retirement from the firm. In recognition that retirement requires more than just pension payments, firms have promised a whole host of other benefits to make the retirement years easier. The next section discusses what some of these benefits are.

BENEFITS INCLUDED

The list of other postemployment benefits is long. It is developed by simply asking the question, "What do retired individuals need or want?" The answers follow:

- Health care benefits, such as medical insurance, mental or psychological insurance, dental insurance, vision insurance, and prescription drug insurance
- Life and disability insurance
- Legal services and financial advisory services
- Tuition assistance and educational benefits
- Housing assistance
- Day care or child care benefits.

Some elements of the list may surprise you. Remember that the typical other postemployment benefits apply to the retired individual and their dependents.

In general, the right to Other Postemployment Benefits arises from the employment contact. The following is an example for Ms. Janine Smith, twenty-five, who just accepted employment with the firm. The part of the employment contract for other postemployment benefits would read: "and subject to change at the discretion of the firm, at retirement age (60), we will fully cover Ms. Smith and her dependent family members with the following benefits: medical and dental insurance, life and disability insurance, legal services, educational benefits, and housing assistance . . . until her death."

As you can see, the coverage of other benefits can be very wide. It is customary for the firm to include a clause that allows them to exercise considerable discretion in the provision of these benefits. Firms maintain the right to change or cancel them at will. Generally, courts have upheld the right of employers to change or terminate these benefits.

OTHER POSTEMPLOYMENT BENEFITS AND PENSIONS FEATURES COMPARISON

It's natural to compare Other Postemployment Benefits to pensions. Both are provided to employees after their retirement. But there are major differences in their features. A comparison of the typical characteristics of each is shown in Exhibit 14.2.

EXHIBIT 14.2
Comparison of Other Postemployment Benefits and Pensions

Characteristic	Pensions	OPEBs
Available to . . .	Retirees	Retirees and dependents
Upper limit	Capped	Uncapped
Paid when	Periodically (e.g., monthly)	When used
Payable in	Dollars	Services
Based on	Years of service	Negotiated
Vesting	Yes	No
Prefunded	Yes	No
Predictable	Yes	No

As Exhibit 14.2 shows, there are few similarities between the typical characteristics listed for Other Postemployment Benefits and pensions. In fact, although both occur at the same time in an employee's life, pensions and other postemployment benefits are really different sets of benefits. To summarize Exhibit 14.2, pensions basically represent monetary amounts paid by the firm during retirement that the employee has earned through years of service. The pension benefit is vested at a point in time, and generally, if covered by ERISA, the firm prepays in advance or prefunds the pension by making payments to a pension fund during the working life of the employee. Most employees will get a set pension benefit and can predict their pension payment as they get closer to retirement. However, OPEBs are basically gratuities or benevolences, which the firm has chosen to provide or has agreed to provide as the result of negotiations. They are not paid in dollars but in services that are provided or reimbursed. The amount of the service is uncapped; it costs whatever the going rates are, and the person gets to consume as much as needed or provided. The benefits are not unlimited, however. Firms do not prefund these benefits, and because the retired employee is receiving services as needed, employees cannot accurately predict their use during the postretirement period. In addition, it is difficult to predict the cost of some of these services in the future. The actual consumption of the services depends on a number of factors.

Based on this comparison, we conclude that there are major differences between pensions and other postemployment benefits. This is an important point to remember as we examine the accounting procedures for other postemployment benefits, SFAS No. 106, because the FASB appears to have adopted many of the features of accounting for pensions.[5] SFAS No. 106 is covered next.

ACCOUNTING FOR OPEBS

THREE ACCOUNTING ISSUES

Three accounting issues arose about other postemployment benefits.

Is there a liability? Does a postretirement benefit plan result in an obligation that meets the definition of a liability? In deciding the answer to this question, what role, if any, should the legality of the promise play? (2) If there is a liability, how should it be measured? If the postretirement benefit plan does result in an obligation for the firm, how should that obligation be measured? (3) When should it be reported? If the obligation can be measured, when should it be reported?

SFAS NO. 106, "EMPLOYERS ACCOUNTING FOR POSTRETIREMENT BENEFITS OTHER THAN PENSIONS"

The FASB issued SFAS No. 106, in 1990. In contrast to the cash basis of accounting for other postemployment benefits, which many firms had adopted because conditions appeared to call for that treatment: The number of retirees were small and the costs involved were low. However, the Board considered these benefits as a form of deferred compensation and decided to account for them in a similar fashion to pensions, that is, to require firms to accrue liabilities over the working life of the employees. SFAS No. 106 had four objectives:

1. To produce a better cost estimate of other postemployment benefits relevant to the service period.
2. To measure the obligation of the firm that promised other postemployment benefits.
3. To enhance understandability through disclosures so that statement users could understand the other postemployment benefit promises of a firm and the financial ramifications of those promises.
4. To increase comparability through more uniform accounting.

Firms had three years to implement SFAS No. 106.

The FASB Answers   The FASB answered the three questions in SFAS No. 106 affirmatively. It regarded postretirement benefits as a form of deferred compensation that represents an obligation of the firm and meets the definition of a liability in SFAC No. 6. These future benefits can be measured by estimation and brought back to the present using present value computations. This liability should be reported from the hire date to the date of eligibility of the covered employees.

Firms take two steps to adopt SFAS No. 106. The first step is to establish a reserve to catch up for the past benefits owed to current employees but not recorded. This catch-up reserve can be amortized over twenty years or taken as a charge in the year it was established. The second element is to record an annual expense and liability for the costs associated with the current year for current employees.

Concerns About the FASB's Answers   There were many concerns raised with the FASB's answers to these three questions in SFAS No. 106.[6] Factors influencing these concerns were the changed conditions that firms found themselves in with regard to other postemployment benefits. For example, in a number of firms, the number of retirees outnumber the current workforce; individuals are living longer and thus taking advantage of the other postemployment benefits longer; and the costs of many of the benefit promises, such as health care, have escalated dramatically. Thus when SFAS No. 106 was issued, the costs associated with the benefits were material.

One concern related to the FASB's conclusion that other postemployment benefits satisfied the definition of a liability. The counterargument from a number of critics was that because many of these promises were discretionary and could be terminated by the firm, the firm was not presently liable, and thus, the definition was not satisfied. Other critics maintained that whether firms were liable for these benefits was a legal question that should be decided in court.

Another concern related to measuring the obligation. Because many of the costs are future costs and are associated with heath care, many critics believed that the resulting estimates would not be relevant or reliable and, therefore, not useful. With many employees' retirement twenty or thirty years in the future and possibly another twenty years of OPEB services beyond retirement, predicting future medical costs is very difficult. For example, the cost of a typical single room (excluding physician fees) in an urban hospital in the beginning of the twenty-first century was $2,400. To help you understand how difficult predicting medical costs can be, what do you think the cost of a single room in a hospital will be in 2040? That information is necessary to comply with the provisions of SFAS No. 106.

A third concern related to the FASB's decision to require firms to report the obligation measured from the hire date to the date of eligibility of the covered employees. Critics believed that the time period should extend from the hire date to the retirement date, which would be a longer time period than the FASB's and result in a smaller annual amortization of the cost. They believed that employees do not receive other postemployment benefits when they are eligible to retire; they receive them on retirement.

THE IMPACT OF SFAS NO. 106

The immediate effect of SFAS No. 106 was disastrous. Estimates appeared in the national media that the total charge for postretirement benefits would be as much as $1 trillion over the next few years.[7] It was expected that the impact of this new standard would be hardest on firms that were unionized and labor-intensive and that have a low turnover of employees and a high ratio of retirees to active workers. Some firms became creative in ways to reduce the financial impact of these benefits.[8]

SFAS NO. 132, "EMPLOYERS' DISCLOSURES ABOUT PENSIONS AND OTHER POSTRETIREMENT BENEFITS"

In February 1998, the FASB issued SFAS No. 132. This new standard was designed to fine-tune the disclosure requirements in SFASs No. 87 and No. 106 as well as to bring more uniformity to these disclosures.

SUMMARY

This chapter demonstrates yet another difficult application of the definition of a liability from SFAC No. 6. Part of the problem arises from the complicated nature of pensions and other postemployment benefits. The basic underlying legal agreements for pensions and other postemployment benefits are complex. The introduction of governmental agencies and legislation into the mix has made the issues even more complicated. The FASB walked right into the situation with its liability approach to this issue. (The APB escaped some of these complications by focusing on the expense side of the coin.) Applying their Balance Sheet approach, the FASB hit those issues head on. What resulted was one of the most controversial accounting standards, SFAS No. 87.

A major accounting problem that is inherent with pensions is the issue of future costs and expenses. Accounting procedures have been developed to record historical events; they are not equally successful in recording future events. This methodological limitation has also added to the problem of accounting for pensions. The pension tension issue has illustrated that.

Similar concerns arose when the FASB addressed the issue of accounting for other postemployment benefits. It appeared to follow the same approach as pensions even though many thought that approach wasn't appropriate because of the major differences between the two. Unfortunately, the reaction of a number of firms to SFAS No. 106 was to cancel their plans, and of course, the FASB was blamed for this. This created another embarrassing situation for accountants—a "lose-lose" situation.

REVIEW QUESTIONS

1. What is the basic question that must be answered about accounting for postemployment compensation? How is that question answered by the cash method? By the matching concept?
2. Define a pension. What are the two types of pensions, and how do they differ from each other?
3. Who are the four parties involved in the typical pension plan?
4. What two federal laws apply to pension plans that impacted the accounting issues involved in pensions? Describe the impact of each law.
5. What are the two major accounting issues related to accounting for pension plans? How are they related?
6. In what ways was APB Opinion #8 an improvement over the cash method of accounting for pensions?
7. What were four concerns that arose over the implementation of APB Opinion #8?
8. How long did it take the FASB to go through its due process procedure to issue SFAS No. 87? What does that tell you about the complexity of the issues?
9. What were the major differences between SFAS No. 87 and APB Opinion #8?
10. What are the two difficult questions about accounting for pensions? How are these similar to the three difficult questions about accounting for income taxes in the previous chapter?
11. What is the "pension tension," and how does it relate to the basic definition of a liability in SFAC No. 6?
12. What are other postemployment benefits? Give some examples of the benefits included.
13. How are pensions and other postemployment benefits similar? Different?
14. What three accounting issues are associated with other postemployment benefits?
15. What were the FASB's answers to those three questions?
16. How have corporations reacted to SFAS No. 106?

DISCUSSION TOPICS

1. Accounting for pensions depends on the notion that current employees are working for the firm for both current compensation and future compensation in the form of retirement benefits. Are today's employees cognizant of the future compensation in the form of pensions, and does this motivate them currently?
2. Describe how the relationships between the sponsoring firm, the pension plan, and the PBGC has muddled the definition of the firm's liability for pension payments.
3. The "pension tension" question relates to the possible conflict between the present obligation of a firm and its future obligation. In accounting for pensions and other postemployment benefits, the FASB expressed a preference for the future obligation when such a conflict arises. Do you agree with this?
4. Are pensions and other postemployment benefits similar? If not, why do you think the FASB adopted a pension approach to accounting for other postemployment benefits? Was this appropriate?
5. If sponsoring firms react to a new accounting standard by cutting back on the provision

of benefits, what pressure does that put on a standard-setting body such as the FASB? Is this just a case of economic consequences or a form of political pressure from preparer firms?

6. **The Longevity Bonuses Case**[9]: "Let me look into my crystal ball . . ."

Paternal Products Company has established a program of longevity bonuses for its employees in lieu of a conventional pension plan. The plan provides that on retirement or termination, employees will be paid a lump-sum bonus equal to 20 percent of their highest annual salary multiplied by the number of years of service to the company. To illustrate, an employee leaving the company after five years of service would be paid a longevity bonus equal to 100 percent of his or her highest salary. Similarly, an employee with thirty years of service would be paid a bonus equal to 600 percent of his or her highest salary. Bonuses are not paid to employees retiring or being terminated with less than one year of service.

Red Turner was hired five years ago at the age of twenty-five at a starting salary of $20,000. He was recently promoted to supervisor and is currently earning $30,000. If he stays with the company until the usual retirement age, he will have accumulated 40 years of service and, with annual raises averaging $2,000 per year, will be earning approximately $100,000 when he retires. However, Paternal Products expects that its typical employee will terminate with only fifteen years of service.

How should Paternal Products base the measure of its liability to Red Turner for his longevity bonus?

7. **Application Problem.** Becky Bookit III is a bright, young, recent graduate of the Central Florida University. She has been hired recently by a Big 5 public accounting firm. Because she comes from a wealthy Bithlo, Florida, family and already has significant taxable earnings from numerous investments, she has agreed to a deferred compensation contract with her employer. She will receive a lump-sum payment of $200,000 at the end of five years as deferred compensation. Assuming Becky was employed on January 1, 20X2, determine the annual compensation expense recognized by the CPA firm to account for this deferred compensation contract plan at nine percent.

NOTES

1 Miller (1987), p. 98.
2 See Wolk, Tearney, and Dodd, p. 597.
3 Wolk, Tearney, and Dodd, p. 608.
4 Johnson and Petrone, p. 7.
5 Thomas and Farmer, p. 102.
6 Based on Thomas and Farmer, pp. 103–112.
7 Berton and Brennan (1992), p. C1.
8 Berton and Brennan (1993), p. A23.
9 Johnson and Petrone, p. 31.

REFERENCES

American Accounting Association, Financial Accounting Standards Committee. "Other Post-Employment Benefits." *Accounting Horizons* (March 1990): 111–116.

Accounting Principles Board. "Accounting for the Cost of Pension Plans," *APB Opinion No. 8.* New York: American Institute of Certified Public Accounts, 1966.

Berton, Lee, and Robert Brennan. "New Medical Benefits Accounting Rule Seen Wounding Profits, Hurting Shares." *The Wall Street Journal* (April 22, 1992): C1–C2.

———. "Some Firms Use Subtle Methods to Curb the Cost of Retiree Benefits." *The Wall Street Journal* (February 24, 1993): A23.

Dankner, Harold, John M. Berto, Jean M. Wodarczyk, and Lee E. Launer. "Your Retiree Health Benefits Plan: Good Design, Safe Funding." *Financial Executive* (March/April): 47–53.

Dankner, Harold, Barbara Bald, and Murray Akresh. "Health Benefits for Retirees— Surviving With OPEB." *Financial Executive* (January/Februrary): 30–37.

Financial Accounting Standards Board. "Accounting and Reporting by Defined Benefit Pension Plans." *Statement of Financial Accounting Standards No. 35*. Norwalk, CT: Financial Accounting Standards Board, 1980a.

———. "Disclosure of Pension Information." *Statement of Financial Accounting Standards No. 36*. Norwalk, CT: Financial Accounting Standards Board, 1980b.

———. "Disclosure of Postretirement Health Care and Life Insurance Benefits." *Statement of Financial Accounting Standards No. 81*. Norwalk, CT: Financial Accounting Standards Board, 1984.

———. "Employers' Accounting for Pensions." *Statement of Financial Accounting Standards No. 87*. Norwalk, CT: Financial Accounting Standards Board, 1985a.

———. "Employers' Accounting for Settlements and Curtailments of Defined Benefit Pension Plans and for Termination Benefits." *Statement of Financial Accounting Standards No. 88*. Norwalk, CT: Financial Accounting Standards Board, 1985b.

———. "Employers' Accounting for Postretirement Benefits Other Than Pensions." *Statement of Financial Accounting Standards No. 106*. Norwalk, CT: Financial Accounting Standards Board, 1990.

———. "Employers' Accounting for Postretirement Benefits." *Statement of Financial Accounting Standards No. 112*. Norwalk, CT: Financial Accounting Standards Board, 1992.

———. "Employers' Disclosures about Pensions and Other Postretirement Benefits: An Amendment of FASB Statements No. 87, 88, and 106." *Statement of Financial Accounting Standards No. 132*. Norwalk, CT: Financial Accounting Standards Board, 1998.

Fogarty, Timothy, and Julia Grant. "Impact of the Actuarial Profession on Financial Reporting." *Accounting Horizons* (September 1995): 23–33.

Hamilton, Jim. "Calculating Pension Obligations." *Management Accounting* (November 1991): 26–29.

Lucas, Timothy, and Betsy Ann Hollowell. "Pension Accounting: The Liability Question." *Journal of Accountancy* (October 1981): 57–66.

Miller, Paul. "The New Pension Accounting (Part 1)." *Journal of Accountancy* (January 1987a): 98–108.

———. "The New Pension Accounting (Part 2)." *Journal of Accountancy* (February 1987b): 86–94.

Scott, Diana, and Wayne Upton, Jr. "Postretirement Benefits Other Than Pensions." *Highlights of Financial Reporting Issues* (Financial Accounting Standards Board): 1–4.

Thomas, Paula, and Larry Farmer. "OPEB: Improved Reporting or the Last Straw?" *Journal of Accountancy* (November 1990): 102–112.

Wilbert, James, and Kenneth Dakdduk. "The New FASB 106: How to Account For Postretirement Benefits." *Journal of Accountancy* (August 1991): 36–41.

Wolk, H., Michael Tearney, and James L. Dodd. *Accounting Theory*, Fifth Edition. Cincinnati, OH: SouthWestern College Publishing, 2001.

Wyatt, Arthur. "OPEB Costs: The FASB Establishes Accountability." *Accounting Horizons* (March 1990): 108–110.

Yamamoto, Dale. "Retiree Health Plans—What Do We Do Now?" *Management Accounting* (April 1990): 21–25.

Zuber, George. "What Auditors Should Know About FASB Statement No. 87." *Journal of Accountancy* (March 1988): 38–48.

CHAPTER 15

MARK TO MARKET ACCOUNTING

LEARNING OBJECTIVES

After studying this chapter, you should be able to

> Understand the advantages and disadvantages of historical cost accounting.

> Identify the factors that led to the emphasis on current market values in accounting.

> Describe how the mark to market approach was applied by the FASB to accounting for marketable securities, stock options, and derivatives.

> Identify the criticisms of valuing assets at current value.

In this chapter the topic of how to measure the economic benefits of an asset is discussed. Recall that the focus in Chapter 10 is on the definition of an asset in the FASB's Conceptual Framework project. In this chapter, the best approach to measure an asset defined according to SFAC No. 6 is emphasized.

Specifically, the mark to market approach in measuring an asset and its application in three topics are examined: accounting for investments in marketable securities, stock options, and derivatives. Stock options are considered as another form of employee compensation, such as pensions and postretirement benefits.

Concentration is on three specific important accounting events and the general development of mark to market accounting.

1. SFAS No. 115, "Accounting for Certain Investments in Debt and Equity Securities"[1]
2. SFAS No. 123, "Accounting for Stock-Based Compensation"[2]
3. SFAS No. 133, "Accounting for Derivative Instruments and Hedging Activities"[3]

A time line of these three standards is shown in Exhibit 15.1.

EXHIBIT 15.1
Mark to Market Time Line

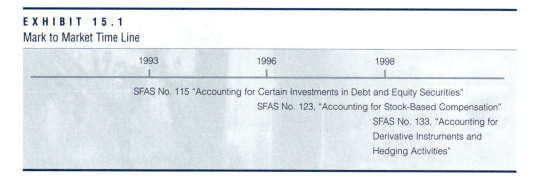

In the Conceptual Framework, assets are defined as probable future economic benefits. There are two general schools of thought on the best approach to measure or quantify those economic benefits: the input school and the output school. The input school advocates exchange values for assets that reflect the sacrifice given up to acquire the asset. The output school advocates values for the asset that reflect some measure of the consideration to be received in the future. In Chapter 10, it was noted that the output school was more consistent with the definition of an asset in SFAC No. 6, specifically, the future orientation of the economic benefits.

It is important to recognize that asset valuation is related to income determination. The choice of an income determination model has implications for asset valuation. For example, recall from Chapter 9 Philip's range of income concepts.[4] Philips described a range of income concepts. The following five different income concepts were in his range:

1. *Psychic income.* This is purely subjective income. Income is what you think it is. It is based on utility, personal well-being, and is inseparable from consumption.
2. *Economic present value income.* This is measured by taking the discounted present value of future receipts. To accomplish this you need to know the future cash receipts and the appropriate discount rate.

3. *Accretion income.* Income is an increase in economic power, measured by the change in the market values of assets. Income is the difference in market values over a time period. Accretion income recognizes income if the increase in value is reasonably measurable.

4. *Accrual income.* This is based on a market transaction and relies on outside exchanges. It recognizes revenue when earned and expenses when incurred. Matching represents this type of income.

5. *Cash income.* This is strictly objective and based on cash inflows and outflows. Cash realization is the only trigger for recognition of income.

Philips believed that as you moved from psychic to cash income, the objectivity of the measurement increased. But as you moved from psychic to cash, the conceptual reasonableness decreased.

These income concepts have asset valuation implications. If you adopt an income concept, it implies an asset valuation approach. For example, if you adopt the accretion concept of income, then assets will be valued at market values. If you adopt the accrual concept, then assets will be valued at historical cost.

This chapter follows the pattern of previous chapters by first examining the background of the issues associated with historical cost and mark to market accounting. Then it examines the accounting procedures for investments in marketable securities, stock options, and derivatives from a theory viewpoint. Once again, the observation reveals that the FASB has had real difficulty in issuing accounting standards for these three elements using mark to market accounting because the standards moved away from historical cost. The FASB struggled to formulate these standards so that the standards would achieve a high degree of acceptance by practitioners and statement preparers. The FASB was not always successful in achieving that goal.

HISTORICAL COST

To many, historical cost has been a dominant paradigm of financial accounting since the 1930s. It was widely supported because it was seen as having many advantages. These advantages are described in the next section.

ADVANTAGES OF HISTORICAL COST

Historical cost has had widespread support among accountants and has become the basis for many accounting standards because it was seen as objective and verifiable. The objectivity was based on the belief that the historical cost generally resulted from an arm's-length transaction, one which actually occurred. The transaction generally had some documentation to support it, which led to its being verifiable by another independent party. Objectivity and verifiability were two major advantages attributed to historical cost.

In addition, historical cost was transaction-based and relied on realization (conversion into cash or other assets) to record changes in the value of an asset. Over time, because of these desirable characteristics to accountants, it took on the appearance of being an absolute value. That is, historical cost was so respected and widely used that accountants began to consider it as part of the core of accounting. Because many accountants believed historical cost to be "a fact," something that actually happened at a point in time, its association with accounting added respect or creditability to accounting, which was welcomed by accountants. Therefore, because historical cost added credibility to accounting, accountants became strong supporters of historical cost. So both were connected in importance: Historical cost was important to accounting and accounting became important to historical cost. A mutual dependency developed.

SUPPORT FOR HISTORICAL COST

Chambers presents a brief history of historical cost and lists three reasons for using historical cost:[5]

1. *Stewardship.* Historical cost reports the property originally entrusted to a principal by another. In the stewardship relationship, the steward is responsible for the proper management of that property and must give an account of what he received and what he returned. Historical cost is consistent with that.
2. *Historicity.* To many, accounting is expected to report what actually happened, and historical cost is consistent with that expectation.
3. *Measurement.* Accounting relies on the basics of mathematics. To complete the mathematical process of summation in accounting, one must add common items (i.e., apples and apples). The original cost of an item is such a common property that its use facilitates mathematical summation.

Another support for the use of historical cost was the past experience of accountants with current value accounting. Historically, accounting departed from historical cost and used current values for some Balance Sheet assets during the period from 1900 until the crash of the stock market in 1929. During that time, the Balance Sheet was the dominant financial statement and often reported the current values of the assets. The inadequacy of this information was blamed partly for the failure of businesses, resulting in the stock market crash of 1929. Users of financial statements felt that the Balance Sheet did not contain the information on which they could rely in decision making, leading to a lack of confidence in balance sheet and accounting. This had three results: (1) an increased reliance on the Income Statement, (2) a rejection of current values as the basis for measuring assets, and (3) an embracing of the use of historical cost.

CRITICISMS OF HISTORICAL COST

However, historical cost has had its critics. Some pointed out that although historical cost preserved an actual record of an event, that record could soon become outdated with the passage of time or the occurrence of subsequent events in markets. And critics contended that timeliness was more relevant to decision makers than objectivity or verifiability.

The classic story to illustrate this concern about historical cost is that if historical cost were strictly followed and if there were no subsequent transactions, the Manhattan Island Company would report only one asset on their Balance Sheet, Land, and at an amount of $24. Reporting $24 for Manhattan Island would clearly mislead any users of that firm's financial statements. Critics of historical cost argued that since markets change, the market price that historical cost records may change with the passage of time and subsequent events; therefore, accounting should "go with the flow," revise the record for such changes, and report the current market price.

Other critics challenged the notion that historical cost was some form of an absolute. To test this, consider a simple experiment of having a widely diverse group of people (composed of males and females of various ethnic groups and ages) assigned the task of going out to buy a specific model of car, with the exact same features (color, body style, engine size, options, etc.). Once the task was completed and the group reassembled, the members would report the price they paid for their cars. It would be very unlikely that any two people had purchased the specified car for exactly the same price. If the manufacturers' suggested retail price (MSRP) for the car, including transportation, tax, and title, were $25,000 and the dealer invoice was $22,500, it is reasonable to assume that the members of our group would pay between $22,500 and $25,000 for the same car.

Given the outcome of the experiment, the question arises: What is the historical cost of the car? Should each person consider the price he or she paid for the car as its historical cost? If so, that would produce wide variation in the original cost of the exact same asset. Is it appropriate to report the same asset at a variety of prices, such as $22,500, $24,500, or $25,000? Is the car more valuable to those who paid more for it? Alternatively, should we compute the average price paid for the car ($24,000) and use that to record all the cars purchased, no matter what the actual price paid? Should members of the group record his or her car at the average cost and then show a gain or loss for the amount each paid that was either more or less than the average? For example, if someone paid $25,000 for a car, the car would be reported at $24,000 (the average) and a loss of $1,000 also would be reported because they paid $1,000 more than the average for the car.

Most accountants would not agree with any of these approaches. Instead, because of the influence of historical cost, most accountants would state that each person should report the actual amount he or she paid as the historical cost for the car. But that would show the same car on a number of different Balance Sheets at difference prices, for example, $22,500, $24,500, and $25,000. That would create a formidable obstacle to comparability. It could easily lead someone to conclude that the cars were different and that the cars that cost more were more valuable. The application of historical cost in this case raises the question, Is historical cost a consistent measurement system for assets?

The reliance of historical cost on transactions and realization has been strongly criticized. Solomons cites a scenario of Kenneth MacNeal in which two investors purchased stock from different companies both valued at $1,000.[6] At the end of the current period, both stocks' market values have increased to $2,000. One investor sells the stock and realizes a profit of $1,000 and ends up with $2,000 cash. The other investor continues to hold the stock. Comparing the two investors, although both started with the same amount and ended with equal amounts, the accounting results for both are different under historical cost. The first investor would show a profit of $1,000 and asset of $2,000, whereas the second would continue to show no profit and an asset of $1,000.

ARS #1 AND #3 AND ASOBAT

As shown in Chapters 2 and 3, two important theory formulations in the 1960s, ARS #1 and #3 and ASOBAT, attempted to replace historical cost with current values. In both formulations, a central feature was the replacement of historical cost with current market values (in the case of ASOBAT, historical cost and current values were both reported). Both theory formulations were rejected by the accounting profession at that time, at least partly because the accounting profession strongly supported historical cost.

Sprouse and Moonitz, in ARS #3, stated that although the cost of an asset is significant, subsequent to its acquisition, events may show that the original cost no longer represents a useful measure of future benefits for that particular asset.[7] When that happens, accountants should use other values, such as market prices, to quantify the asset. Importantly, Sprouse and Moonitz considered market value as objective because it is independent of the plans or expectations of the firm and thus represents a neutral, objective valuation. They considered market price more relevant because decision makers act in the present, not in the past or future. Market price was also considered as superior to acquisition price as a measure of the sacrifice involved in the use of an asset.

ASOBAT stated that although historical cost information emphasizes verifiability, current market prices emphasize relevancy and reflect not only the transactions of the firm but also the impact of the environment on the firm beyond its transactions.[8] As a compromise, ASOBAT recommended that both historical cost and current market values should be reported.

KUHN'S PATTERN

All this controversy over historical cost is understandable when you consider Kuhn's pattern.[9] If you accept his pattern for the way in which a discipline progresses, the development of the controversy fits right into his pattern. Recall that Kuhn stated that at any point in time, a particular discipline is dominated by a particular paradigm (notion or set of ideas that are generally accepted) that is widely supported by the members of the discipline. Although there are some challenges to the dominant paradigm, they are generally rejected by the members of the discipline. This process—periodic challenges to the dominant paradigm that are rejected—continues until evidence contrary to the dominant paradigm slowly builds up, grows in importance, and eventually gains enough support to overthrow the old paradigm.

A critical factor in this process of "revolution" is timing. To some, the right time for the "overthrow" of historical cost came in the 1990s. The emergence of the mark to market approach to accounting and its use by the FASB in issuing accounting standards signaled the beginning of the end of the reign of historical cost as a sole paradigm. The shift to using market values for some items resulted from the previous criticisms of historical cost and the two theory formulations that also attacked historical cost.

THE WEALTH EFFECT

A new criticism of historical cost emerged in the late 1990s that is called the *wealth effect*. This is a new phenomena associated with the strong surge of the New York Stock Exchange (NYSE) and NASDAQ stock markets in the United States from the late 1990s through 2000. The wealth effect is the positive feeling of increased wealth that comes from the rise in the market price of one's security investments. With the strong showing of the stock prices, many people saw their stock portfolios rapidly increase in value. The rise of individual stocks and stock markets was front-page news.

The wealth effect is also the behavioral influence of changes in the market value of investments on the investors. As people's stock portfolios grew in value, they felt more wealthy and based their consumption decisions on these feelings. In effect, more Americans began to calculate their wealth based on the market prices of their portfolios. Although this wealth effect has a negative side, which appeared in late 2000 and early 2001 when the NYSE and NASDAQ fell sharply, the wealth effect influenced the way people measured their wealth. Note: This concept is essentially a market value-based concept, not a historical cost-based concept.[10]

The main question is whether the wealth effect will produce a major lasting change in the economic behavior of people. With the stock market representing a large part of the U.S. national economy, the answer seems to be yes. Market values will continue to dominate the wealth measures of individuals.

FASB'S VIEW ON HISTORICAL COST

Some view the FASB as a strong advocate of mark to market accounting. A number of SFASs use historical cost; however, the FASB was perceived as favoring a change to the mark to market approach. The emphasis on current values is evident when you compare certain SFASs with the APB Opinions they superseded or replaced. As examples, consider that SFAS No. 109, which is more mark to market-oriented, replaced Opinion #11; SFAS No. 87, which is more current market-oriented, replaced Opinion #8; and SFAS No. 123, which is more market value-oriented and replaced Opinion #25. Some consider SFAS No. 130, "Reporting Comprehensive Income," as a response to the many current value standards that caused asset values to change before their realization.

One could also argue that the FASB's current valuation orientation came from following the lead of the SEC. The SEC has long supported current values.

The current value emphasis of the FASB is evident in the Conceptual Framework project. Recall from Chapter 7 that the project was formulated to be consistent with the new view of accounting, which emphasizes the role of accounting in society, capital markets, and the economy as a whole in assisting capital resource allocation. In capital markets, market values dominate.

Corresponding with the new view of accounting, the Conceptual Framework project began with the publication of SFAC No. 1, "Objectives of Financial Reporting by Business Enterprises," in 1978. It identified investors (present and potential) and creditors as prime users of accounting information. The emphasis on investors and creditors is consistent with capital markets and market values.

In SFAC No. 6, "Elements of Financial Statements," issued in 1985, the FASB adopted an asset-liability approach to measuring net income. A major advantage of the asset-liability approach is its flexibility in accommodating current values for assets. The definition of an asset in SFAC No. 6 is more current value-oriented. Recall that an asset is defined as a probable future economic benefit. The future orientation of an asset is inconsistent with a backward-looking valuation approach, such as historical cost. The future orientation of the definition of an asset is more consistent with a forward-looking valuation approach, such as mark to market.

One of the most controversial definitions in the elements is that for comprehensive income. Recall that comprehensive income is defined as a change in equity (assets minus liabilities) produced by transactions and other events and circumstances from nonowner sources. This definition was viewed as setting the stage for an introduction of current values into accounting by the FASB.

The FASB's favorable orientation toward market values (also called *current values* or *fair value*) was not supported by all other stakeholder groups. Auditors were concerned that the emphasis on market values would greatly increase audit risk. Because market values are sometimes more subjective than historical costs, auditors were concerned about their reliability. Statement preparers were also not oriented toward market values. They were concerned that the widespread introduction of market values into accounting would produce a high degree of volatility in accounting measures. Alternatively, the SEC was a strong advocate of current values, and it supported the FASB.

So although the FASB was an advocate of current market values and the mark to market approach to asset valuation, because of the opposition to current values, it was not free to radically change accounting to these views. In light of the opposition of auditors and statement preparer groups and the widespread support for historical cost among accountants and even though it had the support of the SEC, the FASB responded by phasing in the introduction of mark to market accounting. The next section discusses the FASB's first major step in that direction, its standard for accounting for investments in equity and debt securities.

MARK TO MARKET ACCOUNTING

ACCOUNTING FOR INVESTMENTS IN SECURITIES

The seemingly "perfect issue" that would allow the FASB to begin to implement its mark to market approach was accounting for investments in marketable securities, debt and equity. This issue was consistent with the new view for accounting because it involved accounting for capital market securities. It appeared reasonable to assume that because investments in market securities were financial assets that had readily determinable market values, a mark to market approach would be appropriate for these assets. The topic brought together many elements that would fit nicely into a mark to market approach.

Background   Sprouse and Moonitz recognized in 1962 that measuring marketable securities at current market value had two distinct advantages.[11] The first advantage was that the current market price for marketable securities represents objective information about the amount of cash that the firm could realize from the sale of the securities. The second advantage was that it eliminated the anomaly whereby otherwise identical and interchangeable securities were carried at different amounts simply because they were acquired at different prices.

The Savings and Loan Crisis   In fact, the SEC had been lobbying the accounting profession to move to a mark to market approach for financial assets for some time. This harkened back to 1980 when Congress was considering proposals to deregulate the savings and loan (S&L) industry. In making that decision, Congress relied on the Balance Sheets of S&Ls, which showed that the S&L's net worth was in excess of $36.2 billion using historical cost. As the subsequent S&L crisis demonstrated, the historical cost accounting data were questionable. In fact, using a mark to market approach, the S&Ls' net worth was really between $78 billion and $118 billion.[12] This failure of Balance Sheets to accurately reflect the true value of the financial and real estate assets of the S&L industry misled Congress in its decision to deregulate the industry. This contributed to a major financial crisis that developed with S&Ls that eventually cost the public billions of dollars to resolve.

AICPA Accounting Standards Executive Committee   At the urging of the SEC, in 1990 the AICPA Accounting Standards Executive Committee (AcSEC) had been considering a proposal to have financial institutions report the changes in the portfolio value of debt and equity securities in their financial statements. The proposal was soundly criticized by representatives of banks and other financial institutions and accountants. The primary concern of the critics was that this would cause volatile swings in the earnings of financial institutions. The AcSEC retreated from that proposal and instead issued a pronouncement that required banks to disclose the market value of investment portfolios in the notes to the financial statements. This disclosure requirement was not strong enough for the SEC. SEC Chair Richard C. Breeden stated scornfully that the financial statements of banks should carry the caution "once upon a time" at the top of the page because they are essentially a statement of history.[13]

FASB   The topic of accounting for investments in securities became an accounting "hot potato." Nine months after the AcSEC and SEC disagreed, the FASB put the topic on its agenda. The proposal was to require banks and other financial institutions to record investments in marketable debt and equity securities at current market value instead of historical cost.

Many banks and thrifts opposed the change from the historical cost approach. One factor in support of the proposal was that banks and thrifts had been accused of using the historical cost approach to their financial advantage, especially in the case of the investments in bonds. Banks were accused of using a technique called *gains trading* (or "cherry picking") to improve their financial results. Gains trading involved the selection of bonds that had increased in market value to be sold at the end of the year. The sale of these bonds produced financial gains for the bank, but that left the bank with investments in bonds that had not appreciated in value but were still carried on the financial statements of the bank at their historical costs. This gains trading technique would have been curtailed because all bond investments would be marked to market under the proposal.

Other concerns were raised about the mark to market approach to marketable investments. Because there was a time lag between the market value on the statement date and the current market value, some relevancy is lost by the reporting of outdated market values. Others were concerned that marking investments to market value would discourage investments in securities that had unclear or uncertain market values, such as the bonds of local governments. Another concern was that the mark to market approach was piecemeal, in that it focused only on the financial assets of the banks and thrifts. Some felt it would be more defensible if the approach were equally applied to the financial liabilities of such firms. This would appear more evenhanded and would be more extensive an application than what was proposed.

But clearly, the lines were drawn on this issue: On one side were the SEC and the FASB, and on the other side were the statement preparers.

In January 1992 the FASB voted 3 for and 3 against on issuing a proposal to mark to market accounting for investments in securities. The Board intended to issue the proposal as an exposure draft in the first quarter of 1992, hold pubic hearings, and be able to issue the final standard by year-end or early 1993. But the tied vote blocked the issuance of the proposal and delayed the FASB's schedule on this issue. The vote is interesting because the FASB normally has seven members but only six voted on this proposal. An unfilled seat on the Board left the Board understaffed until March 1992 when a seventh member joined the Board. Later in 1992 the Board did make progress on the topic and issued the final standard, SFAS No. 115, in April 1993.

SFAS NO. 115, "ACCOUNTING FOR CERTAIN INVESTMENTS IN DEBT AND EQUITY SECURITIES"

SFAS No. 115, addressed the accounting of and reporting for investments in equity securities that have readily determinable fair values and for all investments in debt securities. It did not apply to investments in equity securities accounted for under the equity method or investments in consolidated subsidiaries.

Under its provisions, SFAS No. 115 required firms to classify debt securities into one of three categories at the time of acquisition: (1) held to maturity, (2) available for sale, and (3) trading. Equity securities should be classified into categories (2) and (3). The subsequent accounting treatment differed between the three categories.

EXHIBIT 15.2
Three Categories of Investments in SFAS No. 115

1. Held to maturity
2. Available for sale
3. Trading

Investments in debt securities should be classified as held to maturity on the Balance Sheet if the reporting firm has both the intent and ability to hold these debt securities to maturity. They should be reported at amortized cost on the Balance Sheet.

Securities that are bought and held primarily for the purpose of selling them in a short time period should be classified as "trading" securities. These can be both debt and equity securities. They should be reported on the Balance Sheet at fair market value, and any unrealized holding gains or losses on them should be reported in operating income.

Available-for-sale securities can be both debt and equity securities. This is the default category for investments that are not categorized as either held to maturity or trading. Available-for-sale securities are reported at fair market value on the Balance Sheet, but the unrealized gains and losses should be excluded from current income and reported in a separate component in stockholders' equity. These were subsequently reported on the Statement of Comprehensive Income under SFAS No. 130, "Reporting Comprehensive Income," issued in 1997.

CONCERNS ABOUT SFAS NO. 115

Two major concerns about the provisions of SFAS No. 115 arose. The implementation of SFAS No. 115 relied heavily on the judgment of the management of financial institutions.

Their judgment was pivotal in the classification of security investments into the three categories. As the accounting treatment of the investment was driven by this classification, the judgment of management became the prime determination of the accounting. Some called this procedure "psychoanalytic accounting" because to audit it, the auditors had to somehow test the thinking of management. Furthermore, this standard was issued to block a loophole through which it was alleged that the managers of banks and thrifts practiced gains trading. In light of this, a credibility issue arose. Could the statement users accept the judgment of the managers whose behavior the standard was designed to correct?

A second concern related to the partial application of mark to market in this case. SFAS No. 115 focused only on one side of the Balance Sheet, the financial assets or investments in securities. It did not apply to the other side, the financial liabilities, and was thus incomplete. Critics believed that the mark to market approach should have been applied more extensively to financial liabilities.

INITIAL SUCCESS

Despite the criticism and controversy, SFAS No. 115 was issued, and this first major effort of the FASB to implement a mark to market approach was successful. With this initial success behind them, the Board moved forward to new opportunities to apply this approach. The next section discusses the second major issue for mark to market treatment, accounting for stock options.

ACCOUNTING FOR STOCK OPTIONS

A second issue that came along and which the FASB adopted a mark to market approach to was accounting for stock options. Recall that accounting for stock options was covered in Chapter 5 with a focus on the politics associated with the FASB's addressing this issue.

BACKGROUND ON STOCK OPTIONS

Employee stock options have been used since the 1960s and 1970s. Firms gave employees the right to purchase the firm's stock for a particular price, which was normally below the current market price, for a period of time. When the employees were given the option, the firm measured the compensation expense element of the transaction by the difference between the market price of the stock and the lower option price. This type of option plan is called a *performance plan*. The accounting procedures for performance plans were established in 1972 by APB Opinion #25. This approach was consistent with historical cost and was called an *intrinsic value approach*. It attempted to measure the cost of the stock option to the issuing firm on the date of the grant.

A new type of stock option emerged in the new economy of the 1980s and 1990s called an *incentive stock option plan*. Instead of providing an exercise price that was lower than the current market price for the stock, firms began to provide option plans with exercise prices that equaled or exceeded the current market price. And, generally, the incentive stock option could not be exercised until a given period of time had lapsed. So for employees with this type of stock option, the only way they could financially benefit from the option was to work to improve the market price of the stock during the exercise period.

This new type of stock option had the following three objectives: (1) motivate current employees and executives to high levels of performance, (2) base compensation on performance, and (3) retain current executives and employees. This plan became significant in the emerging high-tech industry in the United States, especially for the firms in northern California's "Silicon Valley." Many of these firms were startups, and they could not afford to hire experienced executives. So the incentive stock option plan became the standard way for these firms to hire experienced executives at lower salaries but with extensive incentive stock options as a way to pay them in the future.

For many U.S. executives at both high-tech and more traditional firms, incentive stock options became 30 percent of their annual compensation packages (in some smaller high-tech firms it was nearly 60 percent). Unfortunately, these stock option plans did not fit into the accounting mode of APB Opinion #25; therefore, the compensation expense was not recorded and the options became a form of stealth compensation. But once the press became aware of this, it quickly became a public issue and was especially a concern for stockholders and financial analysts.

To resolve this problem, in 1984 the AICPA and seven of the Big 8 public accounting firms urged the FASB to put incentive stock option plans on its agenda. The Board agreed, and this project started through the due process procedure.

FASB'S APPROACH

The FASB adopted a mark to market approach toward the valuation of these new stock options. The approach followed under APB Opinion #25 was called an intrinsic value approach because it valued the option on the comparison of the exercise price and market price on the date of grant. The intrinsic value approach was consistent with historical cost. But no other factors were used to value the option and measure the related expense. Because the intrinsic value approach did not work well for the newer types of stock options, in the opinion of many, the FASB decided to take a mark to market approach toward the issue. It attempted to implement a fair value approach, which measures the market value of the option on the grant data and uses that market value to measure the compensation expense. The fair value approach is more consistent with the mark to market approach because it attempted to measure the market value of the option on the grant date. It also is more consistent with the long-term objectives of such option plans.

EXPOSURE DRAFT ON STOCK OPTIONS

In June 1993, the FASB issued the exposure draft (ED) of SFAS No. 123, "Accounting for Stock-Based Compensation," in which it proposed that firms measure the compensation expense of incentive stock option plans at the grant date. Firms should use the Black-Scholes model, a widely recognized finance model, to measure the market price of unlisted options. The Black-Scholes model attempts to measure the value of the option to the recipient, which is a measure of the expense associated with the incentive options.

As part of the due process on the draft, the FASB received a great deal of feedback. By and large, the feedback was negative. There were two major concerns: (1) Many firms, especially those high-tech firms in Silicon Valley, believed that the proposed standard would drive them out of business by either destroying their profitability or by severely limiting their access to experienced executives; and (2) many believed that the Black-Scholes model was inappropriate to measure compensation expense and was much too complicated to implement. Those in opposition included the Big 6 public accounting firms, the Financial

Executives International (FEI), and the AICPA. In fact, the Big 6 and the AICPA urged the FASB to drop the idea. However, the Board was convinced that the ED was the best way to solve the problem of stealth compensation and measure the stock options at market value.

SFAS NO. 123, "ACCOUNTING FOR STOCK-BASED COMPENSATION"

The debate over the stock option ED quickly became bitter and involved a great deal of politics, as is covered in Chapter 5. There was widespread opposition to this proposal.

As a result of the opposition, and politics, the Board decided to back down on the plan to issue the ED as a new SFAS. So in January 1995, the Board voted 5 to 2 to issue SFAS No. 123, giving firms the choice of methods. The choice given to firms in SFAS No. 123 was either to recognize incentive stock options as an expense at the fair market value of their stock options or to continue to apply APB Opinion #25 for expense recognition and follow the fair market value approach in a pro forma footnote disclosure of the expense associated with incentive stock options.

Although the application of mark to market in the case of stock options was less extensive than it wanted, the FASB did make some progress. But this experience illustrates that even when the FASB loses a major battle over an accounting standard, it still accomplishes something. For the first time ever, SFAS No. 123 required disclosure of the expense associated with stock options in a standardized manner and at market value.

ACCOUNTING FOR DERIVATIVES

Accounting for derivatives is the third example in this chapter of how the FASB is using a mark to market approach in setting accounting standards. As in the previous two examples, accounting for investments in marketable securities and accounting for stock options, the FASB has had a great deal of difficulty in establishing a mark to market standard for derivatives.

BACKGROUND

Derivatives are financial instruments that derive their value from some underlying factor such as an asset, referenced interest or currency rate, or index of some kind, for example, a stock market index.[14] Derivatives generally include futures, forward contracts, swaps, option contracts, and other similar financial instruments. They are often innovative and known as "exotic securities."

Derivatives were developed in reaction to the increased risk of loss from volatility in capital, foreign exchange, and commodity markets. Firms needed some way to protect themselves against losses from the changes in interest rates, currency exchange rates, and commodity prices, and derivatives were developed to fill that need. Many firms successfully used derivatives to defend themselves against those financial risks, and derivatives still serve an important role in the management of risk in global financial markets. Because of the volatility in global financial markets, the use of derivatives became widespread. The "over-the-counter" global derivative market was estimated at $81.5 trillion in 2000. In 2001, more than 3,000 hedge funds managed an estimated $410 billion in assets. Many derivatives are highly leveraged; a small movement in the underlying asset or interest rate can be amplified into very large gains or losses on the derivative. Although most firms use derivatives to manage risk in a defensive way, some firms saw the opportunity for gains.

In the mid-1990s, public attention was focused on derivatives due to the large and unexpected losses from their use reported by many large pubic corporations and financial institutions. Examples of the losses from derivatives reported for 1994 were Orange County, California, $2.0 billion; Showa Shell Sekiyu, $1.6 billion; and Proctor & Gamble, $157 million.

These losses caused a large public outcry for increase disclosure and tighter regulation for derivatives. There were related concerns that unregulated derivative trading posed a threat to the stability of some capital markets. As a measure of the significance of this issue, consider the stature of following list of organizations and groups that became involved in the effort to regulate derivatives: SEC, IASC, U.S. Comptroller of the Currency, U.S. House of Representatives, U.S. Senate, and the AICPA. Of course, one major issue that arose was concerned with who would do the regulating.

FASB'S FINANCIAL INSTRUMENTS PROJECT

The FASB had been considering accounting for financial instruments since 1986. Their efforts resulted in the issuance of three different disclosure standards on financial instruments: SFAS No. 105, "Disclosure of Information about Financial Instruments with Off-Balance Sheet Risk and Financial Instruments with Concentrations of Credit Risk," in 1990; SFAS No. 107, "Disclosures about Fair Value of Financial Instruments," in 1991; and SFAS No. 119, "Disclosures about Derivative and Financial Instruments and Fair Value of Financial Instruments," in 1994. These three standards were considered as interim measures, pending the issuance of an accounting standard for derivatives. SFAS No. 107 provided guidance for firms to use when determining the fair market value of financial instruments. Unfortunately, it is apparent that the first two disclosure standards did not prevent the occurrence of large and unexpected losses reported by firms in 1994.

On the other hand, it is significant to note from the titles of these disclosure standards and the topic of SFAS No. 107 that the FASB adopted a market value ("fair value") approach to derivatives and financial instruments.

SFAS NO. 133, "ACCOUNTING FOR DERIVATIVE INSTRUMENTS AND HEDGING ACTIVITIES"

The long-awaited standard was issued in June 1998. SFAS No. 133 is effective for fiscal years starting after June 15, 2000. This new standard considers derivatives as assets and liabilities and concludes that they should be recorded as such. Fair market value is the most relevant measure of these assets and liabilities. Derivatives that result in cash obligations are liabilities, and derivatives that result in cash rewards are assets. Both should be included on the Balance Sheet, measured at fair value (market value).

Accounting for the change in market value depends on the purpose for holding the derivative. Three purposes for using derivatives are recognized in SFAS No. 133: (1) fair value hedge—using a derivative to hedge a fair value exposure of a recognized asset, liability, or firm commitment; (2) cash flow hedge—using a derivative to hedge a cash flow exposure of an existing asset, liability, or forecasted transaction; and (3) net investment hedge—using derivatives to hedge the net investment in a foreign operation. In the case of fair value hedges, changes in the market value of the derivatives are recognized in current income. For cash flow hedges, changes in the market value are reported in comprehensive income or current earnings. In the case of net investment hedges, the change in value is reported either in comprehensive income or a separate component of stockholders' equity. The standard also establishes special limitations for transactions qualifying as hedges.

EXHIBIT 15.3
Three Purposes of Using Derivatives in SFAS No. 133

1. Fair value hedge
2. Cash flow hedge
3. Net investment hedge

SFAS No. 133 represents a big change in accounting for hedges. Its purpose is to increase the visibility, comparability, and understandability of the risk associated with using derivatives by requiring firms to report all derivative assets and liabilities at market value on the Sstatement of Financial Position.[15] At least part of the controversy over SFAS No. 133 was directly linked to its the mark to market approach.[16]

The accounting procedures of SFAS No. 133 are complex. Its effective date was delayed by SFAS No. 137 (1999), and the standard was amended by SFAS No. 138 (2000). The FASB established a special group of twelve people, the Derivatives Implementation Group (DIG), to assist FASB staff in responding to implementation questions from statement preparers and users.

CONCERNS WITH SFAS NO. 133

In general, the major concern with SFAS No. 133 is the same major concern about the other two accounting standards that adopted a mark to market approach, that is, that adopting SFAS No. 133 will cause increased volatility in earnings and equity. Fluctuations in the market value of derivative hedges will impact current income, comprehensive income, and equity under its provisions.

A second major concern about SFAS No. 133 is the unavailability of reliable and standardized market value measures for some derivatives, especially for the more exotic securities.

A third complaint was that the time and cost to implement SFAS No. 133 was unreasonably high. The FEI projected that the implementation of SFAS No. 133 will cost an average of $100,000 per firm.[17]

SURVEY OF PLANNED DERIVATIVE USE AT FIRMS

Senior executives from more than one hundred *Fortune* 1,000 firms (with annual sales of $1 billion to about $100 million) responded to a survey in 2000 about how their firms planned to deal with their derivatives under SFAS No. 133.[18] (The firms reported using the following derivatives to hedge risk: interest rate swaps, currency forwards and futures, commodity forwards and futures, commodity and currency options, and others.) The executives indicated concern about various features of SFAS No. 133: Approximately 57 percent indicated concern about how to value their firm's derivatives. Thus, the results of the survey shows that the mark to market element of SFAS No. 133 is still a concern.

FURTHER CRITICISM OF THE MARK TO MARKET APPROACH

Although the FASB has made progress, it still becomes the target of criticism. It is interesting that the mark to market approach has begun to dominate the FASB; however, it has become the target of criticism. King believes that the FASB and some academics are the prime supporters for fair value accounting, whereas financial executives and managers are still supporters of historical cost.[19] He lists the following three reasons why financial executives and managers prefer historical cost:

1. Historical cost is well understood and works well.
2. If mark to market accounting is adopted and unrealized changes in market values reported in current income, the unrealized gains and losses will distort net income.
3. Fair value is not exact; it is costly to generate and subject to manipulation.

King states one criticism of fair value that closely parallels one of the major criticisms of historical cost: He claims that there's never a single value that's fair. Applying his thinking to our example of the car purchase described earlier in the chapter, King would ask the purchaser of a car for $25,000 what the fair value of that car was. King anticipates at least seven answers: (1) the cost to reproduce new the exact car; (2) the cost to acquire a similar car, new; (3) the cost to acquire a similar car, used; (4) the amount the owner would get from a used car dealer if he or she sold the car to them; (5) the amount that would be realized from selling the car at a used car auction; (6) the amount the owner would get if he or she sold the car and his or her house; or (7) the original cost of the car, adjusted by some price index. King suggests that all seven values would be different, and he asks, Which is the fair value? He concludes with a recommendation. He believes that fair values should be developed and disclosed when future cash flows are likely from the asset from its sale or disposition. Otherwise, assets that will continue to be used by the firm for the purpose for which they were acquired should be reported at historical cost.

SUMMARY

COMPARISON OF THE THREE MARK TO MARKET FASB STANDARDS

In conclusion, it is interesting to note the similarities in these three accounting standards in which the FASB adopted a mark to market approach. The FASB did not initiate these projects by itself. Instead, all three standards resulted from concerns about current accounting methods from outside stakeholders. In each case, the FASB was simply responding to concerns expressed by their constituencies that conditions had changed and new accounting methods were needed.

    All three financial standard projects became highly visible and attracted the attention of many stakeholder groups, the national financial media, various industrial groups, and

Washington. All three projects became very controversial as soon as it became apparent what the FASB intentions were. The same major concern surfaced about each standard: the increased volatility in earnings from accounting for the changes in market prices in the mark to market approach.

In all three cases, the FASB was encouraged to abandon the project. But the Board persevered and overcame the opposition. The Board had varying success in each of the three cases. It issued standards that put the mark to market approach in the financial statements in two cases (investments in marketable securities and derivatives) and in a footnote disclosure (stock options). Overall, the FASB accomplished what it set out to do; mark to market accounting has a strong foothold in accounting practice today. However, as the comments from King show, the debate continues. The FASB has made progress in its implementation of a mark to market approach to accounting. The FASB overcame strong opposition to give mark to market accounting an important role in financial accounting today.

REVIEW QUESTIONS

1. What are the two schools of thought on the valuation of an asset? Which school appears more consistent with the FASB's definition of an asset in SFAC No. 6?
2. Cite three advantages of historical cost. Which is most important in your view?
3. Do you accept Kuhn's pattern as an explanation for the development of mark to market's dominance over historical cost?
4. What evidence of the FASB's support of mark to market is found in the Conceptual Framework project? Cite where two examples of this evidence can be found in this project.
5. What was the first issue to which the FASB implemented its mark to market approach?
6. How did the S&L crisis of the 1980s influence the SEC's view on historical cost and mark to market?
7. How did the AICPA's Accounting Standards Committee deal with a proposal to change the accounting for investments in market securities?
8. What factors caused the FASB to address the issue of accounting for investments in marketable securities?
9. Why did banks and thrifts oppose accounting for marketable securities using a mark to market approach?
10. What caused a delay in the due process procedures of the FASB in January 1992 when it addressed a proposed exposure draft on accounting for marketable securities? How was this resolved?
11. What are the three categories in SFAS No. 115 for accounting for investments in marketable securities? What accounting treatment accompanies each category?
12. What were two major concerns about SFAS No. 115? Which is more important in your opinion?
13. How did stock options change from the 1960s and 1970s to the 1990s? How did this change affect the accounting procedures for stock options?
14. How did APB Opinion #25 account for stock options? What was the support for this procedure? Why was its approach called an intrinsic value approach?
15. What factors caused the FASB to put accounting for stock options on its agenda in 1984?

16. How did the FASB's approach to stock options differ from the approach in APB Opinion #25? Which do you prefer?

17. What feedback did the FASB get on its exposure draft on accounting for stock options?

18. What groups opposed the FASB's exposure draft on accounting for stock options?

19. How did the FASB react to the opposition to its proposal for accounting for stock options? In what ways could the final action of the FASB on stock options be considered as a victory rather than a defeat?

20. What are derivatives? What makes accounting for them so complicated?

21. What factors caused firms to use derivatives?

22. What is the estimated size of the global market in derivatives? How does this compare to other financial markets, such as the NYSE or the market for foreign currencies?

23. In what way did the large and unexpected losses from derivatives reported by large public corporations and financial institutions cause some concern that derivatives trading presented a threat to stable financial markets?

24. What developments occurred in reaction to these large and unexpected losses? What important question arose?

25. Describe the three pronouncements in the FASB's financial instruments project. What did each address? Did they appear to be a success or failure in light of the large and unexpected losses from financial instruments incurred by firms?

26. What did the FASB conclude derivatives were in SFAS No. 133, and what measure is the most appropriate for them?

27. What are the three purposes for using a derivative according to SFAS No. 133? How does the accounting differ among the three purposes?

28. In what ways was SFAS No. 133 a big change in accounting for hedges?

29. What major concern arose about SFAS No. 133? What was a secondary concern?

30. How did *Fortune* 1,000 firms report using derivatives in the 2000 survey discussed in the chapter? What concern about derivatives was reported by more than one-half of the executives responding to this survey?

DISCUSSION TOPICS

1. **The Asset Disposal Case:**[20] "The sporting thing"

   Early in the year, Sweetspot, Inc., a leading manufacturer of quality recreational equipment, put some idle cash to work by investing in marketable securities, some of which later advanced in price while others declined. The securities were recorded at cost.

   In November, Martin Nicklaus, president of Sweetspot, decided to dispose of all the securities. The securities were actively traded on the Big Board with Sweetspot's holding only a minor fraction of the normal daily volume. As of November 10, the pertinent figures were:

	Cost	Market
Appreciated securities	$40,000	$70,000
Depreciated securities	40,000	27,000
Total	$80,000	$97,000

Because Sweetspot prepares financial statements only at year-end, no gains or losses have been recognized for any of the securities. President Nicklaus is considering the following five possible means for disposing of the marketable securities:

- Sell for cash.
- Use to satisfy liabilities.
- Distribute to stockholders as a dividend.
- Use to pay executive bonuses.
- Donate to charity.

He has told the controller that his decision about which course of action to take will depend in part on how much gain or loss will be recognized as a result of the disposal option he chooses.

Question: How much gain or loss should Sweetspot recognize under each of the five options for disposing of the assets? Should the amount depend on the means of disposal?

2. Which do you prefer, historical cost or mark to market? Defend your choice with the two most important arguments to support your view.

3. Because accountants used current market values unsuccessfully before, in the period of 1900 to 1930, it is easy to argue against their use now by simply saying: "We tried that before and it failed!" Are things different now such that mark to market could be successful? Have conditions changed since then to silence that argument? If so, what has changed and how has the change made the current environment more favorable for mark to market than in 1900 to 1930?

4. **Project.** Using the car buying experiment provided in the chapter as a basis, select some major appliance or purchase and do some research on the buying practices for that item to see if certain groups within society are typically treated differently in buying that item than others. How would this affect the price at which the item could be purchased? As a class project, you could duplicate the car buying experiment and see what range of prices that class members would expect to pay for the identical item.

5. **Project.** Have each member of the class answer the following questions: In the car buying experiment discussed in the chapter, what do you think you would have paid for the $25,000 car? On what do you base your answer. Tabulate the results from the class and discuss.

6. **Application Problem.** The Duece Company has had extremely good fortunes in its operations and has developed a significant cash balance. Because the present cash balance is in excess of its internal demands, it made the following investments during the current fiscal year:

   a. Some vacant land close to a growing retail area of the city. Duece paid $500,000 for the land but has received several offers from potential buyers already. The offers have ranged from $800,000 to $1,200,000. The property is appraised at $820,000.

   b. Shares of stock in General Motors Corporation. Duece paid $300,000 for the shares, and the shares' market value at year-end was $390,000. Duece has classified these shares as current assets, securities available for sale.

   c. Bonds payable of Ford Motor Company. The bonds of Ford will mature in ten years, but Duece has no intention of keeping the bonds that long. Duece probably will keep the bonds for two or three years. Duece paid $500,000 for the bonds, but because of an interest rate fluctuation in the market, they are presently (at the end of the cur-rent fiscal year) only worth $460,000.

d. Shares of stock in the Johns Company. Duece purchased 40 percent of the out-standing shares of Johns Company for $400,000. Since that acquisition, Johns Company has declared and paid cash dividends totaling $20,000 and reported income of $60,000. The market value of the shares of stock in Johns Company at fiscal year-end was $410,000.

e. Land containing timber. The land was purchased for $600,000; land value was only $350,000, and $250,000 of the purchase price was attributable to the future timber to be harvested. During the current year, the trees increased in size and by year-end, the value of the future timber had increased to $270,000. The land value remained fairly constant at $350,000.

   At what amount should Duece recognize the assets on its Balance Sheet from each of the transactions for the fiscal year just ended related to the above investments?

7. Why do you think the FASB has been such a strong advocate of the mark to market approach rather than historical cost?

8. Where on the Balance Sheet do you think the FASB will move next to implement mark to market accounting?

9. Discuss the wealth effect. Have you seen evidence of it in yourself? Other students? Your parents or professor? Do you think it has changed the economic behavior of peo-ple today? Do you think it will be a lasting change?

10. What factors made investment in marketable securities appear to be the perfect issue for the implementation of mark to market accounting? In your view, was it perfect?

11. In 1984, the FASB put accounting for stock options on its agenda at the urging of seven of the Big 8 firms and the AICPA. Why do you think so many groups changed their thinking on accounting for stock options by the time the Board issued its exposure draft? What other groups opposed this exposure draft? What do you think was their motivation?

12. Compare the similarities in accounting for the three topics discussed in the chapter. What pattern of events is evident in each? How can these three experiences help the FASB in future pronouncements?

13. Analyze the arguments that King made in criticizing fair value. Are his arguments against fair value stronger than the arguments made against historical cost? Which dominates in your opinion?

14. Why do you think that mark to market accounting has not been implemented for long-term tangible assets in the United States although it is allowed in other countries, for example, the United Kingdom (see Lee, 1994)?

NOTES

1 FASB (1993).
2 FASB (1995).
3 FASB (1998).
4 Philips, p. 16.
5 Chambers.
6 Solomons, p. 205.
7 Sprouse and Moonitz, pp. 26–28.
8 American Accounting Association, pp. 30–31.

9 Kuhn. For a full discussion of Kuhn's pattern, see Chapter 6.

10 For an interesting article on the wealth effect, see Ip.

11 Sprouse and Moonitz, p. 25.

12 Salwen and Block.

13 See Salwen and Blumenthal, p. A15.

14 This section is based on Evans (2000), pp. 154–156 and Evans (1999), pp. 243–244.

15 Wilson et al., p. 24.

16 Barlas.

17 Wilson and Rasch, p. 25.

18 Solution133.com.

19 King, p. 53.

20 Johnson and Petrone, p. 1.

REFERENCES

Accounting Principles Board. "Accounting for Stock Issued to Employees," *APB Opinion #25*. New York: American Institute of Certified Public Accountants, 1972.

American Accounting Association. *A Statement of Basic Accounting Theory.* Evanston, IL: American Accounting Association, 1966.

Barlas, Stephen (Editor). "Mr. Jenkins Comes to Washington," *Management Accounting* (July 1998): 8.

Beresford, Dennis. "The Need for Accounting Standards, Wisdom from the World of Dogbert." *CPA Journal* (January 1998): 37–41.

Chambers, R. "Historical Cost—Tale of a False Creed." *Accounting Horizons* (March 1994): 76–89.

Evans, T., Stanley Atkinson, and D. Mandal. "High-Tech Hedging, Measuring the Financial Impact of Derivates Under SFAS 119." *Advances in International Accounting* (2000): 153–171.

Evans, T., Martin Tayor, and R. Rolfe. *International Accounting and Reporting*, Third Edition. Houston, TX: Dame Publications, 1999.

Financial Accounting Standards Board. "Objectives of Financial Reporting by Business Enterprises." *Statement of Financial Accounting Concepts No. 1*. Norwalk, CT: Financial Accounting Standards Board, 1978.

———. "Elements of Financial Statements: *Statement of Financial Accounting Concepts No. 6.* Norwalk, CT: Financial Accounting Standards Board, 1985.

———. "Disclosure of Information about Financial Instruments with Off-Balance Sheet Risk and Financial Instruments with Concentrations of Credit Risk." *Statement of Financial Accounting Standards No. 105*. Norwalk, CT: Financial Accounting Standards Board, 1990.

———. "Disclosures about Fair Value of Financial Instruments." *Statement of Financial Accounting Standards No. 107*. Norwalk, CT: Financial Accounting Standards Board, 1991.

———. "Accounting for Certain Investments in Debt and Equity Securities." *Statement of Financial Accounting Standards No. 115*. Norwalk, CT: Financial Accounting Standards Board, 1993.

———. "Disclosures about Derivative and Financial Instruments and Fair Value of Financial Instruments." *Statement of Financial Accounting Concepts No. 119*, Norwalk, CT: Financial Accounting Standards Board, 1994.

————. "Accounting for Stock-Based Compensation." *Statement of Financial Accounting Standards No. 123*. Norwalk, CT: Financial Accounting Standards Board, 1995.

————. "Reporting Comprehensive Income," *Statement of Financial Accounting Standards No. 130*. Norwalk, CT: Financial Accounting Standards Board, 1997.

————. "Accounting for Derivative Instruments and Hedging Activities." *Statement of Financial Accounting Standards No. 133*. Norwalk, CT: Financial Accounting Standards Board, 1998.

————. "Accounting for Derivative Instruments and Hedging Activities—Deferral of the Effective Date of FASB Statement No. 133." *Statement of Financial Accounting Standards No. 137*. Norwalk, CT: Financial Accounting Standards Board, 1999.

————. "Accounting for Certain Derivative Instruments and Certain Hedging Activities—An Amendment of FASB Statement No. 133." *Statement of Financial Accounting Standards No. 138*. Norwalk, CT: Financial Accounting Standards Board, 2000.

Hwang, Angela, and John Patouhas. "Practical Issues in Implementing FASB 133." *Journal of Accountancy* (March 2001): 26–34.

Ip, Greg. "Are Fears Over 'Wealth Effect' Excessive?" *The Wall Street Journal* (March 24, 2001): A2.

King, Alfred. "Why Fair Value Accounting Can't Work." Financial Executive (July/August 1999): 53–55.

Kuhn, Thomas (1970). *The Structure of Scientific Revolutions*, Second Edition. (Chicago, IL: University of Chicago Press, 1970.

Lee, Tom. "Mark to Market: The U.K. Experience." *Journal of Accountancy* (September 1994): 84–88.

McCarthy, Ed. "Derivatives Revisited." *Journal of Accountancy* (May 2000): 35–43.

Munter, Paul, T. Moores, and Thomas Ratcliffe. "A New Look at Market Value Accounting." *Management Accounting* (March 1994): 41–45.

Philips, G. Edward. "The Accretion Concept of Income." *Accounting Review* (January 1963): 14–23.

Salwen, K., and Sandra Block. "Rules Changes for Accountants Worrying SEC." *The Wall Street Journal* (September 17, 1990): A17.

Salwen, K., and Robin Blumenthal. "Tackling Accounting, SEC Pushes Changes With Broad Impact." *Wall Street Journal* (September 27, 1990): A15.

Solomons, David. "Economic and Accounting Concepts of Income." *Accounting Review* (July 1961): 201–211.

Solution133.com [A joint venture of PriceWaterhouseCoopers and G. Fong Associates]. "Companies Focus on Derivatives Compliance." *Journal of Accountancy* (February 2001): 26.

Sprouse, Robert, and Maurice Moonitz. *A Tentative Set of Broad Accounting Principles for Business Enterprises*. New York: American Institute of Certified Public Accounts, 1962.

Steinberg, Joel. "Stock-Based Compensation Issues." *CPA Journal* (March 1998): 52–53.

Wilson, Arlette, and Ronald H. Rasch. "New Accounting for Derivatives and Hedging Activities. "*CPA Journal* (October 1998): 22–27.

Wilson, Arlette, G. Waters, and B. Bryan. "The Decision on Derivatives." *Journal of Accountancy* (November 1998): 24–29.

CHAPTER 16

FINANCIAL REPORTING: DISCLOSURE

LEARNING OBJECTIVES

After studying this chapter, you should be able to

> Define accounting disclosure and describe its role in the accounting process.

> Answer the four basic disclosure questions.

> Describe the work of the Jenkins Committee on disclosure.

> Identify the four issues in the Wallman disclosure proposal.

> Describe the FASB Business Reporting Research Project.

BACKGROUND

BACKGROUND

The last topic in this book concerns accounting disclosure. Accounting disclosure is examined from a theory standpoint, and proposals to make disclosure more effective are considered. In this chapter, five specific accounting developments are emphasized, as well as the general advance of accounting disclosure:

1. 1983 Summary Annual Reports Proposal
2. 1991 Jenkins Committee
3. 1995 Wallman Proposal
4. 1998–2001 FASB Business Reporting Research Project
5. 2000 Association for Investment Management and Research (AIMR) survey

These five advances are shown in Exhibit 16.1.

EXHIBIT 16.1
Compensation Time Line

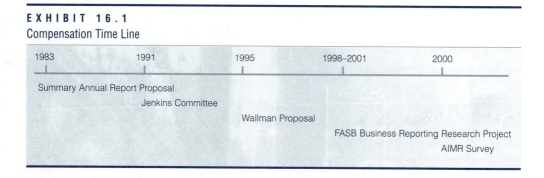

DEFINITION

Disclosure means supplying information in the financial statements, including the statements themselves, the notes to the statements, and the supplementary disclosures associated with the statements. It does not extend to public or private statements made by management or information provided outside the financial statements. Disclosure is the final stage of accounting. After accounting has processed transactions and recorded their impact on the assets, liabilities, and owners' equity of the firm in the accounts, the cumulative impact of these transactions is reported in the financial statements. Typically, the corporation publishes four financial statements: a Balance Sheet, an Income Statement, a Statement of Stockholders' Equity, and a Statement of Cash Flows.

These statements are published in the firm's annual report, which is the major communication vehicle between the firm and outside users of financial information. It also includes additional content, typically, the following information:

- Summary of financial highlights of the current and past two years
- Some key financial statistics
- Comparative financial information for five or ten years
- Management's discussion and analysis of the past year's operations

- Promotional or descriptive information about the firm's products, divisions, segments, and personnel
- The auditor's opinion

DISCLOSURE'S ROLE

Historically, disclosure has had an interesting role in the accounting process and relationship with accounting principles and practices. Disclosure has been linked with accounting practices and principles. It was considered as an acceptable substitute for good accounting practices, and it was regarded as a safety net for substandard accounting practices and principles. Disclosure was regarded as a way to resolve some accounting problems and as a satisfactory alternative to good practices or principles, that is, almost as a "default." The guiding rule was often stated as:

Bad accounting + good disclosure = good accounting

This rule allowed accountants to put less emphasis on the development of optimal accounting principles and practices and instead rely on full disclosure as a way to remedy the situation.

This way of thinking is similar to the thinking in other areas, such as the preparation and sale of food products to consumers. Some would argue it doesn't matter what is added to the food products sold to the public as long as it is disclosed on the label. The counterargument is that care should go into both what is included in the products and the labeling; both are important.

Using disclosure as a safety net for suboptimal accounting practices was not desirable, but it was pragmatic. In the absence of a good solution to an accounting problem, it was considered practical to compromise on the practice but fully disclose what was being done. The disclosure was intended to warn the statement users about what was actually done, and the warning seemed to make the whole situation satisfactory. It could be compared to a local county in Florida that had a road with a sharp curve that caused a number of auto accidents. Rather than going through the expense and trouble of repairing the road and making it safer, they decided to simply put up a sign, "Danger, Sharp Curve, Slow to 10 MPH," to warn drivers as the solution to the problem. However, using disclosure as a remedy for problematic accounting practices is questionable and, fortunately, less important in the development of accounting principles and practices now than in the past.

Today accountants view disclosure as even more important than previously. It is the concluding phase of accounting. It is seen as a way of presenting the results of the accounting process so that financial statement users can utilize accounting information in decision making. In fact, disclosure is regarded as an increasingly important aspect of accounting—even of deserving a new look. This new look at disclosure is consistent with the new view of accounting, because the emphasis in the new view of accounting is on investors and creditors. Both of these groups are outside parties, not part of the management of the firm. As such, they rely on the disclosures of the firm as a primary source of information. There are some concerns that accounting disclosures should be improved to provide more relevant information to investors and creditors and that the disclosures should be provided on a more timely basis. These concerns were underscored in December, 2001, with the unexpected financial disaster associated with the collapse of the giant Enron Corporation. Many concerns about Enron's failure focused on the accounting disclosures of the firm.

FOUR BASIC QUESTIONS

When discussing disclosure, four related questions arise:

1. *For whom is the information disclosed?* That is, who comprises the audience for the disclosure and what parties are involved?
2. *Why are the disclosures being made?* That is, what purpose do they serve? How can they be used by the audience?
3. *How much information should be disclosed?* That is, what is the "amount" of the disclosure?
4. *When should the information be disclosed?* That is, what is the proper timing of the disclosure?

Any proposal to revise disclosure should address these basic questions. In the remainder of the chapter, a number of disclosure topics and proposals to improve disclosure are described. In the following sections, when a topic or proposal addresses one or more of the four questions, the specific question(s) will be identified.

GENERAL DISCLOSURE LEVELS

In general, there are three levels of disclosure. Levels of disclosure primarily relates to the third question in the previous section, How much information should be disclosed?

1. *Adequate disclosure.* This is defined as the minimum amount so as not to be misleading. The amount disclosed should be the bare minimum for decision making.
2. *Fair or ethical.* This involves providing an equal treatment of all parties. No one party's informational needs would be preferred to another's.
3. *Full.* This involves presenting the full range of all relevant information used for decision making.

SEC'S DISCLOSURE LEVELS

For comparison, the SEC has historically recognized three levels of disclosure.

1. *Protective.* This level is designed to protect the unsophisticated investor from unfair treatment and generally requires the provision of a large volume of information.
2. *Informative.* This level of disclosure is designed to provide the full range of information used for investment analysis purposes.
3. *Differential.* This level provides varying levels of information for different needs.

The SEC's emphasis is on informative disclosure; it used to emphasize protective disclosure. Current accounting requires that financial statement users be adequately prepared to understand accounting procedures, practices, and language.

DISCLOSURE CONSIDERATIONS

There are two important considerations when discussing disclosure in general: cost-benefit factors and information overload. These considerations refer to disclosure question three, How much information should be disclosed?

First, an important consideration in deciding on the level of disclosure is the cost-benefit factor, meaning that the cost of producing additional disclosures should be exceeded by the benefits of providing that information. If the cost exceeds the benefit, the information should not be presented. Unfortunately, this is more easily stated than implemented. It is very difficult to measure the benefits associated with disclosures; however, it is easier to measure the costs. Knowing only one side of that equation, the cost, does not permit the cost-benefit factor to come into play in many disclosure situations.

Second, an important consideration in disclosure deals with information overload, referring to providing so much information that the user is unable to process the information effectively. The user is unable to process the volume of information and is stymied. There is a popular idea in communication that the more communication, the better. But information overload maintains that there is a limit to the amount of information that can be processed at a point in time, and this must be considered when communicating. More information is not necessarily better if it can't be assimilated by the receiver.

But it is important that business firms not go to the opposite extreme and provide little or no communication. Limiting communication will create more problems for the firm than it solves. In fact, one principle of communication is that the recipient generally regards the absence of any information negatively and may easily consider that something bad has happened. So when firms are silent, that is not good, either, because it sends a signal that something is being withheld.

THE SUMMARY ANNUAL REPORT

The annual report of corporations is generally designed to be a general-purpose statement. It is designed to supply information for current and prospective investors, creditors, customers, suppliers, and financial analysts. As such, it attempts to serve all these audiences with a general-purpose objective that has been criticized as so much of a compromise that no one party is served well. That criticism is important in light of the time and money that firms spend on designing, printing, and issuing their corporate annual reports. These documents are usually expensive and are filled with color pictures and printed on glossy paper. In fact, in the year 2000, 14,000 firms spent a total of $8.5 billion (and each spent up to four months) to produce their annual reports.[1]

As one way of reducing the cost of producing the annual report and providing more relevant information to investors, the idea of a summary annual report was developed. It is an example of differential disclosure, which involves providing different information to different groups to meet their particular needs. The summary annual report was designed to provide condensed financial statements and aimed primarily at outside investors. Summary annual reports address basic disclosure question two, Why are the disclosures being made?

One proposal to issue summary annual reports came from a study conducted by Deloitte & Touche and supported by the Financial Executives Institute (FEI; now the Financial Executives International) in 1983. Nineteen firms participated in a study of the ways to streamline the annual report. A number of proposals emerged; one was that a "live experiment" be conducted in which some firms would provide users with summary annual reports and other firms would provide the traditional annual report. Users would then evaluate the usefulness and effectiveness of the summary annual reports. The SEC, however, did not support this experiment.[2]

The SEC did allow General Motors (GM) to issue a summary annual report in 1986. In 1987, forty firms were allowed to publish summary annual reports. As part of this experiment, summary annual reports were sent to stockholders who could also request the full annual report. Unfortunately, the idea of summary annual reports never received widespread support from investors, and the practice was not widespread. One major problem with summary annual reports was that the SEC did not revise its proxy rules to allow a summary annual report to be sent to shareholders in place of a full annual report. However, some firms adopted the approach of providing stockholders with a summary annual report and an optional full annual report and continued with it. In general, the summary annual report has half as many pages as the traditional annual report.

JENKINS COMMITTEE'S PROPOSAL TO IMPROVE DISCLOSURES

A major impetus and reason for the renewed importance of disclosure came from the Jenkins Committee, the AICPA's Special Committee on Financial Reporting created in 1991 to study concerns about the usefulness of business financial reporting.

The committee was composed of fourteen members, consisting of eleven public accountants, one professor, and two financial executives. Its report, *Meeting the Information Needs of Investors and Creditors*, was published in 1994.[3]

COMMITTEE'S CHARGE

The Jenkins Committee was part of the AICPA's broad initiative to improve the value of financial information and the confidence of the public in that information. Elements of the initiative were

- Enhancing the utility of business reporting.
- Improving the prevention and detection of fraud.
- Ensuring the independence and objectivity of the auditor.
- Discouraging unwarranted litigation.
- Strengthening the auditing profession's system of discipline.

The Jenkins Committee was asked to make a twofold recommendation about the nature of information that should be made available to others by management and the extent to which auditors should report on various elements of that information.

The Jenkins Committee saw the need for adequate financial information in the economy and capital markets. Financial reporting is the cornerstone of capital allocation and vitally important to national economic interests.

All four disclosure questions were addressed by the Jenkins Committee.

CHANGED CONDITIONS

A major reason for the creation of the Jenkins Committee was the recent change in the way business was conducted. The Jenkins Committee cited two factors that were responsible for sweeping changes: increased competition and rapid advances in technology. In turn, these two factors were changing the whole world of business and creating a new customer focus.

METHODOLOGY

To conduct the study, the Jenkins Committee focused on direct input from users obtained from study groups and from extensive surveys of users (conducted by the Lou Harris organization). Two different user groups—investors and creditors—were created. The committee obtained direct input from 400 people, mostly users and financial statement preparers, and indirect input from 1,200 users (600 investors and 600 creditors) through the survey. The committee also gathered information on trends that were shaping business activity and the implications of those trends on the information needs of users.

To fulfill its charge, the committee held formal discussion groups with portfolio managers, financial analysts, and bankers, as well as with the Financial Accounting Policy Committee of the AIMR.

CONCLUSIONS AND RECOMMENDATIONS

In general, the conclusion of the Jenkins Committee was that financial statement users want more information. Specifically, users wanted more nonfinancial information and forward-looking information. Based on these needs, the Jenkins Committee recommended extending the reporting model. More specifically, the conclusions of the committee were as follows:

1. Users oppose replacing the current historical cost-based accounting model.
2. Users place a high value on segment, or line-of-business, reporting.
3. Users desire information about the stability of a company's earning power.
4. Users want more qualitative and quantitative information about financial instruments and off-Balance Sheet financing risks.
5. Users want forward-looking information on which to base projections.
6. Users want more nonfinancial business information.
7. Users prefer that the information provided is consistent over time and comparable between firms.
8. Users expect the information provided to be credible.
9. Users believe that auditors should provide additional qualitative commentary in their reports.

To address these concerns, the Jenkins Committee made several recommendations on how to enhance financial reporting to meet these needs.[4]

1. Improve the disclosure of business segment information by better aligning the segment disclosures in business reporting with the internal segment information that management uses in decision making. In general, this would result in an increase in the

number of segments included and an increase in the detail of information about each segment.

2. Increase the accounting and disclosures for innovative financial instruments.
3. Improve the disclosures about the identity, opportunities, and risks of off-Balance Sheet financing arrangements.
4. Report separately the effects of core and noncore activities and events. The assets and liabilities of noncore events and activities should be measured at fair (market) value.
5. Improve disclosures about the uncertainty of measurements of assets and liabilities, especially those involving estimates. The committee recommended that firms should disclose how reported amounts were derived and explain what judgments were used to develop the estimates.
6. Report the fourth quarter separately. This would improve financial reporting because many firms report on the first three quarters and then issue an annual report for the year. No separate fourth quarter results are disclosed. This recommendation would improve that by including a separate disclosure of fourth quarter results.

Other recommendations especially addressed standard setters. The most significant ones are discussed next.

- Standard setters should not devote attention to a market value-based accounting model. The Jenkins Committee found little support among users for a market value reporting model.
- Users do not expect management to provide forecasted financial statements. These should not be given any more attention. In general, users seriously question the reliability of forecasted statements.
- Users were divided on the usefulness of the purchase versus pooling methods of accounting for business combinations. The committee stated that the existence of these two methods did not appear to be a problem for statement users; therefore, no change should be made in the accounting for business combinations.

COMPREHENSIVE REPORTING MODEL

The Jenkins Committee designed and illustrated a comprehensive reporting model based on its recommendations. This model was designed to demonstrate the feasibility of the recommendations; it is shown in Exhibit 16.2.

The model consists of five broad categories of information, with one to three elements within each of the five categories. All these disclosures are designed to meet the information needs of users, especially the decision processes employed to make projections, value business firms, or assess the prospects of debt repayment.

The model differs from current SEC reporting requirements in two important ways. First, it includes high-level operating data and performance measurements. Second, it includes more forward-looking information. Both of these provide additional information that users can use to obtain greater insight into what factors create long-term value in the firm and what management's vision is for the future. This information could help users better assess the opportunities and risks of the firm's investment and lending decisions.

EXHIBIT 16.2
Jenkins Committee Reporting Model

1. **Financial and nonfinancial data**
   - Financial statements and related disclosures
   - High-level operating data and performance measures that are used internally by management to manage the firm
2. **Management's analysis of the financial and nonfinancial data**
   - Reasons for changes in the financial and nonfinancial data, and the identity and past effects of key trends
3. **Forward-looking information**
   - Opportunities and risks, especially those resulting from key trends
   - Management's plans, including critical success factors
   - Comparison of actual firm performance to previously disclosed opportunities, risks, and plans
4. **Information about management and shareholders**
   - Directors, management, compensation, major shareholders, and transactions and relationships among related parties
5. **Background about the company**
   - Broad objectives and strategies
   - Scope and description of business and properties
   - Impact of industry structure on the company

Source: Adapted from American Institute of Certified Public Accountants, p. 9.

CONCERNS ABOUT THE JENKINS COMMITTEE

As one would expect, there were a number of concerns raised about the Jenkins Committee concerning its composition and the process it went through to come to its conclusions, as well as those conclusions and recommendations. The concerns are examined next.

Composition of the Jenkins Committee   There were a number of concerns about the composition of the Jenkins Committee. Recall that the committee was composed of public practitioners, financial executives (statement preparers), and one professor. Notice what one very important group is missing from this list—financial statement users. No users were members of the Jenkins Committee. Because of the importance attached to financial statement users, it is remarkable that not one user was a member.

Two other important regulatory groups were not represented on the Jenkins Committee: the FASB and the SEC. As issuer of financial accounting standards, the FASB should have been represented on the committee. Although observers from the FASB were involved in many committee meetings, that was not enough for some critics. And because the SEC is legally mandated to oversee financial reporting, direct involvement of the SEC would have been appropriate. As an AICPA committee, the Jenkins Committee sent its report to the AICPA, which then lobbied the FASB and SEC to adopt its recommendations.

In addition to the issue of missing groups, notice which group had the strongest representation on the committee: public accountants. Of course, the Jenkins Committee was an AICPA committee, and some representation from the AICPA was expected. But with an overwhelming 78.5 percent majority of the committee AICPA members, some felt that the

AICPA was overly represented, especially in light of the absence of representatives of financial statement users and the FASB.

To counter this concern, it should be noted that although financial statement users were not on the committee, many of the procedures of the committee were aimed at obtaining the users' views. To counter the concern about the absence of the FASB, it should be noted that one member of the FASB did attend every meeting of the Jenkins Committee, and the FASB frequently loaned FASB staff to the committee.

The Process, Conclusions, and Recommendations of the Jenkins Committee   Other criticisms focused on the procedures of the committee and its conclusions and recommendations. One critic of the Jenkins Committee was Lee Seidler, who published a review of the Jenkins Committee report in 1995.[5] In addition to echoing the concern that the Jenkins Committee did not include one user, he had concerns about the procedures followed and the recommendations.

Seidler's first concern was that the Jenkins Committee did not provide any documentation for their conclusions. In the 202-page report that was made available in 1994, the Jenkins Committee frequently referred to its research to support its conclusions, but in fact, it simply claimed support for the positions without using footnotes or indexing that could be traced to the research. Seidler considered that justification hollow. Even after reviewing the Committee Database (on four, 3.5-inch floppy disks costing $150), he could not trace the conclusions of the Jenkins Committee to the files in the database.

He did fault the Jenkins Committee's comprehensive model. Seidler stated that it contained little that cannot already be found in annual reports, proxies, and SEC 10-K Forms. Seidler's review was not totally negative. He did state that some of the recommendations were good and, if implemented, would represent significant improvements in current financial reporting.

However, many of the other ideas in the Jenkins Committee report are ideas that are not new. Seidler concluded, "Ultimately, the Jenkins Committee expended a great deal of money and effort to give birth to a mouse. Some of the specific suggestions are reasonable, but they are neither new nor significant."[6]

Another criticism focused on the approach of the Jenkins Committee report in recommending that business reporting be closely aligned with the information provided internally to management to manage the firm. Timmons and Dillon state that this is an illogical conclusion because users want to invest in firms or obtain a return of their loan capital, not to manage the firm.[7] They seriously question the conclusion that information provided internally to management would benefit outside users. They also noted that financial statement users have an "insatiable appetite" for disclosures, and the Jenkins Committee did not adequately consider the reporting costs of business firms when making its recommendations. In support of this contention, another source estimated that if the recommendations of the Jenkins Committee were followed, the cost of financial disclosure and audit fees would rise between 5 percent and 20 percent for the typical firm.[8]

RESPONSE TO JENKINS COMMITTEE REPORT

By February 1997, Noll and Weygandt sensed that momentum was building to implement the comprehensive reporting model recommended by the committee.[9] The first formal action on the Jenkins Committee report was taken by the FASB in February 1996 when it released an Invitation to Comment (ITC) for the report. The ITC was designed to obtain respondents' views on the recommendations of the Jenkins Committee and to provide information on how the FASB should proceed in implementing the recommendations. The ITC Coordinating Committee organized a symposium on business reporting in October 1996. It involved one hundred users and preparers, CPAs, academics, standard setters, and regulators.

Noll and Weygandt reported that a consensus developed at the symposium on the notion that users needed nonfinancial and forward-looking information to assess opportunities and risks of the firm. The need for a conceptual framework for reporting nonfinancial and forward-looking information was debated at the symposium. The symposium concluded with agreement that a coalition should be formed to develop the best reporting practices on an industry basis and that the FASB should lead that effort, with the strong support of the SEC.

WALLMAN'S PROPOSAL

A second major impetus for change in business reporting came from SEC commissioner Steven Wallman in 1995.[10] He spoke on business reporting at the AICPA Annual Conference on Current SEC Developments in January 1995 and subsequently met with CPAs, FASB representatives, financial statement preparers, investor groups, financial analysts, and academics. He concluded that financial accounting and business reporting had not kept pace with the changes in the business world. In addition, he believed that some current accounting policies could interfere with or limit financial statement users' ability to obtain better information. He called for interested groups to work together to resolve these issues within a practical time.

WALLMAN'S FOUR ISSUES

Wallman expressed appreciation for the role of accounting in his speech to the AICPA. He saw accountants as "the gatekeepers of our financial markets." He recognized an important role for reporting by stating that the value of accounting lies in its usefulness to users. Based on that premise, he cited four reporting issues of importance to accounting.

1. *What should be reported in the financial statements? What benefits and obligations of the firm should be recognized and measured?* Historically, financial statements reasonably and accurately reflected the assets and liabilities of the entity. But that has changed. Today, the Balance Sheet does not recognize the major assets of some firms. Examples such as the value of the Coca-Cola trademark or the intellectual property of many firms are not reflected on their Balance Sheets. Part of the problem is that historical cost accounting does not do a good job of reporting these types of assets. But Wallman sees the problem as getting worse as the number and importance of the type of firms with these types of assets increase. He cautioned against a response in which management reports whatever assets it feels are there. But he did ask that the accounting profession explore new ways to reflect such assets on Balance Sheet to make them more relevant.

2. *When should recognized items be reported?* Wallman noted that the timeliness of financial reporting was increasingly important. The traditional timing of annual reports and quarterly reports is insufficient to meet the needs of users and the market and so is in danger of becoming obsolete. But events are occurring so rapidly that something must be done. Wallman cited the case of Barings PLC, which reported a net worth of $450 to $500 million at year-end 1994 but was insolvent by the end of February 1995. These are real concerns that must be addressed; accounting needs to develop a system that produces timely financial information. He believed that an increased flow of relevant financial information to the market in a timely manner would lower the cost of capital for firms by decreasing their risks and the returns that are demanded.

3. *For what entity are measurements being prepared?* Wallman noted changes in the concept of the firm. Public companies with multiple public subsidiaries with joint ventures and licensing agreements defy the traditional definition of the firm. He forecasted the development of "virtual firms," composed of a number of people networked together whose main asset is the intellectual capital of those employees. Wallman considered it a real challenge to account for these virtual firms in a timely manner that reliably takes into account an accurate measure of the income, cash flows, and real assets of that firm.

4. *Where and how are we distributing the information?* This refers to the distribution channels that are used to distribute financial information. Currently, accounting relies heavily on aggregation, the summing of amounts into large totals. Financial reporting typically distributes this aggregated information through the mail, although most firms' financial statements are now also available on the World Wide Web. But increasingly, analysts need the information in a disaggregated form and more quickly. Wallman foresees a time when more financial information will be disseminated by online access.

Wallman's four reporting issues address all four basic disclosure questions discussed earlier.

Wallman's focus was on the future of accounting and disclosure in an evolving world and the resulting need for dramatic change. He believed that corporate financial reporting had to change to keep pace with the constantly changing business world or run the risk of not satisfying its promise to society. Because the value and worth of financial accounting resided in its usefulness to users, financial accounting has a debt to society. Wallman was concerned about accounting's ability to satisfy that debt.

He called for the development of analytical systems for thinking about what the future held and mechanisms for responding appropriately to these future needs. Failure to do this would result in a disservice to those who rely on accounting: participants in financial markets, managers, regulators, and financial analysts. It was his belief that a sufficiently dynamic and reliable analytical framework for anticipating and responding to changes had to be developed. Then, that framework should be translated into a system that would ensure that high-quality information flows would be distributed on a timely basis to interested users.

THE PROPOSAL

To remedy these problems, Wallman called on the SEC, FASB, financial statement preparers, investors, and others with an interest in financial reporting to begin thinking of developing viable solutions to the problems he delineated. He warned that inaction might cause two more problems: (1) a stratification of disclosure in which various groups would be given different information according to their needs and (2) U.S. firms might be inhibited from innovating or taking risks because the accounting and reporting system would not properly reflect the results in the financial statements. To avoid these consequences, he encouraged the accounting profession to design flexible information and reporting systems that would address them. Wallman commended the AICPA for establishing the Jenkins Committee.

Wallman proposed a five-layer alternative reporting model.[11] The first layer included items that satisfied recognition criteria and would resemble current core financial statements. The second layer consisted of items that satisfied recognition criteria but were not currently included in the core financial statement because of reliability concerns, such as the value of a brand name. Items that have both reliability and definition concerns, such as measuring customer satisfaction, made up the third layer. The fourth layer was specified for items that satisfied measurement, reliability, and relevance criteria but do not meet the definition of elements, such as risk-sensitivity metrics. The last layer contained relevant items that do not meet the definition of elements and cannot yet be reliably measured, such as the intellectual capital of employees. Wallman believed that this approach would provide users with a better idea of the quality of the information contained in the financial statements.

FASB BUSINESS REPORTING RESEARCH PROJECT

In light of the Jenkins Committee report and Wallman proposal, in January 1998, the FASB started a major research project, the Business Reporting Research Project (BRRP), designed to consider the types of information that companies are providing in addition to the financial statements to investors and the means for delivering it. The project was organized with a fourteen-member steering committee and several working groups. The steering committee guided, directed, and consulted with the working groups. The Board involved financial statement preparers, financial statement users, and auditors in the project as members of the steering committee and working groups. The Board wanted widespread involvement in the project. The results of the working groups were considered by the steering committee, which published the recommendations for improving disclosure. The steering committee reports are available on the FASB's web site, http://www.fasb.org.

The BRRP addresses three of the basic disclosure questions: Why are disclosures being made? How much information should be disclosed? When should the information be disclosed?

ELECTRONIC DISTRIBUTION OF BUSINESS INFORMATION

The first report of the BRRP, "Electronic Distribution of Business Reporting Information." was published in January 2000.[12] The study was designed to survey the state of business reporting over the Internet and to identify noteworthy practices. The growth of the Internet as a medium for distribution of financial information is also noted. Electronic distribution offers speedy delivery and easy access to the information. It also provides business firms with a less costly way to widely distribute their financial information.

The report describes notable current practices of business reporting on corporate web sites by a wide range of U.S. business firms. The information available online included firms' latest annual report, stock quotes, forward-looking information, and detailed plans about new services and products. Other firms provided transcripts of management presentations, analyst reports on the firm, and archived audiovisual versions of management meetings. Legal issues, technological problems, and other related issues are also described.

VOLUNTARY DISCLOSURES

A second disclosure report was published by FASB in January 2001, "Improving Business Reporting: Insights into Enhancing Voluntary Disclosures."[13] This report is designed to help firms improve their business reporting by providing evidence that many firms are making extensive voluntary disclosures in which the investment community and shareholders have a strong interest. The project's importance is based on the idea that improving disclosures makes the capital allocation process more efficient, which results in a reduction of the average cost of capital to the firms.

The recommendations of the project were as follows:

1. Because of the fast pace of change in business, voluntary disclosures will become increasingly more important in the future.
2. Voluntary disclosures that refer to matters that are important to the success of the firm are useful. An example of this is the disclosure of management's view of the firm's critical success factors.
3. Disclosures of previously reported plans and goals and the results achieved in meeting those plans and goals are most useful.
4. Disclosures about the details associated with unrecognized intangible assets would be beneficial.
5. Voluntary disclosures of the metrics used by firms to manage their operations and drive their business strategies are useful.

The report included an appendix, which lists four projects that accounting standard setters may wish to consider.

GAAP–SEC DISCLOSURE REQUIREMENTS

The third report in the BRRP deals with redundancies between GAAP and the SEC's reporting requirements and ways to remove them. The report, "GAAP-SEC Disclosure Requirements," was published in March 2001.[14] Redundant disclosure requirements are unnecessary and create confusion and wasted effort. The project identifies redundancies in nine areas (shown in Exhibit 16.3) and suggests ways to eliminate them.

The report concludes with a number of recommendations to improve the structure and organization of Form 10-K and other SEC disclosure requirements.

REPORTING IN THE NEW ECONOMY

In response to concerns that there is a gap between the information provided in today's financial statements and the information needs of investors and creditors, the FASB issued a special report authored by Wayne Upton in April 2001, "Business and Financial Reporting, Challenges from the New Economy."[15] The special report, although not part of the BRRP, considered the intersection between the new economy and business and financial reporting.

EXHIBIT 16.3
GAAP–SEC Disclosure Redundancies

- Income tax disclosures
- Disclosures about a major customer
- Disclosure of contingencies
- Disclosure of risks related to financial instruments
- Related party transactions
- Earnings per share computations
- Research and development expenses
- Segment information
- Disclosure of allowances for doubtful accounts

Source: Adapted from Financial Accounting Standards Board (2001a), p. v.

The special project examined two assertions about the interaction of the new economy and business and financial reporting: (1) The economy of 2000 is fundamentally different from the economy of 1950, and (2) traditional financial statements do not present the value drivers that dominate the new economy. To respond to these two assertions, the project focuses on whether business and financial reporting should change, and, if so, how. The special report concluded that the debate over "new" versus "old" economy is not helpful; instead, the more important question is whether business financial reporting should change, and how. The report is based on a review of a range of articles and studies dealing with disclosure and accounting for specific assets, such as intangible assets.

The special report listed three areas that standard setters should address.

1. Inspection of the practical and conceptual issues associated with recognition of internally generated intangible assets
2. Increased and systematic use of nonfinancial performance measures
3. Increased use of forward-looking information

International considerations were also part of this special report. Groups in several nations, including in the United States, United Kingdom, Canada, Denmark, Sweden, and The Netherlands, and the Organization for Economic Cooperation and Development (OECD) were cited for their contribution to improving financial reporting.

EVALUATION OF ACCOUNTING DISCLOSURE

In the past twenty years, there have been a number of evaluations of disclosure and forecasts on the future of disclosure. They are interesting and relevant because they show the status of disclosure at various points in time and explain what concerns have arisen. In general, they respond to three questions: (1) What will financial reporting look like in the future? (2) Does the current reporting model need a minor or major revision? (3) What drives the information needs of users? They are examined in chronological order to preserve the progression of the evaluations.

Balance Sheet Tilt   Among the first of the modern evaluators of disclosure was Ray Groves, who in 1989 was co-chief executive of Ernst & Young.[16] He believed that a shift in emphasis from the Income Statement to the Balance Sheet was occurring. He predicted that the future Income Statement would include not only the operating results but also the changes in the Balance Sheet accounts, leading to more complexity and volatility. He cited changes in the complexity of the business world as a causal factor. He believed that accountants could report realistic and useful information that is complete, but not as complex as it could be, and is subject to change, but not as volatile as it could be.

Financial Reporting in the 1990s   Sever and Boisclair looked at the future of financial reporting and predicted the changes in store for the 1990s.[17] They, too, recognized that financial reporting was shifting from an Income Statement focus to a Balance Sheet focus and were concerned about the resulting volatility. They cited a number of factors (accounting for income taxes, employee benefits, postretirement benefits, off-Balance Sheet financing, financial instruments, and internationalization) as making future financial statements longer, more complicated, more difficult to explain, and more difficult to understand.

U.S. Model Broken   As covered in Chapter 9, Elliott and Jacobson believed that the U.S. financial accounting model was broken and needed to be fixed.[18] If it were not fixed, they predicted that U.S. firms would face higher capital costs, negative financial surprises in the marketplace, and decreasing competitiveness. The problem, as they saw it, was that the periodic, historical cost-based financial statements that served very well during the industrial era were not sufficient for the new information era. They argued that through time, man has developed three fundamentally different wealth creation methods: agriculture, industry, and information technology. Each wealth creation method required a different accounting information system, each of which was increasingly sophisticated. They believed information technology was in place; therefore, accounting needed to change the accounting information system to meet the new needs of information era firms. They called on the FASB to study the information needs of investors and business managers and to lead the push for a new accounting model.

Information Overload   Groves was concerned that the current disclosure system developed incrementally, which has produced a crazy quilt of disclosure rules and regulations. No one has considered the overall impact of all these individually issued rules.[19] Groves believed that the quantity of disclosures had become so excessive that it diminished their overall value.

To support his contentions, he conducted a survey of the 1972, 1982, and 1992 annual reports of twenty-five large well-known firms, including AT&T, Bank of America, Coca-Cola, General Electric, General Motors, and IBM. Disclosures were measured in three ways: the number of total pages in the annual report, the number of pages of footnotes, and the number of pages of management's discussion and analysis.

The results are shown in Exhibit 16.4, which shows the average number of pages for each type of disclosure and the cumulative percentage growth in those numbers. The results for 1972, 1982, and 1992 are then projected to 2002 and 2012. The exhibit shows that in all three categories, very large cumulative increases occurred. When the results are projected into the future, the size of these disclosures expands dramatically. For example, by 2012, the annual report grows to 117 pages, the footnotes take up 72 pages, and management's discussion is 48 pages long. In Groves's judgment, these numbers would intimidate any financial statement user.

EXHIBIT 16.4
Results of Groves's Study

| | Average Number of Pages | | | | |
| | Actual | | | Projected | |
Type of Disclosure	1972	1982	1992	2002	2012
Annual Report	35	53	64	87	117
Cumulative percentage growth		51	83	149	234
Footnotes	4	8	17	35	72
Cumulative percentage growth		125	325	775	1,700
Management Discussion and Analysis	3	7	12	24	46
Cumulative percentage growth		133	300	700	1,500

Source: Adapted from Groves (1994), p. 12.

To solve the problem of information overload, he proposed two ideas: (1) a mandatory five-year review or sunset review of disclosure rules and regulations and (2) two-tier differential disclosures that would package disclosures differently for different users. He believed these two suggestions would result in changes that would help reduce the information overload.

Disclosures Fail Large Investors A multinational survey of the world's leading U.S. and European institutional investors in 1995 concluded that these investors didn't like the information they were provided.[20] In comparing disclosure practices of two hundred multinational corporations (sixty American, forty British, and the rest in Europe, Japan, Canada, and Australia), the investors concluded that they wanted more information on planned expenditures, research and development costs, and forward-looking information. They saw firms as providing mountains of irrelevant information rather than asking investors what information they wanted and needed.

AIMR Survey The last survey covered in this section in which disclosures were evaluated was conducted by the AIMR in 2000.[21] This survey was designed to gauge the current views of investment professionals on various aspects of corporate disclosure practices of publicly traded firms. The survey revealed that 61 percent of the responding financial analysts believed that corporate disclosures were good or excellent; 29 percent rated them as average quality; and only 8 percent said they were below average. But almost 70 percent stated that they were better than in the past. The only negative aspect of this survey was that the results were based on responses from 346 AIMR members, only a 14 percent response rate.

The survey was conducted to focus on areas where publicly traded firms may want to improve their disclosures. Several areas were identified as needing improvement:

- Explaining extraordinary, unusual, or nonrecurring charges.
- Providing information on specific segments.
- Providing forward-looking information.
- Disclosing off-Balance Sheet assets or liabilities.

ONLINE FINANCIAL REPORTING

One of the questions raised by Wallman was, Where and how is accounting distributing financial information? One recent development to answer that question is the development of online financial reporting. This was the topic of one of the meetings of the FASB's Business Reporting Research project described above.

Online financial reporting involves putting the firm's financial report, annual report, or other financial disclosures on the Internet. Kaplan describes the features of the best of them: Java-enhanced cover pages that move and emit sounds; tables of content that include hyperlinks that allow the user to jump directly to each section; animated icons; scrolling banners that emphasize key points; a letter to shareholders in multiple languages with its message punctuated with audio and videoclips featuring top management; narrative in different languages, with audio and video clips; and financial statements presented in multiple languages and currencies.[22]

Some publicly traded firms took the lead in online reporting. Koreto cites Exxon, Raytheon, Intel, and Microsoft as leaders.[23] He believes that the WWW offers advantages to firms over the traditional published annual report. Those advantages consist of more options than in print and plenty of space to add financial pages and audio and video clips. Certainly, the Web provides fast and inexpensive access to the information. Koreto concludes with a prediction that "eventually, most SEC-mandated public company financial statements will be online."[24]

BARRIERS TO DISCLOSURE

Although disclosure is the final phase of accounting, there are some barriers to increasing disclosures that must be considered in order to understand the reluctance of some firms to increase their disclosures. First, disclosure is costly. The costs of annual reports were cited earlier in the chapter. As annual reports have grown in size, firms are concerned that the costs will become prohibitive. Secondly, some firms are concerned that disclosures will aid their competition. That is, as more information is made available about the firm, the competition will gain an advantage over the firm. A similar concern is expressed with regard to organized labor. Some firms believe that disclosing more information will hurt them as they enter into collective bargaining with unions.

Others are concerned that due to information overload, there is a danger that disclosing more information may cause confusion for financial statement users. Additionally, because so much information is available from other sources, the annual report and financial disclosures are less important than earlier time periods, which permits a lessening of the importance of the disclosures.

Perhaps one of the strongest arguments against increasing disclosure is the admission that accounting still doesn't precisely know the needs of users. Without a complete knowledge of their information needs, disclosure is pretty much a "shot in the dark," and a costly one at that. Proponents of this argument believe that accounting should devote more resources to identifying the actual information needs of users, and then the appropriate disclosures can be formulated to meet those needs.

Occasionally, surveys of financial statement users are conducted. These are helpful in providing insights into the decision models and information needs of users. One such study in the mid-1990s resulted from a response from shareholders in fifty states who own at least one round lot of one stock.[25] The results show the following:

- Investors are taking a longer perspective on their investments.
- Stockbrokers' influence has lessened.
- Shareholders believe the annual report is more useful than it once was.
- The Statement of Cash Flows is more important to readers, and the income statement is less important.
- The auditor's opinion is more useful than in the past.
- Management's discussion and analysis is less useful.

Results like these are helpful in revealing trends and explaining the views of users. The survey results deal primarily with the first and second basic disclosure question: For whom is the information disclosed, and why are the disclosures being made? But what is needed is a more comprehensive and widespread study of users. So far, no organization has attempted such a project.

SUMMARY

It is important to note that major impetuses to improve financial reporting have come rather recently. This fact reveals the increased importance of financial reporting and disclosure to the new view of accounting. Disclosure and financial reporting are "hot topics" for the future as the three proposals discussed in the chapter begin to be implemented. At first, the AICPA took the lead in this process with the establishment of the Jenkins Committee, but the FASB took over the lead, as evidenced by its Business Reporting Research project. The proposals to improve disclosure examined in this chapter have many similarities, for example, increased disclosure of forward-looking information, nonfinancial information, and information management uses to control the firm.

These proposals have come at a time when communications technology is changing dramatically. The prospect of using the Web for online reporting has the potential to revolutionize financial reporting and disclosure. Perhaps some of the dire predictions of Groves (see Exhibit 16.4) and others about the growing size of annual reports will not occur because of information technology.

Whatever the final result, it is significant that disclosure and financial reporting are no longer considered as simply the backstops for accounting. Instead, disclosure has been elevated in its own right as a topic and will continue to be important into the future, especially as the widespread financial consequences of the Enron Corp. collapse are revealed in 2002.

REVIEW QUESTIONS

1. How do we define disclosure? What elements are included?
2. What are the elements included in the average annual report?
3. Describe the nature of the relationship between disclosure and accounting.
4. What events caused disclosure to become more important in accounting in the late 1990s to early 2000?
5. What four basic questions arise when discussing disclosure?
6. What are the three levels of disclosure in accounting?
7. What are the three different levels of disclosure that the SEC has recognized?
8. What are the two important considerations when discussing disclosure?
9. It is said that the annual report is a general-purpose statement. In your opinion, in what ways is this good and in what ways is it a negative?
10. Summary annual reports were developed as a reaction to what factor or factors?
11. What factors caused the AICPA to establish the Jenkins Committee?
12. What methodology did the Jenkins Committee follow?
13. What were the conclusions and recommendations of the Jenkins Committee?
14. What were the components in the Jenkins Committee's reporting model?
15. What concerns were raised about the Jenkins Committee?
16. What formal action did the FASB take in reaction to the Jenkins Committee's report?
17. What four reporting issues did SEC Commissioner Wallman raise?
18. What evaluations of disclosure were made by Groves (1989), Sever and Bosclair (1990), Elliott and Jacobsen (1991), and Groves (1994)?
19. How did the two recent surveys of financial statements (Sesit 1996 and AIMR 2000) rate the effectiveness of accounting disclosures?
20. What are some advantages to the firm for having its annual report published online?
21. What are some arguments against disclosure?

DISCUSSION TOPICS

1. How do the three proposals to increase the effectiveness of disclosure discussed in this chapter show the importance of disclosure in accounting?
2. **Project.** Visit the web sites of two or more firms that offer their financial statements or annual report online. Compare and contrast the two firms disclosures on the Internet.
3. **Project.** Select one or two firms from Groves's study and examine their 2001 or 2002 annual reports to see if Groves's predictions on the size of the annual report, the number of footnotes, and the length of management's discussion came true.
4. Discuss the notion that bad accounting + good disclosure = good accounting. What arguments support this notion? Which oppose it?
5. Of the four basic questions about disclosure, how would you rank them in order of importance? Defend your ranking.
6. The importance of disclosure levels recognized by the SEC has changed. What factor or factors do you think caused the change from protective to informative?

7. Which of the two general issues, cost-benefit factor or information overload, is the most important when considering disclosure?

8. What objections did the SEC raise against the use of summary annual reports? Do you think their objections were valid? Discuss.

9. When listing its recommendations, the Jenkins Committee went beyond the topic of disclosure to recommend that standard setters (the FASB) not devote much attention to market value-based accounting. On what was that recommendation based? Do this think this was a proper recommendation of the Jenkins Committee? Why or why not?

10. Which do you think was the strongest concern about the composition of the Jenkins Committee: (1) not having a financial statement user on the committee, (2) not having representatives of the SEC or FASB on the committee, or (3) having an overwhelming 78.5 percent of the committee from the AICPA?

11. Consider the arguments against disclosure. Which are the most valid in your opinion?

12. Do you believe that published financial statements will cease in favor of online reporting? If so, when will that development occur?

13. **Project.** Visit the FASB at http://www.fasb.org, and search any updates and recently available reports on the Business Reporting Research project. What topics are addressed, and what recommendations are made?

14. What do you see as the future of financial reporting and disclosure?

NOTES

1 Associated Press.
2 Cook and Sutton, p. 12.
3 AICPA.
4 AICPA, pp. 11–14.
5 Seidler.
6 Seidler, p. 124.
7 Timmons and Dillon.
8 Berton.
9 Noll and Weygandt.
10 Wallman.
11 "SEC Commission Proposes New Multilayered Reporting Model."
12 FASB (2000).
13 FASB (2001b).
14 FASB (2001a).
15 Upton.
16 Groves (1989).
17 Sever and Boisclair.
18 Elliott and Jacobson.
19 Groves (1994).
20 Sesit.
21 Association for Investment Management and Research.
22 Kaplan, p. 38.
23 Koreto.
24 Ibid., p. 65.
25 Epstein and Pava.

REFERENCES

American Institute of Certified Public Accountants, Special Committee on Financial Reporting. *Meeting the Information Needs of Investors and Creditors*. New York: American Institute of Certified Public Accountants, 1994.

Association for Investment Management and Research. "AIMR Survey." www.aimr.org/infocentral/news/00release/00discsurv.htm.

Associated Press. "Companies' Annual Rite to Go All-out." *Orlando Sentinel* (May 2, 2001): C6.

Berton, L. "Companies Pressure Accounting Panel to Modify Demands for More Data," *The Wall Street Journal* (August 16, 1994): A2.

Cook, M., and M. Sutton. "Summary Annual Reporting: A Cure for Information Overload." *Financial Executive* (January/February 1995): 12–15.

Elliott, Robert, and Peter Jacobson. "U.S. Accounting: A National Emergency." *Journal of Accountancy* (November 1991): 54–58.

Epstein, M., and M. Pava. "Profile of an Annual Report." *Financial Executive* (January/February, 1994): 41–43.

Financial Accounting Standards Board. "Electronic Distribution of Business Reporting Information." *Steering Committee Report Series*. Norwalk, CT: Financial Accounting Standards Board, 2000.

———. "GAAP-SEC Disclosure Requirements." *Steering Committee Report Series*. Norwalk, CT: Financial Accounting Standards Board, 2001a.

———. "Improving Business Reporting: Insights into Enhancing Voluntary Disclosures." *Steering Committee Report Series*. Norwalk, CT: Financial Accounting Standards Board, 2000b.

"Financial Reporting in the Year 2000." *Financial Executive* (January/February 1994): 34–39.

Groves, Ray "What Today's Balance-Sheet Tilt Means." *Financial Executive* (September/October 1989): 26–30.

Groves, Ray "Financial Disclosure: When More Is Not Better." *Financial Executive* (May/June 1994): 11–14.

Jenkins, E. " Letter from the Chairman of the American Institute of CPAs Special Committee on Financial Reporting." *Journal of Accountancy* (October 1994): 39–40.

Kaplan, Ross. "Identity Crisis for Online Annual Reports." *Financial Executive* (July/August 1999): pp. 38–39.

Koreto, Richard. "When the Bottom Line Is Online." *Journal of Accountancy* (March 1997): 63–65.

Louwers, Timothy, William Pasewark, and Eric Typpo. "Silicon Valley Meets Norwalk." *Journal of Accountancy* (August 1998): 20–26.

Noll, D., and J. Weygandt. "Business Reporting: What Comes Next?" *Journal of Accountancy* (February 1997): 59–62.

"SEC Commissioner Proposes New Multilayered Reporting Model." *Journal of Accountancy* (May 1996): 14–15.

Seidler, L. "Meeting the Information Needs of Investors and Creditors, a Review." *Accounting Horizons* (September 1995): 119–24.

Sesit, M. "Disclosure Fails to Meet Needs of Big Investors." *The Wall Street Journal* (November 4, 1996): B11C.

Sever, Mark, and R. Boisclair. "Financial Reporting in the 1990s." *Journal of Accountancy* (January 1990): 36–41.

"Survey Says Firms Need Better Disclosure of Financial Results." *The Wall Street Journal* (February 8, 2000): B25.

Timmons, E., and K. Dillon. "The Jenkins Committee: Where It Missed the Mark." *Financial Executive* (May/June 1995): 11–13.

Upton, Wayne. "Business and Financial Reporting: Challenges from the New Economy." *Financial Accounting Series Special Report*. Norwalk, CT.: Financial Accounting Standards Board, 2001.

Wallman, S. "The Future of Accounting Disclosure in an Evolving World: The Need for Dramatic Change." *Accounting Horizons* (September 1995): 81–91.

Zarowin, Stanley, and Wayne Harding. "Finally, Business Talks the Same Language." *Journal of Accountancy* (August 2000): 24–30.

A

ABBREVIATIONS

AAA	American Accounting Association
AcSEC	Accounting Standards Executive Committee
AIA	American Institute of Accountants
AICPA	American Institute of Certified Public Accountants
AIMR	Association for Investment Management and Research
APB	Accounting Principles Board
APEC	Asia-Pacific Economic Cooperation
ARB	Accounting Research Bulletins
ARD	Accounting Research Division
ARS	Accounting Research Study
APEC	Asia-Pacific Economic Cooperation
ASOBAT	A Statement of Basic Accounting Theory
ASR	Accounting Series Release
ATB	Accounting Terminology Bulletin
BRRP	Business Reporting Research Project
CAP	Committee on Accounting Procedure
CF	Conceptual Framework
CICA	Canadian Institute of Chartered Accountants
DM	discussion memorandum
ED	exposure draft
EITF	Emerging Issues Task Force
ERISA	Employee Retirement Income Security Act
EU	European Union
FAF	Financial Accounting Foundation
FAPA	Federal Administrative Procedures Act
FaSAC	Financial Accounting Standards Advisory Council
FASB	Financial Accounting Standards Board
FEI	Financial Executives International
FRR	Financial Reporting Release
FTAA	Free Trade Area of the Americas